ONCE A HAPPY VALLEY
Memoirs of an ICS Officer
in Sindh, 1938–1948

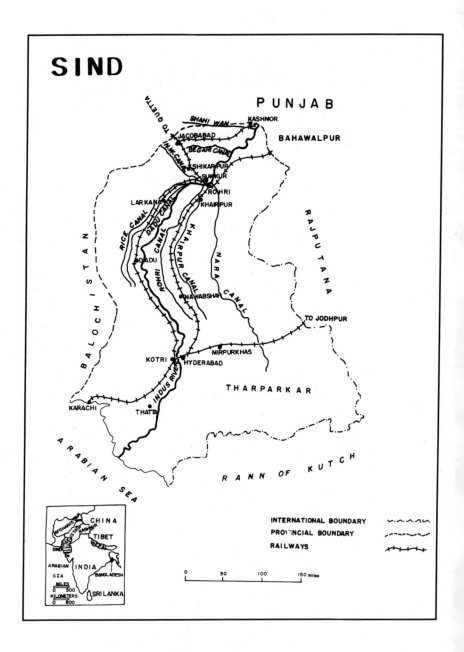

SIND

PUNJAB

BAHAWALPUR

SHAHI WAH — KASHMOR
JACOBABAD
BEGARI CANAL
SHIKARPUR
SUKKUR
ROHRI
KHAIRPUR
LARKANA
RICE CANAL
DADU CANAL
DADU
ROHRI CANAL
KHAIRPUR CANAL
NARA CANAL
NAWABSHAH
RAJPUTANA
TO JODHPUR
MIRPURKHAS
KOTRI HYDERABAD
KARACHI
THATTA
THARPARKAR
INDUS RIVER
BALOCHISTAN
ARABIAN SEA
N.W. CANAL
TO QUETTA

RANN OF KUTCH

CHINA
AFGHANIS TIBET
SIND KASHMIR
NEPAL
ARABIAN INDIA
SEA
BANGLADESH
SRI LANKA
MILES
0 500
KILOMETERS
0 800

INTERNATIONAL BOUNDARY
PROVINCIAL BOUNDARY
RAILWAYS

0   50   100   150 Miles

ONCE A HAPPY VALLEY

Memoirs of an ICS Officer
in Sindh, 1938–1948

ROGER PEARCE

OXFORD

UNIVERSITY PRESS

OXFORD

UNIVERSITY PRESS

Great Clarendon Street, Oxford OX2 6DP

Oxford University Press is a department of the University of Oxford.
It furthers the University's objective of excellence in research, scholarship,
and education by publishing worldwide in

Oxford New York

Athens Auckland Bangkok Bogotá Buenos Aires Cape Town
Chennai Dar es Salaam Delhi Florence Hong Kong Istanbul Karachi
Kolkata Kuala Lumpur Madrid Melbourne Mexico City Mumbai Nairobi
Paris São Paulo Shanghai Singapore Taipei Tokyo Toronto Warsaw

with associated companies in Berlin Ibadan

Oxford is a registered trade mark of Oxford University Press
in the UK and in certain other countries

© Oxford University Press 2001

The moral rights of the author have been asserted

First published 2001

ISBN 0 19 579395 1

Typeset in New Baskerville
Printed in Pakistan by
New Sketch Graphics, Karachi.
Published by
Ameena Saiyid, Oxford University Press
5-Bangalore Town, Sharae Faisal
PO Box 13033, Karachi-75350, Pakistan.

CONTENTS

... ... Inc +	329.58	... ...	− 5.73	
-do- Accum ‡	345.40	... ...	− 6.00	
Portfolio Inc ‡	210.07	...	− 4.09	
N Amer Gwth Inc ‡	969.03	...	+ 4.43	
UK Divfd Inc ‡	489.62	...	− 3.97	

GOVETT INVESTMENTS LTD
020 7378 7979 Dealing: 020 7407 7888
Govett Investment Funds

Eqty Mthly Inc ‡	31.11	... †	+ 0.08	11.40
European Strat ‡	214.22	...	+ 3.48	
FTSE 250 Index ‡	120.28	...	+ 0.96	1.43
Global Opps ‡	197.01	...	+ 2.02	
Japan Index Tracker ‡	89.01	...	+ 0.68	
Pacific Opps ‡	163.01	...	+ 1.03	
UK Equity Safeguard ‡	119.36	...	+ 0.52	0.81
-do- NAV to Mar 16	116.66	116.66		
UK Small Cos ‡	90.98	...	+ 0.32	
US Opps ‡	197.02	...	+ 2.61	

Govett General Funds

Asia Pacific ‡	96.12	... †	+ 0.33	0.22
Corporate Bd ‡	82.34	... †	+ 0.15	3.85
Euro Blue Chip ‡	415.97	...	+ 6.50	
Euro Tech ‡	51.04	...	+ 1.15	
Japanese Opps ‡	110.19	...	+ 0.02	
UK Blue Chip ‡	348.23	...	+ 5.16	1.14
US Blue Chip ‡	401.76	... †	+ 5.85	

Govett Unit Trusts

Balanced Exempt	157.15	163.47†		
Greater China	192.47	205.07	− 0.52	1.73
Money Market	100.19	100.19		4.20
Enhanced Opps ‡	#12.540	#13.172	+ 0.58	3.50
UK Safeguard ‡	143.90	152.61	+ 0.45	
-do- NAV to Mar 16	141.84	141.84		
US Bear	#4.770	#4.943	− 0.04	0.75
US Index	#26.227	#27.177	+ 0.24	1.25

HALIFAX INVESTMENT FUND MGRS LTD
0296 386 386
Retail Shares

...ical ‡	77.39	...	+ 0.48	1.34
...opean ‡	135.35	...	+ 0.55	1.29
... Eastern ‡	288.54	...	+ 1.19	0.96
...d of Inv ‡	275.68	...	+ 1.66	1.36
...h Income ‡	180.44	...	+ 0.51	3.76
... Gwth ‡	173.60	...	+ 1.79	1.31
...anese ‡	24.09	...	+ 0.08	0.25
...mer ‡	258.85	...	+ 4.24	0.73
...can ‡	184.17	...	+ 1.58	2.55
...aller Cos ‡	73.18	...	− 0.31	2.61
...cial Sits ‡	113.53	...	+ 0.80	2.42
...FTSE All-S IT ‡	42.94	...	+ 0.44	2.33
...FTSE 100 IT ‡	67.17	...	+ 0.74	2.23

HALIFAX UT MGMT LTD
Dealing: 01904 611110

...nced ‡	76.56	79.25†	...	2.28
...nced Acc	90.80	94.00	...	2.28
...	38.58	39.93	...	1.24
...wth Acc	42.04	43.51	...	1.24
... Inc Inc	25.22	26.00†	...	5.73
... Inc Acc	26.96	27.80	...	5.73
...	43.61	45.14†	...	3.38
...ne Acc	54.87	56.80	...	3.38
...mulation Tst	36.43	38.46	...	2.39
...er Tst ‡	20.28			1.77

...GREAVES LANSDOWN FUND MGRS LTD
...iries: 0117 900 9000 Dealing: 01392 477 630

...erf Acc ‡	97.11	...	+ 0.89	1.13

...DERSON GLOBAL INVESTORS
...tors Serv: 0800 832 832 Dlng: 0845 946 4646
A Class UK & Europe Fds

...Cap Gwth ‡	1203.10	... †	+16.70	0.31
...mlr Cos ‡	186.20	... †	+ 0.60	

Previously known as Perpetual Funds

Asian Inc	119.39	127.11†	+ 0.80	0.12
-do- Accum	121.79	129.67	+ 0.81	0.12
Corp Bond	86.09	91.11	+ 0.11	5.60
Euro Core	302.76	321.07†	+ 4.62	0.67
-do- Accum	303.81	322.18	+ 4.63	0.67
Global Bond	56.56	59.85	− 0.15	4.48
Glob Smlr Cos	437.88	467.79	+ 2.90	0.26
High Income #	188.64	201.58†	+ 1.51	3.97
-do- Accum #	209.93	224.34	+ 1.68	3.97
Income #	764.00	816.74	+ 5.70	3.73
Intl Core	207.19	220.42	+ 2.52	0.68
Japan Inc	139.64	147.44	+ 0.76	
-do- Accum	139.64	147.44	+ 0.76	
Monthly Inc Plus #	85.38	90.35†	− 0.47	10.25
-do- Accum #	105.23	111.36	− 0.58	10.25
Pacific Inc	251.57	268.79†	+ 2.38	0.48
-do- Accum	259.56	277.32	+ 2.45	0.48
UK Growth Inc	165.73	177.12	+ 0.99	2.51
-do- Accum	199.48	213.19	+ 1.19	2.51
UK Smlr Cos Core	176.00	188.24	+ 0.39	1.53
-do- Accum	200.84	214.81	+ 0.45	1.53
US Core	462.98	488.66	+ 6.38	
-do- Accum	462.98	488.66	+ 6.38	
World Inc #	56.54	60.32†	+ 0.37	1.81
Perpetual Funds				
Lat Am Gwth Inc	29.18	30.92	+ 0.09	1.31
-do- Accum	30.16	31.95	+ 0.09	1.31
Wwide Recovery	680.58	719.21		0.78

INVESTEC FUND MANAGERS LTD
020 7597 1800
OEIC

Cap Acc #	110.24	...	− 0.03	
Caut Mgd Inc ‡	149.02	... †	+ 1.01	3.29
Caut Mgd Acc ‡	172.30	... †	+ 1.16	3.29
European Acc ‡	215.56	...	+ 3.09	0.49
Gbl Free Ent Acc ‡	195.87	...	+ 1.06	1.03
HK & China Acc ‡	97.49	...	− 0.33	0.96
Income Shs Inc ‡	91.43	... †	− 0.04	8.59
Income Shs Acc ‡	163.74	...	− 0.08	8.59
Int Eqty ‡	116.77	...	+ 1.29	0.84
Mthly Hi Inc Inc ‡	73.58	...	− 0.36	9.89
Mthly Hi Inc Acc ‡	90.85	...	− 0.43	9.89
Stg Bond Inc ‡	119.74	...	+ 0.37	4.52
Stg Bond Acc ‡	145.93	...	+ 0.45	4.52
UK Blue Chp Acc ‡	342.76	...	+ 5.06	1.37
UK Opps Acc ‡	699.75	...	+10.57	1.49
UK Smler Cos Acc ‡	515.82	...	+ 0.95	2.91
UK Value Inc ‡	206.63	...	− 2.35	2.32
UK Value Acc ‡	356.74	...	+ 4.06	2.32
Wired Ind ‡	62.72	...	+ 0.65	

JP MORGAN FLEMING ASSET MGMT
Brokerline 0800 727770 Clients 0800 204020
OEIC

Asia A Acc ‡	44.17	...	+ 0.09	0.35
Balanced A Inc #	68.84	...	+ 0.53	4.26
Balanced A Acc ‡	68.84	...	+ 0.53	4.26
Emerging Mkts ‡	38.68	...	− 0.06	
Europe A Acc ‡	392.30	...	+ 5.10	0.21
Euro Smllr Cos ‡	119.90	...	+ 0.80	
Global A Acc ‡	570.40	...	+ 5.80	0.34
Glb Fins A Acc ‡	557.00	...	+ 7.00	0.56
Gl ex-UK Bd A Inc ‡	158.40	...	− 0.20	3.64
Gl ex-UK Bd A Acc ‡	158.40	...	− 0.20	3.64
Inv Trust A Inc ‡	321.90	...	+ 2.50	0.42
Inv Trust A Acc ‡	321.90	...	+ 2.50	0.42
Japan A Acc ‡	189.20	...	+ 1.60	
New Europe ‡	46.00	...	+ 0.77	
Prem Eq Gth A Acc ‡	243.70	...	+ 3.50	1.04
Prem Eq Inc A Acc ‡	474.40	...	+ 5.80	3.50
Prem Eq Inc A Acc ‡	474.40	...	+ 5.80	3.50
UK Corp Bd Inc ‡	45.13	...		8.82
UK Corp Bd Acc ‡	51.81	...		8.82
UK Act 350 A Acc ‡	133.90	...	+ 0.70	1.36
UK Dynamic Inc ‡	46.67	...	− 0.04	0.24
UK Dynamic Acc ‡	46.70	...	− 0.04	0.24
UK Eq Inc A Inc ‡	277.80	...	+ 3.30	

Urbane and loyal diplomat wh...

SIR PETER SCOTT, who ended his diplomatic career as Ambassador to Norway in the 1970s, was among the last survivors of those British officials who saw service in pre-independence India. Joining the Indian Civil Service directly from Cambridge, he served throughout the Second World War in various Indian appointments and was at the side of the last Viceroy as a junior private secretary in the months that led up to independence in 1947.

For 30 years thereafter he made his way in the British Foreign Service, mostly in European or North American appointments. After leaving Oslo and the service, he worked for three years in a royal household, before retiring to the Norfolk countryside, remaining an urbane and slimly elegant figure into his eighties.

Charles Peter Scott was born in 1917 in Japan, the son of missionaries. He was educated at Weymouth College and at Pembroke College, Cambridge. He entered the Indian Civil Service in the last intake before the outbreak of war in 1939 and rapidly showed himself a coming man in a service in which there could be no long-term future for an expatriate. It was to be

expected, therefore, that, hav... ing played his part in seein... Lord Mountbatten and Indi... through to Independence Da... in August 1947, he shoul... transfer to the British Foreig... Service.

His postings in that servic... were, however, less predictabl... for a man who had chosen ... start his career in the sub-con... nent. After two years in th... Embassy in Tokyo, where h... was involved with the negoti... tions of the 1951 Japane... Peace Treaty, he never we... back to Asia again. He wa... brought back from Japan ... the Foreign Office in 1950 ar... dispatched two years later ... the key appointment of priva... secretary to the first Secretar... General of Nato, Lord Isma... He owed the posting to pre... ous acquaintance with Isma... who had served Mountbatt... as Chief of Staff in Delhi, ... he made good use of it ... acquire a commanding kno... edge of Nato in its ea... formative years.

His subsequent appoi... ments, though of less obvi... distinction, involved him ... significant events: to the E... bassy in Vienna; to Brit... Information Services in N... York (arriving there in ... month that Anglo-Ameri... relations seemed to fall a... over Suez in 1956); and ...

onsul-General in Washing-
n at the time of Kennedy's
auguration. He was posted
the UN mission in Geneva,
Rome and, on short-term
asi-academic appointments,
the Imperial Defence Col-
ge (now the Royal College of
efence Studies) and to Sus-
x University's Centre of
ropean Studies.

In 1970 he was appointed an
ssistant Under-Secretary in
e Foreign and Common-
ealth Office with a rather
iscellaneous ragbag of re-
onsibilities. He stayed in
at somewhat thankless job
almost five years, during
nich time he was involved in
e crises in Uganda, Cyprus
d Bangladesh.

A career which had started
centres of power which
ered interest and engage-
ent gradually lost its sparkle
d early promise. Scott, with
ingrained good manners
d modest honesty, got on
th the jobs he was given,
joying the good things that
cities in which he found
nself had to offer. Long
erwards he recorded his
creations as "walking, and
ch as offer". "Such as offer"
s the approach he brought
everything he did, gladly
ing appointments which
re meretricious men might
ve disdained.

His reward was an all-too-
short period as Ambassador
in Oslo, where he served from
1975 to 1977. He brought to the
Norwegians qualities very like
their own. He was straightforward, as they were; he was
modest, unemotional and la-
conic to a fault. They liked
what they saw, and he liked
them, and he left Oslo with
real regret, serving for 20
years thereafter on the Council
of the Anglo-Norse Society in
London.

At the age of 36 Scott had
married Rachael Lloyd Jones,
herself a daughter of the
Indian Empire. She supported
his desire to continue in
employment after his retirement from the Diplomatic
Service, and supported him
through three challenging
years as private secretary and
treasurer to Prince Michael of
Kent.

Scott was appointed KBE in
1978. His services to the last
Viceroy had been noticed
when he was appointed OBE
in 1948, and his diplomatic
career with the CMG in 1964.

He is survived by his wife
and by their son and two
daughters.

**Sir Peter Scott, KBE, CMG,
diplomat, was born on
December 30, 1917. He died
on January 16, 2002, aged 84.**

Balanced Funds

500	498.80	526.40	+ 3.80	1.22
General	420.50	447.40	+ 3.60	1.10
Truslee	291.30	309.70†	+ 2.60	1.14

Growth Funds - UK

Capital	187.40	198.70†	+ 1.50	1.11
FTSE 100	132.70	135.30	+ 1.30	1.33

Growth Funds - Overseas

America	314.30	331.60	+ 5.10	...
Japan	86.97	88.74	+ 1.01	...
Japan Acc	87.97	89.76	+ 1.03	...
Worldwide	247.20	261.50†	+ 2.80	0.30

B2 Cust Service Centre: 0800 626262

b2 Stk Mkt Gth	87.68	88.22	+ 1.67	0.91
b2 Mkt Trk 350	112.10	112.10	+ 2.80	1.55
b2 Mthly Inc	100.80	100.80†	+ 0.30	4.82

BARCLAYS GLOBAL INVESTORS LTD
Barclays Global Investors Funds
Brokerline: 0800 731 2443
Cust Enqs & Vals: 0845 300 4003

American Growth	227.90	241.10	+ 3.70	...
Distribution #	123.60	124.50	+ 0.80	5.09
Equity Income #	196.00	207.70	+ 1.80	3.08
European	86.34	86.68	+ 0.74	1.03
European Acc	87.21	87.55	+ 0.74	1.03
European Gth	276.00	291.50	+ 2.60	0.38
European Gth Acc	304.80	321.90	+ 2.90	0.38
Far Eastern Gwth	127.70	130.30†	+ 0.90	0.13
Far East Gth Acc	221.40	226.00	+ 1.60	0.13
Glt & Fx Int	64.92	67.50	+ 0.25	4.78
Growth & Inc	585.60	623.30	+ 4.30	1.23
Growth & Inc Acc	1325.00	1410.00	+ 9.00	1.23
Int Fxd Int	106.20	109.80	...	2.44
Int Fxd Int Acc	157.00	162.30	− 0.20	2.44
Multintl	71.99	74.37	+ 1.05	0.25
Multintl Acc	71.99	74.37	+ 1.05	0.25
Optimum Income #	92.06	96.26†	+ 0.36	3.94
Smaller Cos	76.67	81.78	+ 1.81	1.50
Smaller Cos Acc	98.92	105.50	+ 2.30	1.50
UK Growth	582.90	616.90	+ 4.20	1.25
UK Growth Acc	610.50	646.10	+ 4.40	1.25

BARING FUND MANGERS LTD
020 7214 1004

American Growth	229.80	241.90	+ 2.90	...
Amer Smllr Cos	183.80	193.80	+ 3.10	...
Eastern	201.30	214.30	+ 1.20	0.20
Equity Income #	113.90	121.20†	+ 1.50	2.60
European Growth	541.50	573.10	+ 7.80	...
Europe Select ‡	473.10	...	+ 4.20	...
German Growth ‡	193.50	...	+ 2.60	...
Global Bond	74.30	78.13†	− 0.08	2.80
Global Growth	200.80	212.10	+ 2.60	...
Japan Growth	82.35	87.51	+ 0.81	...
Korea Trust	88.60	94.37	+ 0.94	...
Portfolio	170.90	181.10	+ 2.20	0.90
-do- Accum	342.60	363.10	+ 4.40	0.90
UK Growth	144.30	153.30	+ 2.80	0.50
UK Smaller Cos	210.10	228.60	+ 1.40	...

BRITANNIC FUND MGRS LTD
0141 223 6020 Dig: 0141 222 8282

Balanced Growth	183.82	194.00	+ 4.91	0.89
-do- Accum	223.61	236.00	+ 5.98	0.89
Smaller Cos	222.74	235.09	+ 7.29	0.46
-do- Accum	259.34	273.71	+ 8.49	0.46
Higher Yield #	67.22	70.94†	+ 1.69	3.43
-do- Accum #	123.76	130.61	+ 3.12	3.43
American Gth Inc	188.04	198.45	+ 3.85	...
European Growth	240.72	254.06	+ 4.32	0.60
-do- Accum	245.87	259.50	+ 4.41	0.60
Mngd Pfolio Inc	66.00	69.66	+ 0.83	2.00
-do- Accum	72.76	76.79	+ 0.92	2.00
Glob Gwth	198.66	209.67	+ 4.04	...
Pacific Grth	168.26	177.58	+ 1.05	0.17
UK General #	114.88	121.24†	+ 2.12	2.84
-do- Accum #	139.56	147.29	+ 2.57	2.84

EDINBURGH UNIT TST MGRS LTD
Client Servs 0800 028 6789 Dlng 0845 606 1111

European ‡	93.11	... †	+ 1.07	
Financial ‡	98.44	... †	+ 0.96	
UK Growth #	389.00	... †	+ 4.10	
UK Income #	272.30	... †	+ 2.60	
Latin American ‡	25.86	... †	+ 0.04	
Mgd Gwth Port	117.20	121.60	− 1.90	
Pacific ‡	70.33	... †	+ 0.15	
UK Fixed Int ‡	23.24	... †	− 0.01	
Tokyo ‡	135.20	... †	+ 0.70	
UK Smaller Cos ‡	371.80	... †	+ 3.00	
Nth Amer ‡	818.90	... †	+10.40	
Global Eqty Inc ‡	89.11	... †	+ 1.09	
Global Eqty Acc ‡	90.22	... †	+ 1.10	

ENDURANCE FUND MGMT LTD
020 7373 7261

Endurance Fd	228.00	242.50	− 5.70	

For Equitable see Halifax Inv Fds Mgrs

EXETER FUND MANAGERS LTD
01392 412 144

Capital Growth	203.37	214.63	+ 0.49	
Global Opps	98.56	104.01	+ 0.16	
High Income #	25.78	27.18†	+ 0.03	
Managed Growth	89.10	94.03†	+ 0.28	
Zero Preference	53.40	56.35†	...	

F&C UNIT MANAGEMENT LTD
Dlg 0845 600 1868 Admin/Val 0870 606 6455

Euro Smllr Cos	197.90	209.80	+ 1.80	
High Income	22.86	24.36	+ 0.16	
UK Smllr Cos	37.99	41.38	− 0.05	
US Smaller Cos	677.50	718.10	+ 7.30	

F&C OEIC - ICV

Blue Acc ‡	50.83	...	+ 0.14	
Corp Bd ‡	50.78	...	+ 0.18	
UK Equity ‡	49.14	...	+ 0.75	
With Prospects ‡	100.20	...	+ 0.99	

FAMILY INVESTMENT MGMT LTD
01273 724 570

Family Asset Tst	165.40	175.90†	+ 1.30	
Charities Eth	425.30	452.30	+ 0.60	

FIDELITY INVESTMENT SERVS LTD
Callfree: Private Clients: 0800 414 161

Wealthbuilder	45.16	47.52	+ 0.52	

Cash Fund

Cash Fund	100.00	100.00†	...	

Bond Funds

Intl Bond ‡	26.25	... †	− 0.01	

Income Funds

UK Balanced ‡	34.41	... †	+ 0.29	
Income Plus #	192.90	... †	+ 2.00	
Mnybuilder Gwth #	42.09	... †	+ 0.51	
Extra Inc ‡	21.30	... †	+ 0.01	
Moneybuilder Ind ‡	40.55	...	+ 0.69	

Equity Funds

ASEAN ‡	7.950	...	+0.126	
American ‡	1301.00	...	+ 9.00	
Amer Spec Sits ‡	544.50	...	+11.00	
European ‡	519.70	...	+ 3.70	
European Opps ‡	153.20	...	+ 2.20	
UK Growth ‡	180.80	...	+ 2.40	
Growth & Inc #	242.20	... †	+ 3.20	
Intl ‡	78.82	...	+ 1.17	
Japan Spec Sits ‡	87.67	...	+ 0.06	
Japan ‡	177.20	...	+ 1.60	
Managed Intl ‡	634.50	...	+10.10	
Mnybuilder Inc ‡	29.85	... †	+ 0.10	
Mnybuilder Glob	124.30	124.30†	+ 1.30	
UK Aggress ‡	86.39	...	+ 0.64	
South E Asia ‡	203.90	...	+ 0.60	

LIST OF ILLUSTRATIONS

but unknowing that life in Karachi was ending. And Candy
being left, behind, and all the others who made their lives.

33. 'Khosas at home': Sirdars, Members of the Shahi Jirga. (R to
L) S. Sardar Khan Khoso, S. Mohammad Khan Dombki, KB.
S. Jaafar Khan Burdi (MLA), SB. S. Abdul Rahim Khan
Khoso, Mr Pearce, Mrs Pearce (with Adam and David), KS. S.
Nur Mohammad Golo (MLA), KS. S. Nur Mohammad
Bijarani, S. Mohammad Khan Mastoi, and S. Khan
Mohammad Khan Bugti.

34. Programme of the Jacobabad Horse Show.

MAPS

AUTHOR'S NOTE

This book has had a long, long period of gestation. The undesireability of my going to Karachi just now has meant that instead of easy consultation in an office, it has perforce been by airmail, fax and, occasionally, by telephone; so, whereas the writing of the book has been the easiest, and certainly the most pleasant part of the process, the Press in Karachi has had all the problems, negotiating with an inexperienced author; and the risks, both financial and moral, of publishing such a book following many comparable works, and doing so in a political climate where women are seriously undervalued.

So I wish to express my appreciation of the patience and unfailing helpfulness of the Oxford Press in Karachi: of its Managing Director, Ameena Saiyid and of her colleagues. For their sakes far more than for mine I hope their trust and courage bring the success they deserve.

Roger R. Pearce
June 2000

ACKNOWLEDGEMENTS

The complete and voluminous correspondence between my wife and myself from 1937 to 1948 still exists, preserved by her for sixty years and over many moves; so to her is due my acknowledgement that without this domestic archive, photographs, and a few other letters and documents from other sources, there would be no firm, factual basis for this book.

I thank Bernard Budd and Jack Phelps, my ICS contemporaries in Sindh, for help on individual points, and Bashir Malik, retired from the Pakistan Railway Service, for information, particularly from his *History of Pakistan Railways*.

I thank the Pakistan Tourism Corporation for useful brochures about present-day Sindh, and particularly for a large-scale map of the province. I had hoped for information from the Government of Sindh about matters pending when I left the province, but even though Mr Masroor Junejo, of the Pakistan High Commission, inquired on my behalf—for which I thank him—none has proved available; this is disappointing, though perhaps not surprising, for in the fifty years since I left, Sindh became a part of the Single Unit and later became a separate province again, which must have played havoc with its records!

When I had given up hope of any word from Jacobabad itself, copies came of careful research done by Professor

Agha Muhammad Ismael of that town, remembered by me more for my pride in serving there than even for its devastating heat.

I owe many thanks to Mr Martin Moir for showing me where I might find records in London, which I did find in a cellar below the Library of the London School of Economics, and for telling me where I might find records in Sindh, which, regrettably, I have not studied, having been very forcefully advised that I should not visit the province just now.

In my own family, my sons have taught me enough of the elements of computing to be able to process my text; for advice and help locally I have to thank Paul Weaving. I am particularly indebted to my son David for his personal account of life in Sindh for his first six years. Though not always accurate, it helped to inspire me to write this, my own account. My daughter has encouraged me from far Brooklyn, and above all I thank my wife Joan, who preserved the letters, who has been a valuable source of confirmation and amendment of memory, and when necessary, a severe critic. I thank them all. I hope their own parts in the story will please them. My sons and my daughter are all Sindhi-born.

Also I count in my family my sister Philippa, whose knowledge and experience of writing and publishing she has lavished on me in an attempt, successful I hope, to make a somewhat disjointed text publishable. Without her help I would certainly have failed.

Finally, I owe much to Lisa Darnell, of the Literary Consultancy, for patiently persuading me to shape my still rather unorganized text into something fit for publication.

If in the following record I have introduced errors in spite of all the help I have received, they are entirely my own responsibility.

PREFACE

Before ever I began to write, I planned to travel round Sindh, to visit the places I knew and see what changes have been in the fifty years since Pakistan was born; even to find one or two of the people I had known. The Pakistan Tourism Corporation sent me a map of the province and some brochures, but was oddly lacking in encouragement. I wrote to the British Deputy High Commissioner in Karachi, who made it clear that the Pakistan Government did not want tourists: it wanted no more murders and kidnaps. At first I was incredulous, but then I read the guide in the Lonely Planet series, and had to accept that Sindh was no place for anyone like me to go.

At the time of Independence, the population of Karachi was about 300,000, about 40 percent Hindu. Now the population of Karachi alone is estimated to be 10,000,000, of the whole province about 25,000,000. Pakistan is an Islamic State, and was so from the beginning: almost all the Hindus left.

In my time, Hindus filled all the professions, and government offices at all levels. In the villages, Hindus were the providers of goods and services and credit. Most of them left for India, and their place was taken by Muslims from those parts of India where they had been the minority community, but had become far better educated and skilled than most Sindhis, particularly in commerce, and begun to threaten the political supremacy of the Sindhi landowners.

It was the rivalry between these immigrants—mohajirs—
and native Sindhis that began the turmoil and violence.
Since then have come refugees from Afghanistan, bringing
with them guns and the poppy business; and most recently
Islamic fundamentalism, which is pushing social
liberalization backwards.

In 1997, both India and Pakistan celebrated fifty years of
statehood. India celebrated with enthusiasm and world-wide
publicity; Pakistan has, just now, less to celebrate. India
invited surviving British members of the Indian Civil Service
to take part in its celebrations. The fact that I had spent all
my service in what became Pakistan, and finally served the
Government of Pakistan, bothered India not at all: my
name was on the Bombay Cadre.

This visit was not concerned with Sindh, but over the
half century there stretch fragile tendrils that bring new
life to that distant past, tendrils that have opened small
flowers both in England on the one hand and in India and
Pakistan on the other. To accommodate them, my Epilogue
also remains open.

Pakistan came to statehood through the trauma and
bloodshed of Partition, without any of the established
central government that India inherited; it is still struggling
with that handicap, and perhaps Sindh suffers more than
other provinces. Sir Richard Burton travelled there a
century and a half ago, and named Sindh the 'Unhappy
Valley'. My book was to have been titled *The Happy Valley*;
but finally that has had to be changed.

INTRODUCTION

Anyone who proposes to record his life story and lay it before the public must possess a measure of conceit in his ability to write with a style that will hold attention, and confidence in there being some general interest in what he has to say.

My confidence was thoroughly tested by many doubts before I was able to suppress them and even to begin writing. Always in reserve was the possibility of abandonment, and if this introduction is being read it must mean that my publisher sees merit in my confidence and has matched it with her own.

I was born at the beginning of the Great War, but I have no intention of burdening the reader with the story of my first twenty-three years, similar to that of any other middle-class boy going to a small public school and on to a university. This was followed by twelve years, the period of this book, when I served in the Indian Civil Service under the Government of India until India and Pakistan became independent; then I, in Sindh, which became a part of Pakistan, served that state for a year and a half before retiring. As was almost traditional among officials retiring from colonial and imperial service, though previously they would have retired after full time whereas I was still young, in 1949 I settled with my family in England in the country. Such officers raised pigs or chickens or something like; I grew apples. We were apt to sit on local councils and become magistrates and run socially useful organizations. Having been used to doing such things professionally, we just carried on, which did not always please our established neighbours.

So only twelve years remain, but they cover the last ten years of the British Empire of India and the first of the new state of Pakistan. (The concurrent Second World War was, in Sindh, little more than incidental!) I hope there is enough in those years to justify the telling.

My wife and I kept no diaries but, although my memory for what happened last month, or is due to happen next week, may be unreliable, for what happened fifty years ago it remains excellent. Letters home have seldom survived, but those between ourselves have done so, even if they are scraps of paper sent with the office post. From the time I left England we wrote almost daily when we were apart, and, looking back, it is surprising how often that was. There are the envelopes, too, usually with a delivery date. The stamps are gone, doubtless given to some collector. My letters are carefully dated, but my wife would write 'after tea' or 'Thursday morning'. A little study has set these in their proper context. They are always there to correct or reinforce memory.

So what facts and memories we have I have set down, and I hope that there will be some readers who will be entertained or informed or both. But do not expect to read of our part in any dramatic or important events when the Indian Empire came to an end. I was very junior in service, and in fact in posts which before the war would have been beyond my years. I was involved in some unusual events, but rather by chance than because I was an important participant.

The British Empire is so long gone that even its end is a matter of history. The Indian Civil Service, whose members were once the 'Heaven-born', is now more apt to be criticized than praised, and sometimes surprise is expressed that any of us still live. In my present home, the acronym

ICS is most readily translated as the Ipswich Co-operative Society. There never were very many of us—about twelve hundred, of whom over half were Indian at the end. But we were the central, tough, able, and incorruptible core of the governance of that vast, varied, uneasy country. At the very top, and at the end, there were a few of my colleagues, British and Indian, without whose wisdom and effort the transfer of government from Britain to India and Pakistan would have been far more difficult, perhaps impossible without general strife.

But I was near the bottom of the tiers of influence. The Empire did not last long enough for my contemporaries and me to rise high. So I write of what happened low down in the structure, where our job was just to keep things running. (Not that that stopped one from having ideas for the new states!) There is here nothing like the dramas in Paul Scott's books, or any place like those in the film *The Jewel in the Crown.*

My story is of one short career, of one family in one small corner of India which became Pakistan. We lived there among the people, they influenced us, and we can hope that in some small way, possibly for good, we influenced them.

We relics of the British in the Indian Civil Service are growing very old; none of us is, I think, under eighty. So I put it on record now that there is nothing in my life of which I am more proud than of being of their number. If there are in this book signs of bias on that account, so be it: such a bias worries me not at all.

1

THE ICS OF COURSE

Even before the beginning of the nineteenth century, the East India Company was consistently trying to improve the quality of its servants, and to reduce the power of patronage.

Haileybury College was founded in 1806 with the express purpose of creating a pool of young men suitably educated to become 'writers' in the Company's service. Gradually, higher educational standards were required and patronage was reduced until, in 1855, with the creation of the Civil Service Commission and the institution of competitive examinations, a university degree became the standard qualification necessary for a candidate to have any hope of success.

After the Mutiny in 1858, the Government of India formally became the responsibility of the British Crown, and competition was opened to Indians, in accordance with a promise of the Queen that 'subjects of whatever race or creed shall be freely and impartially admitted to office in our Service'. The Indian Civil Service was born. But without a long and expensive period of education in England, an Indian had no chance of success: a gamble against long odds. The admission was neither free nor impartial: very few Indians won through, and those few were not welcomed.

Slowly the trauma of the Mutiny faded, and attitudes changed, till a time came when Indians educated in India could sit for the exam in India, and till the point was reached when more than half the members of the Indian Civil Service were Indians, who were perfectly capable of running their own country themselves. Even then there were some who saw this as a sign not of success, but of failure.

I graduated from Cambridge in 1936 with a fairly good degree in History. Britain was slowly emerging from recession, but for someone with a degree in the humanities, and no ready-made job or influence, there were hopes only in teaching or the civil service; or, as one friend pointed out to me, 'you could always fall back on the Church'. For me it must be the Civil Service, and the Indian Civil Service at that. Apart from an uncle involved with textiles in and around Bombay, I had no connection at all with such a service. Even now I find my choice, followed by my determination, a little strange. But I knew Kipling's writing, and was ready to discount his jingoism and his racism, and remember only that there never was such a story-teller. And then there was my uncle.

In other times I could have expected to succeed my Father in his country flour mill, but he was sure there was no future in that; with the growing number of giant mills at ports, he foresaw a swift end.

There was nearly a year to pass before the Competitive Examination, and I had no money, but plenty of time to work for it. I lived at home, and I worked for the Exam with difficulty—so many more attractive things to do. I learnt something of gardening, of pruning and grafting fruit trees, of installing machinery in a mill, of 'extraction rates', and why my Father smelt samples of wheat: a smell of wild garlic, ramsons, meant that the flour would be tainted and the screenings wasted, not to be ground for cattle feed in my newly installed machine. These irrelevant scraps stuck in my mind, to become relevant years later. Otherwise I must have read and read and read: specially I studied economics, and the business pages of *The Times*.

The Commission set a syllabus from the classics to modern languages, from history and anthropology to mathematics and all the sciences. Doubtless the ideal candidate was a polymath, but I could offer history for 500 marks and a hundred more for my new-learnt economics.

To make up the total to the necessary 1,000 there was an interview: obviously this could help along the candidate not quite adequate academically but otherwise just the sort of man needed: it could also fail the man who was too clever by half; for the interview was worth 400 marks.

In my year there was an innovation for the interview: there was a lady on the panel, who would look into the social attributes of a candidate. Was I one of the Pearces of Warwick? I was not. Did I hunt? I did not. (No need to tell her that I had never sat on a horse.) Did I shoot? For pigeons only. Did I fish? I did, and for trout: but with a worm, more useful in our muddy river than any fly. So no help there. I had a relative in India, but he was in trade. I lived in the country, which was to my credit, but my father was a miller, also in trade, cancelling that credit. The lady gave me no comfort: even if I passed, for her I would not pass for a gentleman.

But the other members of the panel were clearly impatient with her, their questions were entirely relevant, and I left them not too cast down.

The Commission reached its decisions very quickly: those unneeded must look for another job. The Secretary wrote to me regretting...and then, before disappointment had faded, he telegraphed: would I after all accept a post, and if so would I present myself at the School of Tropical Medicine for a medical examination? I would surely do both those things.

One man had refused the offer because his fianceé would not go with him. Perhaps she had hoped that he would be rejected.

I thought I had finished with the university when I graduated, but then I came back; back with a long graduate's gown and with unimagined wealth. Before, I had managed on £180 a year, helped by fruit and eggs from home, my laundry done there, and occasional meals. Now I was wealthy! An ICS cadet, with ICS pay: for the year! No more need to squeeze a second boiling from the coffee pot, or wonder if I could afford to dine out for 1/6.

But chiefly there was work, and plenty of it; not burdensome because I—and the twenty or so other recruits there—knew that we were preparing for what we all wanted to do.

There were men from other universities and from India, for now over half the Service was Indian, examined and accepted in India, and in Cambridge for training. (Doubtless also to learn what sort of people the Government of India would like its servants to be.)

There were books, books to know thoroughly, books that from now on would always be with us: the Indian administrator's bible, the Indian Penal Code; the Indian Evidence Act; the Criminal Procedure Code; and, for some of us, the Indian Revenue Act, with a massive tome of Rules Thereunder.

We must know some history, but we could ignore the three and a half millennia of India's record before the British arrived, and not bother about much that happened before the Mutiny in 1857, less than a century before. We were assumed to know the facts—and indeed, there were plenty of books that anyone could read. Our lecturer, G.T. Garratt, was author of our most useful book. His objective was to dispel ignorance and prejudice; we must remember that we would meet people who had lived through the Mutiny, whose relatives could have been killed by the British. We must set aside the undoubted heroism, remember that Indians had not forgotten the other side. We were told to read a little book, *The Other Side of the Medal*, which gave the picture that Indians had of the vengeance that the British took to help them overcome their fright.

Generally we worked together, but for a language we were grouped by provinces; I had chosen Bombay (for that was my uncle's country) and forever after was on the 'Bombay Presidency Cadre'. This whole cadre must learn Marathi, perhaps because it was a language with a literature, and with a hero, the great Sivaji. But for the Presidency there were four languages, Gujerati and Kanarese besides Marathi, all with Sanskrit roots, and Sindhi, totally different, with Arabic and Persian roots, a different grammar and script. Sindh was only joined to Bombay because it was too small to have a cadre of its own.

For months I struggled with Marathi, and then I was posted to Sindh; so cheerfully did I give away my Marathi! But I began my service in a country of whose language I knew no word, whose script was a mystery.

I have great admiration for the Government of India that ordered our training, but remain puzzled by the way it required its recruits to learn a language which, in Bombay at least, had only one chance in four of being useful. For all of us, language would be an essential tool: lack of knowledge would inevitably reduce our competence and make us much too dependant on our staff.

India has two languages, each in its sphere an acceptable lingua franca: Urdu in the north and Hindi in the south, and these two have come to have much in common. Knowledge of one of these would have made us at least a little colloquially articulate wherever we were posted.

No one in England could teach me Sindhi. What a language it was! Fifty-three letters, and different forms if they were initial, internal, or final. Difficult to speak, worse to read, fiendish to write. But, as Defoe discovered of the French, in Sindh even the little children spoke it. There were local variations, too, from Baloch and Gujerati influences.

All of us must be able to ride a horse. The standard picture of an ICS officer was of a young man wearing a sun helmet, riding breeches, and smart boots: it was a true picture. Moreover, it was the only part of our training for which we must actually pass an exam. Some of us were already proficient horsemen; some, like me, had never sat on a horse, and must learn, as it were, from the stirrup up.

It is difficult to believe now, but in the thirties there was a riding school with a covered ring and stabling for the horses in the middle of Cambridge, behind the shops where Hobson Street and King Street join; and there Captain Cooper ruled. He was a retired cavalryman, small and short of patience, insistent on discipline, always dressed and speaking the part. He wore a bowler hat, pince-nez, a butterfly collar, a suede waistcoat, cavalry twill breeches, and perfectly polished boots; to complete the picture he always carried a crop.

We tyros dressed in ways that would have made a cavalry sergeant weep, but then, we were mere civilians, who could not be expected to know better. Some of us had the proper kind of boots, so very bright as to declare their newness. Indians wore jodhpurs, as was only to be expected, and forecast the garment that in India we would find better than any other. I, on advice, wore puttees with my breeches: worn by Other Ranks in the army, but not, I am sure, in the cavalry. Puttees are horrible things. Perhaps the Captain had recommended them just to humiliate me. However carefully I wound mine on they, not being designed for bicycle travel, always collapsed in an untidy tangle round my ankles by the time I reached the School. There came a day when I abandoned the damned things and adopted thick stockings. I should have bought jodhpurs at the beginning, but the cavalry would never countenance such a garment.

Paying for riding lessons was not a required charge on this general training course, but I felt that instruction was essential. In fact, quite soon I realized that, as a means to learning to ride, it was a joke. One did not learn what to do; at best, just a few things not to do.

The School was fine: it was round, with a floor of bark, soft to fall on. Nor can I fault Captain Cooper, with his string of six smart and beautiful, well-kept ponies. We were taught how to mount on the nearside, and to find the offside stirrup without looking down; we learnt how to set the stirrup to the right length, to check girth and bridle, and how to hold the reins. (Little Rao needed a leg up, or to set his stirrup at its greatest length and shorten it to its very shortest once he was in the saddle.)

All this was very well: Captain Cooper's ponies did not dance around as ordinary horses do, and we could have learnt it all on a wooden horse. But the actual riding was another matter: we needed to trot and canter, to learn how to change step and back, even how to 'passage'. So we trotted round a few times, and then the Captain explained how to change step: pressure of knee and rein, the manoeuvre to be executed by each in turn as we rode in a figure of eight across the School, to be done on the word. One by one we reached the chosen spot, he called 'Change step,' and regardless of what any of us did our mounts obeyed; very possibly we did the opposite of what we ought, but the ponies would override our errors and do as ordered. It must have looked very neat and beautiful, and so it should, for they had obeyed that order so very many times.

Horses are very beautiful animals, and I believe can be very affectionate. They are said not to be very clever, but they know how to obey an order they have heard scores of times, and these brooked neither help nor hindrance from the fools who happened to be sitting on their backs.

There came the time to take the test. This was at the Police Training College at Hendon, with full-sized horses, a Sergeant, and jumps at least two feet high. The Sergeant called us all Sir; he said it nicely to those of us who could ride, not at all nicely to those who obviously couldn't. I would prefer to forget about it: I fell off. I preserved my pride by remounting neatly, but that was not enough: I

failed. The Sergeant was very frank: if the horse didn't
know what to do I seemed unable to tell him.

I returned to Cambridge, but not to Captain Cooper
and his beauties: they knew too much. I found a farmer
just outside the town who kept a livery stable, and there I
learned to ride. I went with a group of little boys and girls
and hacked about the countryside and found I could be
happy on a horse which did only what I told it to, even if I
told it to do something that I hadn't really intended. I
learnt that it was fun, too, and next time I went to Hendon
the Sergeant was quite polite, and passed me.

This was just as well. I doubt if failing again would have
cost me my job, but riding competently was truly important
for someone going to be a District Officer making field
inspections—endless field inspections.

Finally, we must know what the India we would find
looked like. The Indian National Congress had been
formed in 1885, the Muslim League in 1906, setting the
scene for the triangular game that lasted, on and off, for
the next forty years. In 1919 the Amritsar Massacre
threatened to destroy Indian faith in British intentions, but
by 1920 there were Indian Ministries in all the provinces,
with elected Assemblies. Then, in 1935, the Government of
India Act promised full independence in the foreseeable
future. So we all knew what to expect. We knew that no
longer was imperial power untrammelled, and we were told
very forcefully that no longer could we be sure of a
lifetime's career in our service. I don't think that worried
us much: we must already have developed the arrogance
for which the Indian Civil Service was notorious, and have
convinced ourselves that an independent India would find
us, even the British half of our service, indispensable.
Perhaps some of us resented the changes, but they had
known the terms, they couldn't grumble. Most of us, all
the Indians, were strong believers in the ultimate goal.

But long before I began to prepare to leave for India I
had faced the parallel prospect of leaving home. I had

stood by the river at Shelford in February and seen the
swathes of snowdrops in the wilderness along the bank,
and watched the water running fast under the old wooden
mill, where it drove the original pairs of millstones. The
turbine that had replaced the undershot wheel rumbled
and whined, the whole wooden structure acting as a
sounding board. On the far bank was the engine room
housing the big gas engine that powered the roller mill, a
tall, gaunt building of pink flettons. The engine generated
its own gas, and occasionally its steady pop, pop waited
when the governor cut in. Then the popping began again;
but occasionally, if one were lucky, the engine would clear
its flue: there would be a bang, and a large black smoke
ring would curl up into the still air, and gradually fade
away.

I loved it; I loved it all. I had always lived in Shelford,
and had been born there. Now I must realize that, if my
Father was right about small country mills like his, I would
never live there again.

In March, on the last day of the Lent term, I asked Joan
to marry me, and she agreed. I asked her to breakfast, and
she came on her way home, cycling to London with a friend
to save the rail fare: she had no more money than I had
before coming into my service wealth. For two years we had
known each other very well; in my mind she was my woman,
I her man (Joan disagrees that there was a marked
relationship) and she seemed to have no doubts. But as I
walked home that night, my feet felt very cold. I had done
something irrevocable, perhaps a big mistake. After this
summer we wouldn't meet for three years, and anything
could happen. Did I really love her? But the telephone
next day told me that I did. So we had all that beautiful
summer, and all I had to do was collect the minimum of
things my uncle said I must take, enjoy the time, and say
farewell to my family, and to Joan.

The *Strathnaver* was one of a fleet specially built for the
P & O for the Empire route to the Far East and Australia;

she carried a vast number of passengers on a hull of draught small enough to pass the Suez Canal. She sailed from Tilbury, but I chose to cross France and join her at Marseilles, just to have my birthday at home and a few more days with my family and my love. It was a serious mistake, for by Marseilles all the social groups had been formed. Probably I would have been welcomed into a group with ICS officers returning from leave, happy to tell their newest recruit all about India. But I was not bold, and I had a group waiting for me: a girl going out to marry a medical missionary, a friend of Joan's, with, as chaperone, a notable officer of the Mission, something of a dragon with a companion called Mabel, mercilessly bullied and sadly plain. We were not a lively group. I was homesick and bored, longing for this voyage to end, when I should have been enjoying this great experience. The highlights I remember are when, twice, a nice girl from a lower deck came up and asked me to dance—on her own deck, of course.

At Port Said there was a simple warning: 'don't buy a *topi* here'.

Then there was the Canal and things became more interesting. The ship must move slowly, lest it wash sand into the channel, and ahead one could see little boats poling madly for the shore, lest they be overwhelmed. When night fell, the searchlight shipped with the pilot was switched on. By daylight I had seen the bare, dry hills of Arabia to the east, and to the west, camels and palm trees, and could imagine the pyramids out of sight over the horizon. The great light bored a hole through the dark. In the Bitter Lakes, the northbound convoy was setting off, ship by ship.

We stopped at every port, and with its own derricks the ship landed cargo, and every time it was crates of gin and whisky. But at Port Sudan a crate fell and a package burst: from it showered shaped flints from Brandon in Suffolk.

They were needed inland for the tribesmen who still used flintlock guns.

More gin and whisky for Aden. I was told it was the ashpit of the East, a great coaling station. But we burnt oil. There was never a drop of rain there. I don't know where its water came from, but without doubt the whisky was welcome. From Aden the course is as straight for Bombay as the great circle allows. The ship stopped moving and the sea began to rush by, making a feather at the bow as it split, turbulence at the stern as it rejoined. The sun moved slowly round us to the south.

In the Red Sea it had been hot, even in November. The India Office booked its recruits P&O First Class B; First Class A was 'Posh', and here the meaning of the word became clear. My cabin was exactly the same as an A class one, but on the sunny side; the A class was on the shady, the port side. So arose the word specific to this great imperial route: Port Out, Starboard Home, POSH. The Oxford dictionary claims that the derivation is unknown, that it first appears in 1918; but anyone who travelled by sea to the East knew, and probably the word first appeared soon after the Canal was opened.

An ocean-going dhow passed us, sailing free for the coast of Africa, its lateen sails boomed out, 'like hare's ears' was the crew's description. We overtook one sailing close-hauled for India. Otherwise the whole Arabian Sea was empty, streaming past day after day. But one day fishing boats appeared, then a smudge on the horizon, and at last the ship itself began to move. The Gateway of India rose ahead, the ship was full of bustle, and in no time we were tied up at the quay: the Apollo Bunder, such a wonderful name.

There were good-byes, and promises to write, probably seldom kept. I was in little doubt as to who would meet me, for my uncle was still in Bombay, but it was an ADC from the Governor who came, and Grindlay's agent who would see my baggage across to the Karachi packet lying at anchor, ready to take me on the next day.

I was taken to the Yacht Club for lunch: the finest Club in all India, to which I would never aspire again. Then I must call at Government House, on the point of Malabar Hill, itself the finest site in all India. Nor did I ever go there again, but I left my card, the first of many, specially printed with 'Indian Civil Service'. But Bombay was not really interested in me, just on passage to another province, even though of the same cadre.

I spent that first night with my uncle in his flat overlooking Back Bay. He was himself preparing to leave for England, foresaw another war, and would not be left out this time. But we were no longer easy together, for now I was one of the bureaucracy for which he had little use.

Next day I set off on the last lap, on a black and white British India liner with a British captain and a deck crew of lascars. I was travelling 'posh' now, and that was a pleasant three-day voyage. There was nothing to see but the ocean on one side and the endless plains of Kathiawar on the other. We stopped in the roadstead of Porbunder and then off Kutch Mandvi; as soon as the ship was sighted, bunder-boats set sail to meet her, bringing goods for export and passengers, and, using the ship's own derricks, taking away passengers and goods—but goods more useful than whisky. Chief of the exports were hides, with their unforgettable smell.

At Kutch Mandvi a young Englishwoman came out asking to be taken to Karachi. She had married a Kutchi who had promised her jewels and a fine house, and it was all lies; hers was a miserable state and she had no money. We passengers were willing to pay her fare, but the captain would have none of it: he could expect fearful political consequences if he helped her to leave her husband. We left her standing in her boat, and ourselves felt guilty, anxious for her fate when her husband heard what she had done. One passenger knew a political officer in Karachi, and would see if there was any help for a woman as isolated and lonely as she.

Next day, Karachi: a very small port compared with Bombay, but with an enormous sheltered harbour. I came to know that harbour well: most of it was too shallow even for the fishing boats. There was one quay, itself created from the wide mangrove swamp behind, and most freighters anchored in the stream to await their turn; but the *Vita*, our mail boat, had precedence and tied up alongside.

At last I had arrived.

I was met by someone from the Revenue Commissioner, head of my own department, my official master, and by another cheerful man from Grindlay's who took charge of my baggage, cleared Customs, and took it to the Central Hotel; finally, when I moved on, he took it to the train that took me up-country. There was, too, on the quayside a small old man in voluminous Sindhi trousers and an enormous white turban. His beard was very black, and so was what could be seen of his hair; indeed, for a man with such a wrinkled and weathered face it had kept its colour well—till the dye began to grow out, and the white appeared. He had a fistful of 'chits', and he wore an ICS cummerbund, though I didn't recognize it. I needed a bearer, and there he was: chits and cummerbund were recommendation enough. In fact, he had served as 'butler' to a succession of sahibs; the latest had just been transferred to Bombay. Perhaps he had been waiting, just hoping that someone would appear, but more likely the grapevine had told him I was coming. I came, I took him on, and his experience helped greatly in the launch of my career: Khuda Baksh. He cheated me over his age, he made a little from me on the side—the customary percentage when he shopped—but he always guarded my interest. His meeting me was lucky for both of us.

2

ON MY WAY

Karachi was a very beautiful city. First I saw the harbour, with the long mole that alone joined the docks to the town. It carried road and railway, and the road ran on through the city and to the Cantonment area where important government officers lived. I was shown the sights by an officer who must have been a Sindhi: no British officer would have known so much. We passed the Merewether Clock Tower, named after a famous officer of the even more famous John Jacob, and drove along Macleod Road past the grand, beautiful offices of the Managing Agents. They had been built of stone nearly a century before, more like mansions than offices, with their pillared porticoes and circular drives. They expressed full confidence in their permanency. They managed the trade between Britain and the Far East, they advised princes on their investments, and then managed the factories that they built. MacKinnon MacKenzie and Matheson Lang; Volkearts, the Swiss who were more recent and handled all the raw cotton trade from Sindh and the Punjab; and Ralli, the Greeks who ran the shipping business. Across the road were the more prosaic offices of companies with which officers like me would be more concerned. Spencer's ran all the restaurants on the North Western Railway; and Phipson's held the licence for imported liquor, and had large cold stores—of more interest to up-country officers even than to those in Karachi.

I was shown the brand new Government House, and left another card. Sindh had only just become a separate province, though I would still remain on the Bombay cadre, liable at some time to be transferred there.

On to the Central Hotel, and there my guide left me. I felt very lonely.

But not for long was I left. My fears of the snobbery and arrogance of an imperial government were proved empty. I was lent a Government House car to do my shopping: a large Daimler with a specially high roof to accommodate a top hat. The driver knew where to take me: to Gangaram's. Mr Gangaram himself came out, expecting Her Excellency, but was unabashed when he found it was only me. I needed no *bistra*, or bedding roll, for I had my Father's, but I needed so many things to go in it: sheets, blankets—Upper Sindh, where I was going, could be cold in winter—toiletries and a *chalumchi*, an enamel bowl with a round leather lid, to keep everything in. Then I must have towels, and Gangaram was agent for Elgin Mills, so I could warm my heart by telling him about my uncle. And, at last a *topi*. With that, bistra, and chalumchi I could travel anywhere. I made very sure that my topi was of the correct pattern for an Indian Civil Service officer posted in Sindh

My posting was gazetted: Supernumerary Assistant Collector in training, Shikarpur Subdivision. The longest entry for the most junior officer.

I left by the Lahore Mail, with Khuda Baksh to look after me. Beyond Karachi was a wide area of garden land, the airfield with the enormous hangar for the R101, the airship that never came because it crashed and burned up in France, and beyond that, desert and dust; dust that could not be kept out even with flyscreen and glass and wooden shutters closed. (I must get used to this!) But later the evening cooled, the dust ceased, and before it was dark I saw the Indus where the railway crossed it at Kotri. All through the night I passed unseeing the newly-won land on the east of the river; in the morning I reached Rohri, where the line passed through a limestone ridge, and there Dermont Barty met me. Instead of my having to change trains for Sukkur he drove me round, with Khuda Baksh, my baggage, and all.

Dermont Barty would be my instructor for the next six months, Assistant Collector in his first charge, a year senior to me. A Scot, and we found an empathy: he also had a fiancée in England, waiting for his first leave. He drove me along the east bank of the river and along the long, long road across the Barrage with its sluices, over the regulators at the heads of the canals, three on each side, watering almost the whole of Sindh. He drove on through the Barrage Township, once housing dozens of engineers, now with only a few remaining; some bungalows empty, some with private tenants. Then came Sukkur town itself, the first real Indian town I had seen. But we drove through and up the little hill on which Dermont's own home perched: the Old Circuit House, stone-built, with a wide verandah all along its front. It had a magnificent view to the River and beyond, to the green jungles of Khairpur. Between, in the middle of the river, was Sadh Bela, an island with a temple sacred to Hindus. Look left, and there was the Lansdowne Bridge, two cantilevers intricately built, towering high into the air, the same design as the Forth Bridge and said to be older; for Dermont it was a reminder of home. The bungalow was built of stone and so would be hot in summer, but he had not been there so long; at this time the very air could have been Scottish.

For the cold weather I would be Dermont's paying guest, and woe betide us if we didn't get on together. There was a more-or-less set rate for a guest to pay his host, and I paid it gladly: indeed, I was feeling rich. From the day I arrived in Bombay I earned Overseas Pay, and from the day I was posted to Sukkur I earned Permanent Travelling Allowance. Total income: Rs. 760 a month, or £750 a year: wealth indeed!

In Sukkur in 1938 I experienced the end of an era for
British officers in small up-country posts. There was what
later became impossible luxury. We had our bath in a tin
tub, with water heated in a charcoal boiler, and used a
thunder-box surreptitiously cleaned by the *bhangi*, an outcaste Hindu, disturbingly servile, hoping, perhaps, not to
be noticed. I wrote to Joan about my unease at the way I,
an ignorant white man, was treated with undeserved
deference wherever I went. But I must have quickly got
used to it, discounted it, and ceased to notice. I was still
worried by the problem of how someone who believed that
India should be independent ought, as an officer of its
government, to behave. But quite soon that was forgotten
too, overlaid by the problems of the actual exercise of
authority, though there remained the conviction that my
actions must never contradict that belief.

I was, in fact, extraordinarily fortunate to be posted
under Dermont Barty: Scottish, a free-thinker, abstemious
as suited his and my finances (though naturally he liked a
good whisky), he was someone I would have been happy to
own as friend, even had I not lived with him.

Luxuries reached us from the cold stores in Karachi:
kippers, bacon, cheese, even chocolate. The chocolate had
been frozen, thawed, melted and frozen again till it came
in all sorts of strange shapes, with a mossy bloom over all. I
never saw Cadbury's; perhaps they feared a bad image.

There was juniper gin from Nasik, beer from Murree,
and imported India Pale Ale, a very old brew popular from
the days of sail, for it could travel through the tropics,
round the Cape, and to the Far East without damage; and
even back again. There was a locally-distilled whisky with a
label just like White Horse, but called White Hart. Dermont,
who knew about these things, said it tasted like a mixture
of wood alcohol and gravy browning.

Within a year all these luxuries were gone: even Indian
gin and beer were rationed, and in Sukkur I ate the last
egg and bacon breakfasts I would taste for years. And,

indeed, our luxuries were so small that they were not seriously missed.

The Old Circuit House was commodious; there was a bedroom with bathrooms at each end and an office. There was a dining-room separate from the drawing-room, and a verandah all round. There were servant's quarters, kitchen, a garage on the hill, with stables at the bottom. There was even a small garden, built up over years with soil carried laboriously up from the river: this part of Sukkur was solid rock.

Servants' quarters throughout Sindh were a disgrace, but this was acceptable because it had always been like that, and even the servants liked what they knew. It was supposed that a man needed no more than room for a cot—he would sleep outside in the hot weather anyway—some nails to hang his clothes, and a locked box. Drainage from the hill was a problem whose solution I have forgotten. The kitchen needed a box for stores, though most were bought daily for that day, and somewhere for pots and pans, somewhere to wash, a small table, and the 'cooker'. That cooker: standard throughout Sindh, even in Karachi, though perhaps not in the newest, richest houses (standard, probably, throughout India at that time). It was a brick-built bench, mud brick in Upper Sindh, and in it was a range of slots, *chullas*, in each of which a little charcoal fire could be built. Pots, kettle, baking tins, frying pan, each could have its own heat, so a lot of dishes could be cooked at once. Even a cake could be baked, with a tray placed over the tin, glowing coal on top, more or less coal as the cook judged proper.

It was marvellous what good and complicated meals cooks could produce from their crude kitchens.

I acquired a horse. I don't know who had owned him, but he arrived, with his syce, Jan Mahommed, and his 'tack'. I paid Rs. 100 for Rajah, Rs. 15 for his tack, and Rs. 25 monthly for Jan Mahommed. Rajah was so cheap there was no point in looking in his mouth... He was in fact very old, as was his keeper. There was no bargaining, I could accept him or not. I needed a horse, and as if by magic one appeared; he looked to be quiet, just right for such a horseman as I, so I kept him.

I have a photograph of Rajah with me in the saddle. His back was hollow, his front was thin and grey, but I grew fond of him. He was my horse almost as much as he was Jan Mahommed's. I have a picture also of Dermont on his horse Bhoop, a chestnut stallion in all his young and virile beauty. I came to appreciate Rajah; I, who never was a great lover of horses. I would pet him, talk to him, see that he was well cared for, though Jan Mahommed would have spoken very firmly had he thought I was neglecting his charge and his companion

We went on tour, beginning the cold weather routine of the District Officer. We stayed first in bungalows near Sukkur, all standard Public Works Department types, with bedroom suite at each end and living-room in the middle. One was a little mud shack, so small that I had to sleep on the verandah; the one at Choi two-storeyed, where we and the staff could live. It was much used by high officials on tour. Dermont's work was mostly field inspections, checking revenue remission applications.

I, of course, rode with him, and he had an escort of the relevant *tapedars*. The tapedar—and there were hundreds of them—was the lowest revenue officer of all. He held all the maps, kept all the records of land holdings; above him was the *Mukhtiarkar;* above him the Assistant (or Deputy) Collector, who must see a percentage of the fields asking not to pay revenue. In the end it all finished with the Revenue Commissioner.

The Revenue Settlement in Sindh was revised every ten years. (In some provinces the settlement was permanent, and it seemed that District Officers had no real need to tour.) So the Assistant Collector came to know his sub-division and its people very well. His decisions on remission applications went to the Collector, his chief, from him to the Commissioner, who could talk with God: even we were only a little below the angels. But these field inspections made a tremendous task, lasting for the whole of the cold weather. Always the tapedars must be there with their maps, each showing the fields, the final units of the Great Trigonometrical Survey of India. (Kim used his post in that Survey as cover for his spying.) Boundaries were marked by stones, and if one were missing there would be disputes for Dermont to settle. First the stone must be found, and if it had been set up somewhere else, the culprit was easy to find; and moving a stone was a serious offence. If it were truly lost the Supervising Tapedar would come with his chain and cross-staff to fix the right spot, bring a new stone, and set it in place. The Survey was safe again.

Dermont had a routine for his remission inspections, his *pertals*. We got up early, had *chota hasri* of tea and toast, met the tapedars, and he chose the route he would take. He was to inspect fields for which remission of revenue was asked owing to failure of the crop. This area was not watered by the Barrage canals, but by old canals that flowed only in the flood period: inundation canals. The crop was rice, and by now it had been harvested, so its quantity could only be judged by the stubble, which might be thin and weak, or more or less strong. One had nearby land not asking for remission from which to set a standard, or occasionally a field where the crop had not been worth the reaping and the thin straw had been left. For years I never saw a field of standing rice. Here, there was a little cotton, easy to judge for quantity because it had been left for the officer to see and agree that it was worthless, because the water had dried up.

I had to learn about remissions, but once I had understood the principles, which were not difficult, it was all rather boring. But there was always the countryside to watch, the people, the birds, and the field work going slowly forward, for the land must be cultivated and the seed sown before the land dried up if there was to be a spring crop at all. An Assistant Collector's touring had changed very little in the fifty years before I first went with Dermont Barty. There were cars now, but it was usually I who drove between camps: Dermont would ride, working on the way. The camp moved with a camel train, staff probably by tonga, the ubiquitous pony trap. The office post might move more quickly than when the *kotwal*, the postman, went by horse. There were buses, *'laris'*, and occasionally a train to bring visitors, official and otherwise, to the Assistant Collector's camp. There was no telephone outside Sukkur except at police *thanas*; a touring officer was peacefully isolated. There was, for emergency, the canal telegraph, but it was traditional for Assistant and Deputy Collectors to disappear, as it were, from the sight of superiors. We preferred to settle our problems by ourselves.

Not every morning had its ride for pertal. There were criminal cases to hear, fixed for camps where parties could conveniently come. I must watch and study court procedure, but since evidence and argument were in Sindhi I could not follow, except when there was argument about translation. As a Magistrate, the Assistant Collector adopted his role as First Class Sub-divisional Magistrate, and must translate the evidence into English acceptable to all parties. He would usually reserve his judgment till the next day, for that must be written in English too. Dermont's Sindhi was not yet very good, so he depended largely on his court clerk, his *Shristedar*. Shristedars were, I was to find, highly competent in the law.

Then there were visitors, with business to discuss or just being polite, and petitioners, coming with their petitions written out in traditional form by a petition writer who knew all the correct forms... 'I, a Poor Man, pray that You, Protector of the Poor, will help me...' to deal with almost any imaginable problem under the sun—with an awkward money-lender, an oppressive neighbour, a policeman, a canal officer, even a bothersome mother-in-law.

It was strange what striking differences there were between one village and the next. We usually camped near one. Lakhi was a poor, mean place, and there even the government bungalow was badly kept. No one could say why. Garhi Yasin was a *taluka* headquarters, the smallest executive unit, with its officer, the Mukhtiarkar. There was a Treasury there, though inspecting that was the Collector's job; but the Assistant Collector could poke his nose into everything, whether or not it was his proper concern. All the villages had their *panchayats*, literally 'councils of five', selected to run village affairs. They would call on the officer formally and tell him their problems and make their requests for help. Usually the help needed was money, and almost invariably they would be exhorted to raise it among themselves. Their activity it was that determined whether a village was clean and orderly, or was not, whether it was like Lakhi or like Garhi Yasin.

The Assistant Collector was ever ready to point out faults he noted, or which were brought to his notice, in village hygiene, the state of its roads, or dangerous buildings. Any faults at all. But sometimes he could give praise, and then everyone was happy.

All this I must remember, for after a year I would have the same things to do myself. Indeed, all over Sindh, and anywhere where there was a revenue settlement requiring officers to tour, the same detailed contacts, the same detailed inquiries and actions went on, providing the administration with an extraordinarily detailed knowledge of the country.

So we moved from camp to camp, and there was a change for me. I began to learn Sindhi by post. There was a language teacher in Karachi, Kishensingh Vaswani, who heard of me—he would soon hear, it seemed that he taught all the British officers posted to Sindh—and with the help of benevolent clerks I began to learn. After a time I could even be a little useful, slowly and with help translating petitions.

We came to a village with a maternity home; usually this would have been inspected by an officer's wife but Dermont had to do it himself, after due warning lest he offend any patient. He must send in a report: a little crockery and cutlery, but no proper stock of instruments or drugs. There was a midwife, but she could do little more than keep the place clean and the patients happy. When Dermont went there were no patients.

The value of these maternity homes was always being questioned. Customarily, birth was at home, accompanied by a 'wise woman' who was accepted as knowing about these matters; if she were at a loss, a hakim would be called in: he might know something of homeopathic medicine, or he might be a charlatan depending on charms.

If the birth were complicated, the hakim would give up, probably after making things worse, and only then would the woman be taken to the maternity home, probably by bullock cart. The case would by then be so difficult that the poor midwife had little chance of success.

There might well be septicaemia, which would spread to other patients, and even without such a disaster, the home would almost certainly have a death rate higher than average. Had there been more hospitals and better communications, it would have been better if maternity homes were closed down and even as things were, a case for closure could be made. But the political shock of such an admission of defeat could not be faced.

Our last camp before Christmas was at Shikarpur, Dermont's nominal headquarters, but first we must go back to Chana. This was a tiny village with a great reputation as a sports centre. Moreover, its *wadero* was the only *zamindar* we had met who could speak English—a great social and official help! He was a modernizing Muslim, had opened a girls' school, though, as he sadly reported, only Hindu girls came. Hidayatullah Khan was a man to remember; he spoke good English, too.

He had arranged a *tamasha*, a sports meeting, for the *Dipiti Sahib*, our presence was enough reason for it. We two and Hidayatullah Khan had chairs; the shristedar and the *Chitnis*, the Chief Clerk, had stools, and everyone else stood or sat around.

There was a juggler and a troop of dancers, their dance a corruption of the *kuttak* dance of the hills. The dancing was followed by a tug-of-war, a magnificent battle, soon hidden by a cloud of dust through which the umpires peered, trying to prevent supporters from tailing on to the ends of the rope.

The chief event was a wrestling match: *malakhira*. The wrestlers were lean and fit, and beautifully muscled. The technique seemed very simple: they wore only their baggy Sindhi trousers, but with specially strong waistbands, and each gripped his opponent in front and over his shoulder to the band behind. Then they struggled. How they struggled! I daresay there were subtleties unnoticed by me, particularly what it was that made them suddenly break off for the end of a round. Anyone could try, but soon there were only two left, local rivals. They fought, covered with dust, they broke apart, and water was thrown over them; they set to again till one was on his back. Three throws were needed, and finally it was over. One was on his back on the ground, and it seemed this was the third time: the roar of the crowd confirmed it. I was not aware. The winner received his prize of two rupees, but it was the glory of his victory that he shed around on all of us.

The Survey of India asked that its Survey Chimney be checked, and it was, of course, the job of the Assistant Collector to do it. This was unique in Dermont's experience, which was not very great, but in the following years I myself never saw another.

Like many other innovations in Upper Sindh, this came from the time of John Jacob. In the 1840s he had settled the Upper Sindh Frontier, first by military action, then by bringing such peace and prosperity as the area had never

known. A proper survey was essential to his settlement, but
the country was quite flat, covered by scrub jungle, so
visibility from one survey point to another was a problem.
He solved it by building chimneys: a fire was built in the
base, some green stuff put on it, and a column of smoke
could be seen for miles. What we saw was one of the last
survivors, still the concern of the Survey. We did not test it.
Even today John Jacob is remembered, by his work and by
the town named after him.

When the railway came, Shikarpur lost much of its fame
and prosperity. It had been the end of one of the great
trade routes from Central Asia to the West, and in the
second half of the nineteenth century was the headquarters
of the Army of Sindh. It was also headquarters for the
District of Upper Sindh before the District was cut in half,
and Sukkur and Jacobabad usurped Shikarpur's position.
It still had the biggest bazaar, and the only covered one in
all Sindh, and was still the entrepôt for Kashmiri and
Persian traders travelling by road to the Punjab, Bombay,
and the Persian Gulf.

There were no Europeans posted in Shikarpur when we
camped there in the Old Circuit House, and there were
ruins all around of what had been the military cantonment,
but since they were built of mud brick, they had melted
away when maintenance ceased. The Circuit House was
badly in need of repair, but it was so large that it easily
held us and also Sir Henry Holland and his staff from
Quetta.

Sir Henry was Superintendent and Chief Surgeon from
the Mission Hospital in Quetta. He knew Sindh and what a
scourge eye disease was in that dusty land, and had
persuaded a charitable merchant, Seth Hiranand, to endow
his Charitable Eye Hospital. For years Sir Henry had been
coming in each cold weather, bringing two or three
assistants with him—when we were there they were
Americans—and performing hundreds of operations. All
treatments and surgery were free. There were daily clinics

to judge whether simple lotions would do, whether trachoma or glaucoma had, sadly, gone too far for treatment, whether cataracts were ripe for surgery or should wait for his second visit after Christmas, or even till next cold weather.

By far the greatest part of his work was the removal of cataracts, and he and his assistants were astonishingly quick and skilful. They showed us their grisly trophy: hundreds of dull, opaque lenses strung on a string that was yards long. We saw patients walking about wearing green eye-shields like medals, and also those pronounced fit, enormously cheerful at having their sight restored, albeit of faulty focus.

The hospital was only a little three-roomed building, but well-suited to its purpose. The recovery area was as simple as could be: brick pillars were the only permanent element; they were arched over with poles and thatched with grass, renewed each year, open all round. Patients brought a wife or mother or sister with them, for they had to feed themselves. There they lay, happy with their eye-patches till the surgeon should come and tell them they could take them off and go home.

Lady Holland came too: she was a proselytizing Christian, and she told us of her successes. Her technique worried Dermont a little. She told us that she would go to a village, find the *moulvi*, and explain Christianity in her basic Urdu. She went on explaining till he was converted, gave him a Testament in Urdu, and left him. He, she was sure, would carry his whole flock with him.

She never came to harm. She seemed not to know that a moulvi knew all the prophets known to her, even Jesus, though he did not accept His divinity. She did not ask if the moulvi had a 'flock' in the ecclesiastical sense. By next year she would anyway have forgotten, though the people had not. Crazy religious fanatics were not unknown, and were tolerated: the English Lady did no harm, while her husband did a great deal of good.

We returned to Sukkur for Christmas. Dermont was not very keen on club life, so we didn't go in till Christmas Eve. Dermont and the horses needed a rest, and I daresay the staff did too. We would all have a holiday.

In Sindh, public holidays were allocated more or less in proportion to the population of each community. Muslims had three, Hindus two, and Parsees one, and each of them, and Jews, had 'sectional' holidays. Christians were perhaps the smallest group, but among them were the rulers, so they had eight days at Christmas and two at Easter. This was considered fair enough, and anyway a holiday was always welcome. In fact, neither administration nor commerce could close down completely: it was too long a gap. So offices opened irregularly, and not for routine work.

Sukkur had its Gymkhana Club, which I imagine was much like a hundred others in small, up-country stations in India at the time. There was still a bar to Indian members, though our Collector, Ansari, who was a Muslim, could have been an honorary member—perhaps a more insulting offer than outright refusal. Anyway, his wife was *purdahnashin*, and he was not attracted to club life, so we were all white. There was a big Railway Institute, and that had no colour bar and was far more lively than the Gymkhana.

The Gymkhana, like the 'English' bazaar, had prospered while the Barrage was being built. It had a concrete tennis court, a swimming pool, and a dining-room with a kitchen—though a member would have to provide the cook. There was a large drawing-room, fit for dancing, and even a billiard room. For Sindh it was old. In the walls were holes for the *punkah* cords, and still the actual punkahs, stacked away in a cupboard: great tasselled frames to hang from the ceiling, pulled back and forth by a man out on the verandah, swinging just above head height and stirring the air till it seemed cool. Had there ever been a long power cut, stopping the electric fans, they could easily be reinstalled, and later, in another place, I sat under one.

There was a shoot, probably several; for this first, I just looked on. For the next, I was lent a gun. I fired off five rounds and killed two birds, an average of 40 percent, which was a low average, so I stayed with it. In fact, I didn't like killing birds and never owned a shotgun in Sindh.

Then, at the New Year, we were all invited to Khairpur: the Mir Sahib invited all Sukkur to a party. No women, of course. There was alcohol, for infidels only, but we all knew that this was an occasion for restraint. I have this vivid memory of bright lights and the State's officers meeting us very cheerfully on their own ground, talking of the problems of a State. We ate a purely Sindhi and Punjabi meal, very long and unhurried, followed by dancers and a juggler. Then there was a *qavali*, a concert of songs and music, entirely strange to me. The songs, I was told, were about love and religion; I came later to understand something of the style and appreciate it, but that talent has left me now. There would be a sudden unsignalled break when, in the middle of a phrase, all the players would stop, not only for a drink, but to have a smoke—even the singers smoked *beedis* made of the rankest tobacco.

The evening ended early, and we all went quietly home, in good, responsible order. And so to bed.

As was proper, we went for a formal drink with the garrison of the Bukkur Island Fort. This was a very ancient site on an island in the River, where the Indus was itself confined in the Rohri gorge. Its strategic importance was obvious, and the British had manned it ever since the Conquest. There was still a garrison, though what it was guarding or threatening was not clear. Perhaps a fortress just demands to be manned.

On another day we were taken on a special trip. Mr Ramchand, a barrister practising in Dermont's court, offered to take us to see Mohen-jo-daro (it is called Moenjo-daro today). It had only recently been discovered, the site of a very ancient town indeed. This was a memorable trip, not only for Mohen-jo-daro itself, but for our journey.

Ramchand's own car took us, but it had a petrol leak and we had to finish by tonga, and we were so late that we could see little of the ruins. We found the car at Dokri on the way back, but it ran out of petrol again, in the dark, near Larkana. The driver, a resourceful man, offered to find the leak himself. He produced his matches, and only just in time were we able to dissuade him.

Ramchand owned a house in Larkana, so we spent the night there uncomfortably, fully clothed for warmth, with a cotton quilt above and another below us on the string bed. We were up at five o'clock to catch the first train to Sukkur.

Poor Mr Ramchand was terribly upset that his hospitality had so badly broken down, he was sure it would convince us that India was unfit for independence if a barrister could be so incompetent. But I think that in the end we comforted him: this sort of thing could happen to anyone, we had enjoyed it all, including the breakdowns; and besides seeing the ruins we had had an adventure that made a welcome break from routine. He was competent in his own profession; India could govern itself with such as him to serve it.

I wrote it all to Joan in detail. I promised that we would ourselves see Mohen-jo-daro one day, and we did.

The most enjoyable times that Christmas were those we spent at home, reading, writing, playing records, exploring the bazaar, the Barrage, the Lansdowne Bridge. I wrote to Joan all about it, even the finding of a workshop where they made galvanized iron buckets to look exactly like factory-made ones. We watched boat-builders by the river, and Dermont inspected the last of the town's custom posts. These internal customs had just been abolished: they were avoided by everything but motor vehicles, they restricted trade, and they made no profit.

Our music was from records, played on a portable clockwork gramophone. The needles we used were of fibre,

and there was a little tool to sharpen them—the dust of
Sindh filled the grooves and could not be brushed out, so
a steel needle would have destroyed a record at one playing.
We got used to the woolly sound—a more expensive
gramophone could do little better. Dermont had all
Beethoven's symphonies, the Emperor Concerto, quite a
lot of Mozart, Brahms while still he was disparaged, and
even modern (in those days) composers like Grieg and
Sibelius. I knew nothing of music then; I don't know much
now, but Dermont's library I came to know by heart, and
to love forever.

3

STILL LEARNING

We set off again in the New Year, towards the border with the Upper Sindh Frontier, moving short distances between camps, so that the camels could arrive in time for the new camp to be set up ready for us, for our comfort. There was nothing sybaritic about this, just the pleasure of finding hot water and a cup of tea waiting. Usually Dermont could find a job to do on the way. At Amrote he had to deal with a threat of communal rioting. A moulvi, said to be bad-tempered and eaten up with hatred of Hindus, wanted to dig a trench to drain water away from his house; he was digging it across the corner of a Hindu temple. The Hindus objected, there were more Hindus than Muslims, and Dermont went with two policemen—and me—and found the villagers ready for a fight. The solution to the problem was simple: the Hindus marked their boundary exactly and to everyone's satisfaction, the moulvi changed the direction of his ditch slightly, and the threat died away. Below the peaceful surface there was always a danger of sudden violence.

Garhi Yasin again, with the usual visitors to see, and petitioners to hear. Here it rained, a notable event in Sindh. We were in a good bungalow, and so were all the staff, so we just waited a day for the roads to dry up. But the rain laid the dust, and at last we could see the countryside, clean, green, and fresh; at last from the roof I saw the distant hills, and on the other side was smoke rising from Shikarpur, and the solid green of jungle along the river.

At the end of the month the Governor was coming, and first he would camp at Shikarpur, where Dermont would have to escort Lady Graham. I would stand by as an occasional dogsbody. We had to think of clothes: the little book with the tour programme said that 'at all official functions morning dress will be worn'. This concerned us deeply. We decided that it was ridiculous: special trips to Karachi to buy two costly suits that might never be worn again. But there was a heart in Government House, and, when Dermont protested, he was told that a decent lounge suit and a white topi would do. We had seen white topis in the bazaar.

When the Governor came to Sukkur, our Commissioner would need Dermont's bungalow; we had to stay in tents in Shikarpur, too, for all the top officers were touring with the Governor. Chief Judge, Chief Engineer, Chief Conservator of Forests, and Inspector-General of Police. That, I think, was all, and quite enough. The Chief Veterinary Officer was there too, just why I don't know, but he examined Rajah for me, to Jan Mahommed's gratification. He found him fit for his age, which was the best we could hope for, I suppose.

Their Excellencies were entertained by the Municipality, and never had I seen so many very fat men together, all the chief merchants of the town. There were no Muslim ladies, of course, and the few Hindus sat closely and safely together, so Lady Graham had to sit apart with them. This was dull for her, but I supposed she was used to it.

I had nothing to do, so could sample all the food, especially the famous Shikarpur sweets, 'mithai'. There were three kinds: the best was made with pistachio nuts and covered with gold leaf, the next was of cashew nuts and covered with silver leaf, and the ordinary one was made with chickpeas, with no cover at all. I just made good use of my time.

Their Excellencies were at home to the Municipality, and next day they all left for Sukkur. Such a move was no problem to these high officers; the Governor had his big Daimler, each of the others was in the care of his department. The Commissioner would move into Dermont's well-furnished bungalow. We were left to manage for ourselves, with a camel train that must toil all the day, leaving us homeless early in the morning, to cover twenty miles and set up camp in Sukkur to be ready for us. We rode all the way. We had plenty of time, too, so had a proper look in the bazaar, and at some place on the way must have found some food. The *naik* drove the car, and both our syces went with him, a pleasant change for them. We took about four hours.

We had our formal lunch with the Governor, and I came then to appreciate Lady Graham. Sir Lancelot was stiff, but she was not. She seemed interested in even someone as lowly as I, and promised to remember that I could sail a boat. Even Sir Lancelot loosened up, so much that I dared ask him how he liked his job. After some thought he replied, 'I do appreciate the amenities'. This phrase travelled all round Sindh, and gained me a small fame.

There were three days in Sukkur; on one the Police and the Boy Scouts were inspected, on the next one would expect a shoot, but that was not His Excellency's pleasure: instead he inspected a Girls' School, while Dermont took Her Excellency to another Zenana Hospital. Only at the school was there any sign that not everyone loved the British: there was a Congress picket, gandhi caps, and cries of '*Jai Hind*'. There was a new wing to open at the Civil Hospital and the Collector, Ansari, was concerned to know how he should behave with a Governor. He was nervous about the etiquette; when we took the matter lightly, he pointed out that it was not so easy for people like him, from the Provincial Service. We said that he was obviously very good at his job to have risen so high, and it was silly to feel nervous, but I doubt if we raised his confidence.

The Boy Scouts made an impressive display; there were Hindus and Muslims lined up in order of size, with no notion of community, which was very heartening. Their troop leader was very dark, and his name was Shidi. This was in fact his tribal name, for his forebears had been Ethiopian, negroid, very black, very handsome, and energetic. They had been brought over from Abyssinia as slaves, and their ethnic root was very clear. Some had married Sindhis, but some were still pure Ethiopian. They had been slaves till the British freed them all, now they prospered, and there could be nothing more respectable than leading a scout troop.

For the Durbar itself I at last had a function: I was to usher guests to their seats. There was a big *shamiana* set up on the *maidan* below the Collector's bungalow, with chairs for all the senior officers, and two very large ones for Their Excellencies. At the side were chairs for all the notabilities to whom the Governor would present honours. There was a flag pole, with the Union Jack folded but ready to raise when the Governor's party arrived, and a police band ready to play.

It was, in its small way, very imperial. It was only a small District Durbar, of none but symbolic importance, but we must take it seriously. I had a list of guests, and was warned that any mistakes in precedence could lead to no end of trouble. Perhaps I was faultless, perhaps someone had been fooling me: there was no trouble.

The honours that were to be awarded seemed slight and frivolous, yet were clearly highly valued. There were *lunghis*, shirts of honour, beautifully embroidered. Some of the visitors came wearing lunghis won by their fathers or grandfathers, faded, very carefully preserved. There were minor titles, swords, even watches and certificates. But the whole basis of the event was feudal: to earn an award, a man must have a minimum area of land or income, or must be a holder of a *jagir*, an outright grant of land by the Government. There had been help in mending a big canal

breach, that was to be rewarded; and rewards for both
Hindus and Muslims for help in the Manzilgah riots just
before I arrived.

The Durbar opened when the Governor arrived. The
Police Guard stood to attention to be inspected, His
Excellency, in grey frock coat and top hat, stood to
attention, and we all stood up as the Union Jack was hoisted
and the band played what was roughly the National
Anthem. The Collector presented recipients of awards, very
much as a headmaster would at school, though in this case
most of those under the shamiana were much superior to
him. Some of the guests were brightly clad, but the British
were a drab bunch, until Henry Frost, ADC to the Governor
and a cavalry captain, arrived in full regimentals, frogged
and tasselled, with sword-belt and sheathed sabre. He
provided the Armed Might of the Raj.

The Governor's party left, and then the Commissioner,
so we would be able to move back to Dermont's home.
There was one more night in tents, and Henry Frost came
to dinner with us, left behind to see that everything was
properly finished, and especially to look after the Daimler.
This car could not travel on our dirt roads, so it had been
limited to Sukkur and the hard road as far as Shikarpur. It
was loaded onto a flat railway truck, swathed in sheets, and
its corners protected from rubbing. A proper job for a
cavalry captain recently converted to tanks. (There was a
strange logic in this switch from horses to tanks, practised
in all armies: the horse was the armour of centuries, the
tank merely brought armour up to date.)

We had no wish to discuss the visit: it was over, and no
faults could be placed at our door. So we talked of the
possibility of war. Possibility was changing into probability,
and our concern was, when? Germany had broken all the
promises given to Chamberlain, had reoccupied the
Rhineland, absorbed Austria, and occupied all but a rump
of Czechoslovakia. Henry was indignant, sure there must
be war, had no ideas about when but was ready whenever

he had orders. We had met an army officer who said six months, and Dermont suggested six weeks, and no time to get his fiancée to come out. I proposed nine months ahead: I had read a lot of history, and learnt that in Europe never did a war begin till the corn harvest was in. It would be foolish to attack when reserves were at their lowest and all the labour would be needed for the harvest.

Once that was settled we all went to bed. In the morning Dermont and I went back home, and the tents were packed up ready for the next tour.

The Commissioner had told me that I was being transferred to Karachi for the final part of my training, so this tour after the Durbar would be my last with Dermont. I was offered tents by a judge who no longer needed them, and I would need my own soon. They were very cheap, but they were also rubbish. I wanted a set like Dermont's, and could wait. These tents were exactly fitted for their purpose: the main tent was like a marquee, with a pitched roof, double lining, and a fly sheet. There was a central living room, with a bedroom and bathroom on each side. In front was a 'verandah' enclosed by blinds made from split bamboo, and the bedrooms had similar windows, with blinds to let down. The floor would be covered by a *dhurrie*, a woven cotton carpet. Their plan was in fact exactly like that of the standard PWD bungalow. With two of us sharing, the office had to be in a *rownti*, a small tent with a ridge pole. There would be two of these, the other for the *patewalas*. They also had fly sheets: seldom was there rain, but a little insulation from the sun was welcome always. (Finally, Dermont didn't want his, and I bought them myself.)

Very comfortable were these tents. Cool and airy by day, and if the night was cold there was space for a brazier. Often the staff would have to fend for itself, and the cook had a difficult time. But the camp sites were well-known, and Mukhtiarkars would have made arrangements. Very heartless we were: the Sahibs were comfortable, which was what really mattered. In fact, Dermont did make sure all was well, and I learnt from him.

I had my own work now, for I must sit a departmental exam, and one for Sindhi, in May. There were still inspections, but I no longer went on all. Moreover, I wanted to consider what I thought of my job-to-be, of India, of Indians, and especially what I felt about British Rule. On the whole, my conclusions were satisfactory to me. I had met intelligent Indians who were yet friendly, and clearly British rule was not oppressive, nor even resented in Sindh, apart from a few staunch Congress supporters. Also, I felt perfectly capable of maintaining a wife on my salary, but Joan felt committed to her job, and adjudged it weak and immoral to give that up in the middle of the school year. So I proposed that she come in October, for I remained convinced that there would be no war till after the harvest. By this conviction I stood. My letters show that I hammered away at it in a way that must have exasperated them all. On occasion Joan told me so. I grovelled—and carried on just the same.

I was due to go to Karachi on 12 March, the anniversary of becoming engaged. It seemed a longer time than that, but was welcomed as beginning the last phase of my training. I proposed to share a flat with Nazir Ahmed when we both reached Karachi: Dermont thought that sharing with an Indian would be seen as a little strange, but doubtless I would live it down. The real problem might be with food, but neither problem worried me. I was filled with self-confidence; it might be that I was over-filled by reason of lack of experience.

I had seen most of the sub-division by now, and was recognizing with pleasure sights that had become familiar from previous tours. Sindh seemed to be poor in plants, which was perhaps natural in a land often semi-desert. But there were plenty of birds. There were those good to eat, partridge and snipe and mallard; and the scavengers, crows and magpies and a fine big jay. Once I saw a jungle fowl,

ancestor of the chicken of the barnyard, and once a
glorious golden pheasant. There were the 'seven sisters',
otherwise jungle babblers, little grey birds, very humble
beings, always seven together, or nearly seven. Wherever
there was a big tree there would be a flock of green parrots.
They would be chatting happily, and then suddenly would
fly off in a panic, circle round, and settle again. The
chattering would begin again, then suddenly, for no
apparent reason, would stop. After a little while, one or
two would pipe up, then more and more till they were in
full throat again. The most beautiful bird of all was the
hoopoe, so graceful, so quick in flight, his crest lying flat as
he flew, and rising in a fan as he landed.

The inundation canals were dry now, but often at a
regulator there was a big pool with fish, and there the
kingfishers collected. There was one just like its British
cousin, another a pretty little black and white one that
would hover over the pool, then suddenly dive. There was
the big, powerful, Indian fisher: I saw one once fly in and
land on an unfamiliar twig. It broke under him, and he fell
towards the water, swearing and fluttering madly. He
recovered and flew to his usual perch, where he sat and
looked round indignantly, challenging anyone to laugh.

Once in camp we were hit by a dust storm, a very nasty
experience, but usually the air was very still. We could sit
on the verandah after work, look out over the fields, and
watch the little whirlwinds, the '*wulliwas*', which would drift
along an erratic course, picking up bits of litter, slowly
dying away, leaving the litter where they died.

Most of the Shikarpur sub-division was watered by
inundation canals, filled when the River flooded, drying
when it went down. So far I had seen of agricultural
methods only harvest, and was going away before the next
seed-time. But at this time the land was being tilled and
sown for the spring crop, *rabi*, which would grow from the
moisture left in the soil. The crops were lentils and

chickpeas, and the work must be done very quickly, though this year there had been rain to help.

As we rode round the fields I had been able to see the rice trusses when they were brought in for threshing. Every little hamlet had its threshing floor, carefully levelled and surfaced with hardened mud, a round space with a post driven firmly in the middle.

The Bible says, 'Thou shalt not muzzle the ox that treadeth out the corn,' and so it was in Sindh. Indeed, it is so still! The paddy brought in from the fields was brought to the post and laid in a circle round it. The bullocks were brought and tied to the post in line abreast, the smallest often a calf, in the middle, and driven round. It did not take them long to learn their role, and when it was judged that the grain was shed from the straw the team was unhitched, the straw cleared away, and the grain swept up; the floor was ready for the next load. Indeed, the bullocks were not muzzled, but he would be lucky who grabbed more than a mouthful of straw.

The grain had to be winnowed before being sent for husking, and this was done by the women when the air was dry and still. I have seen them in the early evening, spread around a village, each with her heap of grain and her winnowing scoop: she would throw the grain into the air with a special jerk and twist to spread it. In the still, warm evening the dust and chaff floated away, and little columns drifted across the fields, several visible from each winnower, till slowly the light stuff fell and the column faded. When the sun went down the work must stop, for a light dew would fall and the dust would stick to the grains. When first I saw this phenomenon I was astonished: I failed to see the winnower at the head of each slowly-marching procession of columns. Every year thereafter, in season, it charmed me, was what I would look for at every camp. One day, I promised myself, I would show Joan.

For this, my last tour, we went to the far north of the district, the boundary with Upper Sindh Frontier District, and even crossed the Begari Canal bridge. It felt like being in a foreign country. We camped in tents at Hamayun, which was a railway station and a road junction where the road from Sukkur to Jacobabad branched, one road going to Thul, an important paddy-husking centre. It was odd that there was no bungalow.

Occasionally through the night we heard a train roar by, lighting the countryside briefly with its searchlight, and when the Quetta Mail passed, its lighted windows glowing in the dark, we felt very isolated. When the slow passenger train stopped I felt like going to the station, just to see people from the outer world. But it was three o'clock in the morning, bullock convoys had been grinding and shrieking past all night on their unoiled axles, I had toothache and had been awake all night; I stayed in bed.

The Mukhtiarkar had told us that there was a good dentist in Shikarpur: Mr Vishindas Wadhwani, 'America-returned', and Dermont drove me over.

Mr Vishindas was a Hyderabadi Amil, one of that 'family' that almost monopolized the professions in Sindh, as the Sindh Work merchants of Shikarpur spread their mercantile webs around the world. Mr Vishindas was just trying to establish himself, he told me. His surgery was in a little open space in the middle of the covered bazaar, and was advertised by highly-coloured placards, one on each side of his door. On one side was a picture of a man with a grossly swollen cheek, positively glowing with pain. Below was a picture of a great fanged tooth with a black hole in it, dripping blood, and below that the face, no longer deformed, smiling happily. On the other side was a man old and grey, his mouth all sunken. Below was, a set of fine dentures, gleaming white, and below again the man, fine and healthy now, with large white teeth positively bursting from his mouth. The pictures must fill anyone with confidence.

The surgery had a large, clean window overlooking the street, and inside one could see the dentist's chair. It was a modern chair, as befitted his American qualifications; there was an electric drill and a glass cabinet full of little bottles and jars on one side and on the other his trays of bright stainless steel instruments. But his surgery was in a mud-brick house, with a mud floor, and only a boy as assistant. His big window displayed his patients to passers-by disconcertingly, but everything was spotlessly clean. He regretted that his house was not of the modern burnt brick, but I could remind him that the old-fashioned sun-dried ones were much cooler.

His professional problem was that he had to persuade people to use his modern but expensive techniques. There was wealth enough in Shikarpur, known to be home to a greater number of rich men—those same Sindh Work merchants—than anywhere else in the province, but they were certainly not open-handed. None knew about filling cavities, building bridge-work, or crowning teeth. If a *hakim* could do nothing with a drug and a prayer, the tooth came out, with strong men to hold the patient down, much banging of drums and gongs, short fierce anguish, and very little to pay. Perhaps if the gap showed it would be filled with a gold peg, which could always be recovered at the end; otherwise, the gap remained empty. There were plenty of tooth drawers, and a short period of pain not much worse than the toothache itself was usually preferred to Mr Vishindas' anaesthetic.

However, the banging of drums was not for me, and Mr Vishindas regretfully agreed that my much-patched molar must come out. Nevertheless, there was useful publicity to be had from treating a Sahib, even if only a very junior one. I realized this, and forebore to object to all the faces at the window of the surgery. He calmed me, as he supposed, by pointing out how very clean and well equipped his surgery was, and then assured me that apart from a prick, a very little prick, I would feel no pain. We were both well aware that if the Sahib screamed and struggled it would do modern dentistry no good at all. As for me, I just wanted the damn tooth out.

So, after all the proper swabbing and rinsing, he took up his syringe and gave me the one little prick he had warned me to expect. I bore it without any damaging quiver, or even a grunt; then he went all the way round that tooth, giving a little prick on the edge of the area deadened by the previous one. Did I feel anything? I did not. So he drove the needle in deeply for the last dose, chatted comfortingly for a bit, took up his pincers, and out it came, a big deep-rooted grinder. He held it up for me to see. The watchers outside could see, too, that it was a veritable tooth, that there was blood on it, and that the Sahib had neither screamed nor squirmed.

Mr Vishindas really was a good dentist. I very much hoped that the incidental publicity my visit gave him helped his practice. We drove back to Hamayun to our tents— Dermont still had cases to hear before moving on.

It seldom rains in Sindh in the cold weather, but while I was in Sukkur it had already rained once, and now it looked as though there would be a heavy storm. Dermont told the patewalas to check all the guy ropes of the tents, and they went round hauling them as tight as they could. He protested that they must leave some slack for the rain to take up, but they told him, more or less, to mind his own business. After they had gone to the village we went round and slackened all the guy ropes of our big tent. We left the two rowntis, one the office and the other the patewalas' home, and went to bed.

In the night it rained; it rained very hard. Before we were up we heard shouting and wailing and went to see the patewalas' tent collapsed on them, all its pegs drawn, and they struggling to find their way out. The office *rownti* was flat too, but our big tent stood, all very neat, ropes tight, the fly sheet without a wrinkle. The naik tried to claim that they must have done specially well for the Sahib, till Dermont explained the miracle.

There was water standing all around: we could feel it squelching under the dhurrie that was our floor. Where the water did not stand there was soft mud, so all morning nothing moved save the occasional train, but it was beautiful. The air was clear, the birds sang, insofar as Sindhi birds do sing, and otherwise all was quiet. No cases, either. The sun was warm, and soon the ground began to steam.

At about noon the first bullock carts began to move through—those little carts could pull through anything in the end. A bus came out from Shikarpur, for the road was a little raised, and motorable, though the *abdar* would have something to grumble about. But the bus was for Thul, and as soon as it left the main road it was in trouble. It swerved and swayed and stuck. The passengers got out and a bunch of men waiting in the village came out and they got it going again; one wheel was in a cart rut so that it couldn't leave the road, and it was keeled over perilously, but with much shouting, entirely destroying our peace, they pushed it wildly on and out of sight. After a while the men from the village came back, very cheerful, covered in mud, reporting that the bus would reach Thul, *Inshallah.* It was in God's hands.

We stayed the night. The cases would have to be redated, and next day we would go to our last camp, and then Sukkur. The end of my touring.

Dermont was happy to stay in Sukkur for a few days while I packed my belongings and said my farewells. Then I left on the Karachi Mail for the last stage of my training: 12 March, one year to the day since Joan and I had become betrothed at that hurried, uncertain meeting in Cambridge. Now all uncertainty had gone, and the only question was, when would she come and join me?

4

LEGACY FROM SUKKUR

The Sindhi bullock cart is a wonderful vehicle: it is small, to suit the small Red Sindhi bullock, it is simply constructed of local materials, it needs no metal at all. It is extraordinarily robust, and any carpenter can maintain it.

Its fitness for its purpose is perfect. Apart from a very few miles, in my time all the roads were of earth, and even now, when there are many more metalled miles, still all but the main routes remain as they were. The earth is either fine sand or even finer alluvial silt from the Indus. With the cart wheels tracking the bullocks, the roads develop deeper and deeper grooves, with an unused hump in the middle. The carts suit the roads, and the roads come to suit the carts; but they suit no other vehicle.

The cart is very small; it looks a pigmy beside the Punjabi carts with their high, spoked wheels. But it is much stronger. It is made from locally grown *babul,* acacia wood, very tough, but easy to work if you don't aspire to an elegant finish. The body is wishbone-shaped, the floor made of planks slotted into grooves in the arms of the wishbone; the shank is elongated through two graceful curves to form the single shaft to which the yoke is tied and held by pegs. The sides of the cart are open, with four corner posts, and in the middle of each side is a much stouter post, slotted right through to form the bearing—if it can properly be called a bearing—of the axle.

The man who invented the movement for this cart was a genius. The simple motion would be for the wheels to turn freely on the axle; but with a fixed axle there is a problem in a country with as much sand and dust as Sindh. Lubrication is not possible, for the sand would quickly make of it an abrasive. So the only treatment for the axle is lamp black, which polishes running surfaces and can be made by burning rags. If the wheels turned on the thin ends of the axle, the wear would be very heavy. If they were fixed so that the axle, four inches thick, turned, then one wheel would have to skid round corners.

The genius who overcame these problems probably lived at Mohen-jo-daro. Clay toys have been found there which are probably models of an embryonic cart, its flat bed and its wheels. He invented a true differential, so that the thick and easily replaced axle would turn, but the wheels could turn independently of each other. He made one wheel free, the other fixed. Turn to the right, the free wheel stood, the axle turned; turn to the left, the free wheel turned, the axle stood. Only when turning was there wear on the free wheel; travelling straight ahead, the axle turned, the free wheel turning with it.

The wheel is cleverly built, too. It is formed of three pieces only, with pegs to hold them together. The middle section provides for the hub and part of the rim for both sides, with a hole, square or round, to take the axle end. Two pieces, cut to an arc, form the rest of the circumference, making the wheel's diameter about thirty inches. The arcs are cut away, left about four inches wide, and an arc cut from the middle section, to save weight. If a wheel breaks it only needs new pegs. I never saw a wheel with iron rims. There is no real bearing for the axle, just the stout post to stop the axle sliding back, a peg in front for if it must go back. Take two pins from the ends of the axle, lift the buck off, and the whole cart will lie flat. It can float!

The usual load for these carts was rice paddy, taken from the villages to the husking mills. This was bulky stuff, carried in sacks, and they had to be roped on, for they overtopped the sides; the same weight of rice, six to seven hundredweight, carried from the mill, would fit inside. But they could carry almost anything. They carried our furniture to and from the station when we were transferred, they could take a piano or a motor-bike, a load of manure or of firewood. For loose loads cloth was draped around; for a family a shade was draped over all, to keep off the sun or, occasionally, rain.

It was after harvest that these carts came into their own. Most *haris* owned one, each with a pair of bullocks taken from the plough and fitting neatly into the curve at the front of the buck, each polishing the frame with his rump. A convoy would collect in the cool of the evening, a *jemadar* would be appointed and given a hurricane lamp; he would get into the lead cart and off they would set. The drivers would climb onto their loads, tying themselves if they were wise, for very soon they could sleep. Only the jemadar must be wakeful, and always show his lamp.

Listening to the start of a convoy was eerie. First there was a little creak as the jemadar set off, then another creak, and another, and another; little by little the creaking grew to a shriek, an ululating high-pitched scream as thirty or forty unoiled axles turned in the most primitive of bearings, as the whole convoy plodded steadily on till morning.

The deep ruts on the road kept the carts on course and the drivers, once securely hooked to their loads, slept. But not the jemadar: the road might fork, and if he slept the whole convoy might finish in the wrong place. Or the lead cart might just leave the road and be in a water-course before he woke up. There were well-authenticated tales of the lead cart, with a sleeping jemadar, being turned gently round, led back in a big circle round the others which, well trained as they were, followed the leader till they were pointed back the way they had come. When the jemadar did wake in the dark he would see nothing wrong till he recognized his own village again. Such trouble there would be: perhaps his justification was the kind that gave rise to ghost stories.

These long paddy convoys would be setting off each evening all over Upper Sindh, some taking paddy to the mills, some setting off home with husked rice for the family for the year, or for as long as the hari could claim without needing credit. From the air one might have seen tangled ribbons of dust, beginning with the tiny light of the jemadar's lantern at the head of each, its dusty track slowly fading away. Imagine oneself floating low in a balloon, and one would hear the faint combined whine of all those unoiled turning axles. And as the sun rose they would all stop, and hundreds of good Muslims would climb down for their morning prayers in the sudden silence.

Retrospect: I have to be careful with the order of events, for less than four years later I was in Sukkur again, in the Old Circuit House, but otherwise in very different circumstances. During this first stay I experienced many things I have not recounted, such as the many shooting parties (for only one of which I had a gun), or all the pleasant times when we went out in the evening so that Dermont could shoot a brace of partridges for our supper. There was the day when mild old Rajah ran away with me: Jan had double-bitted him and caught his tongue between the bits, which made him angry, and in the end he threw me. A tapedar found what was the trouble, so it wasn't my fault, but he wasn't going to spoil the story of the Sahib falling off just for a little accuracy. And Dermont had fallen off, too, though he was a much better horseman than I. Such details remain in memory much more vividly than the Governor's visit, which ordinary people saw as being of much less importance than Sir Henry Holland's clinic.

All this was incidental to the real purpose of my posting to Sukkur. After only three months I felt that, were Dermont to fall ill, I could do his work, provided no crisis arose. This was simple conceit, for I knew little of his office work; on the other hand, I had seen how a sub-division was run. The thought of six months in Karachi with only books and the language to occupy me made me feel very impatient.

I had learnt a good deal about the people, too. The man who approached with all servility was probably not really like that at all: he was merely behaving the way people had told him the Sahibs liked. Once he had discovered otherwise he would be a different person. The petition-writers who came to every camp were the repositories of orthodoxy, and the man who presented a petition professing extreme humility was probably not at all humble, but was boiling with indignation. I had learnt how to deal with petitions, sending them to appropriate officers, hearing how Dermont dealt with some himself. Nearly all concerned someone oppressing the petitioner. Each had a two anna stamp, so was registered, and could not later be denied. It might be *zulum*, oppression, by a zamindar of his hari; by a forestry officer stopping a man from collecting honey, as was his right; by a canal abdar closing a regulator out of turn; these must go to the proper officer for disposal: one mustn't trespass on the territory of another department. A man's wife had been kidnapped by her family, probably a matter of unpaid *daulat*, but it could cause trouble, so they must come to the next camp where things could be sorted out. A moneylender was squeezing a creditor unreasonably, so they must be called and both parties heard. A woman's father claimed that she had been wrongly divorced: here, one must be especially careful, for religious disputes could be full of pitfalls; better refer them to the moulvi. There would be general complaint about cattle thefts by a gang of *patharidars*, rustlers; this was for the Collector, who would talk to the police. Meanwhile, ask the Deputy Superintendent for his local opinion. Then there would be a zamindar asking for a gun licence. This also was for the Collector to handle, but it would be as well

to find out why he needed a gun, what service he had given
to deserve it. The petitions rolled in, day after day, at every
camp. I found them valuable for reading Arabic script, and
for translating. In my own later time I would have
hundreds, all much the same in style and in subject. Their
matter was nearly all petty, often simply domestic, but they
could provide an accurate picture of the lives of ordinary
people, their problems, and the many ways in which the
government, the *Sirkar*, affected them. Never neglect
petitions was the rule, lest small friction grow into violent
resentment.

I had met important folk, too, big landlords, zamindars,
coming to call from courtesy, or, as sometimes appeared
when the needs of courtesy had been satisfied, for more
specific purposes: for a grant of land, or for help in some
case, for action to be taken against a gang of *badmashes,*
bad hats, who might truly be criminals, or the men of some
hated rival. Always care was necessary. There would be
formal visits from the panchayat, complaining generally of
hard times, as a formality, and then presenting the needs
of themselves and their people. These panchayats were
almost entirely Hindu, and they were all competent men,
practical in their complaints and requests for action. On
the other hand, they were perfectly capable of practising
on the gullibility of the simple Sahib: on occasion they
might succeed, but if the Sahib found out...

An Assistant or Deputy Collector was more in touch with
ordinary people than was any other official. He could see
how the administrative machine was working, and after only
a few months I could see that Indians were working it. The
few British in the various services were not essential: in the
ICS itself over half the members were Indian already, and
some of them were right at the top of the government.
Perhaps the British were useful, providing the exemplar
for the long, long tradition of the highest quality of any
service in the world. Or so we saw ourselves!

Quite obviously an independent India could govern itself; could probably govern itself more positively than the British were doing. But I had ideas for what the British might do before they left, had even been so bold as to air some of them. I wrote at length to Joan, happily ignoring my own ignorance and all the political obstacles there might be in the way. I even sought to apply my principles to all India. (Not to the Princely States: I ignored them!) I disregarded the great differences between one part of the country and another, but this was not, in fact, so presumptuous as it may appear, for three-quarters of the population was directly concerned with agriculture, and half the rest was dependent on agriculture, with mills and credits and marketing. Already it was clear that my interest lay with agriculture. Sindh was a small province, with large landholdings but comparatively few landlords, and most of the population was of landless, crop-sharing, tenants-at-will. As if this was not enough, there was Islamic tradition and the Hindu caste system to contend with. I was ready to tackle them all, and though I did become wise enough to confine my ideas to Sindh, I never did abandon my ambitions.

India was anyway due to become independent as soon as the politicians settled their differences: the Act of 1935 said so, and even most Indians believed it. India did not need British officers, and might decide that it did not want such as me, but this didn't bother me much: perhaps I persuaded myself that I would very soon make myself indispensable.

My letters home at this time were almost fulsome in their expressions of love, but I also reiterated my conviction that there would be war after the harvest, that Joan should come out before then. I had been brought up among people who never forgot the horrors of the Great War, I was well aware of the problems facing Europe, and of the dangers that would involve my own family, yet I used my concern solely and selfishly as a means to persuade Joan to come. Perhaps the cynicism of the governments of Europe in some sort justified me.

So I left Sukkur with two immediate ambitions: to pass my departmental exam, and to persuade Joan to come out and join me.

The Indus Valley. The people of Sindh did not speak of the Indus; it was always *Darya*, the River, or *Darya Shah*, the Royal River. Except for a few seasonal streams, it was the only river, and without it Sindh would have been entirely desert. The people of Mohen-jo-daro had depended on it; one of Alexander's generals had sailed down it; and in the seventh century, Arabs had landed in the delta and from there spread Islam all over the valley. There were other invasions from the east, and the last was by the British.

It is essential to understand the topography of the Valley. The River gave Sindh its name, and outside the Valley was desert: to the east was the great desert of Thar and the marshy Ranns of Kutch; to the west were the barren hills of Balochistan and Kalat; to the south-west the sea. There were three main channels, the Eastern Nara, the Western Nara, and the middle channel. Over centuries a channel would silt up, and the course would change. The Eastern Nara had last silted, the western channel was deepest, and once the middle had silted the River would move there. But when the British arrived they built embankments all along both sides: they caught Darya Shah and held him in the middle. When I arrived, the great Barrage at Sukkur had just been completed. The canals all flowed by gravity, for the River was on a slight ridge, and only this made the system operative. There were often small breaches in the *bunds*, which were dealt with routinely, but there was always a danger that an exceptional flood might break through above the Barrage, the River might flow down the Western Nara and leave the Barrage dry. Any breach there was treated as an emergency.

The Sukkur Barrage is one of the last great British engineering bequests to India—though finally inherited by

Pakistan. But one must not forget that almost all those who built it and operated it were Indian.

They say that in America the great dams on the Colorado River are silting up. But a barrage is different: it does not try to hold up a great head of water to drive turbines, but only to fill the canals fed from it. The flow is never stopped, and when the canals are satisfied the remainder flows on. Great quantities of silt come down from the Himalayas, but the sluices, forty-six of them at Sukkur, can be opened one by one and flushed clean.

The snow melts in the mountains, the flood comes down, and when the Punjab has taken what it needs the water moves on, fills the inundation canals, which only flow in flood-time, and still at Sukkur there is a mighty flow. The water can be restrained, but only gently, till the Barrage canals are filled. Even then there is flow enough to fill inundation canals downstream, and ultimately to justify another barrage, built by Pakistan, near Hyderabad.

The River is embanked all along both sides, but the banks are built of alluvial silt, the only material available. These banks cannot withstand any but still water, so the engineers have to try to predict the unpredictable: to foresee that when one year the River is moving towards one bank, next year's flood will breach it. So they build a protective loop behind it. If next year the River moves the same way and breaches the front *bund*, the loop will hold, and all is well. But will the river change its mind? Does Darya Shah have a mind? Anyway, it is as God wills. If it does change its mind, there will be an unnecessary bund, doing nothing. But who knows? Sometime the River may change its mind again.

Officials might drive along these bunds, but must give notice, or they would find them blocked by thorn barriers to stop ordinary traffic: cartwheels would break the surface and the silt would blow away. (But should a driver see a bund without its barrier he should beware: he might be driving blithely along when suddenly there is a huge gap where last year's flood cut through. Furthermore, the roadway is so narrow that there is no room at all to turn the car.)

The maintenance of these bunds and the building of new ones provided a seasonal industry in itself. In the cold weather, whole villages of Pathans moved down from the hills, with wives and children, goats, chickens, and tentage. For transport they had their donkeys, large, well-cared for, and happy. The donkeys carried the soil from the borrow pits to the bund: they were essential tools for the job. These family groups all had their favourite areas, and always there was work for them.

For all my time in Sindh, the River was a preoccupation for my mind, sometimes in the forefront, sometimes only subconsciously; but the River was the life of the province, and my own, and my actions, of little comparative importance.

Corruption. The horror of corruption in government inhibited social contacts from my first days in Sindh. At Cambridge we had all had instilled into us the absolute necessity for the Indian Civil Service to be wholly incorruptible. We had been given lurid pictures of the dishonesty of many Indians we would meet. (By implication there was nothing like that in England, a picture as true, or false, as that we were given of India.) My uncle had told me of the enormous corruption involved in the Back Bay Reclamation project in Bombay, and even in Sukkur we heard of bribery for army contracts in Karachi. On occasion, in affairs involving big money, I was myself to be tested, with the implication that even an ICS officer could be tempted.

But there was nothing like this for an Assistant Collector to meet; seldom was our rather priggishly announced integrity threatened. Indeed, our manual advised us not to accept even gifts of flowers or small quantities of fruit. The possibility of offers of anything of more material value was not, in these rules, even contemplated.

In Sindh rules were not now quite so strict. A basket of fruit might be accepted unless there was some obvious selfish motive in the offer, and it was always wise to rummage a little to see if there were a bottle of whisky in the bottom. Then one had a decision to make: should one return the bottle and keep the fruit, with a gentle rebuke combined with thanks? Or should the whole gift be returned indignantly, with a speech as to the shock one felt at this attempt at bribery? It all depended on what motive was suspected, of what relationship one wanted to have with the donor.

Garlands were traditional presents, and no harm was seen in them. But a garland could be deceptive. I was once offered one with the flowers all tied on with yards of tiny gold chain, almost indistinguishable from tinsel.

More valuable presents could be kept if Government were asked for and granted approval, and the assessed value was paid into the Treasury. Governors and Viceroys were exempt from this rule!

Assistant Collectors were unlikely to be offered more than fruit—and, with Quetta nearby, and money always short, quality fruit was always welcome. But one was selective even then: an obvious motive would result in rejection, and this was sure to be known, and would do the donor more harm than not making a gift at all.

There was a more subtle area of corruption, based on the Sahibs' love of shooting. Possession of a good partridge shoot was worth many baskets of fruit. While I was in Sukkur, Mahomed Khan Drakhan finished a gaol sentence for murder, and almost at once offered Dermont a shoot, for he had good land for partridges, not recently shot over. Dermont refused, indignantly: it had been a very nasty murder. But when the Commissioner was invited a month or two later, he had no qualms about accepting—and Dermont had to go with him. Perhaps the armour of integrity grew thinner as one climbed up the service.

There was a general system of mild corruption we all knew about, tried to limit, but could not stop: it was too deeply rooted in custom. This was *rasai*. In effect, it was a levy on zamindars and merchants and shopkeepers to set up a fund administered by Mukhtiarkars. It was a small levy, so did no one much harm, and its purpose was to oil the wheels of the administration. When an officer arrived on tour, help arrived to set up and service his camp, and it was as if it was all out of kindness. As if the labour was paid. There was a time when it would have been truly forced, from tenants-at-will, the share-cropping haris, but that was long past.

Supplies of food, fuel, and fodder would also arrive, at favourable prices, and it was Dermont's concern, and in due course mine, to see that the prices were not too favourable. What annoyed us juniors was that the discounts were increased for superior officers, whose ample pay could well bear the full costs.

The big inundation canal in Upper Sindh was the Begari, dug entirely by forced labour under previous governance: *begar* means without pay. Jacob the engineer ended that, for being inefficient.

Our patewalas had to be watched. They knew very well how rasai benefited the Sahib, and although it benefited them too, they were known to try to make a little more for themselves: a fee of an anna for taking a petition in; four or five for announcing a visitor; a rupee for a panchayat. So we had heard. Dermont's naik did not try it, for not so long before someone else's naik had been detected and summarily sacked.

So throughout the services, all of them, this small corruption ran. We all maintained that it did no harm, and probably that was true. But none of us could claim to be pure white, which was perhaps just as well. The sinless, self-righteous man is not a pleasant character, and is apt to be too rigid to be a good officer. If such an officer fell from grace his fall would be hard and resounding.

5

THE LAST LAP

The bright lights of Karachi were dazzling after the routine of life in Sukkur. I was to find that there was always this contrast when I came in from the *mofussil.* A month in the Central Hotel subdued that excitement; after that I could settle into a new routine.

Nazir Ahmed and Timothy Crosthwaite and I had all been in Cambridge for our year in training, had all been posted to Sindh, and now all together came to Karachi for our last lap. So we would share a flat, and at last we found one: Number 1, Mary Road, a tall gaunt building very near the railway, almost under the road bridge to Clifton. It was adequately furnished, had two bedrooms and a room to make a third, a large central room, a verandah all along, and a wing at the back with kitchen and store. It was anything but luxurious, but it would do. Moreover, there was what to us was real luxury: a flushing privy, and an enamel bath with water laid on. If we wanted hot water, there was a *'biler'*, a dustbin on legs, with a tube up the middle that would be filled with live charcoal, and a tap. In the kitchen was the usual mud-built range of chullas.

This was a place to work and sleep, not for entertainment. But no one expected much from bachelor officers in training. We would find our own entertainment elsewhere.

We got on well together, but whereas Nazir Ahmed and I became close friends, I never did know—or if I did, have forgotten—where Timothy's interests lay, so we had little

in common except our Service. I liked him, but he followed
a different road. He became ADC to the Governor for a
time, and finished his service as a member of Mountbatten's
staff during the Independence negotiations.

Nazir and I worked and played very much together. I
joined the Karachi Gymkhana, but there the colour bar
still held; Nazir joined the Karachi Club, where there was
no colour bar, and which was well-equipped, for it was
used by wealthy Indians. The Gymkhana was much like the
Sukkur Club writ large, with tennis and dancing, good for
sitting and drinking. But I knew few to talk to, and didn't
want to drink much, for I was saving against the marrying
of a wife. At the Karachi Club there were very few women,
and much drinking of fizzy drinks. At the Gymkhana I met
our fellow civil servants and heard all the gossip; also their
wives who might have young daughters, and were anxious
to look over eligible young men; there were few who were
more eligible than were we.

There were other clubs too: the Boat Club, where 'Sahibs
go to row in little boats for pleasure, for heaven's sake!'
and the Yacht Club, which for me was the one that
mattered, though in this year, when I was so busy saving, I
didn't even become a member. I just let it be known that I
was available as crew for anyone who wanted one, and was
offered all the berths I needed. The clubhouse was a flimsy
shack on piles at the end of the West Dock, shabby and
ricketty and with few comforts, but to me a place of the
fondest memories. The Karachi Club had an Annexe, built
on the edge of the mangroves, and there, I was told, the
serious drinking took place. There was a Railway Institute,
but in Karachi it was different from that in Sukkur. And
finally there was the Sind Club.

The Sind Club (with no h) as I saw it in 1939 was a
genuine survival of Kipling's India. It was large, solidly built,
gloomy, and expensive. It was home to the 'Burra Sahibs'
of commerce, the law, and the Services, the Burra Sahibs,
so important that even the ICS were no more than their

equals. One could live at the Club, spend one's whole life there if one could afford it, and, of course, if one were white. People of such little account as I might go there as a guest. Once only did I enter it. I met men who wanted to be members, but I never felt that strange ambition. Nevertheless, it was the place where matters of policy were discussed by those who would have their execution, where deals were worked out, and a friend on the inside might be useful. There came times when I wished I had such a one.

We settled into our 'chummery'. We acquired servants besides the bearers each of us had: a part-time *dhobi*, a part-time *bheesti*, who heated and carried water, and a part-time sweeper. Since there was no thunder-box here we had a girl, an outcaste Hindu, who swept and dusted after a fashion under the direction of the appropriate bearer. Our bearers were all Muslims, they had no caste problems, but rail at them as we might, they would not dust. They would wash up, they would tidy away, but to dust would dishonour them

Then there was the cook. It fell to my lot to engage him, and to acquire his necessary equipment, so I gave him Rs. 30 and sent him off to the bazaar with Khuda Baksh to buy what he needed. It came to exactly Rs. 30. So Mistri came to us, a Muslim from the United Provinces (now Uttar Pradesh). When we all left our flat he stayed, stayed on when Joan came, stayed on and on. From the first he could cook in western style without the eastern flavour, and equally he could make a curry which, said Nazir, was as good as any you could get in Lahore.

The only people that I knew in Karachi were the high officers I had met at the Sukkur Durbar, in whose circles I did not move in Karachi. My life changed entirely. Nor had I any need for a horse. I wanted to sell him: keeping him for six months in Karachi would cost more than buying another horse when I needed one. I knew a *gharri* driver would buy him, but that would be a sad and cruel end for one who in his time had been a good polo pony. Then he fell very lame and I was told he should be put down, but that would have deprived Jan Mahommed of his friend and his livelihood.

For a time I pondered the problem, and then one day when I went to see them I found another man looking after Rajah. Jan Mahommed had been taken to hospital two days before, with pneumonia, and had promptly died: he had given the hotel as my address, so the news had not reached me till after he was dead. No one knew of any relatives, so I could only pay for his burial, and something for his friends. Rajah was put down. A very old horse, who had once been young and handsome; he was good-tempered and willing, and served me well; the first horse I had owned. I was sad for him, and for Jan Mahommed, who was a very simple man who cared for little but that his charge and his friend should be well and happy.

Naturally my Service took me up. I dined with the Governor and Lady Graham and the Staff; with other guests, too, all white, of course. (But there must have been other Government House parties when there were Indians, of the Service and others: surely the races must have mixed socially sometimes!) There was a ball, and that meant white tie and tails—and forget economy—while I danced with all the pretty girls of Karachi. It mattered little that I was a poor dancer, their mothers would put up with that. But they soon learned that I was not available, and the word spread round. We remained friends, but I was not very exciting company, anyway.

This social life did not attract me; sailing was different. On my first arrival in India I had been to the Bombay Yacht Club, a magnificent building, the Club to which everyone (white) that mattered belonged. There was sailing, but its chief function was to be the centre for the Empire off duty. The Karachi Yacht Club was quite different. There, the only function was organizing and competing in yacht races. There were chairs and a bar, but they were incidental to the real business, and idle onlookers might lose their

chairs to the participants in some fiercely contested protest
hearing. There were a few fixed moorings, and a small
'hard' where boats could be drawn out of the water. No
neatly uniformed boatmen, just *tindals*, boys from the
nearby fishing harbour, wearing decrepit shirts and shorts,
earning a few extra rupees.

There were two racing classes: Tom-tits, rather tubby and
short of sail for their weight, and 'Karachi One-Designs',
which were locally built to International 14 measurements.
They were clinker built, of heavy scantling, and could never
have lived with the current equivalent in Europe. But that
didn't matter: all being one design, there was no problem
with handicapping. Handicapping there was, based on
crews. If a tindal was taken, minutes were added to the
finishing time, because these fisherboys knew every
mudbank, every tidal quirk, every hole in the wind in that
vast shallow harbour. Sometimes a dinghy would sail single-
handed, and would receive an allowance, but usually the
crew would be two, both amateur: Corinthian.

It became known that if I were crew I would not expect
to take a turn on the tiller. But the dinghies mostly had
their regular crews, so usually I sailed with the Burra Sahibs
in the Tom-tits. With luck I would have jib and spinnaker
to look after, as well as the centre plate, sometimes only
the plate. The normal crew was three, of whom one would
be a tindal, and if I could replace him there would be an
allowance for sailing Corinthian. After a time I came to
know those mudbanks and reverse currents pretty well
myself.

Lady Graham was a good helmswoman, and quite often
asked me out with someone from the Government House
Staff, so that she could sail Corinthian. She was easy to talk
to, witty, and knew all the gossip, but clearly passed on only
what she felt was suitable. It was in one of her races that I
found that my report that a girl was coming out to marry
me had reached Government House, for she offered to put
this girl up while we got to know each other: this was even

before Joan had finally made up her mind. It was very kind, and a real honour. Perhaps it was a little churlish of me to say that we knew each other very well, so there was no need. In fact, I think that Lady Graham and I were looking at marriage rather differently. A lifetime in India had accustomed her to the idea that marriages were in some sort arranged, though not so simply and directly as were those of Hindus and Muslims. But situations could easily be arranged for eligible girls to meet suitable men in civilian services or the army, and very often suitable matches ensued. There was some truth in the idea of the 'Fishing Fleet': daughters, sisters, cousins coming to India in the cold weather to meet those young men, though that happened in hill stations, or centres larger than Karachi. (There was the corollary of the 'Returned Empties', the unkind description of those who returned home unmarried.)

His Excellency was not a good sailor. As helmsman he was brusque in his orders and his actions, he might forget to lift the plate, but would be annoyed if it was done without orders. There was a race when he decided to sail Corinthian, with John Corin, his Secretary, and me as crew. He gave us a particularly torrid time, with contradictory orders or none, we being always to blame. Naturally he did very badly, and that was our fault, too. But, as John explained, he had political problems on his mind. Usually he had one of us and a tindal as crew, and we did poorly then, too. He would shout at the tindal, who would grin, and do the right thing if he could. Most important it was that HE should enjoy himself; and in spite of it all, I enjoyed it, too.

It seemed that each of the heads of the main departments of government in Karachi sailed a Tom-tit, *ex officio*. The Revenue Commissioner, Godfrey Collins, and the Chief Judge, Godfrey Davis, both sailed, though neither would have qualified as a good helmsman, but to me that was a minor drawback so long as I could be on the water. Collins was nervous and excitable, given to shouting orders, and quickly changing them in illogical ways. He never won a race with me; I doubt if he ever won a race at all.

Godfrey Davis was temperamentally the opposite; witty, too. He was both bold and careful, but since he sailed, he said, simply for the fun of it, he was always relaxed. He knew all the rules and would seldom risk a foul, like trying to squeeze too close round a mark. As he explained, he was a lawyer, he knew all about evidence, and who was so keen on winning, anyway? I can remember a start when he was at the line, with all the fleet behind him, and he went about lest he risk beating the gun, and lost five places. At this I did protest, but he only laughed: it was only a game, no need to risk a foul, why worry? For a helmsman who was Chief Judge protests were serious: they were in his field of expertise. Before the Protest Committee he would be both judge and jury, prosecuting or defending counsel as appropriate, and he would fight his case to the bitter end. But then, when the decision was announced, and whichever way it went, did he win or lose, he would laugh and take me off for a drink. Sailing was for him an adventure, a pleasure, and a joke, all in one.

The Protest Committee had to sit after practically every race, and as boats came in one could count the rags and handkerchiefs tied to shrouds and tell how long the session was likely to be. No one, I think, protested against the Governor: probably it just wasn't done, or would have been against interest. ('Cross him off the list for the next GH dinner.' That couldn't be risked.) Lady Graham was so careful that I can't remember her ever being in trouble; Godfrey Collins would very sensibly surrender at once; Godfrey Davis gloried in a battle.

None of my Tom-tit skippers ever won a race, but for a few times I crewed in dinghies, and there matters were much more serious. There were trophies, and a monthly league where the top points won a silver tankard. If I ever had the chance, it would be in dinghies that I would race.

In Karachi there were four possible courses: up the main harbour among the shipping and back; up the muddy creek between the islets of Bhit and Baba; straight out to sea past Sandspit as far as Manora Fort and the Oyster Rocks; or a course set with parts of all those three. This left large parts of the harbour unused, but these were very shallow, uncovered at low tide, and mangrove swamp, dank, gloomy, and emitting strange sucking noises and a smell of decay.

The mud, and the complications of the tide, were vital elements in navigation, which was why the help of a tindal was so valuable as to earn a handicap. The wind at least was steady, varying only between south of west and a little north, excessively strong only at the time when Sindh welcomed the last vestiges of the south-west monsoon. Sometimes it would die right away in the evening, and then a race might be called off, because there must be no movement after dark.

Racing in any harbour is difficult. Karachi had its special problems, for its trade had outgrown its docking area, and often there were large freighters moored in the stream. Woe betide the boat carried by the tide into the lee of one of those. Then there were cut-down dhows working as barges, always sailing, never following any western rule of the road, often not even looking out. There were ferries crossing to and from Manora and Sandspit, and sometimes, a lovely sight, a two-masted ocean-going dhow came in from East Africa or the Gulf, foaming along with its tall lateen sails full and free, the crew standing by to bring her to go, as she reached her mooring.

These dhows had been sailing the Arabian Sea for a thousand years, but soon transport using the harbour would come right up to date, with the advent of flying boats. They had a landing area and terminal building at the end of the deep water, but unfortunately, one of the course marks was up there, and often the dinghies would be making that mark and beating back when a flying boat was signalled. Out would come the service launch to clear the course, and each dinghy would signal that it was doing its best, but no one was going to lose a place, or miss the mark, for a plane that was not in sight. The launch rushed around and swore and shouted, but the dinghies knew that they were safe, and anyway got out of the way as quickly as they could. I have watched a plane circle the harbour until the race moved away. They said that one such circuit cost Rs 5,000...

Apart from sailing, I went to the occasional formal dinner, a party at the Gymkhana, or sociable evenings with Nazir at the Karachi Club. But in April Joan had finally decided that she would come, and had given her notice to the school, so my need to save coincided with my need to work. Social life cost money, and I could do without it.

It was different for Nazir Ahmed Moghul, ICS, Punjabi from Rawalpindi, and determined to enjoy himself in Karachi. He was looked on widely and intently as a prospect for a suitable marriage, the most eligible Muslim bachelor in Karachi, but he was determined not to commit himself too soon. We had been friends from Cambridge days, and now he knew I would marry Joan. Marriage was in the air: he would enjoy himself and look around too.

Money never bothered Nazir. While I was saving against Joan's coming, and constantly having to reassure her that we would manage, Nazir used his credit to the full; he seemed even proud of his debt, though I didn't always believe him. Indeed, a few thousands of debt would not bother a mother who saw him as a suitable match for her daughter. But he felt that we should have a car, and his credit would not stretch quite so far. I must buy it. Indeed, we lived a long way from the City Magistrate's office where we had our work and heard our cases, which could be said to justify having one. I found one suitable to my parsimony.

In 1928, when I was at school, I had seen a square-nosed Morris, the successor to the famous 'bull-nose', and it was one of these that I bought, ten years later. It seated two, and had a dickey seat. It had a hand-operated screen-wiper, and a modern accessory: a big lever inside which, when pushed, dipped the headlights, which were mounted on a bar across the front; very advanced. Its paint was a much scratched and chipped grey—but that may in fact have been the undercoat. It would do for running about in Karachi, but it was too unreliable, it had too low a clearance to be of any use for touring.

Nazir used that car much more than I did. When he came to know the Shahban family, he would drive two little granddaughters around with their *ayah*; sometimes he took me, too. Once only I remember: we went to what was then called the Gandhi Garden, the Karachi zoo, and drove right through. A hosepipe crossed the road, and Nazir drove carefully over it. The *mali* came up, shouting with indignation. Why? 'It might have been a man!' But it wasn't. 'No, but if it had been you would have killed him.' That was true, and it was pointless to argue. Malis were good with flowers, but not very logical. That I also confirmed later.

Nazir decided that he should get married, too. I am sure that there was a suitable cousin in Rawalpindi, but he assured me that there was no pressure from there. Perhaps he had announced his intention in the Club; perhaps it was just assumed that it was high time. Anyway, the next thing was, he told me, that the Chief Minister of Khairpur State had offered a daughter; moreover, he had heard of Nazir's western ideas, and would let him see the girl before he made up his mind. This was refused: how could he see the girl and then reject her, humiliating both her and her father?

The real reason for the refusal was his knowing the Shahbans. Mian Shahban had been a member of the Bombay Assembly until Sindh became a separate province, and his wife was sister to Lady Hidayatullah, leader of Karachi society, wife of Sir Ghulam, Premier of Sindh. Her daughter was married to a son of the Bhutto family, one of the chief families of Upper Sindh. There were two little sons, and a younger daughter, Afroze.

Nazir's suit was approved, and now they could go out together. Mian Shahban asked Nazir what sort of car he wanted, and I went with him to buy jewellery and a ring. For the first time I saw real Indian jewellery, priced for design and craftsmanship, not only for the weight of metal. I could not but compare his case with mine and Joan's, but I was not envious: he had so many problems to face, in a society where I very much doubt if we would have been comfortable. Afroze herself had to be very courageous to move in so short a time from *purdah* in a respectable middle-class family. Her friends might giggle and be envious—Nazir said they did—but none of them had made a match with an ICS officer, than whom there could be none better.

The jewels left Nazir penniless, without even enough to pay the *mullah*'s fee. He certainly couldn't pay Afroze the customary daulat, the dowry a husband paid to his wife which she could claim if she divorced him. (The only reason for which a wife could divorce her husband was his impotence.) Afroze assured us that it didn't matter, but that would have looked very bad; I suggested a post-dated cheque would do, for appearances' sake; it could be recovered after the marriage. So Afroze had a cheque for a *lakh* of rupees, with the date carelessly smudged.

The wedding was to be a quiet family affair, but quietness is a relative matter: Afroze's sister was a Bhutto, married into one of the chief families of Upper Sindh. Her aunt, Lady Hidayatullah, could not see her niece married so quietly and, indeed, the Begum Shahban probably felt very much the same.

I was invited to it, being assured that there was no religious problem, and that the real marriage would come later. All Afroze's friends were at the house, which was brilliantly lit, reflecting their bright gold-spangled saris and *shalwars*. Nazir was all alone, so I was sent to the Club to round up some of his friends, to balance things. He sat stiffly in a chair wearing formal Punjabi dress, a beautiful embroidered *achkan*, tight white trousers, and embroidered slippers. He wore a gold-threaded turban and looked shy and nervous: quite unlike his usual self. There was no sign of Afroze, but those pretty flower-like girls kept slipping into another room, coming back giggling and covering their faces. One of them was so bold as to answer my question: Afroze was being prepared to meet her fate.

Now, Afroze was very happy to be marrying Nazir; nothing could please her more, but any sign that this was so would have been contrary to all custom and decency, even among these modern Muslims. So she was taken in hand, clothed royally and voluminously, laughing and calling to her friends to get on with it. But this would not do, so, as she told Nazir later (and which he passed on to me) relatives took a hand, and she was pinched and slapped, and her hair was pulled to make her cry, as was proper in a girl being torn away from her home and handed over to this rough man forever. Indeed, the rough handling, however kindly meant, and the tension, resulted in her truly weeping when at last she was led out to meet her groom. She was being carried rather than walking, so tightly was she swaddled. Her head was drooping, and so well-covered that no face was visible. This was nothing like Afroze!

They sat side by side, the proud if nervous groom and the humble, cowering bride. The ceremony was very short: verses and responses from the Quran, hands clasped, laid on brow and heart and feet, and a blessing from the mullah. Or so it appeared to me.

The timing had all gone awry, with Lady Hidayatullah insisting on a far larger gathering than had been intended, and it was past midnight before it was all over. I paid the mullah his fee (would Nazir ever pay me back?) and we found something to eat and drink. There came to join us a young man, a cousin of Afroze; I had never met him, I could not understand why he should resent me, but then it appeared that he held me at least in part responsible for this marriage, when he had always considered himself to be his cousin's proper husband. Moreover, Nazir was a Punjabi, whereas he was a Sindhi of her own clan. But he was not angry, just sad and disappointed; and with reason.

Afroze spent this time, while Nazir was preening himself with his friends, sitting huddled in her chair while her friends comforted her. In fact, she played her part of the frightened girl right to the end. But she would not accept the custom that she remain *purdanashin* until the full formal marriage in October: next day she was as cheerful as ever when she went out walking with her new husband.

I wrote to Joan at length about the ceremony I had been to. Very priggish I was, about the symbolism of woman's subjection and so forth. I failed to appreciate all the ancient formalities, nor did I relate them to those of the Christian service: the veil, the exchange of rings and promises, the bride being given away. Both ceremonies were much the same, and the omission of the promise to obey was still unusual among Christians.

However firmly Nazir might reject the idea that he must be separate from his wife till after the final ceremony, he was prevented by the requirements of the Service; we were posted to Hyderabad for a course of surveying.

Throughout this time I was learning Sindhi, and for this the three of us worked separately. I at last met my munshi, who had appointed himself already by post: Kishensingh Vaswani. I honour him: he did me proud. I might laugh at him, I might point out how the sweat patch at his armpit spread all over his back and front as the weather warmed up, for each day he cycled from his far-distant house on Bunder Road Extension, but I passed my exam in July, much to my own surprise, though not, he claimed, to his: maybe I was not good at languages, all that showed was what a very good teacher he was. I agreed to go on with lessons, and finally he saw me qualify as an Interpreter. Then he went to Bombay with the other Hindu Sindhis.

Once I took tea with Kishensingh and his family at his home. His father I had met already: he had once or twice substituted for his son, but he was a stupid, lewd old man. I met his daughter, showing briefly and shyly, and his son who was at college. His wife was self-possessed and self-effacing, but very sure of her position: a very proper Hindu wife. Kishensingh was, of course, very loyal to the British—his profession depended on a continuous supply of young Sahibs needing to learn Sindhi or Urdu—but his ambition was to win recognition for Sindhi as a truly classical language, with a literature of its own. His prospects of success were very poor, his foundations insecure, for it seemed to be very much a vernacular language. Karachi was polyglot, and towards the River, where the real Sindhis lived, both words and grammar were corrupted by Gujerati, while in Upper Sindh there was corruption from Balochki. 'Pure' Sindhi could perhaps be found in Hyderabad, the home of the Amils, the intelligentsia of the province. Kishensingh was himself one. He was hard put to find one notable Sindhi author; but he thought only of Hindu culture. Of the Muslim world he knew nothing, except that very few Muslims could, he thought, even read.

He went to Bombay with his family at Partition and must have found his profession overcrowded, with no one wanting to learn Sindhi, and its basis destroyed, with no new British officers arriving to learn any language.

6

REALLY WORKING

Nazir, Timothy, and I found ourselves Magistrates of the Third Class: we had the power to impose a fine up to Rs. 100, or a gaol sentence up to one week. Each of us was also given charge of a *taluka*. Perhaps this was just to give colour to our claim to authority, for each taluka had its Mukhtiarkar, so there was no room for us. It was just a sinecure, for I can remember no work arising from the post. On the other hand, it entitled us to Rs. 100 a month travelling allowance, with no specific travelling. Far be it from us to question the appointments.

Being a magistrate did, however, involve actually hearing and deciding cases. A court clerk was appointed, to be shared, so each had a separate day for his sessions. Only very petty cases came to us: petty theft, assault, driving without lights; nothing very interesting, but better than just listening to cases in sub-divisional courts. I, however, had the good—or bad—luck to get on my list a case, inconsiderable in itself, that caused a real stir in the British community.

There was a Captain Macaulay, left over from the Great War, who was superintendent for a stevedoring company. He was charged by a coolie, backed by his union, with 'assault occasioning bodily harm'. The Captain did not deny that he had knocked the man down—there was the injury as evidence: a black eye and a grazed elbow. The defence was of provocation: the man had questioned an order, and the blow was just a normal and necessary way to maintain discipline. This may have been usual, but was hardly legal, or acceptable as a defence. I fined the Captain Rs. 100, of which Rs. 30 was for the coolie for compensation. (He must have felt the pain well worth bearing, but I wondered if he would ever get a job in the docks again.)

There was a great heat of feeling among the *koi hais* in the city: this young and inexperienced whippersnapper taking sides with a coolie against an experienced officer. My own Service said nothing, but I heard that it was not displeased, and let its judgement spread round.

In August we all three went to Hyderabad for a course on land surveying. For three weeks we stayed, considerably underworked, with plenty of time to contemplate what was happening in Europe, for there seemed to be an inevitable slide to war, and it looked as if my prophecy made six months before in Sukkur might come exactly true. I began urging Joan to come at once, to come by air; but flying was stopped, only an air mail twice a week, and I reverted to the study of surveying.

I drove the three of us to Hyderabad, but not in the ancient Morris: that had gone. One day Nazir had come home, very angry, waving the gear lever, having abandoned the car stuck in the tramlines. We found it, got in, I poked the lever into its hole and wiggled it: a perfect fit, so I started the engine and we drove away as fast as we could. But that was enough. I took the car to the garage for repair, and when that was done and the bill came, I asked what it was worth; when they told me, I told them they could keep it, just paying me Rs. 100 as the balance between the two. I considered that I was well out of it.

This was no sudden decision: I had already arranged a government loan and bought my new car, a Chevrolet. English cars were not very useful outside towns, their ground clearance was too small for earth roads. The Governor's giant Daimler had gone to Sukkur, but that was for a special occasion, and for specially prepared roads.

Charles Clee, my Collector, had an Armstrong Siddeley, but on tour probably borrowed a zamindar's car; and Ivon Taunton, Chief Secretary, had a beautiful yellow Rolls Royce, the only one in Sindh, but his was not a touring job.

The three of us would be posted to Districts in September, and would need cars. Nazir was being given—given!—a new Studebaker, and Timothy would doubtless buy a suitable one. I bought a beautiful, long wheel-base, open top Chev, a most elegant motor, which I came to love dearly. The upholstery was leather, with fitted khaki canvas covers, it had glass side screens, and a large boot with a metal case on it for the spare wheel. (Later, when tyres were scarce, and a blow-out was mended by fitting a 'gaiter', the wheel would not fit in the case, and it had to be discarded.)

This car was suspiciously cheap, only Rs. 1,000. Perhaps it was the front suspension that was suspect. Instead of simple coil springs, there was a big steel cylinder holding a hydraulic ram for each wheel. The system worked very well, until one day when it failed...

There was ample room for the three of us, with our indispensable bistras, and, of course, Khuda Baksh. We drove in great comfort and to my great pleasure. We drove through a hundred miles of Sindh quite unlike any we had seen before. Today the National Highway runs straight from Karachi to Kotri, but at that time the main road went east to Thatta, and then north-east, skirting the great Kinjhar Dhand. Going out of Karachi it passed the RAF aerodrome at Drigh Road, where stood the enormous hangar built for the airship that never came; with it died the hope of an airship service to Australia. Then through the garden lands of Malir and across the dry river bed, with the road made with tamarisk twigs and grass, which would be swept away next time it rained, leaving Karachi cut off by land until the river bed dried and the road could be laid again. All this area is within modern Karachi. This, the chief road of Sindh, was much better than the earth roads of Upper

Sindh, for the soil was mostly gravel. Even on the earthen lengths, where it ran through cultivated land, the soil was well compacted, crossed by 'Irish bridges' (how the poor Irish suffer!). Instead of a proper bridge, sometimes a concrete bed was made in the stream bottom. If the stream flowed only a little, crossing was safe; if the flow were heavy, one just waited.

This was August, and the rice was ripening; water that could not be drained off stood and dried, leaving its salts behind, year after year. Large areas were salt-poisoned—*kalar*—unusable till it could be cleaned. But when the level of the land rose by only a foot we were in scrub desert, out of reach of the River even when it had flowed further west than it did in my time. Driving over the gravel was a pleasure till we hit an area where the wind had blown the surface into ridges like sand on the seashore. That was purgatory.

We soared up the long slope of the Makli Hills, and saw the long lines of tombs and monuments, hundreds and hundreds, fading away in the dusty distance where the little white mosque and shrine of Pir Patho rose above the murk. We descended on Thatta, bypassed it, and crossed a canal by a proper bridge. Then we saw the Kinjhar Dhand on our left and knew that beyond the strip of jungle on the right was the river itself. We passed by Jherruk, crossed a real river, the Barani, and came to Kotri and the railway.

We crossed the Indus by the Kotri bridge, and before we had finished marvelling at its width, were astonished even more by our first sight of the skyline of Hyderabad. As usual for an old town in Sindh, it sat on a little self-made hill, and above the roofs rose hundreds of *badgirs*, wind scoops, all of the same pattern, rising to a triangular peak, all facing to the south-west wind. We drove into the town along a wide, tree-lined road with gardens on both sides, then on to the Mall, in the Cantonment, to the house of Kaikhusro Framji, who would be our host.

K.K. Framji, ever afterwards Fram, Indian Service of Engineers. He was reputed to be brilliant, destined for great things. To us, he was a most hospitable host; and much later Joan and I were to know him very well indeed.

When next I went to see my precious car, it had a flat tyre; the spare proved to be punctured too, and this, as Nazir pointed out, proved that God was on our side: if this had happened on the road we would have been in a rare pickle.

This was the home town of the Amils, with their connections throughout India and the world, and their prosperous houses showed it. It had also been Napier's headquarters for his conquest of Sindh. The battlefield of Miani was nearby, and it was still a military cantonment. At this time a battalion of the Rajputana Rifles was there.

The Rajputs were just being equipped with an artillery section: obsolescent field pieces being modified as anti-tank guns. We were invited to their mess, where all the talk was of war, and very cheerful it was. This was the time when Russia made its pact with Germany, and the Rajputs, having no faith in France, and sure that Italy would be on the German side, saw no harm in Britain's loneliness; in fact, they saw it as an excellent arrangement. I suggested that in these circumstances, in a war on these terms, we might possibly lose, but this was condemned as un-British, unpatriotic, and defeatist.

A picnic was arranged for us, at the Fuleli Canal, and I heard that I was to be ducked, to teach me patriotism. But the picnic never came off: the Colonel had disapproved, so all the guests withdrew. Then the Rajputs received orders for the Middle East. We wished them good luck, and saw them no more.

I dined with the Civil Surgeon, whose bungalow was as it had been built nearly a century before, without even electricity added. We sat under the sweep of punkahs, their musty smell mixing with the smell of the food. All the time there was a squeak from the cord as it passed through a

hole in the wall, and the Surgeon said he liked it: if it
stopped it meant that the *punkah*-puller was asleep, so he
could shout to waken him. He was lit by oil lamps, and
pointed out their advantage over electricity: insects were
attracted to both, but where an electric lamp collected
more and more, an oil lamp killed many as they came, so
there never were any big clouds. Moreover, the gecko
lizards preferred the soft light of oil, and they were his
other insecticide.

The Adjutant of the Rajputs was there, left to clear up
behind the battalion. He claimed that his object in joining
the army had been to play the piano. He saw no prospect
of earning a living as a professional pianist, but the army,
particularly the post of Adjutant, provided a comfortable
living, and more spare time than most jobs. He agreed that
there was an inevitable risk in being a soldier, and that not
all stations were good for his piano, but on the whole he
was satisfied with his choice. Whether or not he took his
piano to Egypt I do not know.

The Surgeon was happy to feed us his grisly tales;
meeting other Civil Surgeons later, I found that their own
grisly tales were often suspiciously similar: they all liked to
make one's flesh creep. But one I heard here and nowhere
else.

It was about a man concerned at the decline of his manly
powers. He made inquiries and heard of a hakim who could
surely help him, so he bought a powder that was highly
successful. There was a splendid erection, but unfortunately
it would not go away. Perhaps the hakim had an antidote,
but he had disappeared. The patient suffered—and being
unable to urinate he truly suffered. He went to the Civil
Hospital for help, but western medicine could only offer
temporary relief; after that, the erection returned. It
seemed that only a continuous course of anaesthetics could
be a cure, and what had been a matter of pride became a
curse. For several days the man came for his injection, but
then he came no more... We pressed the Surgeon, he must

surely know more, have heard more about this strange case. But he was adamant: the story had no ending.

From the professional point of view we wasted a lot of time in Hyderabad; the instruction in surveying could have been completed in a week, given reasonable working hours, but the day began at ten in the morning and ended soon after noon because it was getting hot. An English-speaking Supervising Tapedar had charge of us, and at least he was not overawed by having three Sahibs as pupils. He began at the beginning, explaining the use of compass, cross-staff, and chain. He revealed the mysteries of triangulation. For a Sindhi, a chain was itself a puzzle: he could hardly know that its twenty-two links were the basis for measuring a cricket pitch, and since its origin was from time out of mind it could not be changed. Our Supervisor could not know that when he spoke of a furlong he was speaking of the length of a furrow set by a Saxon ploughman for turning his plough. A twenty-two yard chain would have been awkward to use, so we used half a chain, thirty-three feet, so tantalizingly close to the thirty-two annas in two rupees. But we were assured that such inaccuracy as speaking of a 'two rupee chain' would have put all previous mensuration out of true. A pity. I asked the Supervisor about the problem, but he said they managed: they supposed all the units to be of a different area of numeracy.

We measured survey numbers that had been measured many times before; if we got a different answer from his we argued, quite hopelessly, that he was wrong. But in the end we satisfied him, and each received a certificate stating that we were competent to be entrusted with the Great Trigonometrical Survey of India.

The whole atmosphere in Karachi had changed while we were away. There was a general conviction that war was coming: Henry Frost and Bob Shebbeare, the Governor's son-in-law who had been his Military Secretary, were recalled to their units, and Timothy and I were called to

Government House to learn about codes and cyphers—in strict secrecy, work for British nationals only.

There had been rumours while we were in Hyderabad about the postings of the three of us. I was to have the Hala sub-division, near Hyderabad, and I was so foolish as to believe that. It was the reputed home of Sindhi culture, with a bungalow in the town. I even went to look at it, and wrote to Joan of its possibilities. Then the Commissioner told us that we would go to Hala or Nawabshah or Dadu, but he refused to say who would have which.

Joan continued preparing, and all was well till the shipping office told her that all sailings were in doubt. At the same time I had my second, and serious, departmental exam. I had maintained my opinion that being able to look up the Revenue Rules was as good as knowing some by heart (there were, after all, hundreds of them). But the Examiner did not agree; he failed me, and passing on the legal side was not enough: I failed the exam. This was humiliating, but, far worse, I lost an increment of pay, and would have to confess to Joan my irresponsibility. But at least I was still posted as Assistant Collector, not to any of the three canvassed, but to Thatta. Thatta was a sub-division of Karachi District, with headquarters in Karachi, but no officer's bungalow, so I would have to find somewhere for myself.

Perhaps the Establishment was being kind, but I doubted it. Early marriage was not encouraged. Perhaps Lady Graham had a hand in it, for she knew of my romance. I never knew, and it didn't matter. Joan would not be whisked, as it were, straight into the jungle. But Mary Road was not a welcoming place. Nazir and Timothy went off to their posts, we gave up Mary Road, and I moved into the Central Hotel. There was little point in looking for somewhere more permanent, for we would be touring for most of the six months after Joan came.

On 2 September Joan cabled that her passage was confirmed: the *City of Canterbury*, to Karachi and on to

Bombay. On the next day war was declared. There could be no firm dates for departure or arrival, so I must wait. And I must think of her at sea with submarines prowling, and my family and hers left behind, with Joan's particularly in danger in London. I was rewarded with letters telling of final preparations when I had imagined her already at sea, and with no indication that she would be sailing soon.

There followed in Europe the 'phoney war', though no one knew it was phoney till afterwards. It was phoney in Karachi, too. It was obvious that any patriotic young Englishman must volunteer for war service, so I consulted my Commissioner. He said there was no moral compulsion, and that if I decided to volunteer he could not stop me, and the army would certainly take me. But the Government of India would as certainly ensure that I was kept well away from danger, to be available when the war was over. I would be given a desk job far less interesting and useful than I would find on the civil side. This relieved me of all save a very tiny itch of conscience.

I took over my sub-division: Assistant Collector and First Class Magistrate, Thatta Sub-division. My office was in the District Kutchery, the block built by John Jacob nearly a century before. I could keep all my touring *bundobust* in the godown there.

I had no need for a horse; camels were more useful in this country, but I must have two camel boxes, as was always required, and they must be of a special design. They must have a curved side, to fit round a camel's ribs, and the hinges, straps, rings, and staples must be to a traditional design. They were to be made of mango wood, a strange choice, for it is soft and spongy, but there was no arguing with tradition. I bought Dermont Barty's tents. But I would not leave Karachi till I knew when Joan would arrive. There were cases to be tried, and files to be studied, and matters that I could deal with locally. At that time Malir was a garden suburb. Everything it could produce it could sell locally: all the vegetables that I knew, and others: brinjals (aubergines), *bhindis* (lady's fingers), tomatoes, gherkins, peppers, melons, and all sorts of lentils. There were potatoes, and *berseem*, alfalfa, as a break crop, specially in demand for all the *gharri* horses in the city. Fruits were not good: a low quality mango, a tiny banana, small sweet apples that grew on a bush, though perhaps it was a bush only because it was not allowed to grow into a tree. Then there was the horrible *malta*: an orange, large, tasteless, full of pips, difficult to peel. It seemed to me that if I could get some jaffa scion wood, I might use the trees to graft on good oranges. I knew about grafting: my Father was an expert, using ancient techniques. I had helped him to dig clay from a special spot in the river to plaster round his grafts. It was very old-fashioned, but it worked.

The soil was inherently infertile, but the legumes that fed the horses, and the manure that they returned, changed all that. Only water was needed, and that came from wells, lifted by Persian wheels, mostly wooden ones, a few of metal, modern and expensive. They all used clay jars tied to an endless rope chain. Usually the crown wheel was turned by a blindfold bullock, but I saw one worked by a camel, towering high, looking haughtily round, pretending to ignore his blindfold. There was also a hoist, the like of which I never saw outside Malir. It was for very deep wells, sunk to catch the very edge of the aquifer; a chain of pots would have been too heavy, breaking under their weight. Instead, there was a ramp rising to the well-head, and a rope with a water-skin passed over a roller and down the well. A horse hitched to the rope must back up the ramp, the skin would hit the water and fill, and then the horse would walk forward till the skin hit the roller and decanted its load into a channel. The horses did not like walking backwards, there must be a man there all the time, so it was expensive. But the land's assessment took account of that.

This was agriculture unlike anywhere else in Sindh. The land was held by freeholders, and they were Hindus; their workers were paid wages, and they were low-caste Hindus. Farming was of a far higher standard, and far more flexible than elsewhere. There were endless disputed assessments, and, as I had forecast, no one trusted his memory of the Rules: we always checked with the text.

The Malir River was at this time the sole source of Karachi's water supply; the wells hardly affected this. Most of the time the river bed was dry, but it ran strongly underground. Rain from the hills seeped through the porous soil and supplied a bountiful aquifer. Fifty years earlier, a stone gallery had been built, thirty feet down, cutting across the stream. When I saw it, one end of the gallery had been opened up and extended to trap the last little bit of the flow. This was the business of the City Engineer, but it was in my territory so he consulted me. I could not object to his proposals—I was no expert!—but I was certainly interested. It was always a pleasure to meet someone who knew what needed doing, and was doing it

The Engineer wanted to go much further. Malir could only just supply Karachi as it was. When the city grew, as it surely would, or there were a drought, as there surely would be, real trouble was inevitable. So he enlisted my help for a safe and adequate supply. He would show me what he wanted.

His targets were two big lakes, fed by intermittent mountain streams. Haleji was the nearer, only thirty miles from Malir, but Kinjhar, twenty miles further, was much larger, and very near the River. Most of the land was government waste, but two booster pumps would be needed. The Engineer wanted a pipeline: an open channel would lose by evaporation, and be open to contamination and damage.

Kinjhar it must be. Work began a few years later. I could be proud that, if only as an onlooker, I was there when the pipeline was planned. Then, Karachi's population was about 250,000; by 1960 it was over 2,000,000; today it is said to be 10,000,000. I hope that far-sighted engineer is

remembered, even though this great city is still short of
water.

In England, Joan was having an anxious time. She
collected special things: an air-tight trunk, jodhpurs, short
lengths of beautiful textiles to make covers, all manner of
things. She bought some hand-spun wool and on her loom
wove a length of pale blue wool, and made a costume of it.
Seldom would Sindh be cold enough for her to wear it, but
it was more *swadeshi* than Gandhi himself.

While I was happily getting to know my work, Joan was
filled with anxieties. She haunted the shipping office to
make sure that her berth on the *Canterbury* stood, but there
was no surety: no certainty about anything. She went to the
India Office to see if there might be some other berth, to
see if India would pay her passage, for the only clear thing
was that she would surely marry. But that Office knew that
her passage was already paid: its refusal would not condemn
their officer to a tragic separation. Both our efforts had
failed.

At last there was a firm date for sailing, and my Mother,
whose home was in Bolton, drove her to Liverpool and
there said good-bye. No one was allowed on board, there
were no cheerful, or tearful, partings. My Mother wrote to
me the same day: she stood with a few others at the dock
gate, it began to rain, so she drove away alone.

In Karachi I was told that the *Canterbury* would sail at the
beginning of October. I booked a double room at the hotel
for the end of the month, then was told that the boat
would go straight to Bombay, so I had to arrange for
Grindlay's to meet her, and booked her on the BI packet
for Karachi for I would not go: I was suffering from
dysentery. Why just now, when my wife-to-be was so nearly
here?

I could but listen to the radio and hope that all would
be well. I had a night of real fear when one of the 'City'
boats was reported torpedoed; reception was always poor,
it could have been *Canterbury*, but was not, it was *Mandalay*.

Of course I thought sadly of the ship and crew, but chiefly I was possessed with enormous relief.

After that, and before the letter telling me of Joan's sailing arrived, there came a cable from Gibraltar: 'Safe, slow.' Now it was only a matter of time; but the cable was dated 9 October, so all my careful planning had fled down the wind. I revised my hotel booking, I arranged for John Corin and Tim Crosthwaite to stand by to witness a marriage, and with my office worked out my first tour programme—everything but dates.

And then I must just wait.

7

MARRY IN HASTE

I could at last be certain that Joan would arrive on 11 November— Armistice Day, still properly observed in a city like Karachi; moreover, it was Saturday. Government House must have kept a special eye on its young officers, for again Joan was offered a guest room while we prepared to marry. It was not just a Saturday arrival that was the problem: the Collector—my Collector—was also the Registrar of Marriages, and he had already gone on tour across the River. He was an enthusiastic shot, the partridges were plentiful, and he was certainly not going to come in all that way, spoiling his shooting, just because this girl chose to come at this awkward time to marry his subordinate. I reassured Government House, Lady Graham in particular, that there was no problem: I had a double room booked at the hotel, and as soon as we could we were going to Hawkes Bay. There was no need to worry, we knew each other very well, we would certainly be marrying as soon as we could. But this was in an age, and in a country, that did not accept that a British officer should be allowed to live openly in sin. So a Special Issue of the Sindh Government Gazette appeared, for one item: the Collector of Karachi was deprived of the office of Registrar of Marriages, which was transferred to the City Magistrate. Even this left room for a possible hitch, for his office would not normally open on a Saturday; but I knew Mr Agha, a pleasant and helpful man whose subordinate I had been when I was first a magistrate.

He had agreed to open his office till midday. Let not the Bombay packet be late! I was on the dockside early, with Khuda Baksh and a man from Grindlay's. I had used influence—even the most junior ICS officer could exercise his small measure—to arrange for the Customs Officer to let Joan's baggage through, with an assurance that there was nothing commercial in it. We gazed to sea, and at last the ship appeared round the Oyster Rocks, and as she neared the quay I could see Joan waving, and I waved back.

It was astonishing! After all the time, after all the correspondence, there she was, herself, in person, very real; and there was no more need for letters which were little more than a shadow of reality. Our romantic tale was actually coming to life.

But romance must quickly give way to realism: no one was allowed on board, but a Lascar helped Joan with her bags. We hugged, we kissed, and then I said we must hurry. Why? Because if we delayed beyond midday we couldn't get married anyway. I introduced Khuda Baksh, who *salaamed* to head and heart (his beard was newly dyed for this day). Grindlay's man took charge of the baggage list, we went to the car, the elegant Chev that Joan had heard so much about, and we set off to get married.

With the immediate celebration of arrival completed, in so few hurried minutes, bureaucratic organization had to give way: there might be no long white dress, no beribboned limousine, no bridesmaids, not even anyone to give her away, but the bride must certainly wash and put on a silk dress, even though it came straight from a suitcase, and proper shoes. So we must take the bags and go first to the hotel. Life became a little less hectic: I could even point out the handsome buildings on Macleod Road, and the shining white of Government House. Karachi was not uncivilized.

Washed and changed, we went to that grand place to collect my two witnesses, John Corin and Tim Crosthwaite. Then we returned to my schedule, and set off for the City

Magistrate's office. We were probably the only British people moving at that time in Karachi, for everyone else who mattered was being still and silent for two minutes as we drove through.

It was not yet noon, and indeed, I expect Mr Agha would have stayed on had it been necessary. Mrs Agha was there too, welcome support for the bride, and a small daughter who presented her with a posy. Now there was a kindly thought, and one that I should have had. (All my life I have been too late with kindly thoughts.) It was such an arid ceremony: certainly there was no let or hindrance; yes, we took each other as man and wife. So please sign here. Then witnesses signed and we were firmly married, under Indian law.

Everything was so very unexciting; even the city was half asleep on this Saturday. We four went to the Gymkhana for a celebratory sherry, and then our two witnesses left us for their duties at Government House.

I do wish Joan would tell her tale, of leaving family and friends and braving the submarines, to marry someone she hadn't seen for a year, but she won't. But of this I am sure: in wartime there must have been many hurried weddings, but none so odd as ours; and all to avoid unkind gossips whispering about young men in the Service in these days who lived brazenly in sin.

We went to the hotel for lunch. The other guests looked at us curiously—perhaps we were too obviously self-conscious. I had not even told the manager that this was a special occasion, but by now all the luggage had arrived, and my single room had already been changed for a double one. He had put a big bunch of flowers on the table, and there was half a bottle of wine. We were not entirely unnoticed.

Afterwards we were alone, and could get to know each other again in ways not possible had Joan been a guest of the Governor. It was a time for quiet queries and answers, for just the occasional kiss and caress. After all, we now had before us all the time in the world.

Joan did tell me some of her feelings: rushed into marriage, isolated now in this rather dingy room, in a strange place, with strange noises outside, among strangers, however friendly they might prove to be. And it was hot: even in November it was hot. We decided to have some tea. I found a man who could bring it and asked him, showing off my Sindhi. He replied in English and the tea came, English style, really hot, the milk unboiled. Good tea, for of course India understands tea. (It was usually to be had on railway stations, but that was different. The tea was kept simmering, and so was the milk, lest it curdle. And if one were not very insistent, a cardamom seed would be added for flavour.)

At last we could look at some of the things that Joan had brought with her. All the boxes were in the hotel godown so we had time and privacy for looking. There was so much for me to see and admire, and some things we must keep out, for they would be needed as soon as we went on tour.

Then we went out and about: for me to show off my very new wife, for her to see a little more of Karachi. We could do this properly, for I had been confident enough to have cards printed for Joan herself, bigger than mine, as befitted an officer's wife calling on the wife as well as the officer himself. The first call, naturally, was on Government House, but there at the gate was a handsome stone hut with a Visitors' Book and a silver salver inside. The sentry saluted, I saluted back, we signed, and for the first time Joan left her own card, 'Mr & Mrs R. R. Pearce, ICS.' (Address, the Central Hotel, which let us down a bit, even in brackets.) Undoubtedly an invitation to dinner would follow, but I had arranged with John Corin that we would be left in peace for our honeymoon.

I saluted the sentry again, he saluted back, and I hoped Joan was suitably impressed, but rather was she looking at the beautiful new gardens.

My Collector was away on tour, as we well knew, so the only other compulsory visit was to the Commissioner, my sometime helmsman, Godfrey Collins. He lived in the house built by General Napier a century before. Until recently it had been Government House, and later would be Government House again, when the new Government House became the Governor-General's House. Finally, it became the Commissioner's house once more. My own sub-divisional office was attached to it, and in its compound our camel train would assemble when we went out on tour.

The Commissioner's wife was away, so, no card from Joan: her visit was necessarily informal. We met the Commissioner himself, and he was not so welcoming as we had hoped: astonished to hear that we were already married, expressing his principled antipathy to officers marrying so early. His niece, Wanda Kindzior, whom we came to know later, was there, and she softened the hard words by pointing out that a war made quite a difference. What Collins did not yet know was that the latest ICS recruit, just arrived, was already married, even before he left England.

Our last call, and all others save this could wait indefinitely, was to the Shahbans, Afroze's and now Nazir's family. Here was no western formality: I presented our cards, but no one took any notice of them. No one took any notice of me, either. Joan was at once surrounded by Begum Shahban, the Mian Sahib, several small boys and girls, and Begum Bhutto, Afroze's sister, and, of course, Afroze's old ayah, as much a part of the family as any of them.

The house was filled with excitement and talk and laughter. Soft drinks arrived, and nuts and pakoras and samosas. Bashir Malik came from his job with the railway: now I was married, as well as his friend Nazir, so it was at about this time that he decided he should marry too. He did, and we met his wife Bilqis when we, and Nazir and Afroze too, were all in Karachi years later.

No newcomer, newly married in a hurry with no celebration at all, could have asked for a greater, happier welcome. I think Joan cried a little. I just stood back: doubtless it was good for me to have such a minor part to play.

Nazir and Afroze were coming in from Nawabshah next weekend, and there was to be a party for Joan. I pointed out that we had only a week for a honeymoon, that we were going to Hawkes Bay next morning till the following Sunday, that on the next day we would be going on tour, and all bookings had been made. But it was no good; we must come in for a party on Saturday. Protesting was a waste of breath, and anyway Joan seemed happy about it. Moreover, she would meet Nazir again, the only other person she knew in India west of Calcutta. So the change was made, and indeed, after such a joyful welcome it was churlish to refuse.

So we went back to the hotel for dinner. (Supper was left behind in England, in another world.) After that was just our wedding night.

I have to feel back over fifty years of change in social and marital mores to try to relive our wedding night. For years we and our friends had argued and discussed the rights and wrongs of marriage, of sexual attitudes inside and outside marriage. We had read Havelock Ellis and Bertrand Russell and MacMurray; we had managed to eliminate from our attitudes all the irrelevancies of emotion. Now all the talking and theorizing must end: what we had dreamed for so long had actually come about, and we were alone together.

There should have been a passionate embrace, and a curtain drawn. Embrace there was, but... In these days are there ever two virgins meeting on their wedding night? That is how it was for us; moreover, we were very tired, overwrought, unsure. Unskilled, too. Joan was kind and friendly, and soon turned over and went happily to sleep. I, no longer the strong, competent male, wept a little with

at all, just a slight inward curve of the shore. Our cabin had no glass, but it had a good thatched roof, a verandah, and was only a few yards from a little sandy beach. Behind, a track ran along, and behind that, as it were to shelter the beach, were high dunes, always shifting, never quite swallowing up the huts.

The south-west monsoon wind blew everlastingly. It blew from clear skies, it was cool on the skin, but it was so very damp; everything was damp. We had brought bedding in the ever-useful bistra, and after a day that was all damp too. But it was salty damp, and who ever heard of salty damp doing any harm? When the wind blew off the land it was hot and dry, and blew the dunes nearer to the huts that they threatened to engulf. But always, just in time, the sea breeze arose, and the dunes retreated again. They cut us off from the world on one side, and on the other was the endless sea. As the tide rose, rollers rumbled in; as it ebbed, little wavelets hissed on the shingle. There was no other sound, we were in a wholly private and peaceful world. We had never known anything like it; probably we never would again.

There is no record of those five days. We could eat when we liked, sleep when we liked, make love, bathe, lie in the sun. Joan particularly must have felt it a benison. In little more than twenty-four hours she had landed in Karachi, met me again after a year apart, been rushed into marriage, met a lot of strangers, spent an exhausted marriage night, and now this loneliness. Excepting only me. Was I enough to fill all that empty space? Even now I can feel my anxiety.

Indeed, there was a record, for we wrote home, but those letters have not come back to us. We wore as few or as many clothes as we pleased, more when the sun was hot, or when it sank into the sea. But one did not write home of such things. We have just one picture, a snapshot of Joan on a surfboard, coming in to land on a gentle roller. We had bread and butter, fruit and tinned milk. We had a primus stove and water, so we could make tea: instant coffee there was not in those days, and Camp Coffee was different. Perhaps we had a tin of meat. Water was precious, but there was the whole sea to wash in; when we returned to ordinary life we bore a bloom of salt, but what matter?

So we spent those five days, all to ourselves, in ourselves entirely selfish; they live in memory as a beautiful, beautiful time. Returning at the end to ordinary life, it took a little while to realize that there were other people in the world. We were tempted to forget about the Shahbans' party, even about the tour programme. But even had I been ready to forget, Joan would not have let me: she was always a very conscientious person. Anyway, there were so many new experiences awaiting her.

We drove back from our honeymoon to the drab ordinariness of the hotel. We went to my office, and Joan met my staff: they had been warned, and they were all there, even on a Saturday morning. Rather, they received her. There was a garland for me, as was proper, but so many for Joan that she could hardly see over them. There was no need for work, but disturbing news from the Mukhtiarkar at our first camp at Mirpur Sakro: he had telegraphed that an army officer and his wife had taken over the bungalow without permission. The word had gone back that he must be turned out, the bungalow was needed for an officer on duty: the Assistant Collector had priority. A reply had just come, from the officer himself: 'Cannot move; am on honeymoon.' So what could we do? The bungalow was of the usual PWD touring type, with a large living room and a bedroom and bathroom at each end, and a verandah all along. We would share, my office must be in a rownti. In our own newly married state we could hardly turn them out.

That settled, we went back to the hotel. Whenever we were there, thinking what to do next, the answer was simple: have another look in those boxes. All the things we would need on tour were collected ready to take to the Kutchery next day, to be packed in my new camel boxes. Joan met our cook, Mistri, and she must examine his kitchen equipment. She probably even then thought of improvements, but was too tactful, too conscious of her ignorance of such matters in this new country, to say anything. Then there was bedding, and towels, extra clothing, books—endless stuff, everything for living. Especially we took the Land Revenue Code, and the Rules Thereunder, in which I would receive expert tuition. I had told Joan of my failure, so next time I must surely pass. The prospect of such work cast a small shadow on our happiness.

Dinner with the Shahbans was a wild, rambling affair. Nazir and Afroze were there, Afroze so grown up, now being the Assistant Collector's wife, and senior to Joan as a married woman, too. I was happy to have such friends, indeed, to have all the Shahban family as friends for Joan too. Again, I was of little importance, but now with me was Nazir, and Bashir Malik, and the Mian Sahib himself. There were others who came and went, and it was an evening of light and colour, of continuous chatter and laughter. I doubt if Joan understood many of the words, but the intentions were very clear.

One week of India for Joan, one week of marriage for both of us. I doubted if the future could surpass its happiness.

On Sunday morning we again saw Karachi's Anglican society going to church as we went to meet Gangaram to see his varied stock, and to plan what we would need later. Then we could get in more of those obligatory calls.

It was no good going to see the Brigstocks, who would certainly be in church; later Joan would meet their daughter Elizabeth, who six months before had been guided to set her cap at me; when she found that I was not available she was not resentful, and we remained good friends. (Rather she resented the inadequacies of the domestic intelligence that had misled her.) We met the Thadanis, he an ICS judge, Mrs Thadani an English lady, and their beautiful daughter Barbara, who dressed to her Indian side and was one of the chief ornaments of the Karachi Club. She was much more than just beautiful: she suffered from none of the extreme shyness or even fear of men that afflicted her peers. She was a very special person. She went to Bombay with all the other Hindus at the time of Partition.

We called on Godfrey Davis, Chief Judge; being a Jew, he was not a church-goer (I don't think he was a synagogue-goer either). His wife, a lady of strong personality, was fortunately away, so no card from Joan was appropriate. Godfrey Davis also was ICS, but in an impregnable, special position. He even lived away from the city, on Bath Island, which was only an island during spring tides. He warned Joan against Karachi society with endless scurrilous gossip, and then warned her not to believe half of his tales. The Establishment could not discipline him: he held his post *quam diu se bene gesserit,* for so long as he behaved himself; his behaviour would be judged by fellow judges, not by civil servants and the like. His reward was a knighthood; perhaps he had it already, I don't remember. He was a good friend of ours throughout our service, and, indeed, beyond. His visitors were mostly barristers, other judges, and his Remembrancer of Legal Affairs—there was an office straight from the Middle Ages! A new-hatched ICS husband and wife to talk to were obviously a wonderful gift for a Sunday morning.

From there we went to the Gymkhana, to hear the band. Church being over, we must have met some of my friends there, no one that I remember, but now reports of my new wife would spread all round. The pipe band of the Baloch Regiment always played there at noon on Sundays, and for a short while this continued in spite of the war. The Balochis are a hill people, like the Scots; they play on a pipe, so naturally bagpipes were their instrument. This was Sindh's own regiment, for Balochistan was our neighbour, and thousands of Balochis lived in Sindh. In fact, there

were few, if any, Baloch or Sindhi *jawans* (then, as now,
they were almost all Punjabi). Sindhis were just not warlike,
and Balochis entirely unsuited to military discipline. I asked
an officer about this, and his explanation was that one day
a Balochi would earn a Victoria Cross for bravery, and the
next would run away. Among Sindhis there was the special
exception of the Hurs, the followers of a powerful religious
leader, but again, theirs was not a military discipline.

There remained one further thing to do in Karachi. We
went to the Kutchery to see our camel train away. It left
earlier in the day than it usually would, for it had a long
march to Mirpur Sakro. We stood on the edge of a cloud
of dust, watched the apparent chaos, heard the wild
hullabaloo, and then suddenly it seemed that there was
order: the jemadar shouted, and they were off. One by one
the camels staggered to their feet, unfolding their legs joint
by joint, slavering and squealing as though each joint
needed oiling. They lined up and were tied nose to tail,
each with its driver. Some loads, with trunks and boxes
slung on each flank, looked normal enough, but one beast
had tables and chairs, with legs sticking up and jerking in a
ridiculous way. Our tents were on a camel that needed
extra room fore and aft because the poles stuck out so far
ahead and behind, threatening its neighbours. My office
naik, head office boy, as it were, travelled with the camels,
and so did Mistri, to look after his kitchen stuff, which was
so easily disposable. There went also a dhobi and a sweeper,
an extravagance of servants that was never repeated.

One patewala and Khuda Baksh would travel with us
next day, the office staff would go by tonga. Thus my first
tour in authority, and Joan's very first, was set in motion.

Someone at the Gymkhana must have told Government
House that we had come back early from our honeymoon,
for awaiting us was an invitation to dinner; a note said that,
the notice being so short, we could reply by phone, as if we
might have refused. Even the thought of refusing an
invitation to Government House was out of the question: it

was very like a command, and only a death in the family could justify refusal. It was clear that Their Excellencies wished to inspect the new ICS wife fresh from the egg, as it were, and not to wait till Christmas, when the yellow fluff might have rubbed off.

Dressing for such an evening required careful thought. Not for me—a man's evening wear is very dull and standard. I just had to dress in the Sindhi Service style, black coat with white duck trousers, a waistcoat, not the cummerbund of the hot weather, and a bow tie that I could even tie myself. Occasionally some bold spirit, either very senior in Service or in one of the big commercial houses, might try a coloured tie or cummerbund, but there would follow unfavourable gossip or heavy frowns at such signs of decadence.

Joan had a real problem: only half unpacked, ignorant of local usage—and with that I could give little help—she had to depend on a dhobi for ironing, and he could easily ruin a silk dress. Several of her dresses I remember even now, but only one long one suitable for silk stockings and court shoes, for dinner at Government House. That was the one: it was a dress of watered silk, in candy stripes of darker and paler blue, with a high neck and short puffed sleeves. For a ring, she wore my signet ring turned in. My memory may be faulty, but I remember that dress so very well. Years later it was demoted to become a rather special nightdress.

So we set off, and were relieved to find that this was a small, almost a family, party. Indeed, had we not become unexpectedly available, there would probably have been the 'GH Family' alone. John Corin and Tim Crosthwaite Joan had already met, for they were our witnesses; as well there was Linda Corin, and the Grahams' daughter, whose husband had gone off to war.

I had dined at Government House before, but had been too much concerned to use all the glass and cutlery correctly to have remembered much of use to Joan. But she had dined with a retired civilian in England: she knew the pitfalls to be avoided. The lights shone softly, there were beautiful flowers, and the table fairly glittered with so much silver and glass. Instead of our rather scruffy Khuda Baksh, there were barefoot servants gliding around, white-clad, with scarlet cummerbunds and turbans braided with scarlet and gold. Imperial power at its most gracious and hospitable. However, I doubted if Joan expected us ever to try to compete with this.

Perhaps the food showed signs of austerity: I saw no signs of it. The last shipload of European luxuries had already docked, and although the Governor probably secured a more than fair share from it, and though a diplomatic bag might help, even here the pinch must soon be felt. Not a very severe pinch! And there were local sources for luxuries unknown in England. Peaches, apricots, lychees, and cashew and pistachio nuts. There were beautiful exotic vegetables, and all the meat one might want. For much of the year one could shoot one's own game. All this was fine for Government House, but for me even a ripe mango would not compensate for the loss of kippers and fried bacon.

I cannot imagine that it was a very interesting party, but for Joan it was something of an ordeal. She was, however tactfully, being sized up. Indeed, as an ICS wife she was of an unfamiliar species. She was unashamedly a non-conformist Christian, as also was I, though the Christian side of non-conformity was with both of us a little shaky. However, she knew Mrs Starte quite well, whose husband was something of a hero to the Grahams. He was also in the ICS, in Bombay, notable for having set up the settlement policy for criminal tribes almost single-handed. Knowing his wife helped Joan a lot.

Joan was a graduate from Cambridge, and not many women at that time were knowledgeable in mathematics and economics at that level; certainly not ICS wives. She could not easily be placed in any category. (Indeed, she never was.) Frankly, if quite gently, our pedigrees were examined. Joan's father was an eminent Baptist, and so naturally knew the Startes, which was reassuring to the Grahams. My father was a small country miller, a councillor, and a magistrate. Joan had a sister who had just gone up to Oxford, I one who had just gone up to Cambridge, where my brother worked in a research post while awaiting his call-up. All was reasonably satisfactory, though perhaps a little too intellectual.

We drank the Loyal Toast, the ladies left the gentlemen to their brandy. I don't think any of us wanted it, so we joined the ladies, to hear of Joan's voyage out. Mostly she remembered how long it was, what a relief to reach Gibraltar, how sad she was that I was not in Bombay to meet her. (She has never forgiven me for that!) She told us how the Captain had asked the women to do something to keep the men off the bridge, where their efforts to help the look-outs were so disturbing them as to be dangerous. So Joan played the piano, played all through the heat, till her blouse rotted with her sweat.

I asked about the Thatta sub-division, but no one knew anything more about it than did I. We were not expected to stay late: John Corin gave me a covert sign, and we got up to go. We were given best wishes for our tour, Lady Graham promised to remember us if she needed a crew for her yacht, and we went away.

Joan had brought out a lot of books, heavyweights in both senses. Karachi could supply us with light reading, so we took those we had studied before for a philosophy of marriage, though its reality left them largely unread. With other books she had had a problem: from its beginning we had been members of the Left Book Club, for our ideas were well over on the libertarian left but Indian Customs officers were strict in excluding anything that smacked of socialism, and even the cloak of the ICS might not save those brilliant orange jackets from confiscation. So Joan had disguised them: they were all covered with a drab linen jacket, thoroughly stuck on, anonymous, unless one looked inside and could understand what they were about. In fact, everything passed Customs unopened, and we have those books now, still disguised, the disguise so secure that we have never been able to get it off.

Looking back, I see special significance in this rather ordinary beginning to a tour (apart from the honeymooners). It was the first of over fifty such occasions, spread over the next six years. Usually we moved from one bungalow to another; sometimes we stayed in tents, once or twice in ordinary houses acquired by the PWD for its officers. The Public Works Department was always with us. It maintained all these bungalows; it maintained the canal *bunds* and the roads that ran on them, and the river *bunds* without which Sindh would have been desert. It had its own telegraph system that we could use. Without the PWD our administration would have been static, or no less superficial than it had been just after the conquest. I always felt a certain envy of engineers: they dealt with solid, material things, and saw a solid result from their work. We revenue and law officers saw little but paper files, and perhaps a peaceful community.

So we drove out. Later, when Joan had learned to drive, I might ride between camps doing work on the way, but first it must be me, so I could explain the country as we passed.

I loved the PWD bungalows: they were simple and functional, with no pretensions to elegance, but by reason of their proportions were always pleasing to the eye. Most that I met had been built in the last fifty years, a few were much older, on the new Barrage canals they were less than ten years old. All but the oldest were built of burnt brick—*pukka*—some had fine gardens, with caretakers who could sell anything that they produced. Among the oldest bungalows were those of District Officers, and they were *kutcha* brick, for insulation from heat was the first requirement. Except in Karachi.

We left Karachi, with its noise and turmoil, and the formality of its European population. We were on our own; not like Hawkes Bay—that could hardly be repeated—but by ourselves, with the small community of our touring staff. (We took note of all the Sindhis around us, but they were in a different world, which we, slowly but surely, would come to know.)

We drove first through Malir, a village then, part of Greater Karachi now, and I could tell Joan all that I had learned and that the City Engineer had told me. I pointed out the giant hangar for the airship that never came, and the big hole in the river bed; if it rained the road would be washed away, and we would be cut off—we might welcome that. We left the gardens and crossed a jungle strip to the rice lands at the tails of the two canals, Kalri and Baghar, that served my sub-division. All the rice had been harvested now, and there were areas that would be asking for their tax to be remitted. And there were other areas of the horrible black pollution of kalar, where even camels must tread carefully. But there was none of the real desert that Joan had been told was Sindh.

We had decided that when we met our honeymooning guests we would not tell them how newly married we were, and we made Khuda Baksh and the patewala promise, too. They liked the joke. So when we were settled in, I worked in my office tent and Joan slept on a camp bed. We had tea, and while I dealt with petitioners, Joan went to see Mistri in his kitchen. I had written about Sindhi kitchens, but still it was a big surprise to see one in being, to imagine the sea change in techniques that would be needed for cooking in camp, and moving every few days.

The Mukhtiarkar came to call, and we had tea with him. Then he took us to see Mirpur Sakro, his taluka headquarters. We saw—and to me it was familiar, to Joan all new—his Kutchery, the Treasury, the gaol, a school, and a maternity home, which Joan could inspect next day. There was a little bazaar for essential needs, and a liquor shop that I must inspect to see that it was clean and properly run. With warning, of course it was, and this I would report to the Collector. All sorts of things like that were noted in my Diary, which I handed in every month. This little town was so near Karachi that it was not very typical. It even had a daily bus service to the city. To the south, the road ran on to the mouths of the Indus; to the north, to Thatta. In the middle of the town I met the *panchayat*; I can't remember if they had complaints, which means that they probably did not!

Then we dined, with the honeymoon couple as our guests.

I don't remember what was on our menu, which is odd, for it was our first proper meal at our own table, and with such unusual guests. Whatever we ate it would be better than the bazaar could provide, for the Mukhtiarkar would have used that valuable, unacknowledged *rasai* fund to get what Mistri needed, and at pleasantly low prices. For meat, there was always chicken available, usually mutton, from a young goat, occasionally beef. Never pork or bacon. A place as small as Mirpur Sakro would not produce beef, for there must be a large and ready sale for it to be worth killing an animal: there was no way of keeping it. Always the meat was tough, for there would be no refrigeration outside big towns, and to hang it was unsafe. Perhaps Mistri offered vegetable cutlets, a speciality of his, a favourite of ours if we grew tired of chicken. Then there was fruit, always good in the cold weather; but if we wanted a 'made' sweet it would be caramel custard, until Joan taught him some recipes.

Our conversation naturally turned to marriage, we being supposedly the experienced couple seeking their views; these were orthodox-romantic. Of course those two were going to live happily ever after. As, indeed, of course were we. We certainly wished them well. He was a subaltern, she an army nurse in Karachi. They had a war ahead of them, and we hoped they would survive it. Our future was not so simple, but it was a much safer prospect than was theirs.

After dinner, they retired to their end of the verandah, we to ours. They had only a hurricane lamp, we a pressure lamp, a *bijli butty*, so we could read. He sang love songs to his lady, accompanying himself on a guitar. Joan read the subversive books she had smuggled in, I, the Rules Thereunder of the Revenue Code. We all went to bed early.

Joan and I were up early, had a cup of tea and a biscuit, and were off on our camels. Neither of us had mounted a camel before, but we had studied how it was done when our train for the camp set off, and hoped we could give the impression of confidence and experience. You climbed into the saddle, which was only a heap of rags behind the hump; you could stand on the beast's knee, or was it ankle? to give you height, you grasped the pommel, as it were, and quickly got your leg over, for at once the camel began to unfold. First his fore-end rose, and there was a risk of falling off backwards; then his stern, and you were pitched into the back of the driver, and finally he settled on an even keel. All the time he screamed and bubbled as if being tortured, while the whole camp stood round, solemn, expressionless, just hoping that one of us would fall off. Or, even, *Inshallah*, both of us. We deserved applause, but none came: that would have given the game away.

Once mounted, we found much to be said for camels, and they soon forgot their tantrums. We could see so far, and were so obviously superior to our earth- or pony-bound officers: I could study maps and make notes without dropping the reins, because there weren't any. But there was need for care: at our height the PWD telegraph wires were in range, and one must duck or be beheaded. So Joan quickly learned the meaning of her driver's *'Khabardar!'*

Our two drivers were proud of their beasts, and once we settled down they were comfortable to ride. We crossed a wide stretch of slimy kalar land, trotting smoothly, which reassured drivers and camels so well that they offered to gallop, to show us what they could do. But we refused; we were flattered, we were sure that what they told us of the wonderful smooth ride was true, but we needed more experience. We were not, I think, being offered a real racing gallop. A time came when we saw a race, and it was an awesome sight. It would have had me off in a minute. The camel's pace was like the *pund* of the tapedars' ponies; like them, it gave a fine smooth trot, but, also like them, if pushed too fast the camel had no canter, but broke into a gallop. For a tapedar to do that in front of the Sahib was deeply shaming.

This was, for me, an ordinary pertal like the scores I had watched with Dermont Barty, only now, for the very first time, I was myself making the decision, checking the boundaries, comparing stubbles with those on nearby land. Joan was seeing everything new. (But for how long would the novelty last for her, having not even any need to learn?)

Four hours, at even our gentle and intermittent pace, was enough, and by noon we were back at the bungalow for a real meal, breakfast and lunch combined: brunch, a nasty word, but descriptive. By the afternoon we were finding what the camels had done to muscles we didn't before know we had.

The honeymoon couple were getting ready to go back to ordinary life. Had they had a car, they would surely have chosen a more attractive place than Mirpur Sakro, but I daresay all they wanted was to be alone, and our arrival spoiled even that for them. They took the evening bus to Karachi. As we said good-bye, and wished them well, we gave them one last thought to ponder: they had, in fact, been married a little longer than had we.

We were told that further north there was an Australian who had taken up vacant government waste. An Australian zamindar! Such a wonder, said the Mukhtiarkar. We must certainly see him when we camped near.

Our tour would take us to Ketibunder, right in the delta; and then it would return: there was no road beyond, only

jungle and salt marsh till the border of Sindh, and beyond
that the vast marshes of the Ranns of Kutch. My Chitnis
said there would be no work; my Shristedar said people
couldn't get there for cases, so there was little point in
going. But I would go: no officer had been there for a long
time, and it would be wrong to neglect the place; it seemed
that the taluka office had not been inspected for years.
Moreover, I very much wanted to see what the delta looked
like. In fact, it was not a taluka but a *mahal*, with a
Mahalkari: an anomaly that had come from Kathiawar,
beyond the Ranns, but the difference was only verbal.
Probably at some time it had been a part of Kutch.

Ketibunder was accessible only by ferry, and there was
no bungalow, so we would take our tents. It was entirely
surrounded by a protective bund. The river here was tidal,
though not salt. As its name shows, it is a port, and had
been the great port for transfer of cargoes from and to the
Punjab from ocean-going ships. But the railway, and lately
the Sukkur Barrage, had killed all save local trade. We did
see a few Indus boats. They were of a special pattern, with
high square bows, built to sail before the wind, to drift on
the flood, to float onto shoals and easily off again. They
drew very little water, and had no keel. They floated and
were poled down on the flood, and, when the river was at
its lowest, and using every back eddy and their huge square
sails when there was a favourable breeze, they sailed back.
We saw one making a fair speed under sail, with a man
straining at the enormous steering oar, doing little more
than move sideways.

On the way there we had to stop at a village called
Buhara, on the tail of the Baghar Canal, a big village in a
land where villages were few and small. I had a sheaf of
petitions from the people of Buhara, Hindus and Muslims
alike, all complaining of the *zulum* of the headman, the
wadera, an entirely unofficial title indicating his
acknowledged supremacy in the village.

I took my Shristedar with me; I was not yet confident enough of my Sindhi to try by myself to understand a crowd of vociferous complainants, sort out their complaints, and settle them. As it turned out, we could not even get into the village: the bridge over the canal, only a little ditch by now, was broken down, and this was the core of the problem.

Seth Beharilal did not want to come and talk, and I thought that perhaps he was afraid of violence, but when he came at last to the broken bridge it was clear that he felt no anxiety at all. He was a very large, very powerful, and violent-looking man, red of face; it was clear that it was his violence that was feared. He was quite unlike the pale, deferential shopkeeper I had anticipated. He must have decided that there was no point in fighting the government, in my person, over a little broken bridge.

The indignation and the hullaballoo died down, Joan and I and the Shristedar jumped the little ditch, and we sat down in the shade. We sat on the ubiquitous wire chairs, always on the verge of collapse, and tea appeared: the usual brew, with boiled milk and cardamoms. It was not to our taste, but at least the milk was not likely to give us dysentery. It was a necessary adjunct to diplomacy.

All this was new and fascinating to Joan. While the battle was going on at the bridge, not a woman or child was in sight, but once peace had broken out a crowd appeared, particularly to see a white Memsahib. She offered, through me, to go and see their houses, but this was too much: they preferred to stand off and giggle. Perhaps a time would come when we could make more contact, but not yet, not even in a place with a daily bus service to Karachi.

Meanwhile, we men had a job to do, and it soon appeared that the village was not so violently at odds with its wadera as had first appeared. A little drama clearly relieved the dull round of ordinary life. Moreover, the broken bridge was the only real problem. Yes, it was the Seth's carts that had broken it, but his advice about repairs made recently had not been followed; had it been, he said, the bridge would have stood. No, it was not a PWD bridge, it was the responsibility of the village alone. So we settled the matter, and it seemed that the Seth himself was reasonably happy: he would supply any new material needed, and this time his advice would be followed. The Muslims would do the work, and would be fed by the panchayat. The bridge was all of wood, the Muslims were all haris from round about, all with the necessary skill.

As for the other complaints, it was about the moneylenders who charged too much—collateral there was usually none—but this was the same everywhere. The panchayat complained that the Seth was overbearing, but that was their problem, I could not delve into it. He was clearly a man as strong in personality as he was in physique, too big a fish for his little pond.

We left the village at peace, I a little proud of our success. We came back the same way a few days later, found the bridge newly repaired, and people waved at us cheerfully as we passed.

We made a short camp before Ketibunder, to let our tents get there before us. We stopped at Sanwalpur, a small bungalow with no village near, no sign of any reason why it had been built. It was open to floods if the river ran very high, in the delta itself. I could make a few field inspections, but there was nothing whatever for Joan to do unless she came with me, which posed a problem that we must solve before very long.

We spent two days at Sanwalpur, and there was one special thing about the place that made it memorable: when the office staff, our staff, and even the patewalas had gone to wherever they would sleep, when the last petitioner had been told to come tomorrow, there was not a sign of human life in sight. The little bungalow was stuffy with stale air, and there was a full moon. So we took a blanket and a flask of water and set off walking through the light jungle, where there was not even the sound of animals, and where the moonshine showed us the way. We chose a pleasant spot with tamarisk flowering all round, creating a very private bower. We spread our blanket and sat on it quietly: this was to be a very special interlude. We looked round, and there, a few yards away, stood a man, grinning at us. We waved, he waved back, commended us to Allah, and went on his way. But our deserted country was gone. We picked up the rug and went back to the bungalow, to normality.

Perhaps in the middle of the Thar Desert there are places where no one ever goes, but I doubt it. That intruder was friendly enough, he even wished us well. But for his presence alone I hated him.

After Sanwalpur we were truly in the delta. There were no bunds, but for a long time the land here had been free of erosion. It was very flat and fertile, with no fear of pollution unless a very low-running river met an exceptionally high spring tide. It was highly fertile land, said to grow the best rice in Sindh, 'as good as basmati'. In fact, I learned that in Lower Sindh the usual variety was kangni, high yielding, low quality, the red rice eaten by the poor.

As we drove on towards the ferry we were worried by the bridges over the *karias*, the final canal distributaries. They might be strong enough for bullock carts, but our big Chev was another matter. However, we took them fast, just in case any cracked, and arrived at the ferry in time to see the tents go across. But no way were the camels going to get into that boat, so on the other side bullock carts took over. For the long poles two carts were linked, just like the timber jills one could see in contemporary England.

This stream was the Ochito, one of the main mouths of the River; to the east was the Hyderi, marking the boundary between my sub-division and the other one, Shahbunder; the island so formed was the Mahal. Here we heard more of the Ranns of Kutch: there was good reason for not going there, for it was the abode of devils. What kind of devils they were, who could say? It was too dangerous to go and find out. To the north it was possible to reach the sea, and along the shore there was a direct way to Karachi. Some day we might try to explore this route, but now my work was to please the Mahalkari by a proper inspection of his charge. This I did, with Joan, very pleasantly, travelling mostly by boat, occasionally landing for a closer look at particular places.

Ketibunder was a neat, clean place, surrounded by its bund; there were no straggling settlements, people who lived there did so for their work. It was clean because rubbish could be thrown into a creek on an ebbing tide and was never seen again. We did not go into the question of drainage: we ourselves had a thunder-box, and it was cleaned when appropriate and we paid an appropriate fee; we inquired no further.

Water for drinking was an obvious problem. It had to be taken from the river, but was collected from upstream on a falling tide. Mistri, of course, knew what to do: filter it, and boil it for three minutes. (Only years later were we told that twenty minutes were necessary. We survived, but with more boiling we might have avoided many attacks of diarrhoea.) So we settled to dinner in our tent. Fish, of course, the best, the freshest you would find in Sindh. Water, cool, but very thick. We called Mistri, and he explained that the water was so very muddy that the candle of the filter was clogged so quickly that it had to be cleaned even after half a glass had been through. We had to be content; but a freshwater shrimp swimming in it was too much. How much boiling had been done? None, it was very sweet water. There was trouble. We had to give up the filtering, and afterwards always used alum to clear the water. It tasted a bit funny, but at least you could see through the glass. As for sterilization, perhaps a drop of gin or whiskey was best.

There was little sign in Ketibunder of the trade that had made it famous once. No warehouses that I can remember, and no real *bunder*: just a fish dock and a place for an occasional river boat to unload.

From here we turned back to Mirpur Sakro. We camped at Ghorabari on the way, just to give the camels a break. The tents would stay at Mirpur, so I paid off the two camels, with a retainer so that we could call them again.

A camel ride in the morning, for *pertal*, was very pleasant; we both loved it, and became quite expert riders. But the rest of the day was for Joan empty, and as we had been going this was what she had to look forward to, for weeks, for months, even for years. All her apprehensions about memsahibs resurfaced, and this after only a few weeks, special weeks at that. When, quite soon, we were back in Karachi, something must be done about it, or our future would become darkly clouded.

In Mirpur this time the threat was, by chance, lifted. Mistri had to go back to Karachi for a day or two, so we had no cook. The Office, or the Mukhtiarkar, would willingly have cooked for us, but Joan decided to take on the job herself.

In those two days Joan learned much of the technique of cooking in Sindh—even in camp, in a government bungalow, liable to move every few days. She saw the kitchen, its cooker, its equipment. The little *chullas* in the brick range, the peculiarities of charcoal as a fuel, the use of tongs to move lumps of coal from one *chulla* to another to control the heat. Frying pans and saucepans had no long handles, an oven was a flat iron dish, to be covered by a pan on which more or less coal was placed to regulate the heat. There was an ordinary kettle, the only implement recognizable to a newly arrived English girl.

She insisted still that she should take over. The cabbage was burnt, the potatoes were dry, the tea was smoky. There were black smudges on the plates, on her hands, her face, and her dress, and her fingers were scorched. But everything was edible, and how should I complain? It was a triumph, and indeed the second day saw most of the problems ironed out. Nevertheless, when Mistri returned she was willing to surrender the job to him. But this taught us to appreciate the talents of a cook who, on tour, could produce well-cooked food, clean and neatly presented, if perhaps a little dull because of the limited and unvarying nature of the ingredients he had.

There was one more camp on this tour, and on the way was one of those damnable local-built bridges, more hump-backed than some, and probably the weaker for that, so I took it at a gentle rush, as it were. A long-wheel-base car has its advantages, but this hump-back caught us. We balanced on the crown, and the wheels lost traction. I had to stay at the wheel while the others climbed out and onto the back: it was not enough. We recruited several gleeful men from the fields, told them how to hang on and bounce in unison. They did, the wheels grounded, and the car shot forward. All our helpers fell in a laughing heap, but Joan had cleverly decided that her best place was at the side, beating time. Those cheerful men wanted nothing but thanks: you can't offer a Muslim the price of a pint.

Our last camp was at Gharo, a place on a little sea creek, notable for the stories we were told, the myths about its time of glory: long before Karachi or even Ketibunder were ports, it had been a great port where all the big boats came in from the river, and all the big dhows came in from the sea. Moreover, there was something holy about the place. Were it not that there were the remains of burnt brick near the creek, these stories would have had no evidence to back them: the creek was too small for any boat, the river was nowhere near, and between Gharo and the sea was a waste of marsh and mud. However, before we came again we would, we hoped, find out more. (In fact, we never came again, but there was truth in the folk tales, as there often is: Pakistani archaeologists have proved that once this was the great port of Banbhore, and that here Arab invaders landed and spread Islam through Sindh.)

Our riding camels went to their home; camping gear and staff went to Karachi and to theirs. So did we, but it was to the hotel again.

This provided a flat ending to our first tour. I shall not trace any other in such detail, partly because that would be boring, partly because no other tour would be, in memory, so notable. For this was my first in authority, and for Joan everything about it was new. We saw very little that was at all extraordinary, we did nothing very important. We had been married for over a month, and, once the honeymoon couple left Mirpur, we had met no one but revenue staff, petitioners, and formal visitors. It had been in some sort an extended honeymoon.

Each dawn was fresh and promising as we set off on our camels, or on foot, or by boat, or in the car. Each evening we sat talking and reading by lamplight until we went early to bed. I didn't think we were a very demonstrative couple—the people we met had anyway very different conventions about the married state—but we were very much in love, still very newly together.

There were little clouds threatening: Joan drove me on to work till I knew those Revenue Rules so thoroughly that I could not again fail at the increment bar. She had, too, quickly learnt how empty a woman's life could be for half the day, when her husband had his files and his cases and his petitioners to occupy him. She might be able later to find some purpose special for a woman, but not yet, while she was the new wife of a very junior Assistant Collector. Already she had arranged for Kishensingh to teach her Urdu, a language far more generally useful than Sindhi, and she was determined that at Christmas she would find in Karachi a school happy to employ a well-qualified and experienced mathematics teacher. Perhaps the Service would not like the wife of one of its junior officers doing something so professional, perhaps even being paid for it. If it didn't, we thought boldly, the Service would just have to lump it. For me, there was the gloomy thought that Joan would only tour with me when schools were on holiday, but I could hardly object: she must have something to do, and marriage would soon lose its shine if it involved long periods of boredom. So when inspection tours began again after Christmas, I might go alone. But even if Joan was free to come with me, there would never be another like the first.

Had we expected a Karachi full of joyful celebration, we would have been disappointed: England was at war, which ensured a quiet Christmas. But I knew very few people, Joan none at all. Anyway, we had a more serious matter to deal with. We had to find somewhere to live. We went to the Christmas Party at the Gymkhana, and a cocktail party at Government House. We dined with our Collector, Charles Clee, and his wife, with whom Joan became friends, a friendship which lasted as long as we were in Sindh, and beyond. To Muslim and Hindu friends, this was just a very welcome public holiday; but Nazir and Afroze did not come in. Since we were still living in the hotel, we could not entertain anyway.

Looking for somewhere to live, we joined forces with the Cargills. Peter was the latest ICS recruit, and he would be in Karachi for the hot weather, with his wife Margaret; they were determined they would not live in a gloomy place such as I, unmarried, had had. Peter was an extrovert: he made friends with the Collector, he even mollified the Commissioner who disapproved of young married officers, and he just rode over obstacles that would have daunted me. The Cargills would be in Karachi for the hot weather as I had been, so we discussed and planned together. Not in the Central Hotel, which was a gloomy place that led to gloomy foreboding, but at the Gymkhana. It was a pleasant place, with wide verandahs, wide windows open to the breeze, and bougainvillaea frothing in full flower, drooping down from the eaves. It encouraged optimistic feelings. Peter had already made sure that he would be posted to Karachi, so we just had to find the place. The Club had all the amenities, in particular a bar, and secluded corners for those who wanted seclusion. But nowhere to stay.

India had been taken to war with Britain, it was on the way to independence, so it was inevitable that the Government of India should abolish any colour bar anywhere. All clubs must change their rules. The Karachi Club had no need to: there was none; nor did the Railway Institutes. The Gymkhana passed its amending rule, but it didn't make much difference. So soon after the change, I don't remember Indians going there. Later, Nazir and Afroze went with us, just once. There was too much drinking to please Muslims, and Afroze was still apt to be shocked by the excessive display and freedom of white women.

In the past there had been in the Civil Lines a bungalow specifically for the 'AC Thatta'. A supernumerary under training could hope to be a paying guest with him. But this AC Thatta was married, and anyway there was now no such bungalow, or we would have taken it: the arrival of a Governor with his extra staff had taken it away. Juniors like us were squeezed out.

Neither we nor the Cargills wanted to lodge with anyone, so we looked further afield, beyond the Civil Lines, and found what we wanted. The Indian Life Assurance Company was putting its money into a large block of flats called, naturally, Ilaco House. It was an uncompromisingly rectilinear block, faced with ochre-coloured marble. There was a tower in the middle, a feature essential to a prestige building, a grand entrance, and at each end there was another entrance and automatic lift to flats above. At the northern end we and the Cargills each reserved a flat. The flats would be ready in March, which suited us very well. Two bedrooms, dining room, drawing room, and—what luxury!—a bathroom with hot water laid on. Even the rent was within what Government would pay as allowance in place of my bungalow that had been taken away. There was a wing behind with servants' quarters and kitchen, but still a mud cooker with chullas, no better than those in the poorest of touring bungalows.

The Collector was unhappy, the Commissioner was downright discouraging: it was wrong for an ICS officer, particularly one with a wife, to live so far away from the safety of the Civil Lines, so near to those tall blocks of tiny flats filled with students and clerks and their families. But our Commissioner was from another age, and by the time we moved in, another ICS officer, much senior to me, David Halford, was already there, and Kaikhusro Framji, my friend in the PWD; also a Viennese doctor and his wife, refugees who had left Austria before Hitler took it over: Hugo and Grete Reinitz, who became such friends as one always hopes for but seldom finds. The Establishment could hardly frown at our living among such reputable neighbours.

Then there was one of those serendipitous discoveries that sometimes come to those already fortunate: just behind the flats was a joinery workshop that would make furniture to order, hire it to us, and finally sell it to us if we wanted it; which let us plan our furnishings from pattern books.

This was literally true. Joan had brought with her catalogues from the showrooms of Church Street, Kensington, and from such firms as Ambrose Heal. We searched again through our treasures of china and glass in our boxes, and decided what must be bought and what could be made before touring was finished, saw what we could hire, and foresaw ourselves well-furnished by the time the flat was ready for us. Those ten days over Christmas injected into our lives a new excitement, different from that of just living together. We could expect to be moved elsewhere after a year or so, but would have our own household to take with us. We made no concession at all in our plans to Indian ways of living. Perhaps memory of England was too strong.

We went to Gangaram for bed linen, tea towels, cushions to be covered with fabrics Joan had brought, and he told us of the *swadeshi* shop, the official outlet for hand-spun, hand-woven cotton stuffs that were the ultimate product of Mahatma Gandhi's campaign. We went to the Gaol, where the prisoners' work, doubtless called occupational therapy today, was mostly weaving and carpet-making. I paid an official visit, Gaol Delivery, took Joan along, and we ordered stuffs for curtains, and some of the woven cotton dhurries like those we had for our tents. From the swadeshi shop we bought beautiful, simple fabrics that would have found a special high price in England but here cost only a few annas a yard.

For Joan, house-hunting and job-hunting went on together. We were both sure that work she certainly must have. In Karachi there was a very good convent school, with girls taking English exams, so she met the Mother Superior. In England, had she married, she would have had to give up her job: a woman who was married must not deprive a man of work. In Karachi, being married was equally a bar, but for quite another reason: she would be having a baby, which would interrupt her work. Joan assured the Superior that for several years there would be no child, but that would not do: for that to be certain she must be sinning, and the school could not condone sin.

So there was no job, and till March there was nowhere to live except the hotel. We set out on tour again, together. One goal we had achieved, the other we had missed, which depressed Joan, though I had mixed feelings. She had to console herself with my company and Kishensingh's Urdu lessons by post, helped by one of the patewalas and Mistri, whose language it was.

We would stay out on tour as much as we could; there was now no attraction at all in a hotel room. Nazir, Afroze, and the Cargills had all gone back to their Districts, and there was nothing for us in Karachi.

That first tour in authority had taught me a lot. Now I could take a positive part in planning: I knew what work I must do, could include special things I wanted to do, and anything the Collector required. I knew how far our camel train could travel in a night, so how far apart our camps should be. I knew what stores we should take, whether we would need tents, where we could get petrol. We did not again take our own dhobi or sweeper. With my Shristedar I worked out a programme for case work, trying to ensure that parties and pleaders would find transport to my court.

We expected to be back in Karachi for the hot weather by the end of March. By then the weather in Upper Sindh would be heating up—in April the temperature would be over 100°F. I had left Sukkur before the heat and it was difficult to believe that later it would grow much hotter: we were told that in Karachi it was seldom as hot as 100°F. I would have to be in Karachi in January for my departmental exam, but apart from that we would be out on our own again. After only a few days the memory of the bright lights, of everyone talking English and dressing for dinner, was fading.

8

THE ASSISTANT COLLECTOR'S MANUAL

This is a wonderful book. It was first published in 1905, sponsored by the Government of Bombay, and revised in 1937. I should have had a copy when first I reached Bombay, but was perhaps overlooked, to my great loss, because I went straight to Sindh. I only read it a year later, when I found a copy left by my predecessor in Thatta.

It tells an Assistant or Deputy Collector everything he must do, everything he may do, but very little that he must not do. He is told how he should treat officers of other departments, visitors of various ranks—should they be offered chairs or not—how to deal with petitioners, with his own staff, with subordinates. Then there are all the matters he must investigate: remission applications, schools, nursing homes, water supply. Other matters he might observe, acting with tact: local and municipal board operations, such as roads and street drains, could be reported on, never forgetting that the members of these bodies were elective and could not always insist on what, to an autocrat, might seem best.

Action needed by other departments could only be proposed through the Collector, but within his own department he could insist on knowing everything.

I certainly did not know everything. The Bombay Presidency had a landowning system quite different from the *zamindari* system of Sindh; the Manual only came to Sindh because Sindh was part of the Presidency until 1938, and was subject to the same system of 'temporary' revenue assessments, revised every ten years. I myself remained on the Bombay Presidency Cadre throughout my Service, and beyond. But in most areas the same rules operated. In Sindh we must allow for the social and economic differences between landowning Hindu joint families and the Sindhi crop-sharing zamindari system.

There is a great deal of advice on correspondence but, surprisingly, one kind of letter is not mentioned: the 'demi-official'. This was a personal letter from one officer to another, and unless one wanted one's staff to know what was in it, was strictly confidential, which might have involved typing it oneself and keeping the copy. It was addressed to Dear So-and-So, and signed from Yours Sincerely. So very simple, but I assumed too much: having received a DO from my Collector addressed to 'Dear Pearce', I replied to 'Dear Clee'. Even now I blush to remember it. His response was swift, irritated, and informative: to an equal in Service I could write 'Dear Clee', and if his superior—an unimaginable supposition—I would write 'My dear Clee'. Had we been personal friends, he would be 'Dear Charles'.

It was all very clear and embarrassing. There was no way that I could write to apologize, it could only be done when next we met, which I did. But he seemed not to have remained long offended: he did not call me a young pup, or anything belittling; and I noticed that my next DO was addressed to 'My dear Pearce'.

This by the way. The Manual is about more important matters; it runs to fifteen tersely-written chapters, with no hint of undesirable humour. No detail of an officer's duty is left unexplained. It provides instructions for operating a benevolent autocracy, and it worked for half a century. When India and Pakistan became independent there were enough officers who had been soaked in it, or in similar Manuals in other Provinces, throughout their careers to ensure that the spirit that inspired it, and the conduct that it required, would remain valid, subject to the changes inevitable with the coming of democracy.

We drove out of Karachi on the Hawkes Bay road again, through the Lyari quarter—and surely something should be done to get those poor people a clean water supply; but it wasn't my business, though I could ask the Collector to stir up the City Council. We came to the gravel road to the salt pans and beyond; here Joan should have her first lessons in driving: the only traffic was the occasional camel, or a flock of goats, and there were not even roadside ditches. It was an excellent road for making mistakes.

We would camp on the very western boundary of British India, where it marched with Kalat. But first we came to Mangho Pir. This was a singular holy place. There was a shrine commemorating the Pir, with a holy man taking care of it. There was a hot spring rising in a pool which held crocodiles. There were conflicting tales of how they had got there. I am sure the pool was, as it were, overstocked; they were crowded some on top of others, squirming in the noisome water; they opened their vicious pink mouths to cool themselves, and to my eyes were altogether horrible. I expect there are people who value crocodiles; I do not. It was, I knew, a place for sightseers from Karachi; I just hoped they did not bring their children, the beasts could give them the horrors.

For five rupees the fakir offered to feed them with a live goat. I refused—I was after all the magistrate of those parts, and should have stopped such cruelty, but it was a tricky thing to interfere with anything religious. So I gave a little *baksheesh* only. Khuda Baksh and Mistri wanted to wait and see those crocodiles fed, but I told them that if they did they would walk the rest of the way to camp.

We were camping at the Hub river, the boundary of Sindh with Kalat State. The only road from Sindh to Makran crossed the river here, and there was a customs post: the Hub *chowk*. It was deserted, neither *chowkidar* nor

Customs Officer to be seen. We could have smuggled anything across, had we but something to smuggle. Instead, we walked over and a few hundred yards up the empty road; it wound away out of sight, among low dry hills, and we felt very lonely and insecure, as if the hills threatened us. Very odd: there was no one at all in sight, we could see Sindh and our car just behind us, but it felt a very foreign land, and very dangerous. We walked back and drove on to Bund Murad Khan and the bungalow there.

My Chitnis had not wanted to come here: there were very few people, no cultivation, only grazing for sheep and goats and camels. No one ever came, for there was no water. I said, if no one ever came, then the more reason that someone should; the people might have all sorts of problems for me to deal with. When we arrived I could see his point, but I was not going to change my opinion. On the way we had seen only the temporary huts of herders, but there was this one sizeable village, so the staff would have somewhere to stay.

In fact there was water, and plenty of it: the river itself. It was a perennial stream, beautifully clear, and flowed through a break in the rocky edge of the rising ground. Here Murad Khan—and I must find out about him—had built his dam, his bund. But it had been badly engineered, and had blown out a long time ago. On the Sindh side just the abutments remained, beautiful cut ashlar stonework, with the remains of stone channels leading from it. The water must have been pumped out from behind the dam, but some heavy flood had destroyed it, and now there was no sign at all of cultivation. Nevertheless, it was surely wrong for all that beautiful sweet water to be left flowing wastefully away to sea. I determined to ask the Collector to urge the PWD to look at the site. (Now the whole area has been absorbed into Greater Karachi.)

Otherwise, at this camp there was one other recorded event. For forty seconds I sat in my tin tub, very still, to have my photograph taken by the light of the pressure lamp. There are also pleasant pictures of the river in its rocky bed. The Chitnis was right: there was no work. On the other hand, all the wandering people around would know that the Sirkar had not forgotten them. So I was right too.

We toured on eastwards, and must have camped at least twice for the sake of our camel train. There was little work but petitions and receiving visitors, but it was high time that the Sirkar should appear in person. There were little villages, probably little more than temporary, for usually the name of the *goth* was that of the visitor who called on me. It was a dry, empty landscape of rough grazing, cut by streams that only flowed when there was heavy rain in the Kalat hills. The only cultivation was periodic, with catch crops in land where a bund had formed a pond in one of the streams. There had been no rain, there were no crops, no revenue to collect, no remission claims to inspect. In fact, it was an area hardly worth owning! The only notable landmark was the chimney of the Dalmia Cement Works, standing out stark and ugly, painted in black and white stripes as a warning to aircraft.

We were going to the bungalow at Gujo, on the tail of the Kalri canal, for this was where the Australian zamindar was said to be. And so he was. We were having tea when we heard a loud voice talking a sort of Sindhi with a broad Australian accent, so we asked him in for a cup. Haji Badoola Baloch: pure Baloch, old and gaunt, wearing the green turban to which his haj to Mecca entitled him. He had returned to his ultimate homeland to settle with his young Sindhi second wife and his two half-Baloch but wholly Australian sons, of the large and energetic kind.

The Haji told us his life story. He had gone to Australia as a boy with his father, who took out a string of camels when camels did all the heavy transport for the mine workings of Western Australia. His father married twice, and had no other children, but Badoola married and had these two sons. When his father died he inherited the camel train, and when road and rail took their work away he let his camels go—just let them go to look after themselves. That they did remarkably well, for the outback of Western Australia is very much like the scrub desert of Sindh; they had multiplied and become a serious nuisance.

He had used his savings to buy a 'spread' of grazing land, and reared sheep. When it became clear that war was coming and that Australia would join in, he sold up, at a good price, and came to spend his declining years at home. He was, after all, a Baloch, and he had no wish to see his two fine sons involved in a 'foreign' war. His Australian wife had died, so he came home.

But the complications of farming in Sindh bothered him. He did not like the local zamindars, nor they him. For one thing, he employed paid labour, would have nothing to do with crop-sharing; for another, he worked with his own hands, and his sons also insisted on doing so. He had capital, which upset the local moneylenders; his sons were practical engineers, so he brought no trade to the local *mistris*. He lived in a tent, but his house would be ready for the hot weather. It would be like nothing ever seen before: an Australian outback house, with wooden walls and an iron roof. His difficulties were increased because his half-remembered Sindhi was difficult to understand at best, and shouted with an 'aussie' accent it was worse. There was no sign at all of 'declining years'. It was inevitable that Haji Badoola would get tail-end land, with a good deal of salt pollution, but he was tackling the problem with determination. While the canal was flowing full he washed away the salt, and diverted the foul water from his neighbours' land. When the flow stopped next year he would have a pump ready to use the water still standing in the canal. That anyway was the plan, and the pump was ready to be brought on stream. He gave it a trial run while we were there. *Inshallah* it will work, said the good Muslim. And it did.

His two sons were strong silent types, happy, perhaps, that their father liked talking with us, but a little uneasy, I thought, at the arrival of authority. They just grinned and went on cossetting their machine. (I should have asked where their fuel came from, but did not. Perhaps it was as well: if they burned wood I might have felt bound to involve the forestry officer.) We wished him well, I would give him all the help and advice I properly could, and we would see him again next cold weather, with his first crop. Unhappily, we were transferred before then.

To finish his tale: after a few years he gave up. Local enmity and even sabotage of his bunds and water-courses was too much. He sickened of his countrymen. It was a great pity, for his was the kind of initiative that Sindh's agriculture needed, but it showed the kind of bitter opposition to expect from a reactionary but powerful landholding class when facing innovations such as his. Had I remained at Thatta I might have helped him to defeat his opponents, but probably not. The zamindari was strong and ruthless. I heard later about him. He left the land, and with what capital he had left settled down to retirement. His second wife had a child, a pure Baloch Sindhi this one, and his two sons had no difficulty in getting work in Karachi. We did not meet again.

At Gujo we made a pleasant, unimportant discovery. In our *chalumchi* we always carried a loofah, and I supposed that, like the sponge, it came from the sea. It doesn't! Perhaps I am alone in my ignorance, but at Gujo I was enlightened. In the garden we found a marrow plant, and thought how pleasant steamed marrow would be for dinner. Then we saw that some of the marrows had been left on the plant, and had dried right up. I picked one, cracked the shell, and inside was a loofah. So a loofah is only a sort of dried marrow. Two were ripe, and we bought them off the chowkidar; they lasted us all our time in Sindh.

We returned to Karachi for a day, leaving our camp to move on, for I had my departmental exam to sit. Joan drove, meeting conventional traffic for the first time in Malir; and there, by the road, we came on one of those blessed scenes we were to find elsewhere, always by a lucky chance: a man selling watermelons. We had time to spare, but would anyway have made time for this. There was a whole heap of melons, none of the fancy ones, only the big green ones, without much flavour, but wonderfully juicy. One between four of us was enough: cut in slices, one could just suck the flesh, and the ends poked in one's ears.

Melons turned up in all sorts of odd places in Sindh, in all seasons. They were a speciality of families coming into the plains from the hills for work on the bunds for the PWD, or on the roads, or for zamindars. They would find a patch of sweet, uncultivated land with water nearby, sow the seed they always had with them, and in no time would have a melon patch. Perhaps their animals provided manure, but otherwise they just watered by hand. The fruit ripened, they sold it themselves if they were near a busy road, otherwise in the nearest bazaar, and when the plants had finished they would destroy them and move on. I once asked about seed: they left the first fruit to ripen, of each variety, and they destroyed the plants lest some clever person keep them alive and ripen seed, and so acquire what they had carefully selected.

The whole world was bright as we went to the Haleji Dhand, for I had passed my exam; moreover, I would earn Rs. 50 extra pay. Haleji was a pretty place, the only place where we had seen trees growing big enough for shade. I was there to inspect the fishery, but that was no reason why we should not sit in shade for once, and have a picnic.

We found the fishermen at work. Their method was to scare the fish—and there were plenty of them—into a long net anchored at one end on shore, and then haul the net round in a huge loop to shore again, with men outside the net to scare back fish which tried to jump out. The net, held down with stones, the top edge held up by cork floats, was hauled to shore, and the fish collected. There was no boat, but several enormous copper cauldrons, with narrow tops, on which a man lay and paddled with his hands. If he caught a fish he squeezed it under his body and into the hole. We saw some men fishing alone from cauldrons, spearing fish with extraordinary skill.

We supposed we saw a good catch, of several kinds; but the men said catches were very poor, and indeed, there were a lot of people to share them. Moreover, the merchant who sold their surplus must take his profit, and it was with him that I was really concerned, for he bought his right to sell the catch from the lake from the Revenue Department. Clearly he would squeeze all he could from the fishermen, who would mostly be in his debt anyway. Their complaint was that they were paid too little: if the catch were good, the price was very low; if it were poor they would get very little anyway. I asked a lot of questions, but in the end it appeared that only one of them was literate, that they could perhaps arrange transport to Karachi, that they just might find an honest man in the market who could be trusted to sell for them on commission, but they could not afford to wait for the money, even if there was more in the end. They could not live only on fish, and anyway they were in debt to the contractor.

We parted friends; I would see if there was any way I could help them, and they gave us a big fish, the best kind, they said. It was, too, and a very welcome change from chicken.

Next day the contractor came to see me, as was to be expected, so I listened to his side. He had to pay a fixed contract price, for which he must compete with others. If the fishing were poor, he still had to pay, and if the market price were low he suffered for it. He was not a rich man, he was very generous to the fishermen, who would cheat him by selling to others if they could. (Did he know of the fish given to us?) I would carefully consider what he had said.

We camped a long time at Gujo; it was a pleasant place, with Haleji nearby. I tried a lot of cases, made a lot of pertals—the tapedars must have come to dislike me!—but in the end the work ran out. We had no wish to be in

Karachi till touring finished in April, but my Chitnis argued that there was official work that must be done in Karachi, it would be a good idea to see the Collector, and so on. Moreover, the staff would like to see their families. They were not like me, who had my family with me. So at the end of February I would go in. The office staff could see their families, and I stayed for two nights at Landhi to hear cases.

Landhi was notable for having the only petrol pump outside Karachi in all Sindh. It didn't work. I drove in to see Clee, my Collector, then to Gujo in time for tea. There was the enormous pleasure of seeing Joan again. Only two days, but so very long, justifying a prolonged and close embrace, in full public view, appreciated by everyone. Only the sahibs dared so defy convention.

Of this last tour there were camps whose names only I remember: Luka, Sonda, Hillaya; others had special features. Jungshahi was on the railway, but its speciality was wasps: fierce yellow ones that lived in the rolled-up blinds. After once lowering them and releasing a swarm we dared not touch them again. No flies, no geckos; the wasps left a desert.

The Mukhtiarkar came with maps to look at the route of the planned water pipeline. The land was all government waste, but the problem was to avoid Muslim cemeteries.

Muslim cemeteries were to be found almost anywhere, often unrelated to any human settlement. They might have been abandoned long ago, but were forever holy. Even if there were only little hammocks in the sand, and one wind-worn stone set upright, it must be noted, so that if possible the pipeline would avoid it. These suspect burial sites were a great nuisance, for roads and canals as well as this pipeline. Even the railway, built eighty years earlier, had curves in the line only explicable by there being some cemetery on its route, and that was before people had woken up to the uses of their religious scruples. For our pipeline we did no more than ask the Collector to notify a wide strip within which claims for obstacles must be made by a date. Many were: some old man would come forward and take oath (but not on the Quran!) that his grandfather was buried at such a spot; or a holy man had built a little shrine, but a heavy flood from the hills had washed it all away. I suggested that at one spot, marked only by a very slight mound, we might dig to see if there were any bones. But no, that would be the greatest sacrilege; even the suggestion must not go beyond the Mukhtiarkar, who was himself shocked. I could only hope that the claims within the notified strip were not on the line itself. The pipeline was ultimately built, long after my time, so a way was ultimately found, but I am sure that there are variations from the straight line to show where burials were proved.

We went on, past Makli of the monuments, but we would camp there later. The purpose of the next camps was for me to do a big inspection of the wide river *kutchas*. I suspected that large alluvial areas might be avoiding assessment for revenue. I had no horse, and the land was unsuitable for camels, so I borrowed tapedars' ponies. (I will never forget those iron-framed saddles!) I could inspect one tapa with its tapedar, while I took the maps of the other one whose pony I had, and marked what areas were cultivated, thus forestalling any late changes to the record. I saw again the great efforts being made by the self-employed cultivator, and how little the zamindari share-cropper did. I also discovered discrepancies in the record of the absent tapedar, confirming my opinion that there was little use in inspecting an area where the tapedar had been forewarned that the Sahib was coming, for he had time to make his record fit the facts. If the land were not inspected it could be entered as waste, and the tapedar rewarded suitably by the zamindar or smallholder who had avoided paying revenue. An aerial survey was needed, and the military did such things, but not for the Sindh Revenue Department. However, there was matter for thought.

Jherruk was notable for its bedbugs. That is sad, for it was an interesting place, with a notable history. It was the most northerly point in my charge, and it was a long haul back to Thatta, so, for the only time I remember, we moved camp by bus. The camels could not go back to our next camp, at Makli, in a single journey, so we all, domestic and office staff, reduced our baggage to the minimum, and when the time came we all piled in. We filled the roof-rack with kitchen stuff, office files, and boxes of all sorts.

The approach to Jherruk was notable, for the road wound through a ravine, not very wide or deep, whose sides were not very steep, for the ravine was in stony soil laid down in some past age, and more recently cut through by heavy floods from the hill streams. We climbed out of the ravine, and when we reached the top of the slope and looked across at eye level; the effect was of a continuous flat plain; it was apparently empty, deserted, but in fact cut by ravines into what in Arizona are called mesas. (Sindhi has a word for it, but I forget.) Jherruk had been an important River port, but the River had left it.

As for the bedbugs, they were terrible. The bungalow was a very old one, its walls full of cracks; it was short of ordinary equipment, more particularly mosquito poles, for there were only two. Two *charpoys* there were, but we were perfectly happy to sleep together in one, so we moved the bed near the wall where there was a line of hooks, and with string were able to trice up our net neatly.

So far, so good. We slept, but not for long: we both woke itching, and the torch showed bedbugs in bed with us. Horrible! A squashed bedbug has one of the foulest smells imaginable, and we had to get up and search them out. Then we noticed the source: there were two processions coming from the wall, along the strings, down the net, and so to us. How did they know? Perhaps they sent out scouts to explore; perhaps they could smell a good food source; but they were coming in hundreds. We searched the bed-clothes and ourselves, and moved to the other bed. Next day the Sahib and Memsahib expressed extreme displeasure, and someone spent all day searching. Next night more poles were found, and we slept well away from the walls. Also, I sent a bitter report to the PWD.

So we took to our bus and drove back to Makli, our camp for Thatta. Makli on the Hill, the Place of Tombs. The modern, *pukka* brick bungalow stood on the top. There was no garden, for it was a place of bare rock: it must have been a very hot place in due season! Thatta was only a mile away, so the staff stayed there. On one side ran the road to Jungshahi, on the other the trunk road to Hyderabad, and just on the other side of that road began the Tombs.

There were hundreds, perhaps thousands of them; no one had ever tried to count them, but local advice was that there were several lakhs, and one lakh is 100,000. There may well have been, for down the slopes of the ridge that ran south-west were gravestones, short pillars with a turban carved on top. Along the top of the ridge ran a double row of grand monuments, some old and worn by wind-borne sand, others quite new. One was a mausoleum one might enter, save that it was gated, and this was so modern that the gate was of expanding steel strips, clearly designed for a lift. Some were heavily carved, with flowers and symbols and a profusion of Quranic inscriptions. They were all built of sandstone, but on some were the remains of the blue tiles for which Thatta was famous.

The whole enormous cemetery was secured by a wire fence with a gate, locked, and a hut for the chowkidar. The hut was empty, so we walked along the fence, and a few yards from the gate it was down. We had no trouble at all in getting in, so it was logical that there should be no chowkidar: he would have been wasting his time.

This vast necropolis was something we had to investigate, so that next time we would know what to look for—but for us there was to be no next time. The Pakistani archaeologists have looked after it properly, and now it is a place for tourists. I would like to go back, but I couldn't afford the necessary escort.

Makli was a good camp, high above most of the flies and mosquitoes. We could watch the sun rise, and see it glinting on the River. In the evening we watched it sink, in a blaze of crimson through the dust, but as it neared the horizon the light shone clear over the great salt marsh south of Karachi. Then suddenly it was dark. If we got the time right we could watch the Lahore Mail speed through Jungshahi, the carriages only a streak of gold so far off, and the train noiseless. In camp at Jungshahi we had seen and heard it close to, seen the blaze of light under the smoke as the furnace door was opened, the windows all clear, the headlight boring ahead. And at the station it whistled grandly. Lonely on our hill, we valued it.

From Makli we could look down on Thatta, romantic across its lake; nearer to, we could see the flaws in the picture. It was my nominal headquarters; it was the biggest town between Karachi and Hyderabad; it was the ancient capital of Sindh. Yet there was no paved street, nor any sign of a drainage system.

The Mukhtiarkar could tell me something of Thatta's past, though he depended on local tradition; he had no record, and officers such as he, or indeed me, were seldom in a place long enough to do proper research. Thatta was famous for its textiles, its pottery, and its ceramics. Also for its great mosque, disproportionately large, with its great dome and small ones round it. Tradition said that it was presented to the town in the days of its greatness by the Emperor Shah Jehan for sheltering him in his flight from his father Jehangir. The Mukhtiarkar settled a question for us, unanswered in Jherruk: there was a large building, closed up tight, locked and padlocked. It belonged to the Agha Khan. We knew of him as an excessively rich man who flaunted his wealth round Europe. He was head of the Ismaili sect, his wealth came from gifts from his followers. Both Sunni and Shia hated him. It appeared that he never went to the house in Jherruk, but perhaps a day would come when he would need a safe, unknown refuge.

Thatta was a sad place; its days of glory were long gone, and even its people seemed depressed. Yes, there were still weavers and dyers, and a few old women still doing embroidered mirror work. But the shops were dim and dusty. Shake a piece of fabric and you would be hit by a shower of dust and nasty insects: no welcome to a customer.

There were several potters, selling through one large shop. This shop was even dustier, but here dust was excusable. Again, there was no attempt to attract custom; indeed, the heap of broken shards outside argued some weak and faulty ware. But clearly the trade was local only. There were the large pots we called *chattis*, of three kinds. One was said to be fire-proof, and I daresay it was—for a time. Another was for water, of a pattern used throughout Sindh. For the third, the clay was mixed with a special sand which made it porous, so that evaporation cooled the water.

Those did not interest us *perdeshis*, from outside. But we saw tall stacks of dishes that must be glazed, for the edges of some showed colour; and a little stack of bowls clearly had the famous blue glaze. The shopkeeper gaped at us when we showed interest.

When he had recovered from his shock, he was enthusiastically willing. He took down the plates one by one: no, it was not possible to pull one from the middle, the whole stack would collapse; he would be happy to show them all, he had plenty of time. Moreover, he was happy to see so many people crowding round to see such notable customers, the *Dipiti* Sahib and his lady.

We toiled all through those stacks. There were dozens of dishes with pleasant, even beautiful, designs: there were leaves and flowers, painted on before glazing, there were geometrical designs, but no Arabic texts. I asked why. There was no Muslim potter, and no Hindu would dare to use Arabic, the script of the Quran.

We would have been happy to buy a dozen, even two or three dozen: they only cost a few annas. But there was a problem. When, in England, and probably everywhere, plates were stacked for firing, little clay balls were used to keep them apart, three to each. Although the little balls were well-baked, the spot where each sat, a tiny dot, is visible, is, indeed, a mark of authenticity. In Thatta it was just the same, but either the balls were not baked, or the colour was laid on excessively. The balls had stuck to the plates, so they had to be prised apart, and the little balls, well-baked now, brought a piece, often a very large piece, of the glaze away. So many plates that we would have liked were spoiled. All we could find that were acceptable we bought, and we have them still. Each has its three little marks. We have two of the bowls, very roughly glazed, with the famous Thatta blue. I suggested to the potter that he bake his little balls, for I am that sort of improving busybody; the advice goes well into Sindhi, and the onlookers appreciated the second meaning.

Here was this town, anciently famous, perched on a hillock of the remains of generations of demolished houses, and no one seemed to care for it. There were a few fine houses, but even they were in a deplorable state. The only buildings in good repair were the Treasury and the Mukhtiarkar's Kutchery: he himself was depressed. The school was falling down, and there was no maternity home. There were a few street lights, but none worked. At night the police stayed safely in their *thana*.

The town was so high up that drainage should have been easy, but there were only open gullies in the streets, and from upper floors, channels were cut in the walls, down which the effluent flowed; we could see it flowing, and sometimes solid elements stuck till they dried. It was altogether disgusting. The gullies discharged into a horrid marsh which threatened to pollute the lake, the one feature of their town of which Thatta people were proud.

There was still the great mosque to see. We had heard so much about it, and it let us down badly. It was huge, high up there were still a few blue tiles, out of reach of vandals, but it was near ruinous, and when I asked the chowkidar— there was no mullah—if I might go in, and Joan too if she covered herself, he said he would have been very willing, but it was not safe. The faithful came there to pray, but they knelt outside on the smooth place that he kept clean and holy.

Only the British, in my person, could be blamed for the state of this grand, historic building. One could not expect the Hindus of Thatta to care, and we met no concerned Muslim. The Department of Archaeology in Delhi must be stirred up, for to me, it being in my charge, it was more important even than Mohen-jo-daro. So I reported to the Collector. But there was a war on; I was transferred, and only when Pakistan itself took charge was the mosque restored to its former glory, covered with the lovely blue tiles that Joan and I had hoped to find, and had failed.

I asked the panchayat to meet me. With the Mukhtiarkar to help, I tried to instil some enthusiasm in them for their town. They had to do more to sell their goods, there was not enough local trade. The Co-operative Department could advise and help, it would cost very little: indeed, they had heard of it. On account of the war there were many people who would buy their cloth and their pottery, and the Rural Reconstruction Department had a shop where they could show it. I told them that I had myself built a loom, that my wife had woven cloth on it, but sadly the cloth was in Karachi. I showed them the dishes we had bought, told them we would have bought many more had they not been spoiled. Their potters must improve their technique. Their town was, I told them, a disgrace. They pointed out that Thatta was not a municipality, so could not raise a tax. Surely they could themselves raise the money? What was a panchayat for?

I was speaking to a group of serious, experienced businessmen as though they were students. They probably knew that eighteen months ago I hadn't even seen India, let alone Thatta. But I could show that I knew something of the techniques of weaving and potting; they asked questions, they accepted that I could, through the Collector, help them. I could ensure that my reports were not just sat on. Nor did I forget; but, regrettably, I was moved away.

We all ate sweetmeats and drank cardamom tea; Joan and I collected our plates, and we left with signs that a little enthusiasm had been roused; the Mukhtiarkar promised to nurture it. Perhaps we had changed Thatta a little. In my memory I can see Thatta as it was, nearly sixty years ago. I would like to see it now. But all the Hindus have gone: it must be a very different place. Perhaps it is prosperous now, for its greatness was in an age of Islamic power, and it is now Islamic again, with the great mosque to draw the faithful, and the Makli necropolis to draw the tourist.

Our last camp was at Ghulamullah, where there was to be an agricultural show, and where my most important case would come to trial. It had been long delayed, because the accused was an important zamindar with political influence. My Shristedar had warned me that there might be pressures from Karachi, so I had fixed it as far from the city as I reasonably could. But neither of us had expected that a Government Minister would come.

He was Nihchaldas Vazirani, one of the two Hindu Ministers, the Home Minister, and he had come, of course, just on a courtesy visit to meet me and my wife; it was nothing to do with his being head of the political side of law and order. He was by far the most important visitor we had ever had, and he rated not just a chair, but tea, with Joan presiding. There followed a great deal of small-talk: had we enjoyed our tour? We had, but for Joan there was not enough to do. Surely, for a woman, keeping house was enough? In the first place, said Joan, very little was left for her; in the second, she had not worked very hard at school and college just for that. She wanted to do other things.

'So you were at college? Where?'

'At Cambridge, my husband was there, too; that's where we met.'

'So you must both be very clever. I have heard that Cambridge is the cleverest place.'

'Not everyone coming from Cambridge is clever,' say I. 'We just learn to use the wits we have, or so we hope.'

'I was at college myself, at the university in Karachi.'

'So you must be very clever, too.' He did not deny it; in fact he had to be clever, a Hindu Minister in a Muslim Ministry.

More teasing, and then he came to the point: there was a matter he wanted to discuss. Of course, I said, but he asked that Joan should leave us. I replied that she was very discreet, that her opinion, as an educated person, on whatever we were to discuss might be useful. But she must go. So she went, very obviously indignant, and let him see that she thought him very offensive. (Afterwards I tried to placate her, pointing out that he had acknowledged that she must be very clever, but he was not used to meeting women like her.)

Then we got down to it. This person who would appear before me next day was an honourable man; he was falsely charged by dishonest neighbours. He was a man of excellent reputation, and the charges should surely be dismissed. The Minister acknowledged that he could not order me, and he knew that I would reach the right decision.

I bid him good-bye politely: Joan would not appear. I then joined her, and we both exploded with indignation. We told each other of our feelings so loudly that everyone might hear.

It was, however, a difficult matter. The Minister might well be right: there was nothing unusual about false charges. Those who lectured me had endless tales of false witnesses being paid, of true witnesses being suborned or arrested and kept from court. Even a sound case could be spoiled by the addition of false evidence intended to strengthen it. The police might themselves bring in false witnesses to bolster their case against a true villain, and thereby lose it. There was even a Chief Court circular stating that any conviction depending on uncorroborated police evidence would be quashed on appeal.

In this case that seemed unlikely. Moreover, were I to dismiss the charge, as Nihchaldas wanted, I would leave both police and witnesses at the mercy of the zamindar; and I would become known as a magistrate open to pressure, even if my decision was strictly in accordance with the facts of the case. True or not, I would not like that. Nihchaldas would not like me much, but he was in a Muslim Ministry: why had no Muslim Minister come? Probably because none was a friend of this man, and if I let him off they wouldn't like me much, either. Finally, there was the mystique of the ICS to consider, and I disliked extremely having to consider the element of *politique* in what should be a straightforward criminal case.

Joan and I discussed this, and then I called in my Shristedar, and we worked out what to do. The charges must not be dismissed: unless there was at least superficial evidence it would not have been brought. On this we were agreed; the Shristedar also had his integrity to preserve. But neither of us wanted to annoy the Minister unnecessarily, so the Shristedar suggested, hesitantly, that I plead inexperience and ask the District Magistrate to transfer the case to another court. This I would never do! Did he not remember the Macaulay case? This was only different from that, and a dozen others, in that the sentence might be much heavier.

So the case would proceed. There would be publicity for this one, and the compound filled with people even before the advocates arrived by car from Karachi: the Public

Prosecutor and a barrister, who brought a press reporter. It was a pity that I had no formal court dress, but I put on my best trousers, a white shirt, and, very specially, a tie. The police and their witnesses grouped round the Prosecutor, the accused and his witnesses gathered in a group well away. There was a curtained car said to contain the girl allegedly abducted, with her mother.

We began quite quickly—we had none of the etiquette of a judge's court; I just sat down and the naik called the parties in. There was a little spare space, so the reporter and a few others could sit on the floor. My court was no place for anyone who would sit on his dignity. The Shristedar read out the charges and the defendant pleaded not guilty. The barrister said that his client was an honourable man, the charges were all false and should be dismissed. I refused, and said I would hear the prosecution case. (So the Minister had lost.) The police sighed with relief, the defendant frowned. The Prosecutor read out the details of the charges he would seek to prove: a girl had been forcibly removed from her home, had been traced to that of the defendant, taken away from there by a trick, and restored to her family; all this the police would relate in evidence. As for the theft of cattle, beasts had been found in the defendant's village with the brands of other owners.

This was where I must step in. I told the defence barrister that there was clearly a case to answer. He now had a choice: he could ask for the case to be committed for trial by a judge with a jury, or I could try the case myself. If at the end I found the defendant guilty, I might decide that I could not award an adequate penalty myself, and could commit the defendant to a judge for sentencing.

I adjourned the court while they talked about it, to decide if one side should press for committal, the other oppose it. Was the defendant better off to leave his fate with me, who had definitely not done what the Minister wanted, or risk a jury decision, which was always a chancy business?

I at least could have a cup of coffee. Joan had been listening and was all for committal: we had booked a room at the hotel, and if I tried the case we would be several extra days in camp. I pointed out that she could go 'in' (to the city) herself—and incidentally I would myself miss all the fuss of moving in (so it would suit me to try the case!) But all this was extra-judicial.

It was settled for us: the defence opted to appear before a proper judge, the prosecution did not object, so I wrote a committal order. All the witnesses murmured their annoyance, but could do nothing. The Shristedar and I did all the paperwork, and off they all went. He and I were left alone, and I said I was a little disappointed, it would have been an interesting case. But he wouldn't have it: had we tried it there would have been a lot of extra work, with the special difficulty that my transcription of the evidence must be very accurate in case of an appeal, and there was always a chance that some small error might let a villain go free. I had to agree; let a judge have that problem, he was a specialist. But the man was not a crook till a jury said so. The Shristedar sniffed: he knew better, that meant, but in his profession he must not say so.

That was that. Next day there was a small paragraph in the *Sind Observer*, but the reporter had wasted his time.

Next day came Hassanali Agha, Director of Agriculture, with a display of improved implements and a lecture for any zamindars who might turn up, with pamphlets to hand round. He was an enthusiast, a man I could do with very well. He was high above me, but I was an enthusiast in the same area; I hoped he would find he could do with me.

There was no denying my inexperience, so all my ideas depended on such as him for practical assessment; and then I told him all about them. This was an opportunity not to be missed. I could write to Clee, but he wasn't interested in pottery and loofahs and fish; moreover, I had married much too soon. He would make sharp remarks about these young men who wanted to change the country before knowing anything about it, and would write 'File'. But Agha would be able to see that this didn't happen.

We inspected the implements. There were improved ploughs, even one that could turn a furrow; but it had no coulter to cut through rubbish, and was cast iron, which could not be repaired by a *lohar*. I pointed out the problems, and Agha actually took notes. There was a winnowing machine, but it had far too many breakable parts, it would need a man to operate, standing in a fog of dust, and what about the women deprived of a job, with little else to do? But I promised that next harvest, if he would give me one, I would try it.

We discussed the possibility of improving fruit varieties by grafting, and here I did know something, from my Father. If Agha would get me scions, I would try the technique at Malir, and perhaps grow something better than the malta. How fervently I would pray that the grafts would take! *Inshallah* they would, said he.

Work was finished, and we could go in. Thus ended, very happily, our first touring season, our first six months together, a long step forward in our relationship and in our appreciation of what our life together would be like. Never would there be any touring like it, for never again could everything be new. Next season I would have my work, and following up the things I had begun, but for Joan there would be long periods of boredom between events of note.

Of course, she would have a home where she could stay while I toured; she would know people by then, would have entertainment, sailing, tennis, even a cinema. But she was a serious girl, endless frivolity would not suit her. Our chief hope was that the Mother Superior would put her need for a skilled teacher above her moral scruples.

Meanwhile we became once more conscious that there was a war going on. Our only news was from letters from home: we had no radio, and even so near Karachi we had no newspaper. This was the time when Germany overran

Norway, the phoney war turned hot, children were evacuated from London again. Joan's brother and younger sister were evacuated to a rural school, her sister went to Oxford, mine to Cambridge, and my brother was called up in the artillery. Our parents stayed where they were. By comparison, we in Sindh led a very pleasant life.

1. The Old Circuit House, Sukkur (pp. 18, 47, 283). Old style PWD; grey pukka brick. Alone on its stony hill, with beautiful views; and a special merit in its rough tiled floor.

2. Raja (pp. 19, 59). Hollow backed, thin faced, but a good polo pony in his day. Jan Mahomed's friend and livelihood; there would be trouble if I neglected him. I would not dare, even though I did not myself value him. But Jan died, and Raja was put down.

3. The Elegant Chev: a unique motor; we wore her down; we nearly crashed her, but she remained elegant. Then Sirdar Rahim Khan Khoso had her refurbished, even increasing her elegance with flower vases on the dashboard.

4. Camp Bundobust: 'Total chaos' (p. 95). But loads were roped on, the jemadar signalled, there was screaming and shrieks as the camels unfolded themselves, and they set off. Chair legs waving in the air, double space for the beast carrying the tent poles that stuck out a long way, fore and aft.

5. Fishing at Haleji. Joan, properly topied, supervising. And we were given a beautiful fish; a change from chicken.'

6. Joan sat by the dhand, dreaming, among the only trees in Kambar. But nonetheless, cautiously wearing her topi, shoulders bare—a very foreign gesture (p. 124).

7. Still at Haleji Dhand, Joan botanising, finding spiky blooms.

8. Ketibunder (p. 103/4). A vast bare plain in the Delta, camp just in sight.

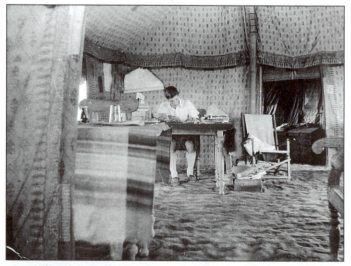

9. Office tent at Ketibunder—or at any other tented camp. Even the bed is visible! Trouble with water: Muddy, and with a shrimp in it (p. 104).

10. Ber (p. 219). Rural Uplift in action. Chaotic mess became a cart-worthy road. Washed away by the flood, it was rebuilt. Did our effort create a spark to flame into self-help?

11. Temples at Chamba (p. 395). The people were Hindu, of a sort, with their own animist gods added. All timber, of course: in the middle of a deodar forest. Beautifully carved, not so tinselly as Sadh Bela. Large lingam and yoni outside; little carved ones inside. And clean everywhere, with the rain. Heart-raising!

12. The Tudor Fireplace (p. 157). Two home-made tables and cigarette box, and two little stools are still with us. 'The wall lights and the Tudor fireplace were included in the approved list. What Glory!

13. The Mango Picnic (p. 187). A very moving and memorable event.

14. 'The Three Sindhi Girls' at Ziarat. Providing a pleasant welcome for three husbands escaping the heat of the plains of Sindh, and enjoying themselves, too (pp. 202-203).

15. Top of the Great Tangi (p. 205/6).

16. Bottom of the Great Tangi (pp. 205/6). We tried to go through; but there was the unknown middle, where we might be trapped. So we left it; next time we would bring a rope (but there was no next time).

17. Kambar Subdivision, under water (p. 257). I stood with a man who was crying. His house had been washed away, his kharif crop was lost, how would he live? I swore that the Sirkar would get food to him and all like him. His family was safe, gone with his few goods on that wonderful little cart, which would float if it must.

18. 'The Kambar Ferry' crewed by the two Mamoos. A private ferry behind us. To eat our snack, we just tied up to a tree (p. 270).

19. Bahram Hethion Station, North Western Railway (p. 216). Here Joan's counselling settled a threatened marriage, and made the parties happy. And here the Quetta Mail stopped just in time, and reversed all the way to Kambar. And Shahdadkot was isolated.

20. I left the trolley, climbed the water tower and saw my domain, water to the horizon (p. 244).

21. The Ruins of Shahdadkot (p. 248). All the husking mills fell down. All the paddy was lost – and how it stank! A broad river through the middle, and here I came near – not very near – to drowning.

22. Joan and the Twins, at one month (p. 266). She had the freedom of the grand Government House gardens. Lady Dow was little; she found the Memsahibs patronizing; but Joan was not like that. She could laugh. She was not proud; they became friends.

23. At the Eminson Bungalow, with Candy (p. 292); a little older.

24. Adam and David in their dungarees and topis (p. 413). Enjoying their beautiful woodland, not aware how special it was.

25. Afroze: a paragon of her race (p. 339). And our very dear friend.
    A bold girl, too. Even danced with me when Nazir Ahmed danced
    with Joan. But would have none of that western hugging business:
    elbow length was best. Nor do I know if she still lives.

26. Nazir Ahmed in his office. Another dear friend, even from
    Cambridge days, and until we left Sindh.

27. Neza-bazi: myself up on Prince; 1945. But in 1944 the peg fell off (p. 348). Never mind: the ferocious charge, with the lance slowly lowered, was the same. Win or lose, the thrill was the same.

28. The Officers' Race (p. 348). A polite race; run along proper lines. Nothing like the ferocious heat of the Baloch Races.

29. The Baloch Races (p. 350). A fierce battle; no holds barred. In fact, as Joan's note on the back, discovered when taken from the album, shows that it was a race from years back, at Ghulamullah.

30. Not judging; just watching (p. 345). Notable ladies looking at cattle. Mrs. Das, Executive Engineer's wife, with two daughters. Jane Holt, wife of Collector of Sukkur, with one son, Joan, hostess; baby sons elsewhere. Chaperoned by Andrew Davies, D.S.P.

31. Camp-fire at Dalhousie (p. 392). Stories for the children of the bitter cold, of wild animals scared off by the fire. They believed none of it.

32. Near the end in Karachi, did they but know it (p. 481). Adam (behind,) and David, proud with baby Judith. A happy time, but unknowing that life in Karachi was ending. And Candy being left, behind, and all the others who made their lives.

33. 'Khosas at home': Sirdars, Members of the Shahi Jirga. (R to L) S. Sardar Khan Khoso, S. Mohammad Khan Dombki, KB. S. Jaafar Khan Burdi (MLA), SB. S. Abdul Rahim Khan Khoso, Mr Pearce, Mrs Pearce (with Adam and David), KS. S. Nur Mohammad Golo (MLA), KS. S. Nur Mohammad Bijarani, S. Mohammad Khan Mastoi, and S. Khan Mohammad Khan Bugti.

JACOBABAD HORSE SHOW.

24th to 29th January 1944.

PROGRAMME.

Monday, 24th ...	10-00 a.m. ...	Horse Show Classification.
		Cattle Show Classification.
		Classification of Agricultural and Industrial exhibits.
Tuesday, 25th ...	10-00 a.m. ...	Horse Show Classification.
		Cattle Show Classification.
		Classification of Agricultural and Industrial exhibits.
Wednesday, 26th...	10-00 a.m. ...	Horse Show Judging.
		Cattle Show Judging.
		Judging of Agricultural and Industrial exhibits.
Thursday, 27th ...	10-00 a.m. ...	Horse Show Judging.
		Cattle Show Judging.
		Judging of Agricultural and Industrial exhibits.
		Ploughing competition.
Thursday, 27th ...	5-30 p.m. ...	Distribution of prizes to the winners in the Horse and Cattle Shows and Agricultural and Industrial Exhibitions.
Friday, 28th ...	2-30 p.m. ...	Police Sports.
Saturday, 29th ...	3-15 p.m. ...	Baluch Races.
	7-00 p.m. ...	Distribution of Race Prizes.

R. R. PEARCE,

Deputy Commissioner, Upper Sind Frontier,
and President, Show Committee.

KARACHI: PRINTED AT THE GOVERNMENT PRESS.

34. Programme of the Jacobabad Horse Show.

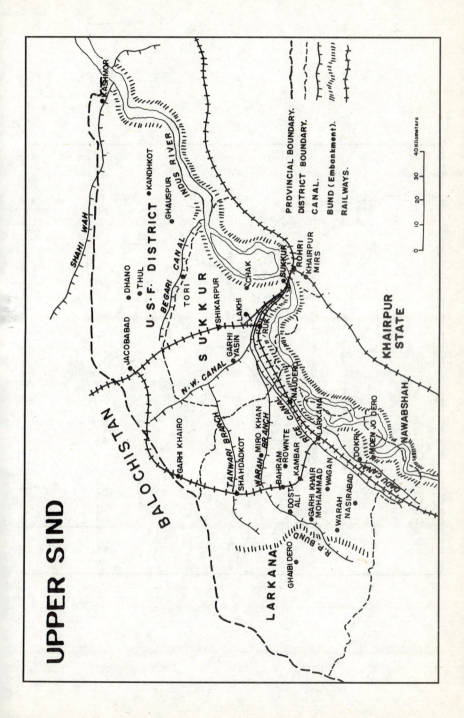

UPPER SIND

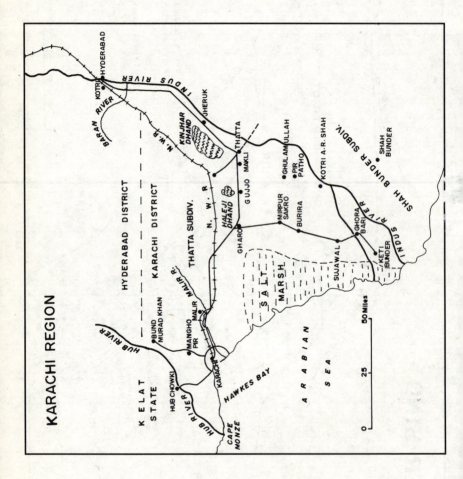

KARACHI REGION

9

HOME IN KARACHI

We were in the hotel again, but only for one night. Our hired furniture was moved into the flat, but there were no beds yet, nor curtains or carpets. The camels weren't due in till next day, but we had our bistra, and we slept on the floor. Then the beds came, one double and one single, charpoys with webbing pulled so tight on the double one that the sides bent. One mosquito net over all. Next, the camel train was reported in the compound, which worried me, lest the camels misbehave. We needed the big boxes, so one camel went to the front; the driver was unworried— camels and Karachi traffic knew each other, and it all pleased the small boys and idlers. They gave the driver scraps, some for him, some for his charge, so everyone was happy. The rest of the train went to the Kutchery to unload into the godowns, and everyone was paid off, except for the two beasts which went off to Mirpur Sakro for the tents.

We slowly got our home straight; indeed, we spent much of that hot weather making furniture and curtains and cushions, with teak from the mistri behind the flats, cloth from the swadeshi shop, and Joan's special weaves from England, to cover cushions specially made by Gangaram. Our style was strictly English, with patterns out of books from Ambrose Heal and Church Street, Kensington, with little concession to Indian ideas.

But first I must necessarily meet my Collector. My enthusiasms did not stir him, nor did my proposals to stir up other departments—not in wartime. In fact, he had little to say, but at least had no cause to criticize. I told him of the visit of Nihchaldas Vazirani, and he referred that matter to the Chief Secretary. I heard later that Nihchaldas was told that, never mind that he was a Minister, interference with a magistrate was a 'negation of good administration'; very gently, of course, just to help him to be a good Minister. But it would make him even less fond of me.

There was a clear indication that my files would be sat upon. I was glad I had met Hassanali Agha.

Our corner of Ilaco House filled up, and became highly reputable: three ICS officers, two of them married, the other very senior; Framji the Engineer whom I knew already, and who became a very helpful friend; and Hugo and Grete Reinitz, Jewish refugees from Austria, who had left Vienna before the Nazis came, and so had brought their furniture with them, and specially their long-haired dachshund, Fipsi, more precious than everything else. They had come to Karachi round about: they had wanted to stay in England, but although Hugo had been the best doctor in Vienna, which had the best medical schools in the world, he would have had to spend a year there training, and could not afford that loss of income. Moreover, they would not surrender Fipsi to quarantine kennels. For a time they had been in the States, and then had come to Karachi, where Hugo became the fashionable doctor. For a time they were interned, till Hugo's patients demanded, and secured, their release. They bore no resentment, they accepted that such a security measure was a proper precaution in wartime, but they were always uneasy, knowing that some security officer kept watch on them. Before leaving Vienna, Grete had taken courses in cookery and corsetry, arguing that wherever they settled there would be a demand for good clothes and good food. They even brought away their electric cooker, but that was no good to an Indian cook, and it stood in the kitchen, symbolic of greater sophistication, but used as a cupboard.

The Reinitzs became our friends and generous helpers for all our time in Sindh, they were always there when needed, always affectionate and understanding, not laughing too much at our youth and inexperience. Never did we have dearer friends.

I had imagined that in the hot weather I would be over-burdened with work, and, indeed, I went to the Kutchery every day. There I wrote reports to be sent to the Collector, responses to government circulars about every kind of activity. There was one that allowed me to sit in the office in shorts, but in court I must wear long trousers and a white shirt. There was daily and weekly routine to be noted in the Diary, and all the taluka revenue returns to be collated, and remissions to be justified, if possible. There was always a list of references I had made which had not been answered, of references made to me that I or my staff had 'sat on'. The Collector on his side would have made a note, 'Expedite', and on my side I would note the same for my office. There was a great deal of Indianized office jargon, which meant that I must draft important letters myself—there was no shorthand writer, though we did have a typewriter. My Chitnis would respond to a note from me with 'Disposed off', 'Filed in error', or even 'Lost in error'. 'He is in error' meant that a man was lying. There were many similar phrases, and endlessly people apologized to me and I to my superiors. But no longer was I 'Your humble and obedient servant'. Not that I should forget it. The proper subordination remained.

Apart from hearing cases in court—and even then I could write the judgements at home—it soon became clear why touring was preferable to being in headquarters. In a sub-division such as mine, few visitors and even fewer petitioners would come into Karachi. Indeed, several times I felt it necessary to drive out to see the people and places I was supposedly administering. There was trouble at Buhara

again, and I saw rice actually growing for the first time,
some land already planted, some where women paddled
about sticking plants into the mud. There were still the
seed beds, fertilized with cow dung and with the ashes of
burnt rags. (Cloth must be ragged indeed before it was so
discarded!) To me it seemed that there was a great need
for lime in this sour soil, so I had another query for the
Agriculture Department. I asked if there was any response
to my previous proposals, but there was neither response
nor apology: clearly he was sitting on them all.

As I had been, so Peter Cargill was given a taluka, which
gave him the welcome benefit of travelling allowance, but,
as I pointed out, made him my subordinate, which pleased
him not at all. He went with me on some of my short trips
to the *mofussil*, but then it rained, the roadway across the
Malir River was washed away, and we were cut off in Karachi
until it was relaid. Joan went with me to see a disputed site
on the route of the water pipeline, when we could see the
Haleji fishermen again in that welcoming oasis. We were
pleased to meet again: they had heard from the
Department, so even though Clee had sat on my proposal,
Hassanali Agha had not. We picnicked again at the dhand,
and again the fishermen gave us a fish.

That was pleasantly hot weather. Our catering was joint
with the Cargills, and it was we who had the cook. Joan
took cookery lessons from Grete Reinitz, and passed them
on to Mistri, so that he could venture beyond the chicken
and caramel custard cuisine.

Kishensingh had most of his income from our corner of
Ilaco House that summer, for he had two Urdu and two
Sindhi pupils: I aspired to higher grade Sindhi, for there
was an increment in it. Peter Cargill had a departmental
exam to come, and I managed to persuade him that those
Revenue Rules Thereunder must be learnt: he felt as I had
that such rote learning was nonsense, but I persuaded him
that the parrot should be his model; I saved him from my
own downfall.

May, and Joan had her birthday, with a cake from Grete, and presents of some of the endless things we needed. Then the Germans invaded France, followed by Dunkirk; we were expecting any day to hear of a landing in England. It seemed inevitable, nor did we know then how little resistance could have been offered. Dunkirk was a victory, that was the tale we British must tell, looking always cheerful and confident. We did not believe it was a victory; we all heard from our families, yet even they, even Joan's in London, remained confident. The bombing of London began, we worried, but there was nothing we could do about it.

At last we were asked to sail with Lady Graham; first Joan, with a tindal, then both of us together. Lady Graham must have felt a special responsibility for Joan, and when she passed her test as crew the Lady could sail corinthian— never, she said, done before. Joan took fore-sheet and spinnaker, I the centre plate, and standing by the main sheet. We didn't win, but with our time allowance we came second, which was the best ever, and the Lady was jubilant. HE had never done so well. But we weren't asked to crew for him; not yet: he was dubious about taking too much notice of a very junior officer. We were, though, invited to one of the informal dinners at Government House.

We naturally dined with the Clees. I always behaved rather formally, I don't quickly become familiar, but Joan began a lasting friendship with Merrie Clee. On occasion the Cargills were there too, and for Peter it was very soon 'Charles'. (I waited several years before I so ventured.) With us they dined with our Commissioner, Godfrey Collins, that joyless man, with Wanda Kinzior as his hostess. (But perhaps he was not wholly joyless; perhaps he was still disapproving of our living in the wrong place, marrying at the wrong time, yet obviously enjoying it, and not noticeably incompetent.)

Then there was Godfrey Davis, now Chief Judge and Sir Godfrey. Several times we went to see him: his wife was

away, and he liked company; his careless—carefree
perhaps—talk was always fascinating to hear. I asked him
about my *zamindari* case: it was safely finished, and the
time for an appeal had passed. Five years for cattle theft,
two for kidnapping. It sounded wrong, but he explained
that cattle theft could easily lead to violence, whereas in
the particular families concerned, a money payment would
have settled the affair of kidnapping; it was just that the
silly man had refused to settle. (It still did not seem to me
to accord with strictly British principles, but India was
different.) Nihchaldas had been to see him about the case,
but Sir Godfrey was clever at avoiding political pressure.
Nihchaldas had called on him ostensibly to wish him a
happy Good Friday, an unusual way to celebrate that day.
Perhaps he was just ignorant of Christian customs, but
perhaps he was being very subtle: perhaps he knew that Sir
Godfrey was a Jew, and was celebrating for him the death
of the man who was for Jews a false Messiah.

When we were in our own flat the atmosphere lightened
happily. In the hotel the party walls were so thin that we
could hear every sound made by our neighbours. As
someone went in there would be a bang as the door closed;
a low murmur of voices, creaks as bed or chair was sat
upon, voices raised in sudden disagreement, and so on.
Doubtless our neighbours heard every sound that we made,
so we were quiet as mice. Here, there were solid walls all
round, all was quiet: sometimes too quiet, till we opened
the window for the cheerful sound of traffic in the street
below.

It was usual at this time of year for there to be rumours
of transfers of officers not firmly fixed. I did not want to
move: apart from our flat, which was still hardly as we
wanted it, there were all those proposals I had made, and
wanted to look after. But rumour became hard fact: I was
posted to Kambaralikhan, in Larkana District, in Upper
Sindh. I knew little of the place, except that it lay between
the River and the hills, had a railway running through, was

a rice area, and had the Agricultural Research Station at Dokri, which pleased me. There was also Mohen-jo-daro, which I had seen from Sukkur, and which I hoped would please Joan. It had a big old mud-brick bungalow, with electricity, but no other of the amenities we had, for a short time, become used to.

I could, perhaps, have asked to stay in Thatta, pleading unfinished work, but my Collector wasn't interested in my ideas, and my motive might have been misread as a desire to stay with the fleshpots of Karachi, or at least with proper bath and closet. Nor was mine the spirit to fight authority. Not yet, anyway. So we prepared to leave. It was all very well for me, with a new charge, new country, new people, problems and possibilities. I wished Joan would stay in Karachi, but she didn't want to, without a job. Teaching was still denied to her. She asked at the Censor's Office, but that would not take on the wife of an officer on transfer. Anyway, we couldn't really afford to run two households; nor had we been so long together that we would welcome separation. Joan would certainly come with me.

10

LARKANA

We had ten days' 'joining leave', to pay bills, suspend our club membership, say goodbye to friends, and pack up. There were also the formal calls and cards to be left. The sad part was dismantling the flat and saying good-bye to friends, but Larkana was not so very far away: Framji might well have work there, and the Reinitzs promised to come to stay. David Halford had been posted there before, and he told us about the bungalow. It was large, old, with very thick walls. It sounded as if our furniture, made for a small urban flat, would be lost in it. But at least it would be cool in the hot weather. We would be going back to a thunderbox, a tin bath, and water delivered in a pail and taken away by a bhangi. The refrigerator in Karachi was fixed in the flat, and we couldn't afford to buy one. We bought an ice-box instead.

Khuda Baksh decided to retire. He would not go to live in the heat of Upper Sindh again at his age. He had some land near Karachi, and money saved. (How could he save on the wage that we, and his previous employers, had paid him? Better not to inquire. The bearer of a district officer was a man of influence.) As was to be expected, a replacement appeared: Nawab, a much younger man, smarter in every way. Instead of baggy trousers and a large turban, he wore tight Punjabi trousers, an achkan, and an embroidered cap wound round with a vestigial turban. A man from the United Provinces, Uttar Pradesh today, in central India, speaking Urdu, which suited Joan very well; he was to a degree, a very small degree, literate in English. He could read a shopping list, he had served with memsahibs. He was a cheerful and friendly man, and we were happy to have him with us. Then we found that he was a friend of the Cargills' bearer Mahomedali: they came from the same place. So the grapevine was not so very long. However, we could suppose that Mahomedali had given us a good name.

I handed over my charge to the Collector, with notes about staff and confidential papers locked in the safe, the key left with him. I didn't meet my successor, nor had I met my predecessor. This sort of transfer often happened, because of the need for a certain time for officers to move. Even the government did not demand that one hand over and rush off to take over one's new charge on the same day, from someone who must himself rush off, and so on… Ridiculous! Nor did the administration seem to suffer. At least the Office had time to get everything in order.

After the sad goodbyes to friends, I said goodbye to the Office. I wished them good fortune, and congratulated the Shristedar on passing his departmental exam. He knew far more about my work than I did, and in a year or two might hope to become a Mukhtiarkar. By the time I was a senior Collector he could hope to be a Deputy Collector. If the Raj lasted so long. If it did not, and the likes of me retired early, his rise would be much faster, and I don't suppose these able young men were unaware of that. We were garlanded, but with none of the enthusiasm of our first arrival. Our short reign was ended, and the garlands were just for politeness.

Bashir Malik came to see us off at the station. He was Divisional Commercial Officer now, and made easy the loading of our furniture in a wagon; he found a flat truck for the car, and booked space on a west-bank freight train: there were not very many till the rice was ready to move. He even found a way to pack our long tent poles, which had caused a furore when they went through the city, with red rags hanging from their tails.

Then came the bad news: our bungalow in Larkana was not fit to live in, it was falling down, so we must go back to a hotel. But Larkana had no hotel. We could stay with the District Superintendent of Police, who lived in a bungalow next to ours and exactly the same.

It was a gloomy start to a new post. Again, no home. We left with Mistri and Nawab, and jogged along in the slow train that went along the west bank of the River, the first line to be built. Through the night we could see nothing of the hills on our left, and the river on the right was behind high *bunds*.

In the early morning we reached Larkana, and here there was no fuss, for I had not yet taken charge. Eric O'Flynn the policeman met us and drove us all to his bungalow, where we would be paying guests with him and his wife Eleanor till our bungalow was ready. Tea, toast, and our admiration for their garden. So we could have a garden! Their cook welcomed Nawab and Mistri, who doubtless learned more about the place than did we.

We could see our own bungalow, just beyond a little hedge with a convenient gap in it. There were heaps of bricks and builders' rubbish around, but it did not appear to be falling down. We crossed over, and there waiting for us were the Mukhtiarkar of Kambar and my new Chitnis, with a paper to sign to show that I had taken over my new charge, so at once I was responsible for any disaster that might befall. Our new naik, Allahdino, arrived hotfoot from the station: the wagon would arrive later in the morning, and he had arranged bullock carts for transport. As well that we had packed carefully, and had nothing like a piano!

We had an enormous compound, with a few trees and a tumbledown wall round it, good quarters for staff, a stable, a garage, and two godowns; in fact, better for its purpose than was this decrepit bungalow. Once our stuff arrived we would sort things out, but first we looked inside.

The bungalow was not really decrepit, but it looked a mess. The walls were crumbling from the bottom up, for the salt had got into the *kutcha* bricks and had risen two or three feet up the walls that they were turning to mud. All round, the walls, eighteen inches thick, were being dug out, two or three feet at a time, and underpinned with a burnt-brick foundation topped by a damp course. Above that there was *kutcha* brick again, to keep the heat insulation. Clearly it would be a very long job.

Inevitably we must stay with the O'Flynns: the only other possibilities were Abdur Rashid Kazi, the Executive Engineer, and Nur Mahomed, the Deputy Collector, but both kept their families in purdah. There was also my Collector, Rahim Ali Mahamadi, and his wife was in purdah too—local purdah; she was not in purdah in Karachi. Mahamadi was also ICS, far senior to me; he was a small, forceful man, arrogant perhaps because he was small. When we stood he had to look up at me, so we sat down. Whenever we met he sat down, and told me to sit too—not, I thought, out of courtesy. Once when I was on tour, he told Joan he would keep me under his thumb, which annoyed her extremely. Perhaps that was why she jeered at him—mildly—for keeping his wife in purdah. Had we known them longer I think she might have persuaded the Begum to rebel. (Afroze once told us how indignant she was that when she visited Nazir Ahmed's family in Rawalpindi she had to wear a *burqa*.) So we stayed with the O'Flynns for a long time. They were kind and hospitable, but somehow we could not come to like them much. Eric was the son of an army officer, born in India, and had never been to England, which he felt was a fault. His wife Eleanor had been a missionary, and felt that this put her at a disadvantage with Joan, no matter that missionaries were the heroes of Joan's youth. They kept chips firmly fixed to their shoulders, but generally we managed to circle round these prickly matters without getting too badly pricked.

They knew far more about India than we did, and were only too happy to share their knowledge.

The result of our unease was that we toured very conscientiously. I bullied the engineer to hurry work on the bungalow, met my staff, dealt with what needed doing in the office, booked several bungalows for a short tour, and set off.

First, naturally, we went to Kambaralikhan, my nominal headquarters, looked round the town, and met the Mukhtiarkar, Ali Ahmed Yusifani, whose name I remember because he was the best. There were no cases fixed, so after camps with only pertal, visitors, and petitions, we returned to Larkana and stirred up the builders. Joan had word that Lady Davis was starting a school for local children, so she went down to Karachi to see if there was a job. There was nothing to keep me in, by now there were cases fixed, so I went back into camp.

Letters began again. I complained about the stupidity of the Mukhtiarkar of Mirokhan, she replied with funny stories from Karachi life. She stayed with the Reinitzs, and as hopes of a job waxed and waned they urged her to stay on and on.

'Framji sent in a live duck yesterday, and it's sitting in the sink. When Ali has nothing better to do he fills the sink with water and lets him have a swim. Grete wants to fatten him with twelve suet dumplings every day until Christmas, but then it would mean killing an old friend...' Another of those tales without an end.

At Mirokhan was that rarity, an incompetent Mukhtiarkar (I judge from the future, too: I never met another.) I was there at the specific request of Hugh Lambrick, Census Officer: he could not order me, his was a different department. He was very much my senior, and a direct descendant of John Jacob. (When he retired he wrote a definitive biography of his forebear.) He asked me to sort out a census muddle, which I did, and at the same time dealt with a muddle with the revenue remission claims.

The Mukhtiarkar, to show how efficient he was, had refused to allow any, so I was given a large sheaf of appeals. I went to look, and allowed a lot of them; it was assumed, of course, that I, new to the country, was soft, so there came a whole lot of fresh appeals against decisions that had been accepted before. I rejected the lot. Nor was there any complaint.

Lambrick was pleased to have his precious census returns put in order. He gave me another job: to report on the material, economic, social, and demographic state of a typical village. What he imagined would be the value of my report I don't know, but I typed it out laboriously on the fragile yellow cartridge paper we used for office notes. I really let myself go; I brought in my pet ideas and theories as well as facts. I produced a document whose size I remember, if little else. This is just as well: I had been in India just two years. It was very strange: there were plenty of Deputy Collectors, even Mukhtiarkars, as competent and far more knowledgeable and experienced than I, but he picked on me. I can only suppose it was because I would be less prejudiced than were they, which was a proper consideration. Also, we were both in the same Service, whose mystique enwrapped us and gave us this special talent. Maybe. Those others only lacked our arrogant self-confidence, so assured that it was sometimes intimidating.

Kambar was in so many ways different from Thatta. My first discovery was that no longer could the camp *bundobust* travel by camel: this was the rice bowl of Sindh, and there was nowhere for camels to graze. So I had to accept bullock carts, and indeed they did very well. Barrage water now flowed in what had been inundation canals, so that the rabi crop could be watered. But the zamindars did not change. They continued to grow rice and millets, would not consider cotton and wheat, and their rabi crops were still pulses.

Sometimes I toured alone, sometimes Joan came with me, but mostly she was either in Karachi or supervising the repairs to our bungalow. I had a horse now for my inspections: Dermont had lent me Bhoop, for he was Secretary to the Governor, and Bhoop would be better in Upper Sindh for the cold weather than idling in Karachi. I could avoid the O'Flynns by touring, Joan could not unless she came with me. She would not ride Bhoop, and indeed he was a very powerful animal. She could borrow a *tapedar's* pony, but the saddles were not made for a woman. Once the teaching in Karachi failed her she had an unhappy time, with little to do, and the O'Flynns for company. I kept away from Larkana, learning my district, new techniques for assessing crops, new ideas for what might be done to improve agriculture, calling cases to camps convenient to parties though not to pleaders from Larkana. But here there was the railway, and buses.

It was always assumed that an ICS officer, whether British or Indian, would develop some special interest. It might be archaeology or Sindhi literature, Indian music, Persian poetry, or just shooting. My subject was beginning to appear, and it would be agriculture. In Larkana I began to clarify my ideas. Listening to petitioners and zamindars, trying cases about land tenure, evictions, water supply, damage done to crops, I was working towards principles that I thought should be adopted. There was scope for machinery, but used as a means to increase output, not to save labour, and the machines should be such as could be locally maintained. Everywhere there were good *lohars*, and mechanics who maintained the zamindars' cars could surely learn about tractors. My chief target remained the share-cropping system. Still I advocated the creation of self-employed smallholders, but here I was in a land of big zamindars, who were well aware of the basis of their political power. My advocacy of changes did me no good at all. But in my sub-division was Dokri, the only Agricultural Research Station in Upper Sindh, so at least I could discover what was going on.

I carried on with inspections. Riding Bhoop was a pleasure, but now he was a gelding, and sometimes he was awkward, when he mourned his lost balls. But for the tapedars with their little mares the change was a godsend. After a time he recovered his spirits, and on occasion I could give rein to them. Inspections in one *deh* were finished, and I set him to the canal bank to move on to the next. He dashed up it happily, and there was this long road, with little thorn hedges. He set off, and I was happy to let him go, with just a check for each hedge—they were only a foot high, and he was happier than I had seen him before. The road went on forever, the tapedars soon dropped behind, and Bhoop wanted to go on forever too. But I was afraid that in his enthusiasm he might founder, so in the end I gradually pulled him up. I wasn't being run away with this time; this was something old Rajah could never have done. It was marvellous, and he thought so too. Once or twice we did it again, but if Joan was with us she wouldn't let us go. I daresay it did look dangerous, from outside. But that first gallop was the best. Bhoop stopped, snorted, and looked around. He thought of going again, but I discouraged him, so we turned and walked back to the tapedars, Bhoop giving a little skip at each hedge. I received a rebuke from the PWD for the big hoof-marks that had broken the precious surface of their road. I apologized, I regretted it, I couldn't help it—the engineer was to think that Bhoop had bolted, but the fiction didn't hold: tapedars and canal abdars were always chatting together. I couldn't even humiliate myself.

By Christmas, part of the bungalow was ready to use. I had my Office there, and room to bring in all our perishable belongings, away from the godown where moth and rust threatened corruption. We lacked wardrobe and drawers, chairs and china cupboards. We did inherit a pair of long, caned chairs called *aram kursi*, rest chair, found in all the touring bungalows. These had swivelling extensions to their arms, so that one could lie back and perch one's legs on them. Some had an extra, a bracket with a hole in it that swung out and would hold one's drink within reach without the trouble of sitting up. Someone in some past time had studied the art of relaxing. There were, too, several *mooras*, little tub chairs made of tightly bound jungle grasses, with goatskin seats.

In the bazaar was a Sikh joiner, reputed to be good. We went to see him, with our catalogues. This *mistri* would make our furniture to order. He had pattern books of English furniture, of the style of about 1870, which was not, in our view, an era notable for good design. Joan showed him her Ambrose Heal book, and he could build to her design. But whereas he would make us an *almira*, in teak, to his own design for Rs. 100, one to hers would cost double. She pointed out that hers had a much simpler carcass, and none of the extra decoration, but it was no good: a special job must necessarily cost double. So we hired all we needed, of a style that our grandparents would have admired. But he made a set of six dining chairs from a Rowley pattern: he had no pattern of his own for setting a double price. These were ladder-backs with goatskin seats, but the dimensions were too slight for teak, and one by one the backs broke. Only one survives.

The underpinning was finished, and the walls were replastered. Joan reported that Eleanor wanted the walls papered, but we did not. We wondered what a room would look like, twenty-five feet square, nearly fifteen feet high, with paper flowers all over. Moreover, we wondered how soon the climate and insects would destroy the paper. Fortunately it would anyway have cost far too much. But the engineer, Bhojraj, was receptive of ideas that did not cost money, so by wily diplomacy Joan got most of what she wanted. It was difficult for Bhojraj: in the nature of things a woman was weak and silly, but this woman clearly was neither. Nor was it easy to be rude to a lady; moreover, this lady was perfectly capable of being rude herself if necessary. So by the time the bungalow was ready most things were as

we wanted them. There were wall lamps instead of flexes
dangling from the ceiling: Joan managed this by pointing
out that the old fittings could be sold for more than the
cost of the new ones. The fireplace in the drawing-room
had to be rebuilt, and the PWD pattern was much like the
entrance to a pharaoh's tomb. This, we pointed out, would
need a lot of time-consuming mud-work, where all we asked
for was a simple red-brick arch. Joan drew a careful scale
plan of it, and it was built. So the bungalow of the Assistant
Collector, Kambar, if it still stands, has in its drawing-room
an exact replica of a Tudor arch. Gradually the filth was
cleared away. The doors were scraped clean of many layers
of varnish, the little towers built by the termites through
cracks in the floor were swept away, the cracks were filled,
and, almost unbelievably, the job was done. We met, we
thanked the contractor, and apologized for the trouble we
had been, we thanked Bhojraj, and signed acceptance.
Then it was he who had a present for us: the wall lights and
the Tudor fireplace were officially included in the patterns
for bungalow repairs. This was glory!

So we at last moved in. Joan went off for a teaching job
in Karachi, and I began to prepare for the Governor's visit
that was due in January. My part was minor. Once
Mahamadi set his shoulder to the wheel it began to turn
rapidly. This would be a very short tour, with interviews, a
duck shoot, and a camp at Ghaibi Dero, in my sub-division,
the home of Nawab Bahadur Nawab Ghaibi Khan Chandio,
chief Sardar of all the Baloch tribes. I would be a small
wheel, escorting Lady Graham to schools and the hospital.
But Joan would be back, and she could do that, she would
have informed ideas, and anyway I could not enter the
zenana at the hospital. In fact, Lady Graham must have
made dozens of such inspections in her service life, she
only needed an escort and someone to pass on her
comments. It should have been Begum Mahamadi, but she
was in purdah.

Security was a police matter, and so was the arrangement for the duck shoot on Drigh Dhand. Eric O'Flynn had to set up hides, arrange for boats, and for there to be guns on other small lakes to turn back the fleeing ducks. There was a much bigger dhand near Dadu, Manchar, but shoots never went there. I was told that there was no cover, whereas at Drigh there were several little islands covered with light jungle. (Look in a bird book about migrations: all the ducks from Central Asia for the winter come to Drigh and Manchar—many thousands of them.) Later I met some fishermen from Manchar, who told me that it was possible to shoot a few; it sounded as though their technique was much like that of the Fenland punt-gunners in England.

Nur Mahomed, Deputy Collector of Naundero, the other sub-division, was to arrange all the interviews; there were none, I think, from my side except for the Nawab. On his side were the Bhuttos, and I was happy not to be involved with those powerful people.

I had the problem of setting up a tented camp for the Governor and his party, with us local officers, at the Dero, which was thirty miles from Larkana along a dirt road, and beyond the Flood Protection Bund which guarded my sub-division from flash floods from the hills, and on the very edge of those hills. This camp must go off without a hitch, and to exact timing.

Governors, and the Viceroy, issued little grey books for tour programmes, with details of staff, journeys, people to meet, and exact times for everything. Sub-divisional officers were not on the distribution list, but I had detailed notes of my duties, and woe betide me if there were any hitch, if there was no hot water at the right time outside Their Excellencies' tent in remote Ghaibi Dero. Mahamadi would have briefed the Governor on what should be discussed with the Nawab. His had been a real desert village until a canal from the Barrage was built nearby. Then he had plenty of water, but didn't know how to deal with it. The polluted water draining from the rice paddies at the tail of the canal was creating a horrid marsh close to the village, and he must be persuaded to ask for advice on how to deal with it, either himself or his two sons. But he was over seventy-five, and had no use for modernity. Moreover, he had just married, a girl of sixteen, a relative, for it was necessary to keep her property in the family. He was enormously fat and had been supposed impotent, but the girl was pregnant, which could pose problems in the future as there were already two grown sons.

All was ready, done with the help of a little *rasai* lubricant; *Inshallah* all would go well. Joan came home from Karachi to a beautiful clean bungalow, and we were ready. There remained only the important question of dinner at the Dero, and to settle that I must consult an ADC.

I was at the station to meet the train—I would not miss a chance to wear my white topi—and discovered what Their Excellencies would or would not like to eat. Anything of good quality would do. I had discussed the matter with the Nawab's Vizir, and we had finally decided that there must be both Balochi and English dishes, knitted as it were. So the menu for a grand dinner was settled. Would we lend our cook? Of course we would. Would Mistri go? He would not. Among those wild men? He might never come back. What if someone choked on a bone? Or had a stomach ache and suspected poison? They might blame him, and kill him. We pointed out that he would undoubtedly be well-rewarded, and should have our toughest patewala to protect him. So he agreed.

All went well with the arrival at the Dero, probably more to the credit of the Government House butler than to mine or the Vizir's; certainly not to the credit of any of the Chandios. All the guests must stay the night, for the entertainment would go on very late. We were staying in our own tent, with some other officer. Did we all have a bath? I expect so, it was a long and dusty road to the Dero. It would be usual to wear medals at dinner, we were told, to honour the Nawab Sahib, but we had none.

There is only one word adequate to describe that dinner: it was grandiose. It was laid in the Nawab's *otak*, furnished with nothing but trophies of the chase. None of the beautiful woven carpets hanging on the walls that tradition hath it should decorate such a tribal centre. There were just the heads of animals that the Nawab had shot, some mere skulls, some with rags of skin still hanging from them. Some were quite recent. There had been no troubling of taxidermists. The favourite method of mounting was to drive a large spike through the skull. And the freshest heads smelt.

We were called to dinner by the Vizir, and the Nawab met us in all his glory. He was crowned by a Baloch turban, the most enormous one I ever saw; he wore an embroidered *khamesa*, and appropriately baggy Sindhi trousers. He was himself enormous, yet he had small feet in embroidered persian slippers, so once he had himself been slender. There was a table set across the hall for the Governor's party, the Collector, and the Vizir. On each side was a table, on one side the O'Flynns, Nur Mahomed, and one Chandio son, and on the other we sat, with Kazi of the PWD, the other son, and other minor guests. So there were three women, all white, of course. The Mahamadis had considered the Begum's coming, but had decided that she should not, since she was in purdah in Larkana. To 'come out' in such a place as Ghaibi Dero would be 'Unhelpful', and she had agreed heartily. She offered to visit the new wife, but there was heavy official disapproval of this marriage, so there would be no visit. Poor girl; but she was no worse off than most other Baloch girls with an inheritance, and to help them a whole culture would have to change.

There was no alcohol, of course, but a variety of so-called fruit drinks. They were all aerated, and there was a general idea that the fizzier they were, the more sure was the sterilization. We knew it was nonsense, and that the water was unboiled, but one must not be impolite; anyway, we had all had our inoculations, and boiling would have done nothing for the filth that collected round the marbles used as bottle seals.

Throughout there were breaks for a smoke, and for those who might have an urgent need for privacy there was somewhere outside.

The Vizir's idea of knitting English with Balochi dishes worked like a charm. We had wondered with Mistri about a soup, and decided against it: the problems of these heavily bearded men ingesting it would be too great. But good river fish there was, delivered on ice, the English crumbed and fried, the Baloch curried. There followed lamb cutlets with cauliflower and baked potatoes, balanced by spiced lamb with pulau rice, or half a sheep's head if one preferred it. My neighbour did, and offered me the choicest bit, the eye. I asked him not to deprive himself, so he popped it in, and as it went it seemed to reproach me. I heard it crunch. This was the Nawab's other son, and he was greedy. He saw that his neighbour on the other side also had an eye, and he neatly speared it away with his dagger, thus doubtless asserting his tribal authority.

I don't know what they ate at the top table, but we favoured the Baloch menu. Always we felt anxious lest the food run out before it reached us: two or three of the Nawab's henchmen stood in the short passage from the kitchen, and levied tribute from each dish as it passed. Our watching them bothered them not at all, they grinned and winked at us. Indeed, they may well have been official tasters for the Nawab.

With the double menu, and several rests, the meal took a long time. The speeches that followed it were admirably short. The Vizir had to translate for both Governor and Nawab, so there was little said save flowery compliments, followed by prayers for long life and many children, not really appropriate for either party. Probably the Nawab was unaware of his part in a war, or he might have prayed for victory. However, the news of the Nawab's new wife gave the Governor's good wishes a little reality, though he was doubtless hoping that the child would be a girl, for the sake of tribal peace; or, best of all, that there would be a miscarriage.

Then came the entertainment, which was outside, so we all went to our tents for more clothes, for it was very cold. There were, of course, fireworks, but to see the special honour done to His Excellency we should look towards the hills, to the *Kutti-jo-Kubr*, the Dog's Grave, the highest mountain in Sindh, right on the border with Kalat. Precisely to its hour a beacon blazed: a tiny yellow light, hardly brighter than the stars on that moonless night. It blazed and faded, we all expressed our astonishment, and then went to our tents.

Joan and I had often looked to those hills, and determined to climb to the top: they were not so very high, and seemed to have no face too steep to scramble. But the Dog's Grave was 6,000 feet up, and this night we were told that for fifteen miles there was no life anywhere, only arid soil and rock, fissured by nullahs that were short-lived raging torrents when it rained. The two men who lit the beacon had taken all day to get there. They had taken food and water and a load of fuel, and a watch to get the time right. It would be very cold, so they would come down to a little sort of cave, and shiver there till it was light enough for them to come down in the morning. Our bold project died.

I daresay there were a few drinks in other tents, but we would have a busy tomorrow, so we went to bed. In the morning there was ice on the pail of water at our tent door, the only time I ever saw natural ice in Sindh.

For Joan and me this was a notable event: a tribal chieftain at home in his village. From an anthropologist's point of view it was quite unchanged by modernity, except for the arrival of a motor car, and water by canal, and this sign of progress could by bad management result in regress if the Chandios failed to deal with all the salt. There was no electricity, the *otak* was lit by paraffin and torches. Our tent was heated by a charcoal brazier—we took special care with ventilation. It all depressed us. Here was a man who, with his sons, would be very influential in the independent India that was surely coming, but as an exemplar of the Baloch tribes along the frontier, he preserved a rather nasty feudalism. But Nur Mahomed reassured us: the Nawab was only tolerated because he was so old. (But would his two sons, Sirdars-in-waiting, be any better?) There was nothing typically Baloch about the Chandios; indeed, tribes further north did not accept that they were true Baloch at all. So, as so often, we must reserve judgement.

The Governor spent the next day granting interviews, mostly from Nur Mahomed's sub-division. First, of course, were the Bhuttos. We met Khan Bahadur Nabi Buksh and his brother Kadir Buksh later. Their father, Sir Shah Nawaz, had been a prominent politician in Bombay before Sindh became a separate province; now he was Vizir to the Nawab of Junagadh, a tiny state on the coast of Kathiawar with a Hindu population but a Muslim ruling family. There was a much younger son, not old enough to meet officials: he was Zulfikar, who became Prime Minister of Pakistan long after we had left.

Lady Graham went to a purdah lunch with Begum Mahamadi, where she met the *purdahnashin* wives of all the other officials. Joan went, of course, but had little to tell: domestic talk, and Lady Graham deliberately teasing the ladies who tried to copy her western table etiquette. Our opinion of her sagged a little.

Next day would be the duck shoot, and then the 'tour' would be over, and Their Excellencies would leave for Karachi.

Eric O'Flynn allocated the guns to their hides, and went with them. Lady Graham took a gun, and so did Eleanor. But we did not: we went along, ostensibly in case anything went wrong, but in fact for a picnic. We went with the Deputy Superintendent in charge of security, who had a boat, poled by a Mirbahar. These Drigh boats were a little like an English punt, but with the bow end sloping steeply up so that it could ride over reeds and small scrub. The Mirbahars were the fishermen of inland Sindh, cousins to the Mohanas of the sea coast.

The policeman had brought a gun, for he had promised his wife that he would get her a bird. But first we must wait: we sat quietly floating in that peaceful place, all embowered with young tamarisk, with clockwork moorhens pottering about near cover, and the white-faced coots cruising aimlessly with their silly cluck. We would have been happy for the peace to last for hours, but not the policeman: he wanted to bag his duck, but must not fire till the guns sounded. At first came a single shot, then a fusillade, and ducks rose into the air from all sorts of secret spots. One rose quite near us, and our gun went off, but it missed; probably it had not been aimed at all.

The birds were all flying away, and so once more there were only occasional shots. But the ducks found that the little dhands they knew were no refuge today: Eric's other guns shot and turned them back. They returned in small groups and were shot at; off they flew again, were turned again, and this time insisted on staying in their known home, regardless of the danger.

Our policeman was still trying for his bird, but no duck came his way. The moorhens had hidden from the uproar, but the coots seemed not to care, so he would have a coot. There was no nonsense about waiting for the bird to fly, and anyway coots don't fly much. We and the boatman had great fun chasing them till one was in range—very short range. Even in spite of the white shield a coot wears, he couldn't hit one. They swam about as if unconcerned till one was fed up and dived; and now began the real hunt. Our gunman could see his quarry through the clear water, and conned the boat to keep in its wake. In the end it had to come up for air, and he shot it as it took breath. He shot it with his 12-bore gun at a range of about two yards. There was not much of it left that could be retrieved, but enough, he hoped, to satisfy his wife with his sporting skill. I never heard if she cooked it. The policeman excused himself: he had no ambition to become a member of the Armed Squad. Poor coot: it had fought gamely against a determined foe, and had lost. But it had died quickly, and was only one odd victim among the dozens that died that day. That was the end of our duties. Sir Lancelot thanked me, thanked Joan, and gave us a photograph of himself and Lady Graham, in a simple silver frame with a heraldic S at the top, appropriate to go on the piano. Only we didn't have one. Instead, I enlarged a photo of Joan, put it on top, and showed that instead.

The Governor left, and routine was reinstated. Joan went off to Karachi to negotiate her teaching job and I went on tour alone, to finish off my pertals. In the end Joan got her job, but not with the convent—still sin could not be countenanced. So she taught eight-year-olds; she forgot her Maths and Economics, and taught English Literature and History. She wrote of learning much more herself as she prepared her lessons. In the end, it was a job. It was not really what an ICS wife should do, but that bothered her not at all. It hardly paid her expenses, but that didn't matter either, at least to me. I was well aware how boredom could send her into deep depression. It would do that to anyone; and Upper Sindh was growing hot.

It was for no luxury that British women, wives of officers serving in the heat of north-west India, went to the hills: had they stayed, and unless they had some very clear purpose, there would have been many broken marriages, far more than arose from the highly exaggerated philandering in the cool. The provinces of Northern India all had their hill stations, except Sindh, the hottest of them all. There was Karachi by the sea, but it was not very cool, and was very humid. There was Quetta in Balochistan, which was favoured by wealthy zamindars, but that was not really cool, and its officers themselves sought greater cold in Ziarat, high in the hills, near the Afghan border. We met Reggie Simpson, Police Superintendent in Upper Sindh Frontier, and he knew Ziarat; it was cheap, and we could stay in our own tents and cater for ourselves. So we would go there, and the Cargills and the Bartys would go too. Between us we could collect enough tents, we could camp together, and Reggie would supply a cook, for he would be leaving no one behind.

There was a shuffle of posts in Sindh; Clee became Commissioner, which might be useful. Or not, depending on what he had thought of my time in Thatta. In Larkana we had a new Collector, Khan Bahadur Rahim Buksh Khan, a Sindhi, and a cheerful, conversible man. 'Call me RB,' he said; so we did. He was obviously sick; we heard later that he was diabetic, and Larkana in the hot weather was a bad posting for him.

Everything around us in Larkana was peaceful, but across the river it was different: the Hur rebellion reached its height, and Lambrick left his census post to become Special Commissioner to deal with it. It was not anti-British, but the fanatical followers of the Pir Pagaro, held by them to be a direct descendant of the Prophet (PBUH) were against all government. We must all take care. There were patrols along the river to stop anyone crossing, to turn back or kill any suspected Hur. I bought a pistol from the police, but there was no ammunition for it. I put out a word, and acquired some; I did not inquire its provenance as I should have done—in fact it was entirely illegal, but at least I paid for it. The histories of the cartridges were varied and obscure: some were bright and new, some were dull, some even had verdigris on the case. I did not test them, for if one failed, why should the next one not be all right? Or not. That pistol was a great embarrassment to me. Because of the heat we were sleeping on the roof, and I would take it up and put it under the pillow: there was no point in having it if it were not ready to hand. By day it was hidden under clothes in the wardrobe. As was bound to happen, one morning I forgot it, went to fetch it, and found the bedding had been taken in. So perforce I must ask Nawab where it was. 'It's all right, Sahib, I've hidden it where you always do yourself.' A very secret place.

The police also defended us, and while we slept on the roof, a small picket kept guard at the foot of the outside stair. I protested that they were only armed with *lathis*—the Indian equivalent of the truncheon—but I was assured that it was all right. They were only recruits, for trained men could not be spared. It was assumed that if there were an attack they would scream and yell enough before they died to give me time to cock my pistol and defend the stairhead.

We all liked RB. He seemed to like me especially, and often called me to his office, seemed to need to see me without real cause. He liked to put his arm round my shoulder, he openly admired my fresh pink skin, the little golden hairs on my arm. It bothered me: there was Joan, very good to look on, and she didn't interest him at all. Joan laughed at me, but I was worried. How should I deal with such a Collector? Coming and going he liked to shake my hand, and I noticed that his middle finger was missing. Each time I squeezed his hand hard, and it hurt him. But perhaps he liked the pain, or took the pressure as a sign of affection. I don't know: he never went far. And in spite of his preference for me we all liked him. Probably it was clear that I did not like the special attention.

In Kambar there were two bungalows. The older one, in the town, had electricity, but I preferred the one on its edge, that looked away across the fields. I heard a lot of cases there. On this occasion Joan was in Larkana, getting ready to leave for Karachi. She was feeling the heat, but as I pointed out, she had electricity while I did not. But she had awkward builders and was not comforted.

All remission inspections were finished, taluka records had all been checked, and any schools and maternity homes could be inspected from Larkana. It was time to finish touring, and very conveniently Dermont asked to have Bhoop back, to get him away from the heat. I had grown very fond of him, but was glad to see him go to somewhere cooler; nor would I need a horse till touring began again. I would finish all fixed cases, and set down future ones for Larkana. And then trouble blew up. A panic-stricken shopkeeper ran in from the bazaar, where he said all the Hindus were being murdered. Well, maybe. But one didn't wait to confirm, it was better to chase a wild goose than to wait for the real thing. I collected my naik and a waiting policeman and we ran off. For the Sahib actually to run was not a usual sight, for he must always keep calm, but this was unusual.

Very evidently there was trouble: the shops were hurriedly being boarded up and all the Hindus were indoors. There was a big crowd of Muslims in the middle of the bazaar, some just shouting, others asking what it was all about. All this meant communal trouble, though I had not met it before. The Hindu said a massacre was being planned, and it seemed he had cause for panic. On the way I had collected two more sepoys, and we all shouted even more loudly than the crowd till they saw who we were and gave way. We found the cause of it all: a Hindu selling sweets, nearly dead with fright, yelling men and children pressing in on him. Things calmed down, and we found that he had sold sweets to a Muslim in a piece of paper which was said to be a leaf from the Holy Quran. If that were true there would surely be trouble. The writing was certainly Arabic, but no one there could read it. There were two necessary steps to take: I collected all the bits of paper he had used, and all those still on his stand. Then I arrested him, and told someone to ask the mullah to come. (I would never order a mullah!) We waited; everyone grew chatty, and with the little Hindu under arrest the real danger was past. There was small-talk, just to pass the time. Yes, it was very hot. Was the rice doing well? It was. As for this miserable man, was he not just ignorant? Would he have deliberately blasphemed by knowingly wrapping sweets in the Quran *Sharif* in the middle of Kambar? It was unlikely: he might just as well cut his own throat at once. The man who had sold him the paper was to blame.

The mullah came and heard all about it: better he hear from his own people than from me. He took the paper and said it was not from the Quran, and a sigh of relief went up. Even the death of a Hindu, of several Hindus, would not cleanse Kambar of shame if the Holy Quran had been blasphemed against there. I asked the mullah to take away all the paper, and let me know what it was. Before I took the shopkeeper off to gaol, Allahdino asked what should be done with the sweets? But the owner said, let them be, so the crowd cleared them up for him very quickly. The man, still badly scared, had done nothing wrong, and I told him he could go, but he asked to stay in gaol at least till dark. I advised him to leave Kambar for a day or two, but he said he would leave and never come back. The mullah came to see me at the bungalow. We had a cup of tea, and he told me that the leaves were from a book of stories; nothing holy.

So ended my first riot, that was not. Of course, it might have become serious had I not been camped nearby, and had people not been so restrained. If it happened today the matter might not be so easily resolved—but perhaps today there are no Hindus in Kambar anyway. Joan wrote from Larkana that reports had reached there of my great courage that had prevented a massacre of Hindus. I saw no reason to deny the reports, except officially; and who believes official reports?

At last Joan was called to Karachi to teach, and left all in a hurry. Our plans for Ziarat stopped. Nawab, Mistri, and Allahdino were sure there had been a fight, and that I had turned her away. They were very sympathetic, and it was several days before I discovered why they spoke with so much indignation of all the doings of womankind. This business of the position of women when one was living in a Muslim environment was very difficult. I only put things right when they saw letters coming and going every day, and I began again preparing for Ziarat. They all liked Joan, they would be sorry if she never came back, and I had the pleasure of making them feel foolish and contrite at once.

To their relief she did come back, but not till near the end of June. Tents, boxes, crockery, bedding, and books had already gone to Ziarat in the care of a patewala; we would be very late there, but would find everything ready for us. Even our mud-walled home was very hot, and would only cool a little as the humidity rose very high, which was in many ways worse.

I met RB and told him all he needed to know; most things Nur Mahomed could deal with, and I would in turn do the same for him. I cleared my office, and the staff went on leave, except for a skeleton. The bungalow was wrapped up and our own staff went on holiday—with pay—except for Nawab, who would come with us to the hills. Allahdino drove us to the station, and we set off.

We had to wait at Ruk for the Quetta Mail, the night mail through Jacobabad, across the desert, and up through the Bolan Pass. So far everything had gone as planned, but now it all fell apart.

We had two berths booked in a four-berth compartment, everywhere else on the train was full, but before we could climb in the police stopped us. The Deputy Superintendent from Sukkur was there, Faruqi, with his wife. He was going on sick leave, and his wife was in purdah, so only Joan could go in, not me. Excluding me was against railway rules, this was not Ladies Only, and anyway Faruqi was there. But there was a loyal Inspector with several sepoys, and they made their own rules. There was a great deal of heat and indignation, but we had to surrender. We saw them off with a curse: might their rabbits die. I cannot remember ever seeing a rabbit in Sindh, and it was most unlikely that Faruqi kept tame ones, but it relieved our feelings. Nawab had to wait with us, too.

So we waited two hours for the slow train. The station was completely deserted, breathlessly hot. Half a moon, a brilliant sky, and the rails stretching away, shining like silver. We found a heap of sleepers near the water tower and sat there, dozing and sweating. Water dripping from the tower made a cooling noise.

At last the train came, and we boarded a compartment where already were a young Hindu with his wife and baby boy, a refreshingly uncomplicated family group. We stayed awake to see the train cross the three great canals that watered our district, very straight, right in the path of the moon. Joan took off her blouse, to sleep in her underslip, I took off my shirt, the father already wore only shorts, but his wife conceded nothing; she sat cross-legged at the end of the berth, looking cooler than any of us. The baby slept holding all that he could drag together of his little shirt up to his nose. His father climbed to a top berth, and we all slept. The train rumbled along, stopping at every station. Shikarpur was noisy and woke me up; Jacobabad was noisy, and I hardly stirred. Joan never woke at all. I suppose we stopped at Jhatpat, and after that just rolled on and on across the *pat* to the hills.

In the dawn we began to climb, and with the train's motion the air already felt cool. We all woke up and dressed ourselves decently—the girl had always remained a model of decency. The little boy's name was Hira, he began to cry, and she told her husband to quiet him.

The child, naked save for his screwed up scrap of cotton shirt, went on bawling till his father played a game with him. For our benefit he played it in English: he darted his finger at the tiny penis and cried, 'I'll have your man! What a fine man you have! Don't let me steal your man!' And so on, and the child loved it. He laughed, he protected himself, and then he ate the little balls of rice his smiling mother fed him. Hindus are known for their relaxed views on sex, and we saw a lesson in early education, one that would have struck horror into the minds of many Christians.

The train began to labour on the grade. At Nari it stopped: this was not a station big enough for a restaurant, but there was time to buy food from the platform. There was tea, well brewed, with boiled milk and cardamoms, but we preferred our flask. There was curry on leaf plates, and fizzy drinks with a deposit to pay on the bottle. I bought hard-boiled eggs and chapatis—surely they must be safe, and if Joan didn't want hers I'm sure I ate them. There were grapes, huge bunches, very small, very sweet, very cheap: *kishmish.* They had no pips, one could fill one's mouth and suck. We had a huge bunch each, and ate them all; we have never forgotten them, eaten early in the morning, cool for the first time for weeks.

The steep rise to the Bolan Pass itself began here, and we waited while another engine, a 'banker', was coupled on behind. We set off again with these great monsters roaring ahead and behind, forcing clouds of steam and smoke straight up in the still air. There was an infectious excitement about our progress as the line twisted and curved so that sometimes we could see both engines at once. The little boy was awed, he needed no more amusement.

This railway to Quetta is a marvellous line, an extraordinary feat of engineering. There are bridges and tunnels and cuttings without number, and there were many setbacks in its building. One could see abandoned sections and tunnels at a lower level, where floods had swept the line away and it had to be rebuilt at a higher, safer level. As a result, there were gradients steeper than anywhere else in India worked without racking. There was another danger, whose solution puzzled us till it was explained. At two places we saw branch lines curving away and just ending in a sand dune. They were for the reception of runaway trains. There was a spring switch on the main line which opened of itself for the climbing train, and closed behind it. But if the engine lost adhesion and began to slide, it would be diverted into the slip line, gradually slow as the line rose, and finally bury itself in the sand dune. Dignity lost, but no harm done.

The tunnels had grand ashlar-cut stone entrances, with turrets pierced for guns; up the hillsides here and there were the ruins of little forts. A hundred years before, troops had marched this way, and the area was still not so very safely settled. The troops had marched in the rock-strewn valley bottom, in their good serge uniforms no matter how hot, wearing their heavy packs, and menaced by snipers in the heights above. We rode by in the train, cooled by the wind of our passage, and thought of those men, marching on up to Quetta before ever Quetta was built, up to the *Dusht-i-bedaulat,* the Poverty Plain. That valley was grim in its rocky chaos.

The train entered the plain, no longer poverty-stricken, and rolled on into Quetta. We were astonished to see how little of the destruction of the earthquake of 1935 still showed. But the town was a great military base, growing fast in the face of the threat from the west if the Germans rolled up Russia, as seemed likely.

Our spirits rose. We were out of the oven of Upper Sindh, the sun shone mildly, it was cool, and we were on holiday.

11

ZIARAT

There was nothing to worry about now, except for finding the bus: we had come by the slow train, so there was no time for sight-seeing.

The buses we saw in Quetta lived an even harder life than those we saw in Sindh. The practice was to buy a chassis and get a local carpenter to build a body for it. There were no rules that I knew for safety and reliability. The chassis was usually of a Chevrolet light truck. It would be worked hard in terrible conditions, inadequately serviced, and when it failed the body would be taken off and put on a new chassis. Before that happened, most of the fittings would be long gone or broken: selfstarter, screen-wiper, the engine would run without them; ashtrays, handles for doors and windows might or might not survive. A bulb horn was as good as an electric one, and didn't strain a tired battery. Usually one headlamp was kept in order in case a breakdown involved night driving.

The body of the bus was filled with wooden benches; by the driver was room for two passengers, and this was the first class, for the seats were padded. Also, there was less dust than further back. There was a ladder to the roof-rack, and sometimes people travelled there, too: I can remember only one bridge over a road in the whole of Sindh, and that was in Karachi. Nor was there any over this road in Balochistan.

Mrs Holland, daughter-in-law of Sir Henry the eye surgeon, was travelling with her child, and I, always the gentleman, offered her my first-class seat, but she didn't want it: the door didn't look safe, and on the other side the driver was too smelly. That was fine for us: we could hold the door on, and would have a better view. We didn't mind the smell of sweaty man and rank tobacco, for the sake of padded seats and no dust.

The row of pictures of gods and goddesses strung across the wind-screen told us the driver was a Hindu. (A Muslim would have had no pictures, but a string of *suras* from the Quran). He was also hooked on *beedis*, the local, very rank cigarettes, burning with a highly distinctive and to most Europeans horrible smell. Mrs Holland sat just behind him, and caught all his smoke. She asked him to stop smoking, but he pointed out that it was very tricky driving, and his beedi helped him to relax and be attentive. She persisted, insisted, and in the end threatened to get his licence cancelled if he didn't stop. With the threat he stopped. Perhaps his beedi came from a liquor shop and had been spiked with hemp, as sometimes happened, but he was no longer relaxed, he was very angry, and he drove. How he drove! He would show this memsahib what he could do. We just hoped that the lady, the cause of it all, was more scared than were we.

Petrol was short, and our driver had developed a method of economizing: the road wound steeply up and down, and as he went down one side of a valley he would switch off his engine, wrench the wheel round the corner at the bottom, and coast up the other side, finally letting his speed start his engine again. I doubted if it saved much petrol, but it certainly demanded skill, and the wrecks down below showed its danger. The road was new then; perhaps it is safer now, and anyway there is less need to save fuel.

There came the longest, steepest slope, and at the bottom, on the turn, was a great boulder at the edge of the road. He switched off, and down we went; we could only hold tight and hope. The front wheel hit the boulder, the steering wheel whipped round in the driver's hands, and we were sweeping up the other side. We breathed again, and I suggested to the driver that we had been lucky. Not at all, he said: it was all skill. If he hit the boulder just so, he would get round safely, coast further up the other side, and save more petrol. So far he had never missed. Which, obviously, was true. (As I wrote this I wondered: could this tale be true? I asked Joan, and she confirmed it. She is a truthful person.)

These mountains lacked the grandeur of the Himalayas, nor were they barren like the dry hills of Kalat. The valley sides were gashed and crumbling, and we could see crops growing in the valley bottoms, and in terraces built up with stones cleared from narrow strips of land. The terraces were watered by channels built into the sides of the valleys, fed from sources higher up. A channel would appear round a shoulder, following the contour, sometimes interrupted by a *chakki*, a water mill, grinding wheat grown in the bottom. The population was very thin, each family guarding its crops. We saw not a single village.

Ziarat, the place of pilgrimage, was a big centre by tribal standards. It was important as a retreat from what Quetta called heat, and had a customs post on the road into Afghanistan. There was a rest house, a hospital, a bazaar, and even a club. There was also the town itself, for there were permanent residents. It was on an ancient trade route, and on the route of those British troops who had fought their way up the Bolan and passed on the way to Kandahar.

The arrival of the bus was the event of the day, and there was a crowd to meet it, welcoming friends, collecting goods, or just watching. Mrs Holland was met and carried off to the rest house; we saw our driver talking with his mates, and making rude gestures behind Mrs Holland's back. We couldn't blame him; I thanked him, but we were determined not to travel with him again.

Margaret and Anne were there, and Reggie who had helped to set up the camp, so we had help with our baggage. We walked together up to our camp. It was a beautiful site; comparison with camp-sites we had known in Sindh made it the more astonishing. It was right in among the junipers, there were junipers on the hills all round, everywhere smelled of junipers, and the tents were half hidden. The air was warm and blessedly dust free; clearly it would be cold at night, so cold that two people would be glad to lie close for warmth instead of apart to avoid being bathed in sweat.

Joan and I were tired; coming from the heat of Sindh, the thin air at eight thousand feet bothered us. We just wanted to drink, to sit quiet, not even to eat. Once past that first reaction I could feel an enormous release from tension. Of course I was concerned for my sub-division, and we had made several friends in Larkana, but just then I felt I had had a bellyful of India and Indians. I expected that by the time I returned I would have vented my spleen, but now I was happy to forget it all and just revel in the company of these three girls, one of them my own dear wife, another the most beautiful woman I had ever met, and she tough and cheerful with it. For a time I was unashamedly racialist.

My week was spent exploring the *tangis*, narrow gorges made in earthquake cracks scoured out by torrents. We sat in the shade of the junipers round the camp, we bathed in the little pool at the club, we looked in a tangi where the shoulder of a mountain had cracked from top to bottom, so narrow that the light hardly penetrated. We climbed to Prospect Point and looked across to Tsut, and beyond that to Khalifat in the distance, a real mountain, 13,000 feet high. When I came again—and having seen Ziarat I would surely come again—we would climb it.

First we had had a beautiful short honeymoon, then a second one on tour in Thatta, and now this, our first real holiday together. Perhaps, looking forward to how life could grow complicated as time passed, we should enjoy it as the most beautiful we could ever have. The memory of Sindh as we had left it, and as it would be when I returned, coloured that time with roses. Joan was the chief element in it; without her the place would have been of little account. She would stay on, and for her those first impressions would become commonplace. But I hope that the first week is still for her special.

We said good-bye at the bus, and now I felt no reason to be cheerful. The bus travelled down dangerously but safely, the train rushed easily downhill, towing a banker behind it to await the next train needing help. At Nari the *kishmish* were not so sweet, and in the plain were warm before I could eat them all. I changed at Ruk in the small hours, and there heard that the sick policeman had died in Quetta. This was far worse than anyone's rabbits dying, and I had a quite irrational feeling of guilt.

At Larkana Allahdino met me with the car, all shining bright, but with news that the *mistri* must have it for a proper service.

It was perhaps the contrast that made the heat seem far, far worse. But the bungalow, freshly clean, furnished as we wanted it, was very welcoming. There was breakfast with coffee and toast with honey and white buffalo butter. Before the real heat hit me I could sit on the verandah and smoke, and daydream, and remember.

But the Chitnis arrived with a week's post and all the current files to be dealt with, followed by the Shristedar with cases and jirgas to fix. The routine of official life was reinstated. And there was Mistri, too; I was happy to see him, for I must do my own house-keeping now.

So I forgot my sour feelings after a time; I met friends again, and liked them again. It was a good job that I had to do, well worthwhile. But it was very hot indeed, and I missed Joan: I told her so, and she asked, would I spoil her holiday? I would not. I stopped complaining, and went on tour.

I met officers who always wanted to know what the
Secretariat view was; others who looked far back to the
days when a man on a horse was the swiftest way that orders
could travel, and when it took six weeks, even by the
overland route, for news from India to reach England. It
was not quite like that for us, but only the Collector had a
telephone to Karachi and to the police. Railway and PWD
had their own telegraph. I had no phone and didn't want
one. If the Collector wanted to see me he must write a note
and send a patewala; if I were on tour he must look at my
tour plan, decide that his need was great enough for him
to disrupt my work, phone the nearest police station, and
then... In fact, Rahim Baksh called me over often when I
was at home, more often than when Joan was with me. I
didn't like it, I didn't like his greetings or his farewell with
a caressing half-embrace, but there was nothing I could do
about it. Come the need, I could probably have got away
with an insubordination that Mahamadi would have
stamped on very heavily. Often now I went to the Club. I
went first when Joan was in Karachi, and liked it; when she
came home Joan did too. It was the sort of club one seldom
reads about, quite unlike the Gymkhanas of places like
Sukkur and Karachi. There must have been scores like it
all over India, with small funds and little equipment, its
membership from Collector down, not up. There never
had been a colour bar. In Larkana, when O'Flynn went to
Kashmir I was the only white man there, but this society
absorbed me easily. I knew Sindhi well enough to fit in
with a society that spoke largely in officialese anyway. There
was no objection to 'shop', indeed, it was the staple topic. I
was the authority on the war, but since we all had the same
censored news, my only advantage lay in my far better
knowledge of geography. I had an atlas which was endlessly
studied. We could even talk of Independence, its prospects,
its problems, and when would it come. I pointed out that it
would end my career, but everyone was kind and reassuring:
of course India would want to keep such fine officers as

me. There was a small question: there were many
Mukhtiarkars competent and willing to step into my shoes.
So we just laughed about it.

We hired a little house, and had a mud tennis court,
that was all; but we had real fun. We were not all officials,
but there was always the worry lest someone not official
might use his club contacts for his own ends. There were
politicians who visited us occasionally, and with them the
worry pricked both ways: he might want something from
one of us, or he might suspect that our hospitality hid
some plot to influence him. We had few non-official
members: ordinary zamindars would not have been happy
with us, and the Bhuttos were too grand. There were a few
advocates; and there was Ram Motwani.

Ram Motwani was our intellectual, and a great friend.
How he earned a living I don't know, I never met wife or
daughter, they were not so sociable as the families of
officials, though Muslim officers' families were, of course,
in purdah. Ram was a staunch Congressman, he had met
and loved the Mahatma, he owned a little garden that he
called the Gandhi-bagh, and he had a large English library,
for he loved the English, and hoped that Independence
would make no difference. A large room in his house was
his library, with stacks of books, hundreds and hundreds,
and Joan and I searched them thoroughly. Never had we
seen so many, with so few that even people short of books
to read would want. How had he collected them? Well,
here and there. Had he read them? Not yet all. There were
old government reports, collections of speeches, of Hindu
philosophical essays. Never a novel. We must take
something, for politeness: we don't remember Joan's book,
but mine were Prescott's books on the Spanish conquest of
Central America. Now, what would that gentle man, a
disciple of Gandhi, a vegetarian, confirmed non-violent,
want with those brutal conquistadors? Well, Ram Motwani
would never claim to be consistent. He showed me once
the secret of the Gandhi-bagh. He lifted a trapdoor in the

ground, and we went down some damp and mossy steps, and there at the bottom was a little room, his refuge from the heat. There was electricity, and it was cool—shockingly cool by contrast. We didn't stay long and even so the heat nearly knocked me out. The garden outside was a gloomy place, haunt of dark evergreens and bromeliads, with a dank, graveyard feeling even in that heat.

The Collector, RB, would come, my opposite, Nur Mahomed, and the Executive Engineer, Abdur Rashid Kazi, but not their families, of course. RB had a daughter, Kamalia, about twelve years old, who, he said, was keen to come, if her mother would let her. She would come when the other girls came, and come she did, but she was very shy, almost frightened, and never came again.

Kishenchand Punjabi was a barrister, and the Public Prosecutor; he had two pretty daughters, Indra and Vimla, who often came. They wore trousers and *khamisa*, so could play tennis, but not very well. Their mother never came; she was enormously fat, and when suddenly she produced a baby son we were all amazed: we had not realised she was even pregnant, there was no unusual swelling. Kishenchand was in a sense a 'wide boy', which hardly suited a barrister in Government service. His family had nothing against the Raj, and were far removed from Hindu orthodoxy. His two daughters were lively, charming, and intelligent. They spoke good English, too, so that they need not over-strain my Sindhi. Indra later married Illahi Buksh Soomro, nephew of the Prime Minister, Allah Buksh Soomro, head of one of the chief families in Sindh, who was murdered later. It was a cross-religion marriage, a true love match, very unusual. Kishenchand was determined that in some way he would make money out of the war: he decided that imported cosmetics were sure to become very scarce, and stocked up accordingly. He showed me little cupboards built into all sorts of corners of his house, full of face creams and lipsticks, toothbrushes and eye-shadows, and little tweezers for pulling unwanted hair, and depilatories for places where there was too much for tweezers (I was sorely puzzled by his word, till I read the label). This was an odd choice of market for an Upper Sindh profiteer. His targets were women, whom he could seldom meet; and outside Karachi women used little make-up, and that traditional and locally made. I doubt if he made even a small fortune. Kishenchand was wholly liberated. I once travelled up from Karachi with him, and Joan had packed for my supper some rare and beautiful ham sandwiches. I assumed that Kishen would abhor meat, so offered him one. But not he: he was happy to accept, and I lost half my supper. So I learned that prohibitions are not always absolute.

Nur Mahomed was a strange amalgam of solemn orthodox Muslim and cheerful, conversible colleague, highly intelligent, widely experienced: a valued friend. His family kept strict purdah, but he was surprisingly ready to talk about his marital life. He seldom indulged in sex, he said, because it drained his energies, which he managed to sublimate into augmenting his official activity. Did he perhaps think that I sent my wife away for that same purpose? I dared not ask. He had a son, and a daughter who was betrothed to a young man of whom he approved. As he told Joan: 'He has no habits, no habits at all.'

Then there were the Shivdasanis, and they were special. Hiranand was the Chief Officer of the District Local Board, in charge of all the roads, many of the bridges, and the maternity homes, schools, and the like leased to the government. The Board was always short of money, but he managed to remain hopeful. Once he had octroi, income from internal customs, charged at chowks on the road, so much for a bus, a car, a cart, a camel, each at its special rate; also on many goods. But not all chowkidars were honest, and all traffic that could turn off the road before the chowk did, which damaged the roads themselves. This levy had been abolished just before I arrived in Sindh. He thought this might even have saved money; and anyway the government paid funds in compensation for the nominal loss of revenue.

There were two Shivdasani daughters, both at Calcutta University: Kamala and Sunderi. They were purely Hindu, proud of their Amil roots, though they spoke very good English. Their heroes were, of course, Gandhi, Jawarhalal Nehru, and Rabindranath Tagore. Active Congress they were, and their father was embarrassed by them, but they had some respect for the English because Tagore wrote much of his poetry in our language. They were polite to me as a guest, but perfectly ready to argue with me about the evils of imperial rule.

These girls were not perhaps conventionally beautiful, with their strongly arched noses, but never did I meet any other Indian girls so vividly alive, so sure of their feeling for their country. I think that at first their parents were anxious: they should not talk like that to a British officer, but when they discovered that I read Tagore, and looked forward to independence, and knew many in the ICS who felt the same, all was well. It was sad that Partition lost such people from Pakistan.

Khan Bahadur Nabi Buksh Bhutto invited me to visit him and his brother. I need not worry lest he want a favour from me, not a Bhutto. He lived in Naundero, not in my sub-division, he was very wealthy and politically powerful, though he did not choose to exercise that power himself. But he loved dogs and horses, and he knew all the English were the same. So I went to his house, not to the part where his family lived in purdah, but to his *otak*. We sat in a large hall decorated with portraits of his forebears round the walls, trophies of their guns between. His own generator provided power for electric fans, and there were chairs and couches of high Victorian design, set exactly, round the walls. We sat dwarfed by the grandeur, and drank tea and ate little cakes. The Khan Bahadur compromised his orthodoxy by offering whisky—all the English liked whisky—but I assured him that I surely did not, that hot tea was the most acceptable drink on this hot afternoon. We talked of the heat, the weather, of the Governor's visit.

When it was cooler we went to see his kennels and stables, and they were just as they should have been for such a man: well-built, cool and airy. His dogs were very happy to see us, and I was all for petting them, but he himself would not touch them: he loved them, but they were unclean. It was not their fault, he regretted it, but it was so. He had spaniels for his shoots, and Afghan hounds for coursing hares. The hounds were beautiful, with their long legs and narrow heads. They had long hair, and it was silky, but not like the silken fleeces of their relatives in English shows: those were pretty dandies, whereas his were working hounds.

He had three polo ponies, but little scope for using them, and riding horses, some of which looked as if they might race. I denied any expertise in polo or racing. Did he race them? Only in private races, for a wager. He would never send them to Karachi or Lahore, where there were proper tracks, and most of the people were crooks. He asked, would I like to borrow one? This was an idea that I had hoped to plant myself, and here it was, full-grown, from him. (He had probably heard that I had sent Bhoop away). I said, I could not just borrow, but could I not...perhaps...hire? No, but I could pay the syce and the horse's keep, and look after them well.

So we left it, but I made it clear that I must make a suitable gift at some time.

Joan wrote from Ziarat that Peter Cargill jeered at me for camping in the hot weather, which annoyed her but didn't bother me. It was hot, but more interesting than staying in a bungalow which was not much cooler. Chiefly I heard cases, which was much easier for the parties and I could drive out in the early morning and back as the evening cooled. If I had to stay overnight it was more difficult, but there was always the bistra. The Mukhtiarkar would know the best 'hotel', and Naik would buy food there for us, or perhaps I would eat with him. I made myself unpopular because I would not take a long midday siesta, which made me wake feeling stupid; I always wanted to finish quickly. I used the bus to get to Kambar, the train to Shahdadkot, and then for the first time saw the young rice, bright green, glittering where the water shone through. This was truly the Sindh rice bowl, and it stretched to the horizon, though not a continuous carpet, because the little bunds were everywhere, dividing the fields into small patches for sharing the water evenly. Once the rice was planted there was little work to do, so a hari would camp on his land, and his wife or a child would bring food. The water supply itself must be protected: battles over water brought many cases to my court. If a case was dragging on, if there was no letter from Joan, and if it was very hot, I could be brusque. A visitor when I was in such a mood might be warned by Allahdino to be very careful. I once heard him: 'The weather is very hot, and the Sahib is not used to it. The witnesses have been very stupid, and he is in a bad temper. It would be better to come on another day.' I wrote to Joan of such a day:

> God, I get annoyed with people who talk of their own virtues and abilities and achievements... Today came a zamindar who wants to be a Khan Sahib. I asked him to think of any special service he had done, apart from taking too much water so that small khatedars lost their crops. If I don't look out I shall become unpopular because of my hatred of their greed and ignorance, their pride and servility... men who think it undignified to be educated or to work with their hands.

This was after only two and a half years in Sindh, eighteen months with a charge of my own. How could I be so pompous? So arrogant as to try so soon to apply my own standards of a sort of puritanical imperialism to a society of which I understood so little? My excuses were not really valid: it was hot, I had had a trying day, I was lonely for my love, but it was not his fault. And at least he had not offered favours, he had come straight out with his request.

I met hundreds like him, and generally was polite. But I could not love them. There were some like the Chandios, some like the Bhuttos, who were civilized in their own culture. But already I was blaming them all for the dead hand on agriculture of the crop-sharing tenancy system, a judgement that experience was confirming. Agriculture was becoming my special interest, and always this system stood in my way. But government was averse from stirring up trouble in wartime, and afterwards the Government would be India's anyway. Moreover, the system was the basis of political power in Sindh. I had chosen a truly formidable target. The haris themselves did not question the justice of their servitude. They were used to it; they trusted what they were used to and feared what change might bring. They worked, and, *Inshallah*, there would be a good harvest, and their share would be enough to pay off the *bania* and leave enough for their families.

To Mirokhan I could go by bus, but to Warah there was no bus, and I must drive. Sometimes I would take a pleader with me, but he must understand that if he said a word about the case I would at once turn him out of the car to walk the rest of the way.

Kambar also had its Club, but it had no tennis court, not even a club room. The members used an empty room in the Mukhtiarkar's Kutchery, so naturally he was President.

I was a guest, not a member; I was invited for a particular purpose: I must be there; I was instructed that I only need take a towel. There was to be a picnic, but nothing like an English picnic, with which I associated sand in the sandwiches. The object was kept secret from me; all that was needed was tea and sugar and a *maund*, perhaps two maunds, of mangoes from the bazaar. A bus was booked— and finding one in good order took some time—and off we went, along the Ghaibi Dero road to Gharhi Khair Mahomed where it crossed the Warah Branch canal; and there we stopped at the PWD bungalow.

We were in holiday mood, so it must have been Saturday or Sunday, and my presence seemed to bother no one, which more than anything made my day. We could use the bungalow, because we had the Assistant Engineer with us, and first of all made tea: no milk, plenty of sugar, one cup each. More than one was bad for the health. That was strange: considering the bulk of some of our members, and our intention to eat mangoes all day, it was difficult to see why tea should be picked on as specially dangerous.

The engineer borrowed the tin tub from the bungalow, and it was launched in the canal, half filled with mangoes; we all stripped to our underpants. Some slid in, some jumped in, some, including me, essayed to dive. The largest among us were keenest to jump, and there were some almighty splashes. There was no need to swim, the gentle current carried the tub along, and we stayed near it. A knife was tied to the tub to cut a mango so that it could be torn open. We milled around, solemn men acting like children, joking and splashing. (I must play my part, but again, *Inshallah*, I must not overplay it.) We gently drifted along, sucking mangoes, discarding skins and stones into the water. (Would there some day be a grove of mangoes at the tail of the canal?) Ali Ahmed Yusifani, the Mukhtiarkar, remarked that this was far the best way to eat a mango: no messy face or hands, no annoyance at stains on one's shirt or the table-cloth, it all came off in the water. When the tub was empty we all climbed out, ran with it to our starting point, refilled it, and jumped in again. But this time I didn't either dive or jump. The sun was very hot, so I put on my topi and slid in, which delighted everyone; it was a comical sight. Someone suggested that he should wear his, but I pointed out that they all had beautiful thick black hair, far better protection than my thin fair thatch. That began a somewhat unscientific discussion: if a man with black hair wore a topi too long, would his hair become fair like mine? If I discarded mine, would my hair turn black? I suggested that well before that I would be dead of sunstroke. Anyway, there were enough experts among us who knew about genetic inheritance to sort it all out. If my wife had dark hair—but it was known she hadn't. If one of them married a girl with fair hair...I told them the limerick about Starkey's affair. That was certainly appreciated, but then Ali Ahmed felt it was getting a little too personal, he ducked the speaker, and we all went back to eating mangoes.

That trip finished the mangoes. We ran about, we lay in the sun, dried enough to get dressed. It was odd how these men, all alone, were very modest about dressing, and about going into the jungle 'of necessity', as they put it. Young Englishmen, with no women about, would probably have been mother-naked. We lay in the shade, chatted or slept, smoked, and had a final cup of tea: a second after so much exercise was all right; but again I was not allowed another, in my own interest. Then we went home. A very splendid picnic it was. No sand in the sandwiches, indeed, no sandwiches, no mess, the canal cleaned all; no bother of any kind. We drove back to Kambar and I said I was hungry; could we not buy *samosas* and *pakoras* and *kababs* in the bazaar and all go to the bungalow, where I had lemon squash and even a little whisky for those who liked it? That was considered a very clever thought. (There is a certain advantage in not having to report home to one's wife). We sat on the verandah, we ate and drank, we were all pleasantly tired. Members drifted away in ones and twos; Ali Ahmed was, of course, last, and thanked me with emotion. I pointed out that he and his friends had paid me a compliment I would never forget. And I never have. I am sure the club had picnicked before, and did afterwards many times. It was just that with me there it was different, and because my presence did not spoil it, it was special.

Letters came from home. My sister finished her first year at Girton, and reported that they remembered Joan. Joan's sister finished a year at Lady Margaret Hall, and was a heroine for pulling someone from the river. My brother

was called up in the artillery; my Mother was full with
problems of billeting and evacuees at the same time; my
Father was running three shifts in the mill, on orders from
the Ministry of Food to supply flour for a mill that had
been bombed out. Joan's Mother and Father were in
London running a big chapel, and all that involved in
wartime. Now that Russia was in the war the bombing was
much less.

The war had little effect on Sindh, but we were told that
there would be a War Week in Larkana in August, and we
should procure as many recruits as possible for the army by
then. Sindhis were not generally a warlike people, so
volunteers were not easily available. (Balochis were
different, but equally impatient of discipline.) However, we
had many good businessmen, and a specialized trade soon
grew up. An agent would explain to a zamindar that
Government would grant a gun licence to a man who
produced recruits for the army. This was not strictly true: a
man who produced recruits would be remembered, there
was no promise. But wishful thinking and a clever salesman
even drew up a tariff: thirty men for a shotgun licence, fifty
for a rifle, a hundred for a pistol. We in the Districts
disliked even the suspicion of it. The agent would collect a
gang of men whom he fed and kept, promising a reward
for any 'booked' by a zamindar. We tied the scheme in as
well as we could: the prospective licence-holder must be a
man of good repute, with no criminal convictions, and his
recruits must be finally accepted, at least for a labour
battalion.We hoped to prevent a racket becoming a scandal.

Perhaps to avoid gloomy boredom, I became a
conscientious officer. There was satisfaction in keeping
work up-to-date. This was the time of year when
Government wanted reports on everything: crop prospects;
state and usage of maternity homes, much in need of
equipment; school numbers by age, sex, and community:
older boys mostly Hindu, some girls, but none Muslim (but
a note: almost all the Muslim boys went to the *madressah*, to

learn the Quran). The state of the roads, of liquor shops, of bazaars. Fire precautions (probably only when a fire in a bazaar had been reported in the Press). Cholera precautions: check availability of inoculum—the Civil Hospital had plenty; all staff must be certified as inoculated. There was no cholera, but there surely would be, and indeed there was. For that, instructions were routine: all sales of green vegetables and fruit were stopped; people must not move from the cholera zone to others; people were discouraged from entering it. Perhaps there was no power for this, but no one wanted to harbour anyone from the area. There was a saying: 'Hindus starve, Muslims have only mutton and boils.' Joan never had a cholera injection, for it was not a cold weather danger.

The hot weather ground slowly on; just occasionally things of note happened. Trying cases in Kambar, one defendant, a 'right villain', absconded from the court itself, and the magistrate himself set off with two policemen to catch him. We searched all around, but lost him. No matter: I confiscated all his property, so his family was sure to turn him in. I fixed more cases for Shahdadkot, travelling there by train, and seeing the rice coming on, high enough to hide the little bunds, looking more and more like a green lake with a small breeze blowing over it. There I met Gobindram Advani, from the Government of India, researching into the habits of locusts. I had never seen a locust, but he assured me I would. He had found grape-fruit in the bungalow garden, and wanted the Sindh Government to grow them commercially; he told me of others in the garden at Dostali.

A certain Musmat Darya Khatun came to my office for a certificate to help her enter the brothel at Dadu, to urge no one to listen to false aspersions on her character. Another lady asked me for a lift to Shahdadkot. Her motive was not very clear, but when she heard that I was going by train with Allahdino and my Shristedar, her request died away. One must not make jokes of others' problems.

In that hot weather, domestic arrangements were inevitably bisected. Nawab stayed in Ziarat with Joan, and I kept Mistri. I had a patewala who had acted as bearer for Sahibs before, so Khudu took the job on. He could lay the table for one, could wash up very slowly and thoroughly, and I needed no more, save that he should make tea without cardamoms. Sometimes there was unusual noise from the pantry, as Mistri and Khudu argued about how a dish should be presented. Khudu came on my short tours anyway, and somehow food appeared, if only from the bazaar. There they made good curries; add pulau rice, and who could ask for better?

We had a garden patch, but English growing seasons were no guide for Upper Sindh. Brassicas and roots like carrots would not stand the heat. We were too late getting our bungalow for the first growing season, but tomatoes and aubergines grew well, though the mali trained them like melons; however, it was too hot for slugs and similar vermin, so they took no harm. Why did I not grow melons? Perhaps it was too easy; more likely, they were too cheap. The same was true of onions. In memory, in that hot weather I had no other vegetable but onions, and them every day, till Joan went to Quetta. I did not waste space in so small a plot. We grew some flowers: cannas, inevitably, already there; from seed came marigolds, once introduced, ever arriving, petunias, and zinnias; never have I grown zinnias like those we grew in Larkana.

One pleasant thing about gardening in Sindh was that a weed-choked patch need only be left dry for a week or two, and the weeds died. But Hubba's equipment exasperated me. If, as Kipling says (always Kipling), 'Half a proper gardener's work is done upon his knees,' then Hubba was excellent. For a hoe he had a spud on a very short handle, for a spade he had a *khudr*, a sort of entrenching tool. I found a dutch hoe that I put on a longer handle, but a spade would have been useless to him: he worked with bare feet. We made compost, but he only put stuff on it by

handfuls. More exasperation: I made a wheelbarrow; I
bought wood, cut to shape, from a mistri, who cut out a
solid wheel. It was a very heavy barrow, and Hubba didn't
like it much. I expect that when I was not around he still
used his hands. I was very proud of that barrow: I have a
picture of it. The wood is unplaned, it is not elegant, but
acacia wood is long-lasting, so very likely it is still there. I
used to claim that it was the first, and very likely the only
wheelbarrow in Sindh. (I built a foot-powered loom, too;
this followed us round, dismantled, until I gave it to the
High School in Jacobabad in return for their spinning some
wool. It was operable; I don't know if it was ever used.)

We grew English vegetables in the cold weather:
cauliflowers, parsnips, carrots, beet, and spinach. For them
I made a drill, just like my father had: a long handle with a
cross-piece on which were set wooden blades, eight inches
apart on one side of it, a foot apart on the other. For
things like parsnips and beet Hubba was to drill both ways,
and sow seed at the intersections. But he misunderstood,
and when the seed came up, he had sowed full rows in
both directions, a sad waste of seed. I didn't waste precious
space on onions and potatoes. While Joan was in Quetta
she sent me baskets of fruit and vegetables, so I did very
well till my own brinjals and tomatoes were ready.
Otherwise my fruit was dried apricots, also from Quetta,
and very good, though after a time they palled. Sindhi
mangoes were all very well for a picnic, but were of poor
quality.

Visits to the Club, and above all writing to Joan, kept me
from moping. I kept my table clear, dealt with cases as they
came due, and was a conscientious officer. I went on with
my summer camps. Perhaps Peter Cargill would find how
much better they were than sitting in an empty bungalow.
If one liked drinking alone it was another matter, but
neither of us could afford it, anyway.

In Kambar I abandoned the little bungalow, not because
I didn't like the squeak of the punkah, but because I

wouldn't have my *bijli butty* for a single night, and needed
the electricity of the circuit house. I tried mostly jirgas
there and at Shahdadkot, and had a whole new judicial
code to learn. Shahdadkot had electricity, too, which meant
fans as well as lights. And it was there that my absconder
surrendered. His family made him, lest I really hold his
property. In fact, I had no power to do so, but he wasn't
quite sure. This villain, this badmash, claimed to have been
tried by jirga under the Frontier Regulations; but they were
for Balochis, and his name was Shah Nawaz Junejo, and
Junejo is a Sindhi clan. Moreover, the charge was of cattle
theft, a crime not dealt with by jirga. He was reputedly a
habitual cattle thief, and the police had asked that he be
required to provide sureties for his good behaviour.

Chapter VIII of the Criminal Procedure Code was a
valuable provision of our legal system; and very dangerous,
too. A man who was unpopular, or had incurred the wrath
of a powerful zamindar might well be innocent of any
crime, but under s. 117 evidence of general repute was
admissible, and such evidence might easily be procured:
he would have to produce sureties for his good behaviour
who his enemy could ensure would not appear. He would
go to gaol till sureties appeared, which meant till his enemy
let them. There were court circulars about the dangers to
justice involved, about the great care needed by the court.

But this was a clear case; only one or two witnesses came
to defend Shah Nawaz, and they proven relatives, whereas
his whole village was prepared to testify against him. I had
only the problem of setting the level of security. It must
not be so high as to appear oppressive, nor so low that he
could at once produce sureties. Perhaps I set it about right.
He went to gaol, and in due course I reduced the level of
security so that he could find sureties, and was released. To
be good thereafter, one hoped.

Looked at legalistically, Chapter VIII was, of course, very
oppressive, a great *zulum*. But it was highly valued by district
officers, and, indeed, by most law-abiding people, who were

more concerned with good order than with the niceties of the law. Its threat hung over any attempt to set up a protection racket, limited the activities of patharidars, and gave people a feeling of community strength. If subsequent information showed that a conviction was unsound, the man could be released with minimum security, his reputation not seriously damaged, for he had not, after all, been convicted of any offence. In this country, in these sophisticated days, there would be claims of wrongful arrest and detention, but I never heard of that happening in Sindh.

Oddly, Joan became involved in the case. In Quetta she met Tony Drake, Assistant Political Agent in Balochistan, and he wanted Junejo for some offence. He asked Joan to ask me to turn him over. Just like that: using the wife of the Assistant Collector to avoid all the red tape. But we in British India always suspected the Politicals, even though many of them were from the ICS. When they changed allegiance they were apt to cut corners, or worse. They were apt to cut great swathes through the rule of law if it suited them.

Junejo was a crook, but he was a Sindhi crook, and Drake could not have him till he had served his time in Sindh, however long that might take, and even then I would want a proper extradition order, from a judge. So no more was heard of it. If a wife could not persuade her husband to do a friendly act, in the interests of good order, to help a colleague, then, well...so be it. Joan had not at all liked being used in such a way.

Our Chevrolet had lost much of its elegance during its hard life. Its petrol use was very heavy, so when I could I travelled by rail or bus. The buses were very unreliable, they were hot and horribly dusty. As in Balochistan, they had lost most of their inessential trimmings, but their faults were sometimes far more serious. Seldom was there a mirror, to show the driver if there was anyone behind him, but perhaps this didn't matter, there being such a fog of dust behind. In a car, it was useless to overtake through this fog; one had to keep well back, and hope that sometime the bus would stop for passengers. Extraordinary measures could be taken to keep the bus running. Often the self-starter was broken; there was a starter handle, but it needed a strong man to use it; and one driver had broken his arm using it. Once I travelled in one whose driver had damaged his left leg, but he carried a boy who squatted down by me, ready to work the clutch pedal on orders. A mistake was not very serious, the engine would stall, and we would stop with a jolt.

A more extreme improvisation made me anxious. The driver's mate squatted on the wing, with the engine hood off. I asked the driver his purpose, and he explained that the lock-nut on the petrol feed pipe had lost its thread, so his mate had to hold the joint tightly together. Now, those chassis had the petrol tanks in front, feeding the engine by gravity. It is true that the driver drove very carefully, but there was a strong smell of petrol, and if that hand slipped petrol would pour out onto the hot engine. In fact, we arrived safely, but I had checked that the door would not jam, and for the whole way was ready to jump out, regardless.

The Chev was badly in need of an overhaul. It had been driven over horribly rutted and dusty roads for twenty months, and though it had been routinely serviced, this time the mistri came to me with a long list of parts that needed renewing. Its elegance was badly faded, but nothing could be done about that. I went on one last journey and considered things. I struggled home at about twelve miles an hour, which was poor even on a bad road; average petrol consumption was 10 miles per gallon and I seemed to have used a gallon of oil in the last hundred miles, most of it burned off in smoke. There were very many Chevrolets in Sindh, he could get all the parts now, but they would soon dry up, with nothing new coming in. There was the touring season to come, so I told the mistri to go ahead. It was

rumoured that petrol would be rationed, and I didn't want
a hard-drinking car. Last of all the mistri heaved the car up
on its side; he showed me two gaping cracks in the frame.
As he said, one good bump, and the engine would have
fallen to the ground. Those mended, Allahdino and his
mates polished her as for a wedding. But a Minister was
coming, he would want a car, so I sent mine back for
further repair. Mistri looked, and as soon as the Minister
had left he returned her: he could find no other fault.

The rumours of petrol rationing were true. I received a
highly confidential order through the Collector to set up a
rationing system. Just like that. I was to seal all retailing
tanks, issue coupons to priority users, and so on. We all
knew it was coming, so we all had what reserves we could
store: I had four two-gallon cans, kept on the back
verandah, as the coolest place not actually indoors. I found
all the big tanks; of course they were empty, but I found
them all; there was no point in sealing them. We had
nothing so sophisticated as a pump. Next came a large and
precious package of coupons, followed by a Rationing
Officer, but with no rules. And finally the Instructions. The
Collector called a conference, and we heard what the
Rationing Officer would do. (And where did they dig him
out from? asked Nur Mahomed.) Sub-divisional officers
were not, thank heaven, to administer the scheme. One
trade profited by the petrol shortage. An age that Sindh
had generally missed was revived, and bicycle sales and
repair shops boomed. The bicycle was not suited to the soft
roads of the *mofussil*, and traditional male dress, with hugely
baggy trousers, was not suited to the bicycle. So the model
sold was the ladies' pattern, with a dress guard, though of
women only Joan had a cycle in Larkana; she tried to hire
one in Ziarat, and in Karachi she cycled everywhere, but
that was unusual; it made her well-known, but she didn't
care: there was no better way for short distances, couldn't
everyone see that?

After I 'went down the hill', Joan's letters began again. She wrote of walks she would show me when I came; of people we might, or might not, meet. She was trying to teach geometry to two Sikh girls; was offered a puppy, but if that were to be her reward she would refuse: she wanted money, not gifts; we were always chronically short of money. The other girls had puppies, the camp was organized round them. Perhaps it was this that lit a maternal fuse in them all. They were all three about twenty-five, high time for a woman to start a family.

Babies at this time? It was crazy; moreover, they had not consulted their husbands. All Europe, from the North Cape to Gibraltar, and round through the Mediterranean, was fighting Britain. Ships were being sunk every day, there were bombs raining down on our families every night, and supplies were being bought with the last of Britain's gold. There was Russia but the Germans were smashing a way through to Moscow, and beyond that might well drive through to the Middle East, to the oilfields, and finally to us in India. That was all reason enough not to encumber themselves with babies, but there was no security for their husbands' jobs, either. Yet they had decided that it was high time to begin. (Perhaps it was the altitude, as well as the puppies?) They had even decided to make a race of it, with handicaps to account for the early or late availability of the essential husband. I still think it was crazy, and the fact that it all worked out well does not change my mind. (Anne Barty dropped out of the race, but nonetheless her family began at about the same time).

Joan went down to Quetta and stayed with Jean Lowe, whom we had met at that Christmas shoot. She lived in Quetta when she was in from her tours as Inspector of Schools in British Balochistan. She travelled about in tribal areas, sometimes with an escort from a Frontier Militia if one happened to be going her way, sometimes alone, by car, by bus, or on horseback. She travelled the wild roads between such places as Harnai, Fort Sandeman, and Sibi, in areas where the militias wanted no man to travel alone, still less a white woman. She would come in to rest at Jacobabad or Quetta; all the tribes knew her, no one harmed her.

Joan stayed with her in Quetta, ostensibly to buy stores, but also to escape from tensions in the camp. Three grass widows alone, with the husband of one or another of them arriving in his turn, made for a society certain to suffer bouts of friction. And she could send me fresh fruit and vegetables, and little presents of nuts. She stayed a week, so my letters went astray. I was sweaty hot, with prickly heat, with verbose witnesses, and judgements to be written on cases being decided on the balance of reasonable doubt, or not, which might as well have been settled by the toss of a coin. And there was my wife, pleasuring herself with all the delights of Quetta.

It wasn't like that at all. Certainly she had stores to collect, but she was deliberately leaving an atmosphere that threatened to damage their group; with her away, the others could blame everything on her, and disparage me, with no harm done. (So she wrote; but why should they disparage me?) She stayed on to nurse Jean Lowe, who had come in with an ulcerated leg. Those ulcers, tropical sores, Sindh sores—the name depended on where they struck— were debilitating, crippling, and very difficult to cure. Joan applied fomentations, shopped, and ran the house until she had persuaded the cook that there was nothing unclean about the fomentations and shown him how he should apply them.

Alone, reading about Joan in Ziarat and Quetta, I pondered on our marriage. It was going on well. Quarrels in Ziarat, a flock of officers in Quetta, could not damage it. Only if there was no proper work for Joan was there cause for worry, and dealing with that must await the cold weather, though this idea of a family might change everything. But she was quite different from the girl who had reached India less than two years before. She was now perfectly capable of running a house in up-country Sindh, of handling building contractors who had never met a tough woman who knew what she wanted. She was an experienced teacher, and surely the time would come when a school wanted her. I must have changed, too, and she was largely responsible for that. I decided that we were together well-integrated in our life; and there was no one to dispute it with me.

But Joan was much concerned with our future postings. For her, a post in Karachi would make teaching a far better prospect than it was up-country. For me, there was Government House or the Secretariat, but by then I think we had already disqualified ourselves for GH: an ICS wife who openly sought paid work, paid, moreover, a proper rate of pay, and an officer who openly expressed belief in the coming of independence were hardly suitable. Although there could be no official objection to my opinion—it was, after all, the statutory goal—there were many who did not like to hear an ICS officer talk about it. So with no hard feelings at all, we felt that a post with the Governor was not for us, nor, from what we knew, did we want one. We just needed a post for Joan, for her own contentment.

As the humidity and heat grew less, the rice became a yellowing ocean, and by September I didn't want to leave Larkana. We hardly knew our own home yet, and I certainly wanted to know more about my District. I hoped that Joan wouldn't want to leave, either.

12

MOUNT KHALIFAT

My desk was clear, cases were fixed for two weeks ahead, our staff was paid, and I had collected my petrol coupons, lest it be argued that I wasn't using the car, so didn't need them. Allahdino drove me to the station. With a very clear conscience I boarded the train. It left very late at night, the same train we had taken when we went up together, which from Larkana went straight through to Quetta. I wanted to go through the Pass by daylight, as before. I dozed, but was fully awake when we crossed those three grand canals. But the train ran on as if for Sukkur, and another passenger explained: it could not make a right-angled turn at Ruk, but ran down a spur line to reverse back and join the line from Sukkur...and I had never known this, on a line I supposed I knew well. A fresh engine took us on, leaving the first one behind, for it was at the wrong end of the train.

I slept; I woke as before at Nari, cool, with the sun rising over the low hills, and *kishmish* still for sale. As before I bought a *chapati* and two hard-boiled eggs; this time I had brought a twist of salt with me; no flask, but I had brought a mug for my station tea, cardamoms and all. We picked up our banker and with the two engines roared up the grades. I could almost feel the vitality returning that I had lost in those hot months in the plain as we rolled into Quetta.

There was no Mrs Holland on the bus, no beedis, and a cautious driver who needed no help from the big boulder. It was still there, stained by rubber from tyres that had hit it. I could watch the country pass, so steep, barren on the hillside, green in the valley bottoms. But as the road wound on the junipers appeared, and we were in what was called the juniper forest, though every tree must have its own space, the ground was so rocky, the rain so scarce.

As we climbed out of Quetta I realized where I was: a little cooling breeze blew, refreshing here. In Larkana we often had a breeze, but it was dust-laden, like a draught from a furnace; it dried the sweat on you, it dried your mouth and cracked your lips, it brought the plague of prickly heat, people were irritable and short-tempered, ready to quarrel and fight for a nothing. But here the breeze greeted one like a blessing, it stroked the skin like velvet, and it presaged real cold when the sun went down.

When the whole population turned out to greet the bus there was no very great crowd. Joan was there waiting, looking wonderful, brown, unworried, her hair bleached by a friendly sun, altogether my own dear wife. We embraced heartily, to everyone's satisfaction. Not often did I have the chance to overcome Joan's shy avoidance of any public display of affection. My *saman* and my box of things I had to bring were unloaded, and Nawab found someone to carry them up to the camp.

Then we went to the little club-house where Anne and Margaret were waiting. They looked wonderful, too. Everything was wonderful. There was nothing to look forward to but two weeks of beautiful days and nights.

We talked; as with other husbands, the newly-come husband's wishes were paramount. I wanted to walk through the Great Tangi, to climb Tsut and Khalifat, and, since they had already decided the principle, see what could be done about this baby. But there was no hurry, I had only just arrived, and there was all the time in the world.

Khalifat is 13,000 feet high. They hadn't climbed it yet, and I certainly wouldn't be fit for a few days. Instead we walked up the near tangi, far enough from the camp to be really alone, and there we, as it were, caught up with each other, confirmed that the loving letters were not just words.

Joan had very clear ideas about the baby. First, she was now an enthusiast: all the pros and cons had been argued through and rationalized. It was the same with Margaret, so it looked as if it really was to be a competition. There I was, so we would have a slight advantage, for Peter wasn't due till I left. Anne was still not quite convinced, and Dermont had been and gone, with no decision, so she had handicapped herself. It all seemed to me, the stuffy civilian from the plains, unseemly, frivolous. But who would not be light-hearted in such a beautiful place?

First supper, and then there were things to decide. Did we agree that we want a boy? At least for a start? Yes, we did, though the civil servant required a caveat, that a girl would do just as well, and the chances were even, anyway. Not so, said Joan. She had read van der Veldt's book, which indicated steps one might take to decide the sex of the child; and Mrs Bedi's old mother had very specific instructions, culled from Sikh philosophy. (Good heavens, had these three girls been discussing such private matters with the whole of Ziarat? Old Mrs Bedi was the biggest gossip north of the Bolan!)

I didn't much like the pseudo-science, but was willing to go ahead with it. Van der Veldt and his even chance sounded much better. We would follow the Sikh regime without much faith in it, and anyway we would be far away, in space and time, before we knew whether Mrs Bedi's recipe worked; even then we would only know certainly if it didn't.

Reggie Simpson came to stay: he had a right, some of the tents were his, and it was all his idea. But it seemed that his presence had led to an idea that this was a Sindh camp, that anyone from Sindh could come. Bernard Budd, whom we all knew, who was on transfer as Deputy Commissioner, Upper Sindh Frontier, arrived. He was thinking of marrying, and we thought perhaps he was briefing himself. He had a young Christian called Robert as his bearer, and wouldn't allow him to go with the others to the bazaar; poor Robert, there was little scope for wickedness in Ziarat's tiny bazaar. We all liked Bernard, and Reggie was going to the same District as Police Superintendent, but they made it clear that Bernard was a guest. Later came David Halford, far senior, and they charged him board and lodging, which displeased him but made it clear that the camp was not for everyone.

We set about preparing for our expedition for the conquest of Khalifat. This was not just a day's walk. We would have to camp, we would have climbing, of a sort, and we would need porterage. It was not quite so lavish as a Himalayan expedition, however. We needed a man to help carry enough for an evening meal and some bedding, so that we could spend a night at the foot of the mountain; in the morning he would carry back to camp everything we would not need to reach the top, come back down, and return to the tents by the evening. Reggie assured us that we would not need ropes, which was a relief

So we ate a meal, together with our porter, at the very foot of the mountain, and all slept happily there. It was cold, but fine to feel that we five were quite alone.

I had seen the mountain before from Prospect Point: a rock buttress, sheer on three sides, bare rock, with precipices too steep for anything to grow. From its top one looked down on a valley on each side very far below, green in the bottom, watered by a perennial stream, with scattered junipers growing on the flanks. It was a wild and beautiful land, seeming to be wholly deserted, very lonely. Our guide told us that in winter the stream froze up, and there was deep snow everywhere except on the tops, where the wind blew it away. Khalifat was ahead of us, with its double peak, but we could see no sign of precipices, nor of deep gorges.

There was nothing that an alpinist would call climbing; just scrambling.

At first light we made tea and then set off. We wore no special clothing, we were shod as we would be for tramping the fields in Sindh. We carried nothing but my precious camera. Three went ahead, I was not yet very fit, so could be excused for trailing, and of course Joan stayed with me. My thighs had ached even after the little walk up from the bus, more after the short walks since, but now, walking up steeply, I remembered how valuable was the hair of the dog, and I walked off the stiffness. On Khalifat the thin air was more troublesome than unused muscles, but I never doubted that I would make it to the top. Given time.

Just below the top, where we had to creep on a narrow ledge round a big buttress, Joan and I rested. Then we crossed a saddle in the mountain, all rough ground and spikes of dry plants, as if unchanged since the beginning of time, and there, with the others out of sight, and very near the top, Joan found a little crevice, very private, very suitable for the need of my begetting a boy child. We made the attempt, successfully we hoped, and then went on to find the others.

We stood in a group on the very top, and there were only mountains to be seen, ridge beyond ridge, till the haze hid them. To the west and north was Afghanistan, to the south-west was Quetta, out of sight, hidden because its plain, so high from Sindh, was too low to be seen from here, and to the south, beyond all the hills, was the burning plain of Sindh. To the east the mountains, though hidden in the haze, rose higher and higher, till a long way away, beyond the Hindu Kush, beyond the Karakorams, they joined the true high Himalaya. We all contemplated it, we thought of it, we wondered. None of us had ever been so high before; Joan and I at least would never be so high again.

Then we set off down, very careful at first, growing less breathless as we descended, and reached the foot of the mountain. We collected our gear and walked home. We were all quiet, perhaps just tired, perhaps still subdued by the memory of that stupendous view. For Joan and me there was a particular, private reason.

My holiday so far had been anything but restful. But first the journey, then this climb, and being securely with Joan, had smoothed away all tensions. Now we swam, we walked, we swam again, in the little pool, or in a wild pool in a tangi, created by a rock fall that made a waterfall for us to play in. We behaved very much like children.

There was time to read, and I must read James Branch Cabell. Particularly, I read *Jurgen*, and I think it was to point a moral. It is like a story from the *Decameron*, and I discovered why when I reached the end of the story: Cabell would have nothing to do with lovers who lived happily ever after; his heroine found a lover who 'made her a good husband as husbands go'. Joan introduced me to the children who so charmed her, and the Sikh girls who were so slow, until suddenly they got the hang of geometry. There were days when we did nothing but read and play the gramophone. There were people I should meet, 'politicals' mostly. It was interesting to hear their ideas about us of settled Sindh. But there remained our other ambition: to explore and walk through the Great Tangi.

The Kirthar Range was—is—unstable. 'Geological times' were now. The earth moved. It moved violently in 1934 and destroyed Quetta, and all round us in Ziarat were signs that movement was still going on. There were old tangis whose sides had all broken down; newer ones still sharp-edged. The Great Tangi was different. A whole mountain, albeit a small one, had split and one half had slipped, was said to be slipping still, down towards the valley bottom. Not, we were told, so quickly as to be noticeable. The gap was fifteen or twenty feet wide, and no one had ever been through. Well, maybe.

We had been into the lower end, to a rock fall that we thought we could climb down, but not up—even after Khalifat we were not ambitious climbers. So we talked with local people, walked over the top, and found the beginning of the tangi. It was so wide that there was light all the way in. Deeper, the walls rose sheer above us, to a greater and greater height, and the light grew dim. But the little stream hurried on, so there must be a way through; there were small rock falls, but so far nothing to worry us. Then there came a very big fall, it fell forty or fifty feet, but the stream found a way through.

We went over, very tentatively, and began to climb down, till we came to a steep rock face; we could slide down, and there was a convenient shelf at the bottom, but we thought we had better stop and think. We would never be able to climb up again. If further along there should be another dam, one we could not climb down... We had no wish to cause panic, to need a search party. So we turned back. Perhaps next year, with a rope, we would do it. (But perhaps not: there might be a little baby by then.) It was a sad defeat.

So we met friends for the last time. Before we left I found that preparations to have a baby had gone further than I had thought. It was by no means a decision based on simple emotion, on a sudden upsurge of maternal instinct, coupled with the excitement of a race. Anne, in fact, pulled out of the race: she would make a decision with Dermont. She would have a family, yes, but when was their business alone. Perhaps that was Scottish caution. But Joan had already examined the matter in detail, it was no sudden exuberant flush of youth. She and Margaret had been properly examined and pronounced medically perfectly fit to conceive and bear a child. She had worked out dates, had booked a rondavel for next hot weather, the one she most approved of, furnished with shisham wood, straight from the Bible, which pleased her. (I rather spoiled it by pointing out that it was the same as our *jungli* acacia in Sindh. But no matter). It was booked provisionally, but could be cancelled by March—so there was at least a thought that I might not do my part exactly punctually.

The baby would be born in June, in Quetta, cost Rs. 300.
Of course we could afford it. As for afterwards...

It was a beautiful programme: it showed that Joan's
previous plan to go home to England was dropped, and
she was not depending on a transfer from Larkana, which
was very unlikely, and which I did not now want, for Ziarat
had made me forget that shocking heat.

But I bore a heavy responsibility! The moon must wax
and wane and wax again before we could know if I had
fulfilled it, and if I had not, the hot weather in June was no
time for a heavily pregnant woman to be in Larkana, and
by October Ziarat might be deep in snow. There must be a
fall-back plan, changeable from month to barren month.
There must be no publicity. The plan must be kept quiet
until the change of shape made it undeniable; and even
then the competitive aspect should be kept hidden.

So we left that pleasant place, those pleasant people.
Afterwards there was almost endless correspondence—
unexpected bills, patterns and photographs to be
exchanged. Margaret would make a housecoat like Joan's,
scarlet-patterned cotton with big scarlet buttons, all sewn
by hand, finished specially for me. There is a photograph
of her wearing it to surprise me, which it did, pleasing us
all. Later it was worn a lot, then passed on to the next
generation, and I saw it a few years ago, still in use, in
Brooklyn, still elegant, defying fashions.

We went down the hill. We said good-bye to Jean Lowe
in Quetta, and caught a train that would take us through
the Bolan in daylight. We travelled in luxury, with Nawab
to look after our bags and boxes and bundles, while we sat
idly by, as Sahib and Memsahib should. I don't think that
ever happened to us again.

We reached Larkana in the very early morning, but
Allahdino was there with the car, thoroughly repaired,
bright and shining. It was pleasantly cool, too, though we
knew it would warm up soon, but not to the fierce heat I
had faced a month before. Nor was it so humid, for the

rice was ripening and the water was being drained from the paddy fields. It was bearable, and anyway we were together.

The bungalow was bright and shining too. Nawab passed it as fit, and Joan was anxious and excited at the same time. The height and size of everything was daunting after the tent with its low roof and canvas walls that she had grown used to in Ziarat, and the smell of juniper and the soft light of lamps that she knew better now than this place. But I saw her run her hand secretly over the silky teak of the big table, and straighten two cushions she had covered with stuff from England. It was all right.

First I must see the Collector, and 'RB' was as effusive as ever, beyond the needs of a superior welcoming a subordinate. But I could ignore it now. I collected my pistol from the police, for the Hur trouble was as bad as ever, but by day from now on it would be locked in the safe. Then there was a need to contribute to the War Fund. I talked with Nur Mahomed, I argued that it was only nominally his war, so he should not give as much as I. I decided to give Rs. 50, which was quite a lot to us; what he gave I didn't ask.

As I knew, Larkana was to be honoured with a Special Demonstration by the Indian Army to encourage Sindh's war effort. Little enough was Larkana aware of any war, so a little propaganda seemed a good idea. Its organization was the Collector's job, but he insisted that I be there for the show. So I heard some cases at Kambar, where Joan was very bored, except for the evening when she met the Club for the first time, and heard from Ali Ahmed the tale of the mango picnic. We would go to Larkana just for the day, saving petrol by using the bus. We sat high enough for Joan to see standing rice for the first time, ripening to harvest, dull gold in the sun, reaping already beginning. The harvesters reaped with little saw-edged hooks, the very same that I had seen at Mohen-jo-daro; I thought of trying to introduce a scythe, but perhaps it would not do: water still stood in the fields, and the straw stood in little bunches, not in rows like English corn. Besides, they were used to their little hooks, they had two or three thousand years' practice with them.

We arrived in time to see the whole show. It was all very informal: the Army had not set up shamianas for important people like the Collector, as was usually done for a tamasha. The maidan in front of the Collector's Kutchery had been levelled, and enlarged by filling in a ditch. A unit of the Indian Army had arrived with a field gun and a light tank. There was a tent bedecked with recruiting posters, and another for the doctor to examine recruits. We were interested to know how many recruits would arrive: that might indicate how many gun licences Rahim Baksh had promised.

The Demonstration did not, in fact, instil into onlookers, including ourselves, much hope of success for British and Indian arms. The recruits lined up, put their marks each to his piece of paper, and then were passed on to the medical tent. At one time there was uproar from inside: a man who had been assured that he would fail the test, so that he could collect his fee and go away, had been passed. He was in the Army, and the Army had no intention of letting him go. He was one of the few who could be passed as even minimally fit.

Then we were to be given a demonstration by the quick-firing field gun. Onlookers were advised to cover their ears. The action was not very quick, but the officer explained that this was not his regular team. It certainly made a very satisfactory bang. There was a recruit being examined in the tent when it first went off: he gave a yell and ran out and away, stark naked, never to be seen again; not till the Army had gone, anyway. More seriously, Joan was taken by surprise, and burst her precious brassiere.

Next, the tank was to show its paces. It started up with much roaring and shaking and clouds of smoke, and people were told to stand back. It charged about the maidan scaring the children. Now, that ditch had been filled very neatly;

no difference was detectable between hardpacked gravel and very soft sand. The tank charged at the ditch, threw up great clouds of sand, stalled its engine, and stuck. All the soldiers began to push, but with no effect. Then someone stopped a passing bullock cart, and the driver hitched his team to the tank; at their driver's signal they pulled the tank out without any real effort, chewing all the time. Some wag suggested that the Army recruit the bullocks, but their driver was not one for joking: he was indignant at the idea, and anyway he needed his team every day.

The show calmed down after that; it proceeded smoothly according to plan, but from the public's point of view, if there were to be no more bangs it was boring: just a few sepoys marching up and down. As a demonstration, it realized no one's hopes. Perhaps we should have stayed to entertain the troops, but we were in camp, and the bungalow was empty. We did not wait. I contributed my Rs. 50, and we considered that we had had a worthwhile day; hilarious, if not inspiriting.

The Collector would certainly be asked to report on the demonstration, and he would surely ask for my comments. I hope I was bold enough to report adequately my feeling for the damage that such an inept display did, that only made people laugh.

When we had news from home of the war we always felt a little guilt as well as anxiety, especially when we were in Ziarat. Joan would write home about what a beautiful place it was, and her family could only tell her of bombs and evacuation and shortages of every kind. For me it was not so bad: I was in a hell-hot place with little but hard work, and my family was in the beautiful countryside of my home. It made us feel uncomfortable, as, indeed, it should. We never heard a bomb burst, nor a shot fired in anger. It was not our fault; we could do nothing about it. But still we sometimes felt shame for it.

A few more days in Kambar, and we were back home. Joan had to go to Karachi for her Urdu exam, and by the end of September we knew she wasn't pregnant. Our first attempt had failed, all Mrs Bedi's instructions were void, pure chance would order things. Then Margaret wrote in triumph that she was pregnant: she didn't know if it would be a boy or a girl, but, as she put it, Peter was rested and very well, they had been half-tight, and they had made love at the bottom of a coal mine. Only there were no coal mines in Ziarat. She called Joan a 'sterile old cow', which was not fair, since it was probably my fault anyway. It was a pity that her news could not be passed on in the Larkana Club: for one thing, her language would shock, and for another the jibe at an old cow would be expected to make a permanent end to a friendship. The gulf between English and Indian humour must not be ignored; if one tried to overleap it one would almost certainly be tripped, and this was true in both directions.

I paid my first visit to the Agricultural Research Station at Dokri while Joan was away, and I was terribly disappointed. I was there for the annual show, and found little sign of scientific research, and the judging of cattle, of crops, and of ploughing I found pitiful. Certainly I was inexperienced, and my little experience was from England, but there should have been some sign of testing seed for improved strains: there was not. Buffaloes, the milch cattle, were judged by size, with no records of milk yields. Draught cattle were not needed too big, or they might not fit the Sindhi cart. (But perhaps a bigger cart should be tried?) However, the Red Sindhi was a strong and handsome animal, some even had pedigrees. The Sindhi plough was small, too, and there was no sign that the improved plough I had seen a year before at Ghulamullah was being tested. There was a special Stud Bull, so all the scrub bulls around Larkana were to be castrated—if they could get hold of them! On the other hand, any cow offered was put to the bull, be she never so scrubby herself, and no breeding records were kept for such. The offspring of such a cow would be sold as 'half-stud'. There was a strong bench kept handy to put under a cow's belly if she were not strong enough to stand to the bull; I thought that service should at least be reserved for those that could stand. But I daresay the fees were useful.

I wrote all about it to Joan: 'If someone will give me two lakhs, I'll give up the ICS and try to farm practically and scientifically. Or maybe I won't.' Perhaps I was remembering Haji Badoola.

I had to write a report on this show. I could be very critical, but on the other hand I very much wanted to know more about Sindhi agriculture, as it was and as it might be. So I held my report back. I could not require anything from another department, but I persuaded Dokri to invite me again after the show, when the Director was coming. So I met Hassanali Agha again, with the Director of the Station, and we could talk almost as equals, he telling me of his ideas for Sindh, I relating what I knew of English practice in very different conditions. He showed me his stock herd of Red Sindhi cattle, not on show, disfavoured for being too big for the plough and the cart. He was hoping to get a bigger cart built, to display its advantages, and to try his bigger plough, but a rigid conservatism was against him. As we talked my report, still in my head, grew less and less acid.

He wanted to breed new strains of rice and millet and wheat. It was, he said, shameful that people in Sindh who wanted really good rice must send to Patna for it. The yield of wheat, with an assured and controlled water supply, was a quarter of that in America, only a tenth of that in England. And so we went on. Perhaps one day I would be working with him.

The Station had a tractor, a very heavy crawler, with a 'prairie-buster' plough. The Station Director was very proud of it, though he agreed that it had very limited use. It was used to plough up soil near the river bunds, for repair work, and could clear jungle from river *kutchas*. But it was a disaster for ordinary ploughing: it cut so deep that it turned up dead and salty soil, and ruined the land for years. My contribution was the description of a new light tractor being made in England, the Ferguson: as I had told Agha before, it could increase the area cropped without displacing labour.

Almost unconsciously I moved into becoming a specialist in agricultural reform, not with any idea of displacing the Director who was the expert, executive head of the department, but with a plan that, if I were to be moved to the Secretariat, the administrative side of the Agriculture Department was the place I would choose.

I stayed several days at Dokri, with pertal and cases, for it was convenient for parties and pleaders. Also, Joan was coming up from Karachi after her exam, and would meet me there. It also gave the Director time to finish his own report on seed selection and fertilizers for rice. He had promised me, in strict confidence, a copy of it.

Joan arrived, we had a cup of tea, and set off to see Mohen-jo-daro, the Place of the Dead. It was the one place for which Sindh was famous worldwide. It was an awe-inspiring place, not because it was big, but because it was obviously so very old.

We drove along the river bund, and looked across at it, isolated in a barren, *kalarish* plain, a large mound crowned by blocks of burnt brick where then no burnt brick was used. It was dominated by a Buddhist stupa, old itself, but young in the presence of ruins from four or five thousand years before. There were walls, but no more than four or five feet high, obvious streets with gullies running down the middle; rooms with blocks that might have been tables or altars, gaps in the walls for doors and windows, marks where stairs had perhaps risen to an upper floor. At that time even the archaeologists had not decided the purpose of the various remains, nor why the site had apparently been abandoned suddenly. In the little hut were most of the artefacts that had been discovered—the few precious pieces had been taken to a safer place. What fascinated me most were the clay rings named as spindles, and flat clay trays with knobs underneath labelled children's toys, for it appeared to me that they might well be the wheels and platforms of toy carts very much like the full-sized ones we saw every day. The place was impressive only if we imagined all those years that had passed, could truly realize that people had lived and worked there, even though so far no one had thought why they came, just how they lived, and when and why they went away and disappeared. Now there is a great deal more to see, but one needs an armed escort to get there. We just set off from our car on the bund, walked round with the chowkidar, and drove back through a quiet and peaceful countryside.

Next morning we went back to Larkana, just for a day, for Joan to feel at home again, and then set off on our first long tour, first to Mirokhan, where I found my horse: I had reached agreement with Nabi Buksh Bhutto, leaving the arrangement for final remuneration till I returned him. The camp called him Ghoro, which just means Horse, so I call him that. My tack had been collected and polished up, his stall-to-be and his syce's quarters were cleaned and readied, and all his and his syce's *saman* was with him at Mirokhan.

In the evening before we set off from Larkana, Gobindram's prophecy came true: the locusts arrived. Near sunset, in a clear sky, a cloud appeared between us and the sun, over towards the western hills, and, as he said, the swarm really did darken the sky, or, more accurately, it darkened the land below its passage. The swarm was much deeper than its head which we could see, and as the sun set the locusts came to ground. They landed on Larkana, in our compound, in a vast area to north and east, wherever the sun left them.

The known method of getting rid of locusts was by creating a huge noise, by beating tin cans and drums, by shouting, by doing anything very noisy. We proved that this method was completely useless: all the hullaballoo made no difference at all.

Where they landed, there they began to eat, whatever was edible. If there was nothing, they crawled about or rested. All the bungalow doors were closed, but they got in; they even came down the chimney. There was no sleeping on the roof or the *thalla* that night. We walked on them and crushed them, and our shoes were in a horrid mess (And when finally they had all gone they left their nasty shit behind.)

Next morning there was a grey desert. In the evening we had heard the champing of a million jaws, quite different from the hissing of their flight. The champing had stopped, for there was nothing left to eat, not a blade of grass, not a leaf. The evening before, all the parrots and pigeons had come to the feast, eating till they were bloated, making no significant dent in the numbers. Before it was dark the birds had sickened of them, they stayed in their bare trees and let them go. We were told that some people caught them and fried them, but who that was I don't know. We just wanted them gone.

But the field crops were already ripe and safe; and thanks be to his god, said Hubba, our seeds were not yet up. I don't know which in the Hindu pantheon was Hubba's god, but he received full credit.

As the sun rose the locusts began to wake and to fly on. We wanted to leave early for Mirokhan, and as they flew they covered the car, they smashed on the windscreen till we could hardly see, they spattered the body all over in front till we feared lest the radiator be blocked and the engine overheat.

The Mirokhan bus had left earlier, when the locusts were still resting, lying everywhere on the ground, and the bus had marked its passage by tyre tracks of crushed locusts. Very odd: satisfying, too, to see that some of the invaders had paid with their lives. But so few. Before we reached Mirokhan we left the track of the swarm, which flew on towards Shikarpur.

On this tour there was one memorable event, and that at a camp whose purpose was only for pertal and receiving petitions. Petitioners came at every camp, with every sort of problem: thefts, interference with water supply, *zulum* by a zamindar, quarrels over property—in fact, anything where the poor petitioner hoped the *Dipiti* Sahib, Protector of the Poor, might help. They were valuable to the officer, too: he could glean all sorts of information about his charge, and how the small people felt, and how the powerful were misbehaving. There was this general feeling that a benevolent Government had its eyes open to everything. But this camp at Bahram Hethion (Lower Bahram) was not even at a village. It was just a wayside station on the loop line to Jacobabad. Here a girl petitioned me, and for a woman herself to come was most unusual. She wanted a divorce from her husband. This could not possibly be my business, but clearly I must see her, so she was called, and appeared, with her husband standing beside her, looking embarrassed. Such a matter was clearly for the moulvi, for Quranic law would be involved. On the other hand, a disputed divorce could lead to a breach of the peace, and that would be my business.

I decided to look into it. The law, as far as I understood it, allowed a man to divorce his wife for almost any reason. He only had to say *'talaq'* three times, and off she must go back to her parents, who would be greatly shamed, and might well react violently to it. For a woman, though, the only reason for which she could divorce her husband could be his impotence.

There stood this fine young man with his fine black beard; he certainly looked virile enough, though he didn't deny the charge. But he had his own complaint to make: at present he must live with his wife's family, because his house had burnt down and he was building a new one. Her father kept asking the girl if she were pregnant, and when she was not both father and mother reviled him. He was unhappy there, they kept insulting him, how could he be happy with his wife? Also, her father and mother could hear everything that happened.

I sent them out while I consulted with my Shristedar. We agreed that I had no power to grant a divorce, even if that were desirable: interference with religious matters could be very dangerous. He tried to think of some way of proving whether or not the man was potent. There had, he said, been a predecessor of mine in the District who dealt with a similar case by calling a whore from the brothel and telling the man to get on with it, to prove himself. He did not know if the method worked or not. I ruled that it was unfair, such a test might make any decent man recoil, it was immoral and disgusting. He withdrew the suggestion, said he was just reporting, not recommending it. I called them back: I was going to consult with my own wife, they should wait. They would certainly wait; they had all day.

This was a matter not for law or for custom, but for counselling. We agreed that this young man, living with nagging in-laws, had no chance. Joan proposed to talk with the girl, hoping that Sindhi and Urdu could inter-communicate. She must be persuaded to get her husband away from her parents, even if only for a short time; she must lure him away for at least one whole night, and there seduce him. She was a very pretty girl, there should be no problems, she must use all her charms, and I daresay Joan demonstrated some. But she must not let him or her parents know what she was at.

Somehow Joan had put her proposals across the language barrier. At first the girl had been bare-headed in a most aggressive and improper way, but when she came back after her counselling, her *dupatta* hid most of her face, and she peered out shyly and modestly. Before me her husband looked puzzled. I made her bare her face, and she had a secret and excited look which was itself a seduction.

I dismissed them to think things over, to do nothing about the divorce before I came again in two or three weeks, and then I would decide.

Their tale need not wait three weeks. We came back, the man and girl came in, the man tall and straight and proud, the girl well-covered, all modesty. I asked what was her decision; she replied, very quietly and submissively, 'Mursi attus', which meant; in telescopic Sindhi, that he had found his manhood. Lest I fail to understand, my Shristedar translated for me: 'He has satisfied her'. She whispered to him, and he said she wished the memsahib to know that she was grateful. I wonder if she had told her husband what she was being grateful for? But anyway, that was not enough, so I asked Joan to come—I would not order my wife! She came, and was thanked very prettily. She embraced the girl and then, startling him considerably, the husband. The blessings of Allah were called down on her, and might He bless her with many strong children. Joan was happy to reciprocate. Blessings of any sort, from any source, were welcome just then.

Next, Shahdadkot, where, over near the hills on pertal, I lost my signet ring, given by my parents before I left home. It had come off as I was riding, my finger had grown so thin. It had sealed all my letters home, though most of the seals had broken off. It had served as Joan's wedding ring. We went home for a few days.

Out again, to see my Warah taluka, and inspect its records, and do my stint of remission claims—pertal again. Thence to our southern boundary on the Dhamrau canal, an old inundation canal now linked to perennial water. Beyond was Dadu District, where the Cargills were posted, but at its southern end, out of our reach. We camped in an old bungalow on the canal. In its compound was a vast and ancient peepul tree, with a hermit living among its aerial roots. The chowkidar said he had lived there since time out of mind, so he paid no rent.

The canal ran out through the Flood Protection Bund. There was a sluice there to control it.

This bund ran right through my sub-division, cutting off any sudden rush of floodwater after heavy rain in the hills.

Hardly anyone lived beyond it, though there was occasional cultivation of catch crops after rain. Ghaibi Dero was the only village on the hillside, and was the only place I had been to there.

We camped at Wagan, a dirty, unfriendly place—and that is all I remember about it. But as I rode out on pertal, I came to the little village of Ber, which was anything but unfriendly, and it had a problem. It was small, and very old, so sat on a high hillock of past collapsed mud-brick houses. There was a water course, and a bridge across it to the road; bridge and road were the responsibility of the District Board. From there people had to climb up a steep slope to the houses, and if it rained even that was impossible. I told them I would come back next day to see what could be done. It seemed a perfect opportunity to practice a little of the rural uplift, community help, about which I had questions to answer for the Rural Reconstruction Department.

So we went. We persuaded the people that they could build a road across and up the slope, cutting into it and building up the cut soil to give it width, like the roads in the hills. No one had ever seen roads in the hills, but they got the idea. The shopkeepers and their like would pay a little to those who worked, the Muslims would dig out the soil, and Hindu workers would carry it and stamp it in place. Even in the middle of the day it was not too hot now, but we all took a rest; the Muslims offered their midday prayer, and we others drank tea in the little bazaar, sitting on little wire chairs, with cardamoms in the tea as usual. By evening the job was done, and the first bullock cart was driven ceremoniously up the slope. We went back to camp, and as we passed next day on our way to Kambar we looked at it proudly. People were waving furiously, we hooting, and children chasing the car and trying to get run over.

This was the same method that had succeeded at Buhara, in Thatta, but again it seemed that such self-help must be organized and evoked from outside; within these small villages there was no one with the necessary disinterested authority to ignite the fuse, as it were. English communities seemed to breed that sort of person, indeed, our own parents, in their own spheres, were of the kind: Joan's with a large chapel community, mine with a village and all its wartime needs. The people needed must be part busybodies, part social consciences. We had seen no sign of any such in Sindhi villages, but perhaps they would appear, given official support and encouragement. Anyway, Ber had its new road, the people had built it themselves, and the very fact that they were pleased with themselves was a step forward. Were it not for Collectors and Commissioner and Ministers, I might become a thoroughly undemocratic but essentially benevolent tyrant.

On the way home, disaster struck. Had we been capable of higher speed it could have been a catastrophe: the front suspension broke, the wheel jammed, and we nearly ran into the canal. But there was never long to wait for a bullock cart. We got the wheel off, hitched up behind the cart, and were towed home on the brake drum. Surprisingly, spare parts were no problem—so many Chevs were bought, ruined by ignorance, and scrapped—and we soon had the car again. The PWD received profuse apologies for the furrows in its precious road.

I called on the Collector, as a matter of course, and he told me officially that the Viceroy would camp at Larkana at the end of January. RB would, of course, be chiefly and generally concerned, but there would be a visit to Mohenjo-daro, and a duck shoot at Drigh, which were both in my charge. I saw the little grey book produced by the Government of Sindh with every detail of the Viceroy's tour; but a mere Assistant Collector was not on the distribution list: I was given only excerpts for my own duties.

Only good news for Joan: she had passed her Urdu exam with 80 per cent marks, which was 'highly honourable'; wrote Kishensingh—and better than any of the army candidates. Margaret reported that Bernard had failed his

Sindhi. I could sympathize with him, he had not had, as had I, six months of intensive teaching from Kishensingh in Karachi. Bernard strongly disapproved of the way Margaret and Joan discussed the merits of Marxism, read books about it, and, specially for Bernard's benefit, condemned the evils of British Imperialism. Joan was much more tolerant than was Margaret, but it was probably as well that he did not stay long in Ziarat. Now he was Deputy Commissioner in Jacobabad, so we would meet him again at Christmas, would see how he practised authority. I was ready to feel sorry for him, with those two termagants after him. (Jean Lowe wrote to me. She had asked Bernard, did Margaret scare him? 'Yes, but Joan Pearce scares me more'. Well...) There had been times when Joan had been not altogether gentle with me.

Joan came on tour again, to Kambar, where I met her as I came in from a special trip with the Mukhtiarkar to talk about the Viceroy's visit to Drigh. We camped at Garhi Khair Mahomed, of the mango picnic, and on to Dostali, a pretty bungalow with a chowkidar who was himself a keen gardener. Here it was that Gobindram had found grape-fruit, and so did we. It seemed to be like the orange and lemon, with fruit and flowers on the tree at the same time. We bought two off the chowkidar, and I began again to think of a citrus industry for Sindh. The malta, that disaster of an orange, flourished at Malir, and could be grafted over to something more worthwhile; here in Upper Sindh was the grapefruit; lemon and lime I had not seen, but they were cousins, where one was happy the others probably would be. I saw myself as Secretary for Agriculture, acquiring land and setting up an experimental farm for citrus fruit at Dokri. That would do for a start; for now, we had two beautiful juicy fruit to eat.

We went back to Kambar, and there the tour was disrupted, for Joan developed jaundice. Why, who could say: it was not uncommon, perhaps it was something to do with the water somewhere—whenever some place was lauded or condemned the judgement seemed to depend chiefly on the quality of the water. But Ali Ahmed seemed to know just how to treat it: pomegranate juice. I only knew the plant for its brilliant scarlet flower, but the juice was a sure cure for jaundice, and fortunately it was in season, cheap in the bazaar; he bought up the whole stock. Joan was to chew the pips, and Mistri made a very pleasant drink. It must have been one of the traditional homeopathic medicines, and contained a vitamin, perhaps A: like carrots, good for the eyes. Anyway, after two or three days of gloom in a bungalow with all the *chiks* down, the whites of her eyes lost their yellow tinge, she could bear full light again, and could be considered cured: a triumph for Ali Ahmed's treatment, for homeopathy. Or perhaps she recovered by herself.

We moved on to Rownti. Now, Rownti was a bungalow of no repute; in fact, among all those we knew it was about the meanest, and would have been forgotten except for one thing: it was here that Joan conceived. At Christmas we worked out the arithmetic that led us to that conclusion, and now, over fifty years on, I see no reason to question it. Had I wanted to create some pretty and romantic place, I would never have chosen Rownti, or a time just after an attack of jaundice. But we decided then that Rownti was the place, so it must remain.

This was December. We stayed in Larkana, and so many things happened in that month. Joan's Urdu triumph became known; by Christmas we were sure she was pregnant; and she had news of a temporary job in Karachi, beginning conveniently just after the Viceroy's visit. We would be in Jacobabad for Christmas, but RB would not let me go to the Horse Show, which would almost overlap with the Visit, and Joan would not go alone. At Christmas all the Ziarat Sindhis would meet again, and all three girls would have finished their race for families. (I think Anne Barty had, though she had disowned any race.) The one failure was that the Reinitzs refused to come and stay with us.

Looking more widely round the world, the Japanese bombed Pearl Harbour, Germany declared war on the United States, refusing any longer to accept a neutrality that helped Britain but damaged itself; and the Viceroy, without consulting his Advisory Committee, declared war on Japan for all India. This led to serious trouble in Hindu India, with often violent civil disobedience, but the Muslim ministries of Northern India remained 'loyal', and Sindh was one of the few places where the Viceroy could camp in reasonable safety. Even the Hurs were coming under control.

Joan had come back from Karachi with all the gossip. Dermont Barty was there, called for an interview with someone from Delhi, hoping for a post there. Tim Crosthwaite was interviewed too, and had the same hopes, which were realized at some time: he finished on Mountbatten's staff. The Grahams had gone, and in their place were Sir Hugh Dow and his Lady. Joan found him perfectly willing to discuss the economics of India, and even of the world. Lady Dow she found a little overawed by her position, but Joan got on very well with her. Several times she dined at Government House—her social life was leaping ahead of mine—and was forever putting in a good word for that young officer in Larkana. She was enthusiastically in favour of Indian independence, even though it would lose her husband his job, but such wild talk, all right for Governors, did junior officers no good. I also aired my views unwisely.

We travelled to Jacobabad on our loop line; we saw our kingdom in a different condition, for all the paddy had been taken to the villages to be threshed and winnowed, and when we were near a road, we saw the convoys of carts taking the grain to be husked; the land was being ploughed for spring crops—mostly pulses and gram, for the zamindars seemed still not to appreciate their perennial water. In the Upper Sindh Frontier we saw wheat being sown for the first time.

I remember very little of that Christmas, which is strange. Joan had instructions from Margaret concerning what to take, stores and tableware, and we had all agreed that there should be only small presents. All of us who had been in Ziarat were there, all of us men had proved our manhood. There was a shoot, but since neither I nor Joan had a gun, we only looked on. I have some large group photographs to remind me, and a memory of sitting by the fire with Reggie and discussing whether we would try to keep a dog. There sat George, a spaniel who had adjusted himself to the climate. Joan protested that Reggie was cruel to him: whenever the dog came near, he spoke roughly, but he explained that if he were to speak kindly, George would take advantage of it; he proved it, too. George was cowering on his mat, and Reggie said quietly 'Good boy!' In a flash, George had leapt to his lap and was licking his face, and in no way could he be put down.

It is very odd: that little incident, more than any other that Christmas, has stuck in the memory of both of us.

13

VICEREGAL VISITATION

RB, the Collector, was ill, and within a day or two was sent to hospital in Karachi. I was told to take over, even though Nur Mahomed, Deputy Collector, was able and had long experience, whereas I had very little: the charge must go to the Imperial Service. It surprised me that Nur Mahomed accepted that as normal, in no way to be resented. Perhaps that was at least partly because of the imminent arrival of the Viceroy.

All preparations for the visit had been made, I just needed to go through the little Book, to check everything, to talk to the Collector's Chitnis about the ordinary District work, to see if there was anything urgent I should do: there was not. It was a holiday period, anyway.

The Begum Rahim Baksh had gone with her husband, so for news I had to phone the Civil Surgeon in Karachi: When will my Collector return? Not for a month or two, which set me a problem: I could not 'hold charge' for so long, the District could not just stand still, with no District Magistrate, and certainly His Excellency would not wait, and must be met by someone of sufficient authority. I asked the Chief Secretary if someone was coming soon, but it appeared that there was no one to spare. That was fine! So I asked, what about my position? With a little urging he agreed that I would have to be posted as Acting Collector, pending RB's return. This was what I had hoped for, as much for the extra salary as for the good of the District.

The *Gazette* wouldn't really make much difference to the District, nor to the Viceroy's comfort when he came—we all behaved just the same—but it felt grand.

The *Gazette* was published. Joan was pleased, too. She thought maliciously of being Chief Lady of the District, and what Eleanor O'Flynn would think of that. I had not met such malice in her before, but, indeed, the extra pay was what pleased us most, more than the honour. Moreover, we must be very tactful with the O'Flynns; true, we would be their superiors for a short time, but then I would revert, and the position would be reversed; they shouldered enough chips already. With Nur Mahomed there was no problem: he was quite simply pleased for me, and it was easy to point out how much I would be dependent on his experience.

The Viceroy was Lord Linlithgow, last of the aristocratic Viceroys. With Begum RB in purdah there could be no lunch given by the Collector, and our bungalow couldn't entertain so large a party. Nor would there now be any troublesome Purdah Party.

Having settled that, we set about amending the Book; but I left that to the Chitnis, myself just being consulted. He knew the Book by heart. I gave myself the job of checking arrangements at the station, for Their Excellencies would live on their train. It would be the Viceregal Special, but a war-economy train, only five coaches instead of the full nine. The Railway was happy to provide a siding. In fact, an old siding was refurbished, a roadway laid to it, lined with plants in pots and whitewashed stones. They would have an extra siding, and an untidy area cleaned up, all at Central Government expense.

The Governor would stay in the Circuit House; would we have to supplement its meagre furnishings? Fortunately, not: RB had arranged what of his furniture could go there if needed.

Inshallah, they would not want to go into Larkana town. It was in such a bad state that we had just secured the appointment of a Special Administrator to put it right.

The people to be interviewed had all been invited, and had, of course, accepted. But all their biographies, prepared by RB, were locked away in his safe, so, in great secrecy, Nur Mahomed, Eric O'Flynn, and I, worked up new ones to give to His Excellency's Secretary.

Nur Mahomed dealt with the matter of interviews and the trip across the river to shoot partridges in Khairpur, Eric and I with the duck shoot at Drigh Dhand, and I had to check the state of the Dokri Farm, and see that all was ready at Mohen-jo-daro. The Director of Archaeology was coming from Delhi, and the Visit would be in his charge once they reached the site.

We ourselves could not entertain at home, but Joan had an ambitious idea. There had to be tea served between the partridge shoot and Mohen-jo-daro, so she would provide a picnic. She was sure that, with help with chairs and tables and other stuff, she could do much better than could a bare room at the Farm.

The shoot at Drigh would be the same as it had been for the Governor the year before—the poor ducks!—and otherwise Eric, Nur Mahomed, the Chitnis, and I just hoped that no disaster might befall.

To relax, there was the Club. Joan was welcomed back, and congratulated. Now, how did everyone know that she was pregnant? To my eyes there was nothing to show, and it was not a matter usually talked about among men. But she wouldn't play tennis, she felt a little insecure. Ram Motwani was there, and I asked him, please, as a friend, not to put on an anti-British demonstration, but he explained that, friendship aside, he must. It was a matter of principle. This was no surprise, and indeed it was better to have him organizing one than to be branded a traitor and replaced by someone far less reasonable. He agreed that there should be only a small picket, and that it would be entirely non-violent, and with that Eric agreed that he would not object to cries of *'Jai Hind'* and *'Hindustan Zindabad'*. And so it fell out. In fact, Larkana people were not so very hot for independence, but they could not afford headlines suggesting that they had welcomed a Viceroy of India, the very symbol of Imperialist Dominion.

My last duty was to find out what arrangements had been made for the shoot in Khairpur, including the river crossing. The Vizir, the same man whose daughter had been offered to Nazir, assured me that all was well. If it wasn't, that was not my concern. Three cars had arrived a day early, to be taken in charge by the police. I remembered Lady Dow's digestion, and phoned Dokri: was the cow that would supply milk for the party all right? Certainly she was: she was being kept in isolation, given clean straw every day, her udder washed for each milking, and I could have her milk for myself if I would send for it. I could not, but was reassured.

There was a sort of OC Train with the Viceroy: he saw that it was the right way round in the siding, and that the engine was sent away. (If it had been wrong, what would he have done about it? Put the steps on the other side?)

The train arrived, settled down. Eric and I were there to welcome it, he in full dress uniform, I with my white topi. In the background were Nur Mahomed and the Mukhtiarkar in case of need, Joan and Eleanor stood further back, also in case of need, or just to see. Their Excellencies came out, all four of them, and shook hands. This was the signal for the anti-British demonstration, led by Ram Motwani. He would himself, I thought, have preferred to shake hands, but he shouted *'Jai Hind!'* with the rest. The ADC whispered to Eric, who shook his head, the Viceroy went back inside, and the Governor's party set off for the Circuit House with a police escort. And that, for the moment, was that. I met the Viceroy's Secretary and gave him a list of the changes necessary because of RB's being away, but they didn't amount to much. At least I didn't ask for any changes in his precious timing.

Lord Linlithgow was to be the last of the old-style aristocratic Viceroys, and he filled the role admirably. He was six feet seven inches tall, and Lady Linlithgow matched him, well over six feet. He had a long thin face and a long thin nose, and as a result he must always look down on the people before him, appearing supercilious and arrogant when probably he was not so. It was Sir Hugh Dow's misfortune that he was a little short, and Lady Dow even shorter. I don't doubt that His Excellency knew that I was very junior, Acting Collector by an unfortunate chance, but he was going to be entertained by the Office, not by the person. He asked questions about Sindh and the war; I could tell him that Sindh rarely thought about it, but had very much enjoyed the Display, considering it a good joke. Perhaps he took the hint that, in his interviews, the war might not be a useful subject for conversation.

Apart from the planned engagements I have only small, incidental memories; the list of Staff: butler, valet, major domo, and cook, each with his assistant; Lady Linlithgow with her lady's maid and housekeeper; the staff for the Staff; and the pinman. What his function was I do not know, but perhaps that is why I remember him. I talked with an ADC, an Elphinstone, no less, with a name from the past of the Indian Empire. He remarked how lucky we were to have such a pleasant railway station and I agreed, but pointed out that the platform had been rebuilt for the Visit, and the road too, all at government expense, and all the pot plants would go back to their owners afterwards. He seemed surprised, but I wonder if his naïveté was not assumed.

There was to be no Durbar, which would have been disproportionate in a place as small as Larkana. Here were interviews, and otherwise Their Excellencies would entertain themselves.

The first expedition was across the river to shoot partridges as guests of the Mir of Khairpur. The Mir Sahib provided a luxuriously caparisoned boat for the short crossing, and on our side the PWD had cut a road through the young tamarisk, and had built a fine, serviceable jetty. I did not shoot, but knew that there were not many partridges on our side, so did not expect a very big bag. But the Mir Sahib had many resources to deploy for such an important guest, and a competent Vizir to deploy them. He had put an Inspector of Police and three or four sepoys on special duty, had levied birds from all the zamindars around, and had them caged. His men had been feeding the area of the shoot for a month, to ensure that all the resident birds would stay there. As a result, there was a very handsome bag, and some very odd happenings.

Two rides had been cut through the tamarisk jungle, with stations for the guns at intervals. The birds were to be driven up to the guns, and they flew up in such ideal numbers that very few escaped. The guns moved back to the second ride, the beaters crossed the first, every three or four with a jemadar a little ahead, and again a lot of birds rose. But as the beaters neared the second ride, birds began to rise seemingly out of the ground, and then some began to scuttle across the ride and into safety.

Perhaps the Viceroy knew what was happening; I saw him smiling, so at least he was not annoyed. His ADCs did not understand, and were amazed and happy to shoot at any bird that dared to leave the ground. But we made them stop, the beaters were too close.

I learned what had happened: it was a tactic often used for the Mir Sahib's shoots. The jemadars had filled their so baggy trousers with birds, and shook out a few whenever necessary. But when they closed the guns, the birds had had no time to recover from their confused state, and could do no better than walk: there was no space for a take-off.

Nevertheless, it was a highly successful morning, and perhaps the best, certainly the funniest, act came last. One of the jemadars waiting to collect his reward had not released all his birds; he stood in a patch of new tamarisk near the water, he said there were birds there, told the guns to be ready for a quick shot, and shook his trousers. His birds recovered their wits and began to fly. They took off straight up and very fast, and I doubt if anyone had time to fire, which was just as well—there were a lot of people around. HE was saying good-bye to the Mir, he saw what was happening, and laughed. So he was to that extent human: he could take it as a joke. But I cannot forget the startled faces of those young men of his Staff at the sudden eruption of birds.

Then came our entertainment of the party, which was very much Joan's business, and she made of it a triumph. I had only been concerned with the guests, and with the doubtful approval of the Secretary I had invited Abdur Rashid Kazi to come and be presented, for he was responsible for the river crossing, and, indeed, for the picnic site. Also Nur Mahomed, for he was responsible for much of the comfort of the Viceregal party. This was not usual, but I had chopped a little logic: if it had not been for the real Collector's absence I would not have been there myself, and nor would Joan, so there would have been no picnic. I would have liked to invite other officers, but judged it unwise to try.

Relative to what was happening in the world, even in the rest of India, our entertainment of the Viceroy was of little account. We were well aware of this, we were no lovers of aristocrats (this was the first one we had ever met) nor could we love an officer who simply by birth outranked even the Heaven Born like us. But the young and inexperienced wife of an inexperienced and very temporary Collector was not going to need to have anyone making excuses.

Rashid Kazi had cleared a spot between the river and the little so-called museum of Mohen-jo-daro, and there the Mukhtiarkar of Warah, helped by raiding the *rasai* fund, had set up a shamiana, and collected tables and chairs and a portable toilet, just as he would for an officer's camp. We provided all the tablecloths, crockery, cutlery, teapots, and jugs—everything necessary for something far more sophisticated than an ordinary picnic.

What was most unusual of all was the food. Recipes were those from Vienna which Joan had learnt from Grete Reinitz and passed on to Mistri, working under her supervision. Mistri accepted the challenge of producing something that would make even a Vicereine stare, and very well he succeeded. He had biscuit crumbs and honey, chocolate and nuts ground up, dried fruit and real butter, eggs and cream guaranteed to be healthy. So much cream! There may have been a little flour, but not enough to notice. He made cakes and biscuits and little sweets; we just added cashew and pistachio nuts.

The whole affair went off without a hitch, though Lady Dow of the delicate stomach asked if the milk was safe. I was ready for this, and told her of the cow cosseted in purdah at Dokri, vetted, washed every day, the milker's hands and pails sterilized: in all India there could be no safer milk. She hesitated, then decided: 'I don't think I'll risk it, I'll have lemon.' We had prepared for this, too, and had a fresh lime sitting by.

It was all very satisfactory, and Lady Linlithgow was properly impressed: 'Rumpelmeyer in the jungle!' was her comment. (Rumpelmeyer was, I believe, the best confectioner in Vienna, so probably some of the recipes really were his). Happily, she asked for Mistri, and congratulated him herself. My opinion of the aristocracy improved a little more.

We dined with all Their Excellencies on the train, and Joan remembers more about that than I do. Her conversation with His Excellency was about universities, subjects read, and where, and so on. Joan was particularly closely questioned: economics and mathematics, were they suitable subjects for a woman? Was higher education suitable for a woman, anyway? Would it be of any value in India? Both Their Excellencies had been briefed, but could not know that Joan was pregnant, or that as soon as they left she was off for a professional teaching job in Karachi.

Joan, who is a serious person, recalls how very silly were those well-born sprigs of ADCs, and afterwards we pondered on what they had all thought of the daughter of a Baptist parson and the son of a small rural businessman. But after all, Viceroys must mix with all sorts, and we must not assume them to be social snobs just because they were so intimidatingly tall.

Next day, as a rest from killing birds, was the visit to Mohen-jo-daro. Joan and I had both been there, but would certainly go again; I must, anyway. Last time we had had to guide ourselves round the ruins; for the Viceroy, the Director-General of Archaeology for All India was there to welcome him. This was Rao Bahadur Dikshit, a short, fat, knowledgeable, and friendly Bengali. His name was unfortunate. Sir Hugh Dow, my Governor, was inevitably outfaced by the Viceroy, which made him familiar and chatty with me as he never would have been otherwise. He had made a serendipitous discovery which he must share: the Rao Bahadur's name transliterated neatly into English as Richard the Turd. He insisted on using that name, but I hope the Rao Bahadur never heard it, it would not have made him happy. On the other hand, perhaps it was not so very original, for it was so obvious that he may have heard it a dozen times, and just put it down to these uncivilized British.

It was interesting to hear what this or that piece of brickwork indicated; everything was very theoretical. Several times HE insisted on climbing to the top of a ruined wall, where the Rao Bahadur joined him. Then he asked about another wall, across a narrow alley. He, of course, just strode across, but the short RB must scuttle down and up the other side, arriving breathless, to find that HE had moved on. Several times this happened, it could not but be deliberate. What with this and the nickname, I awarded the Empire a Black Mark.

What Joan and I really wanted to see was the museum, for all the precious artefacts had been brought back from Delhi. We saw the beautifully incised scarab seals, no bigger than a postage stamp, the necklace of polished semi-precious stones, and other jewels. There were fragments of writing, untranslatable but fascinating. (More of the writing has been found since then, but still it is not translated.) After the Visit the museum was packed up and went back to Delhi.

A duck shoot at Drigh was something we knew about, we had been through it all the year before for the previous Governor, and my being now Collector made little difference, except that now it was I who had to ensure that the police had everything properly organized. Eric O'Flynn was subordinate to me, but only for a short time, so I had better not make it too obvious: I would ask, not order, consult and defer to someone who in fact knew much more about it than did I. It was Joan who had the real difficulty, with precedence over Eleanor the policeman's wife, who felt it severely. But there was nothing we could do about that: the real problem would be when I reverted, but by then Joan should be away in Karachi.

I forget how many guns there were on this shoot. Out of sight were guns on other dhands to turn birds back. I left Eric O'Flynn in charge, happy to avoid asserting my very temporary authority. I just waited idly, and very pleasantly, too.

The firing waxed and waned, but it was always possible to detect the Viceroy's hide: his valet was also his loader, and no one else had one. He had two guns, so whenever there were four shots at once, it must be himself.

In the end the firing died down, or perhaps time ran out: the shoot ended, everyone came out from the jungle, and the bag was counted. Well over a thousand, and a record for the Dhand. I hoped the summer hatch in Siberia would not be too much reduced, and was thankful that the other great migration dhand, Manchar, lacked the cover to make this kind of shoot possible. Their Excellencies naturally had by far the biggest share, and their birds went straight back to Delhi for storage, and production there or in Simla, with a useful tale to be told. I expect there was an entry in the Viceregal Game Book. All the other guns, on Drigh and other dhands, had their birds as a reward.

The Collector and his Lady had not a single one.

The Viceroy was to leave that night, to be hitched to the Lahore Mail in the morning. The Governor left soon after him, in the other direction. An official—a pinman, perhaps?—was left to tidy up, to settle accounts, and to see the Viceregal cars onto a train.

So we have nothing but memories to show that we entertained the Viceroy of India. No photographs, no press reports. But perhaps, if anyone cares to search, there are records of that Visit. We discussed it, and even Nur Mahomed agreed that it was an affair of no significance, except for those honoured with interviews. Work went on in field and shop and workshop; none of the party looked at a village, or even into Larkana town. The impression of cleanness and neatness round the train that we had established was, it seemed, accepted by its occupants as normal. All that ordinary folk saw was that there were more police about than was usual, and some colourfully-dressed strangers. Some of the shops did extra trade. Cars sped along cleared roads, raising the dust, annoying people because the bus was forced to the side, smothered in dust, and delayed. People looked up, wondered a little, and then got on with their ordinary lives. Seldom did anyone not an official ask me about it once the Visit was over. I was real, the Viceroy was but the decoration on the cake. Except for a few things like declaring war, dismissing Ministries, and arresting Gandhi, he was irrelevant.

Joan began her teaching, and before I went on tour the new Collector came: Isvaran, much senior to me, freshly up from Bombay; I never learned his given name. He was a bustling, energetic man, forever wanting to see me or Nur Mahomed to tell him about the District. I disliked being called in, particularly as it upset casework, and after a month felt like suggesting that he go on tour while the weather was still cool, and see for himself. But I decided that caution with my new master was the better policy.

I carried on with my touring, bored but grinding away at routine, doing my case work and seeing Isvaran when I must. I went to Ghaibi Dero because the Nawab had complained that he was short of water. I rode over from Garhi Khair Mahomed, and stayed in the *otak* decorated with decayed animal heads. It was hotter and dustier near the hills, and I found that the Nawab had neglected to fill his big water tank, and had used all his water for extra cultivation. I was very angry, but his people could not be left waterless, so I consulted with Kazi. Remembering the underground aquifer of the Malir river, I suggested the sinking of a borewell. I left the Chandio to talk with him, and came away.

This was a period when little of note happened in the District. In Karachi the teaching went on well, though there were 'management problems'. Joan might stay there for another term, or she might not. Lady Dow became a friend, perhaps as much as anything because she disagreed with those who said a wife should not leave her husband for a job. But she did feel that it would not be wise for Joan to follow her plan to have her baby in Quetta, and then stay in a rondavel in Ziarat in September. This was soon settled: no rondavel would be available, and certainly tents would not do. I was out on tour when news came, much delayed, that she had developed appendicitis; but by the time I reached Larkana and phoned, the appendix was out. Joan urged me not to go, all was well, I would only lose half my hot-weather leave, and the baby was all right. Outside the envelope was a note from Hugo: 'She is OK.' So I didn't go. All the ICS rallied round with flowers every day; even if it didn't approve of everything Joan did, the ICS looked after its own. And anyway, she wouldn't be riding that old bike around for some time. The Ziarat plan had failed, but Joan set up another: the Trotmans, up from Bombay, Pop and his wife Pip. The names suited them, and Margaret maintained that he was far too soft to be Collector of Karachi. They claimed that even a Collector was underpaid, and Joan suggested herself as a paying guest, when she could be there to have her baby. That was a very satisfactory idea: a pregnant ICS wife made the best possible paying guest, and it need not look like having a lodger at all.

Back in Larkana, we went to the Club together, and now that Joan's state was undeniable it was treated with due solemnity, and I was properly congratulated. Joan pretended annoyance, pointed out that my part, though essential, was very small. She went further: there were Hindu gods, Greek gods, and even the Christian Jesus who needed no male; that that kind of birth was so common that the Greeks had a word for it: parthenogenesis. But this was too disturbing an idea, she was taken too seriously in the society where we lived, which was a long way from granting equality. So we left it.

It was odd how easily Joan and I could fit into that Club. Eric O'Flynn tried to be witty, with a very heavy wit, at which we all laughed politely; Eleanor was clearly a somewhat superior being who favoured us with her presence—we tried to be away when they were there; Isvaran could not stop being the Collector and sitting on his dignity. But Joan was never dignified, and I could keep dignity for my office. So we were treated as ordinary people, and we had fun. We and Nur Mahomed could tell of the funny things about the Visit, which rather shocked the O'Flynns and Isvaran. The two Punjabi girls were there, and Joan could talk of their school, which interested her. The two Shivdasani girls came, and told us about life at Calcutta University, which was so very different from the

Cambridge we could describe, but in many ways the same, too. And they had actually sat with Rabindranath Tagore, and talked to him! I think that, as Joan looked at those four very pretty girls, she was a little anxious about the coming time when she would be in Karachi and I was alone, meeting them. But perhaps she realized how very careful their families were of their virtue and reputations. Burn I never so warmly, I would have no chance to philander.

Isvaran sent Nuru and me out to patrol the river, making inquiries and finding people who could give intelligence about the Hurs. Hugh Lambrick and his special force were closing in on the Pir Pagaro, and we didn't want a lot to fly from him across the river. Whether we were very clever, or no Hurs fleeing the military tried to cross, I don't know, but we caught none. A few came in flight from other Hurs, we held them, and they gave us useful news.

Then we went into camp for the last time in that season. Over the same routes, doing the same things as before. We landed up at Shahdadkot, which was, after Kambar, my favourite camp, and there we met the LeMesuriers. He was the Settlement Officer, busy revising assessments. My camp had been booked there before he came, but he, being by very many years the senior officer, took precedence and the PWD bungalow. We had to camp in the little old bungalow near the town. Joan had met them in Karachi and approved of them, if for no other reason than that Mrs LeM had thoroughly approved of her taking a job, even if it meant deserting me for long periods.

Algie—and I have never met anyone else whom I could address as Algie—of course invited us to dine, and of course we dressed in our finest, which for Joan was a blouse and a wrap-around skirt, adjustable for her increasing girth, and made by herself from a pair of my grey flannel trousers. I had a good pair of grey flannels, my standard evening wear on tour, and they would do for dinner; it was a pity there was a patch on the seat, but Joan had sewn it very neatly. Also a collar and tie. We found the LeMesuriers in full evening dress, himself with a starched shirt—it was not hot enough to justify a soft front—bow tie, and short black jacket and cummerbund. His wife wore a long dress, as was proper. Joan's figure was no longer elegant, my jacket was clearly for riding, with wide skirts and two vents. Our shoes were a disgrace, but nothing could be done about that.

They met us on the verandah. We had never dreamt that anyone on tour nowadays dressed like this, but no one made any comment at all. Which was surprising, for usually Joan could not have restrained herself from laughing at such a ridiculous contrast of styles. Perhaps it was this baby that made her discreet.

One sherry on the verandah, and we moved in to dine. The china was standard PWD, but glass and silver were their own; plate maybe, but the glass was such as we would never have risked on tour. Our own smoky Danish glass was much too precious. There were, of course, finger bowls. No rose petals, but bougainvillea did just as well.

What we ate I cannot remember; probably no fish, for canal fish was very muddy, and Shahdadkot was about as far as one could get from the River; roast chicken, with fresh vegetables down from Quetta, not so good as ours from our own garden; caramel custard for a sweet, and the recipe must have been the same for every ICS cook. For fruit there was a special treat: a musk melon. Of course we were appreciative, and the ginger made it special. But we had seen the melon patch grown by a Brohi family near the canal, and had already eaten a watermelon.

The ladies left us to our nuts and port and cigars. Well, they walked through the arch which divided the room into two, standard PWD style. We could still see them, but in theory they were invisible. We drank our brandy, ate our cashew nuts, and smoked our cigarettes. We could now talk shop, and I mounted my hobby-horse. I was anxious to discuss my ideas for improving agriculture, and surely there was no better audience than the Settlement Officer, concerned with anything that would increase land revenue.

He must appreciate my idea for settling self-employed leaseholders on government waste: men who would use the last drops of water in the tails of canals, who would reclaim *kalarish* land, and who in the *kutchas* would clear and cultivate land as no zamindar with his share-cropping haris ever would. I grew indignant about the dead hand share-cropping laid on Sindhi agriculture, and I daresay Algie listened sympathetically. Certainly he would like to increase revenue, but I am sure he pointed out all the political difficulties.

We joined the ladies. No need to tell them what we had been talking about—they could hear it all through the arch anyway.

After the LeMesuriers left we moved into the bungalow and stayed on for a few days. Mostly I heard jirgas, for Shahdadkot was a largely Baloch area, and made *faislas*, settling disputes that would ordinarily have gone to the civil courts, with heavy costs and endless delays. Delay might lead to violence, which was my concern, and gave my action justification. The panchayat called. We talked about the town's problems—none serious—and the working of the paddy-husking mills, the availability of rail transport, and what about this rumour that the Government was going to buy all the rice? I knew nothing of it. (But soon afterwards I did.) We met Satramdas Tolani, new to me: the ne'er-do-well cousin of the Larkana Tolanis, so disreputable that he was disowned by them. But he was a much more interesting person than were they.

We passed through a countryside as it were resting, on our way to other camps and back to Larkana. The paddy had all gone to the mills, the rabi crops were nearly ready for harvest, and the seed beds were ready for the rice. Bare land that had dried before it could be cultivated and seeded was my target, that and all the kalar areas. Had there been a light tractor like the Ferguson, so much of the bare land could have been seeded. I collected figures—I would not dignify them as statistics—to take to Dokri.

It grew warm enough for Joan to prefer to stay at home, so I stayed too, going out to talukas to hear cases. Once we went together to Kambar, and met the Club, but no picnic: the mangoes were not yet ripe. I heard all about her friends in Karachi, now so many, people I had never heard of before. April Swayne Thomas was an artist with her own 'studio', who made a charcoal portrait of Joan which we still have. There was an Intelligence Officer who had been a master at my school, and school contemporaries. Fram was still in Ilaco House, now with his wife Jeanie, and new to me was a policeman, Andrew Davies, who seemed to be, as she put it, something of a light-weight compared with such as Reggie Simpson. Seniors were apt to be critical of her lifestyle: teaching, cycling about alone in her condition, speaking Urdu well enough to argue in the bazaar. But those who knew her best valued her, especially Lady Dow. She had been annoyed not to hear at once of the appendix operation, and had responded by sending a giant bunch of Government House flowers. Joan thought that she needed sympathy, felt she was belittled because she was in fact small and lacking the elegant figure that a Governor's Lady needed.

The Shahbans were special friends, but she had a problem with their kindness. They urged her to go and stay with them for her baby, and how could she refuse without hurting them? Somehow she managed it: surely they must see that wholly different customs and methods could not be coped with by a mother-to-be? Afroze came in with her baby, and that helped.

The Reinitzs were our friends above all others, and they introduced Joan to an entirely new circle, refugees from Europe, people with ideas entirely different, and refreshing, from those of the insular British: Donath, the Austrian radiologist; Levy, the furniture-maker from Berlin, Nemenye the Hungarian, and others we can remember, but for their names.

Another short teaching job turned up, and in May Joan was back in Karachi. The Mother Superior could now tell what were the limits of her availability, and that now there was no sinning with contraceptives; perhaps most importantly, she had some girls taking the London Matriculation (External), the equivalent of GCSE today, but she had no one for their mathematics, so Joan had just the job she wanted, ending in July. After that, a baby, and then she would see.

So she went back to Karachi for four months at least. This time she would stay with the Trotmans, and could be there for the birth and after. This was the time when Margaret had her baby, at the Civil Hospital. She wrote to me, and of course I telegraphed. She told me the baby, Simon, was a great comfort to her. She did not explain why she needed comfort. Perhaps because of its huge ten pounds of weight.

Staying with the Trotmans was respectable, for Joan as well as for them. But somehow Joan could not avoid offending Karachi society. She would not go to the Civil Hospital to have her baby. Instead, she would go to the Goolbai, the Parsi nursing home: not even a hospital! But Hugo Reinitz's opinion was what mattered, and he said she would be well looked after there, the midwife was better than any at the Hospital, and there were neither fleas nor bedbugs. 'Just what Joan Pearce would do! How does her husband let her do it?' Well, her husband wasn't there, and couldn't have made her change her mind. Anyway, there was time for Karachi to get used to the idea.

How futile was all the forward planning! The teaching went well, knitting and sewing went well, and Joan herself, growing larger and larger, was very well. I arrived for my leave, well ahead of the birth—I could get compassionate leave then as well. Then, on 18 July, Joan went into labour. There was just time to pack her bag and call Hugo, who took her to the nursing home.

How should a mere father judge of the pain and anxiety of a birth, particularly of a long-time premature birth? In fact, all was well; the baby weighed only four pounds, which perhaps made it unusually easy: it was a boy. I was near being a nervous wreck, was told to pull myself together, there was a lot to do. Then, after a few minutes, came the shock. 'There's another!' Another boy, less than four pounds.

Two of them, and so tiny! We were prepared with two names, Deborah and Adam—Bible names are always best— but now we needed another for a boy. In fact, there was no problem, David was from the Bible, that would do very well.

I thought it was mere chance who got the name-tag for Adam, and so became the firstborn; there were only fifteen minutes between them anyway. But Joan is sure she knew, and that today's Adam was assuredly the first.

In a modern maternity hospital, those two tiny premature objects would have been put straight into an incubator. In the Goolbai there was no such thing (nor was there in the Civil Hospital, or anywhere else in Sindh). But there was a clean, cheerful, and airy ward, and total, careful nursing.

Joan's part was done: she just lay there, relaxed and happy, with a son on each side of her, a very beautiful picture. I had to set to work. First, the births had to be registered, and I did that so quickly that I see from the register that we had not decided on the second name. It reads: '2 boys, both alive.' No names at all. Cables had to be sent to England, news had to be given to those people in Karachi who would most quickly spread it round. Poor Pip Trotman: she had expected one baby, six weeks later, whereas there were two, both long premature. But Grete Reinitz settled that: Framji had been called urgently up-country, where the river was threatening to burst its banks, and Jeanie had gone to Bombay, so Joan could have their flat, next door to the Reinitzs.

Joan had already been thinking of a nurse, so that she could go on teaching. She had consulted with the Mother Superior—they were good friends now—and she had found Candalina Miranda. Joan was determined that she would not have an old-fashioned ayah, but a girl she could train, who would wear western clothes and learn western ideas about babies. She would wear a blouse and skirt, and a white nurse's coat withal. Candalina was very dark indeed, though clearly from her name she was partly Portuguese, but from a very long way back, from Goa, where the Portuguese had ruled the first European colony in India and had encouraged inter-marriage as a matter of policy.

So I had to find Candy, and tell her that she was needed six weeks earlier than she had expected.

I was dazed; good wishes poured in, but at least there was no problem about presents. Joan had equipped herself handsomely for a baby of either sex, but now, and very early, she needed clothes, and nappies, and binders, and everything else for two, for two boys. The Clees and the Trotmans, Commissioner and Collector, gave her a beautiful twin pram. So her offences against social mores were forgiven: she was ICS, and the ICS appreciated success.

Cables from home. A telegram from Margaret: 'God Almighty!' Just that; she had won the race, but Joan had pulled back some of the deficit, and had certainly won in quantity.

The first time I saw my sons naked I was scared: after a day or two their faces were quite human, but when I saw those tiny bodies, they were like skeletons, and red; they looked flayed. I stayed in Karachi long enough to see Joan out of hospital and installed in Fram's flat, then I had to leave.

14

FLOODTIME

Although my hot weather leave was only half done, Isvaran wired urgently for my return: the River was running dangerously high, and the canals were above the safety level. No matter that my sons were only a few days old, I must go. The River bund was cut through near Chak, above Sukkur, by this abnormal flood. Framji had gone to close the breach, but could do little so long as the full force of the stream flowed that way. What he could do was collect timber and carts and labour to be ready when the river decided to flow away, as at some time it surely would. (Some weeks later it did: had it not done so, disaster would have become catastrophe.) He wrote to Joan, staying with her babies in his flat, relieving himself of his frustrations with contractors and officials who would not look ahead.

Three of the canals on the west bank had been cut at Ruk, and the railways as well. I could write to Joan that my subdivision was still safe, but not for long. Straight from Larkana I went with Isvaran to cut the west bank of the Rice Canal: the regulator at Naundero had blown out, at the Larkana regulator the level was 25 per cent above normal, and if that blew out Larkana would assuredly flood.

So we cut the bank and saved Larkana, but that condemned my own taluka of Mirokhan and also drowned a great deal of Bhutto land. The Bhuttos sent men to close the breach, and Isvaran had to send police to guard it. I met the Executive Engineer, Parwani, busy cutting breaches in his precious canals to avoid general over-topping, and weeping as he did so. Yes, Mirokhan was sure to go, Shahdadkot probably, Kambar perhaps. So I should evacuate Mirokhan, get all the foodgrains above the water, and cut all the distributor banks to hurry the flood along.

From then on I was on my own, sometimes with a tapedar, sometimes with an engineer, sometimes just with Horse. I was ahead of the water at Mirokhan, and found the Mukhtiarkar urging people to leave, to go north to higher land, and locking the stores of rice and wheat away from possible looters. Mirokhan had no high centre: there would be very little left above water, but the Mukhtiarkar with a few police would stay.

I wrote copiously to Joan. I wrote as I stayed the night in Mirokhan, and somehow the letter reached her. My letters alone provide a good picture of this great flood: 'Mirokhan, the river is rising again. Now I'm off to see to Mirokhan town, and to find food.' Later:

> I've got all the food possible for the town, and Mirokhan will probably be under water tomorrow. So also this compound, for certain. We shall have to wade out, I expect; we can hear rushing water all round, though we can't see it, except a vague pale sheet. We shall certainly wade out. It is damper than in Karachi—cooler too.
> ...It's coming with a terrific rush now. I feel rather a coward going, but still, it's my job to keep just ahead of things. I'm wondering if you'd like to be here or not. It's rather terrible, but thrilling also. And very sad.

After sending that letter I did not again send her a complete picture. Hugo Reinitz sent me a wire, via the Governor no less, that Joan's alarm was threatening her milk supply and the babies' health. Dramatic episodes were omitted, but fortunately it is those that stay most vividly in memory.

I had three specific jobs to do, and anything else that might turn up. I must persuade people to move out from danger areas. That applied to the whole of the Mirokhan taluka, and for a time I could requisition buses for Ratodero and Kambar. But the buses had no intention of being cut off: very soon no more came, and the people left on foot or by cart.

All the foodstuffs we could secure would be needed for the famine that would surely follow the flood. I had no money to pay, but never mind: I concocted a requisition order for the Mukhtiarkar; I had no power to do that, either. We filled and locked godowns, and put small stores at PWD waystations along the canal bund.

My other job faced me as I left Mirokhan to the water and rode towards Shahdadkot. On the way I saw to the breaching of canal watercourses and distributors in the path of the flood, for I was anxious to hasten it on its way. There was no hope of stopping it for more than a very short time, and even then it would spread more widely over the countryside, destroying more crops and endangering more villages until the obstacle was overtopped.

I and the tapedar with me were not popular. We could easily collect a gang to cut a channel and let the water off their land, but we had to face another gang bent on stopping us, stopping the water from flooding theirs. There were some awkward times, but never any actual violence. Moreover, as soon as a channel was breached, its defenders turned and became the attackers of the next downstream obstacle.

I was told that all was well in Shahdadkot; the water was several days away, and if the worst happened there was a large, high-level town centre that would hold the entire population if it must. But it posed a problem because it was a big grain storage and processing centre, the hub of the grain trade of the area. It was on the railway and had become the last link with Quetta. So the Army was involved, but at least the Army realized that it couldn't stop the water, and was rushing stuff through as fast as it could.

I rode in and found the Mukhtiarkar embarrassed by the presence of a Minister, Rao Sahib Gokaldas, with Pribdas Tolani, who had land and trading interests there and a fine brick house, and a Congressman unknown to me who was forever filing dramatic reports for the Press. Also waiting were messages from the Collector: I wrote to Joan:

> Why is it that the high-ups are all so late with their information? I've just had a wire to hold a canal which was overtopped three days ago; to evacuate a village that was flooded two days ago; to hold as second line a canal overtopped yesterday, and a third one that doesn't exist!

The telegraph belonged to the Railway—there was no telephone—and the telegraphist was being required to send off long screeds for the Minister at all hours. And who, he asked, would pay? So I ordered him to work only regular hours unless instructed by me or the Stationmaster to do otherwise, and always to give priority to Government and Railway messages. (I had no authority to do this: I just did it.)

The first message was from Isvaran: to cut and evacuate, and go to Shahdadkot. All had been done. He must have sent the message after I had left Mirokhan, so perhaps he was providing himself with *ex post facto* authority! It was this message that inspired my irritated report to Joan.

I began to organize the evacuation of Shahdadkot, using the railway while it was still working. Bashir Malik was there, to organize freight movements, and would run refugee trains too as long as possible. He allocated to me a lot of wagons for grain. I offered their use to any merchant who would sell his grain to the Government, its price to be determined later, but I don't believe any did. (Some may well have booked space from Bashir.) At the last Bashir had to send the wagons away—he didn't want to have them marooned—leaving me just a few for emergencies.

The politicians talked endlessly, but their indecision resulted in my getting only a few hundred people away. Just before the railway was breached all this top brass left.

I had nothing against the Hindus of Shahdadkot: they sat tight in the bazaar, they didn't help much, nor did they hinder. There were large quantities of grain at risk from flooding, but they seemed not to worry: I discovered that the wheat was safe above the expected flood level, and the rice in the lower town belonged mostly to outside merchants. There was nothing I could do about it if they would not or could not sell to Government in the railway wagons.

Shahdadkot was peaceful; in a way, it was quietly awaiting its fate, which reads more dramatically than it was. We expected the Quetta Mail to go through, and then the rail line must go, and only the telegraph would keep us in touch with the rest of the world.

It was a great relief to be rid of Gokaldas, who was shouting at me that I must save all the rice, myself shouting back that I would rather lose a thousand maunds of rice than one little child, and that anyway I had offered to buy it in the wagons and no one had accepted. All very noble and authoritarian. Unwise, too, to shout at a Minister, and to know that the Press was there—and, at that moment, not to care.

I rode about the town. The district bungalow and the Circuit House were flooded and culverts under the railway were letting water into the lower town. Ghulam Akbar was Deputy Superintendent, an excellent policeman and very valuable to O'Flynn, who was not. As I rode by, people were walking along the railway towards the Tanwari Bridge and the north. Akbar had organized evacuation there as soon as the last train left for Kambar. People were wading through the water, which became shallow away from the railway bank. As I got there the railway bridge over the canal blew out. The backed up water flowed away fast, and the route become much easier for the waders.

But what I envisaged was the Quetta Mail reaching Shahdadkot, unable to go forward, and finding the line breached behind it. The Mail with all its passengers, cut off in Shahdadkot! So I set off back for the station. Water was flowing fast through the lower town already, and people on their way to Akbar's escape route were having to turn back, with much wailing and crying of children. I thought I might have my claim to Gokaldas tested: would I sacrifice the Quetta Mail to rescue one child? But the test failed to arise.

As I neared the station the stream grew deep and strong, and I had to cross the current on my way. The water was near my knees, and Horse grew worried: he couldn't see where his feet went, there might be deep holes. But he struggled on, we got through the deepest water, and he was happier. During the whole of the flood period that was the most worrying time I had—really worrying: certainly not to be reported to Joan.

We made it to the station. There they were preparing to receive the Mail, and on my news at once tried to stop it. But it had already left Kambar, and there was no manned station in between. So we just had to wait. A trolley was sent out along the line, and after three miles found it under water, and no sign of any train. At least we were not going to have a great train-load of all sorts to deal with. We supposed we could manage ordinary people like us, or so claimed the Stationmaster. But there would be troops, and officers, and, may Allah preserve us, sahibs and memsahibs! The train might have got itself bogged down, but that would be Kambar's headache. I pointed out that in fact it would be mine too: they were properly sympathetic, they pointed out that anyway it would be some time before I could get out, and would I like a cup of tea?

About four hours later came a wire that the Mail had stopped before bogging down, and had laboriously reversed all the way back to Kambar. I went back to the Tanwari bridge, but this time I rode through the bazaar; there the

shops were open, and people sat about chatting. There was
a smell of cooking, though most of the women and children
had gone. The men would look after their property. I rode
on, envying them.

At the other side of the breach a train stood, and Akbar
was still guiding people across to it. I could see Bernard
Budd, the Deputy Commissioner, there, so I crossed myself
to talk to him. He agreed to organize another train next
day, and would keep in touch, so that whenever enough
people were ready to leave, a train would be sent. He would
also tell Karachi that all was well, and ask that Joan be told
too. My ride to warn the Mail would not be recorded in
any letter to her!

Soon afterwards the telegraph line fell into the water,
and that final contact with the outside was lost.

The next crisis in Shahdadkot was news of a threatened
raid from the hills. Towards the hills the water was very
shallow, and here was a heaven-sent opportunity for loot.
An alliance of Mengals and a Brohi tribe planned a raid,
but Ghulam Akbar had intelligence well in advance, so we
could prepare our defence. For this was far more dangerous
than the rumour that had previously arisen and died away,
and with the road and railway cut, and now no telegraph,
we could expect no help from outside. We decided we
could manage anyway.

We had a section of police with muskets, and persuaded,
or perhaps forced, all licence-holders to produce their
weapons. We settled on a line of defence, based on the
Tolani house and the police post, which were on either
side of the road to the bazaar, with deep, rushing water to
the north, south, and east. Then we mobilized our troops.
I was surprised how many Hindus had shotguns, and
beautiful weapons at that. But they were scared of firing
them. There were a few legal Muslim guns, and a surprising
number of Muslims with no gun but able to shoot. We
tried a few Hindus, but when they held their weapons,
loaded and cocked, wavering about, we found it dangerous

to be anywhere in front of them. So we developed a simple tactic: since the Hindus wouldn't lend their guns, each gunman had a marksman posted behind him, who would take his gun if he were hit, or offered to run away, and I would be in the Tolani house, and Ghulam Akbar in the police *thana,* to discourage any thought of knocking a man on the head to get his gun. This satisfied those Hindus who were suspicious of some of the Muslim townsfolk.

We were all prepared for an anxious night, standing-to expecting a dawn attack; then another spy came in. The Brohis had heard that there was a large armed force under a Sahib waiting for them; moreover, a Mengal had run off with a Brohi girl; furthermore, rain had fallen in the hills. So they had all set off home.

So many congratulations there were, for everyone, even for the man with a bad shoulder who had fired off both barrels at once before the butt hit his shoulder. But I often wondered what would have happened if the Brohis' intelligence had been as good as ours.

I stayed for another day. Ghulam Akbar and I camped on the verandah of the police post, at one end of which the police cook set up his kitchen, so we all ate together. With anxious moments in the past, Shahdadkot safely flooded, and the tribesmen gone, I felt pleasantly relaxed. I enjoyed the food, just grilled goat's meat and chapati, with tea and tinned milk. For those who didn't like tea there was water with 'pinkie' in it: the well was polluted. They didn't like that either, so I raided the bazaar for bottled drink. (In fact, the aeration did not bother any germs, but we overlooked that. A drop of whisky would have been much better, but anathema to our good Muslim police.)

I toured the lower town in a little skiff borrowed from the canal, so that I could make a proper report. No deaths, we thought, till we found a body floating. But it turned out that it was a corpse on which the doctor had been doing a post-mortem when the side of the mortuary collapsed; not a flood victim after all. He had been a Muslim, so was given decent burial. I found, too, a big glass bottle: very big, about four gallons, and rather amateurishly blown. It was— is—a beautiful green with a narrow neck, the kind the police said was used by liquor smugglers, and they wanted to know where it came from. I still have that bottle. Just how it travelled from water-bound Shahdadkot to here I cannot remember. It is my only memento of the great Sindh flood.

All seemed well by now. Ghulam Akbar was happy to be left in charge, said his boss, O'Flynn, was welcome to the rest of the District, and Shahdadkot was clearly a post of danger. Straight-faced, I agreed with him. But I had the rest of my sub-division to see to. I had left orders with my naik, instructions and money for him to get Horse round the flood towards the hills, to Kambar. This news spread about, and he soon found himself the proud escort for several other horsemen. So I crossed the breach again, this time with a little bundle of my toothbrush and such things essential to the orthodox escaper. I went on the refugee train to Jacobabad and met Bernard Budd: we settled about the flood. There was no more need for refugee trains, but he was anxious to get the wheat out. For that, I saw no solution till the water had gone. We had no boat apart from a little skiff.

His only outside contact was with Quetta by telegraph, and by a plane service being run by the RAF for the army. A plane was in Jacobabad on the way to Karachi, as a gesture of goodwill taking the Deputy Commissioner's mail. The pilot was willing to take a civilian passenger too, so long as he signed the proper forms: the RAF disclaimed any liability for damage or loss to the person or his possessions. I certainly wanted to go, so I signed, and asked for my parachute. No parachute! Still, I wanted to go, and presumably the pilot would be as careful for my skin as he must be for his own. The pilot flew me over Shahdadkot so that I might see what a mess it looked, then we were flying along the edge of the hills.

I had never flown before, and I wanted to see those hills, but I went to sleep. I slept the whole way, and only woke when we were coming down to Drigh Road, and my head hit the roof.

Bernard had signalled Clee that I was coming, so I went first to see him. He had only very sketchy information about what was happening in Larkana, because Isvaran had not been far outside the town. He had his troubles with the Bhuttos, and he and O'Flynn seemed happy to leave the flooded area to Ghulam Akbar and me, just occasionally wiring orders which were out of date or (in our opinion) silly.

I could tell Clee that everyone, Revenue, PWD, and Police, had done very well; that no lives had been lost, or were likely to be. Security was good, Kambar could probably be made safe, and Dadu District too, if Gallagher would help to hold the Dhamrao Canal, and we could divert the water to cuts we would make in the Flood Protection Bund. Then we would have to wait till Framji had closed the river breaches and the water had drained away.

He had had no word of the threatened Brohi attack on Shahdadkot, but plenty from RS Gokaldas and the Press about my high-handed actions in that town.

Clee could tell me that the high levels reported at Attock had now passed Sukkur, and Framji reported that the river had moved away from the breaches, so that he could get to work.

This first phase of the great flood was clearly over, but at once there was the future to consider, and I wanted to begin work on that now, when we could already see the kinds of problem that would have to be dealt with. In my area, most of the *kharif* crop was lost, and we would need money for famine relief; there was no shortage of grain just now, but the haris would have lost their winter harvest and so their food supply. Also, on the positive side, I

estimated that there would be scope for very large areas of
rabi crops, areas previously kalarish and desert now being
washed clean of the salt. I suggested that it would be a
good idea to have very large stocks of seed ready, of pulses
like *muttr* and *chunna*, oil seeds like *djambo*. And if Dokri
could get a light tractor to move from village to village
cultivating these large new areas quickly...? I knew there
was no hope of this, but saw no harm in floating an idea
that might bear fruit later.

There would clearly be need for a Special Officer. And
who better qualified than I?

No word that I was in Karachi had reached Joan, but
Candy had dreamed that I was coming—and there I was.
And there was Joan feeding her babies, one tucked in each
arm, and now looking truly human. They were only three
weeks old, but it seemed very much longer since I had seen
them being born. Sadly, I had to go away again next day.

I had time to see that Joan was comfortably settled in
Fram's flat: as comfortably as she could be with two
premature babies. I had a civilized meal, I was clean, we
were for a time very happy together, and then I went to
sleep again.

Trains were running as a shuttle service to Larkana, so I
went on one. I found Gokaldas on my train, going to
Larkana. After hearing of the tales he had told about me
in Shahdadkot, I could hardly be friendly; in fact I cut him
very pointedly, which I considered justifiable, though not
very wise.

At Larkana I reported to Isvaran. Gokaldas had reached
him before me. I had at last the chance to explain what
had happened in Shahdadkot, to justify my rudeness.
Perhaps it was acceptable. O'Flynn was there too. I thought
it strange that he should be there all the time, as also was
Isvaran. They were at the centre for receiving information
and issuing orders; I supposed it was the best place, but
they depended entirely on having that information, and I
personally seldom had time or means to send the daily

reports, he wanted. As for his orders…they had generally proved irrelevant. But, to be fair, they could not ride about as I could, dealing with each problem as it arose, or seeking to foretell and prevent it arising. I left them to their discussions, with the simple order to save Kambar. That I would certainly try to do.

I had left my charge without notice; I pointed out that there was no way I could ask. I also pointed out that the Governor had considered the situation at Shahdadkot so serious that he had arranged a plane to fly over the place; at a cost far greater than the travel claim I made for my return to Larkana. What I did not tell was that HE had arranged for that plane, which we had seen and waved to, on the insistence of Joan, who threatened that if her anxiety for me were not allayed her milk might suffer, the twins fall ill, and it would all be the Governor's fault. After I left Isvaran I went home and greeted everyone. I collected my camera—I would have a record from now on—a jar of marmite, and some permanganate of potash, 'pinkie'. At the Hospital I had a cholera injection, for an outbreak was surely coming with all the bad food and bad water there was about, and I took a trolley from the station.

Following the flooding of Shahdadkot, I found life a little flat. At last people had realized that it was no good trying to stop the water, that the best thing to do was to open up its way and send it on quickly, or divert it from one area to another.

Now I was always at the edge of the flood, or ahead of it. There were still distributaries to be breached or overtopped, covering the land and all those standing crops. When we had cut a way through for the water the men would stand sadly by, watching the ruin of their harvest and their homes, and comforting themselves, if it was a comfort, that it was the will of Allah. But I never found that this belief stopped them working as long as they had any hope at all.

The water was irresistible, but no longer was there that dramatic, rushing torrent. Instead was this horrible creeping on, hissing when it came to dry earth, carrying a fringe of rubbish ahead of it. Once as I looked upstream I saw a house collapse; it was only wood and thatch, with one mud brick wall, but the man beside me was crying: it was his house. Yes, his wife and children had got away on his cart, with all his pots and pans. But now he had neither crops nor home.

Those little bullock carts were a great boon. The cultivators in huts and hamlets could get safely away to higher ground, and from around Shahdadkot hundreds had gone off into the foothills; there they were safe, but would soon need food. The Brohis would not attack fellow Muslims, many of them Balochis. So, leaving their families there, they were doing very well as carters for those with goods to move. The little carts could go anywhere; if the water proved too deep, they could even float.

In towns under threat there was little co-operation. Kambar I found full of intrigue. Would I order a breach here and not there? Inquiry showed that this would save the petitioner's land, and flood that of a rival; that other breach would do the opposite. But there I found Rashid Kazi, the Executive Engineer. Regardless of these interested prayers, he had opened breaches in the right place to take the water north of the town, and Kambar was safe. Ali Ahmed Yusifani was still there as Mukhtiarkar, and Mahomed Khan Halcro, the local gang boss, otherwise something of a scoundrel but now with more to lose than anyone, was a reliable lieutenant to Ali Ahmed. I left with Rashid Kazi to see what could be done about my last taluka, Warah.

The people of Warah were apathetic, immovable. Kazi tried to get men to cut distributors north of the town, to divert the water, but none would go. They expected the middle to be above the flood, and those living lower down had built little bunds round their houses, bunds of soft earth which even still water would waste away in a few minutes when it came. Moreover, the proposed breaches would flood the lands of big zamindars, and they would have men on guard.

So Kazi and I and a few men left the town at the dead of night, found no one at the chosen spot, so made the breach untroubled. Next morning a tapedar was sent to the nearest zamindar with an official warning from me: anyone who tried to close the breach, or otherwise interfered with it, would be liable to immediate imprisonment. I doubt if I had such summary powers, but as a bluff it worked. Nor did I ever have any complaint about the damage the breach had done, doubtless because the zamindars were not fools: the channel would have overtopped anyway.

Perhaps Warah was safe now, perhaps not. We could do no more. So Kazi, the Mukhtiarkar, and I left for Nasirabad, in a group with two or three tapedars.

Nasirabad had no hope at all: it had no raised middle, and the Railway beyond it, and the Dhamrao canal to the south would hold up the water. But the people refused to go; they claimed that the water was a long way off and would never reach them. In the end we convinced them that they must go. I left police in their thana, to prevent looting, and moved on. We proved right about the Railway: it certainly held the water, for there was little force in it here; and although Nasirabad was drowned, Dokri, and above all Mohen-jo-daro, were saved. Maybe I would have sacrificed a lot of rice to save a child, but I felt no qualms about a whole village so long as a bit of archaeology was safe.

From Dhamrao I could telegraph O'Flynn to tell him what I had been doing with his police, and Isvaran with my latest reports. I sometimes wondered if Eric knew about the PWD telegraph system.

The water was coming to the end of my territory: the Dhamrao Canal was my boundary with Dadu, though Kazi was, of course, responsible for the whole of it. He hoped that if we could strengthen it here and there, and cut the big Flood Protection Bund at the far western end, we could save his canal and Dadu District itself. We rode along it, noting weak spots, and I wired Gallagher, Collector of Dadu, to get men to these spots to strengthen it, otherwise it would probably overtop, for the flood was most certainly coming. His response was that it was my canal, my responsibility, but that he was preparing for refugees.

This was stupid: the canal was the PWD's, for the revenue department it was just a boundary. We found men on my side prepared to breach the banks to let the water off their land: they certainly knew the flood was coming, if Dadu didn't. They proposed to pass it on as fast as they could.

We made the men promise to wait, and persuaded some of them to come with us to cut the protective bund. I suggested that Kazi stay to guard his canal, but it was only an inundation one, he said, not like his precious Barrage Canals. (But in fact by that time it was fed with 'Barrage' water!) He came on; if Dadu wasn't bothered, the protective bund was more important.

We reached the bund in the dark, as the water was rising. A busload of men came from Kambar with several hurricane lamps, and were very happy to see us—we gave legal colour to what they had intended to do. The bus went straight back, on the hill side of the bund, lest it be cut off when the breach was made.

The water was coming surprisingly fast—we could hear the hissing round the fringe as it came. The men worked hard, in shifts, cutting deep and narrow grooves, leaving a thin dam in each cut. Once the water broke through the cuts widened fast, they joined up, all so quickly that one man was left on the far side. He wasn't worried. The top of the bund was swarming with snakes, it was no place to delay, so once the water was running well we left. They all got home, some way.

Later we heard that the Dhamrao had overtopped and a large section of its banks had been washed away. I was sure, and I reported it, backed by Kazi, that with help we could have held the Dhamrao while we cut the bund; but I couldn't expect people from my side to try: the breach was just what they wanted. Later I asked them about it, but they swore they had done nothing, had just watched, but no one at all had come from Dadu.

Along its course the flood was running in the ancient bed of the river, the Western Nara; for most of the way this was hardly detectable, except by the depth of the water. After we cut the Protection Bund the flood had a clear way along the edge of the hills to Dadu, where they came close to the River, and the water went through a sluice in the bund and so home. The railway crossed this sluice, and the last joke of this great flood was to blow out the sluice and so cut Larkana's final rail link, leaving it isolated. As for Dadu, Gallagher had ample opportunity for practising his relief plans.

Once the bund was cut, the whole of my sub-division was under water, except for Kambar and the strip beyond the railway, and Ghaibi Dero. The Nawab had plenty of water now! And his people had an easy refuge in the hills. Most of the people leaving Warah and Nasirabad had gone off to test Gallagher's relief plans, and Mohen-jo-daro was reported to be safe.

The little bungalow of Garhi was quite nearby, and I went there for the rest of the night. I had to be my own syce, unsaddled Horse and rubbed him down, and tethered him near the big peepul tree. The hermit had gone. Horse had been grazing on lush green paddy, and was a little loose, but I found some chopped *juari* straw and gave him that. The bungalow was raised on the canal bund, and had a well: polluted, no doubt, but I had my pinkie. I found a charpoy bare of any quilt, lay down, and just went to sleep. I wanted nothing to eat.

I felt emptied; I was literally emptied: even pinkie had not been enough, and I had acute diarrhoea. I need no record to remind me of that! I was mentally exhausted too, my mind like a motor suddenly out of gear. Kazi could

look after his canals, O'Flynn could see to keeping the
peace, and Isvaran couldn't get in touch with me. I wanted
to have nothing to do with administering anyone or
anything. I would just wander off wherever the water was
shallow enough and see what was going on in all this
flooded waste of my sub-division, with no intention of doing
anything about it.

First I had to saddle up, something I had never done
before. But there was one thing Captain Cooper had taught
me at Cambridge: if the girth tightens before its usual
notch, don't trust it, a horse likes to blow himself up so
that if you mount and he decides to let out his breath you
will have a very loose girth, and at the slightest peck you
and the saddle will slip sideways. I remembered, I waited
till he had to breathe out, and got his girth good and tight.
So perhaps all my time with the Captain had been
worthwhile for that one tip.

There were still a few people about, who happened to
have built their summer huts on top of a spoil bank, or
some such place. They stayed there to protect their crops,
though there was nothing to protect now. They always made
me welcome, glad of news about the floods. They had
noticed the level receding after the Dhamrao and the
Protective Bund were breached. Their families had moved
out of their homes on their carts; they had food, plenty of
water, they saw no need to move. Their question always
was, how were they going to live, with the kharif harvest
lost, and so all their food for the next year? I promised
them, I assured them by Allah, that I would get them food.
And I certainly meant it. I would eat a chapati with marmite,
drink *lassi*, or perhaps water doctored with pinkie. A man
would try the marmite, when I assured him it was not *haram*,
but I found no one who liked it. If there was no *lassi* I told
them to drink my water, which was safe, and I doctored
their water jars. I expect they threw the bitter stuff away as
soon as I left. I offered to pay for the food, but none would
let me, so I left a coin by which they could remember the

flood. I promised help in getting seed for the rabi crop, and help for rebuilding their houses. Their bullock carts were all away, being used by a son or a brother, a very profitable business.

I hoped that I would be able to fulfil all those promises.

I went to Warah and stayed the night with the Mukhtiarkar, who was busy securing food against the time when merchants might try to take it out to more profitable places. The middle of the town was safe still, but all the little *bunds* on the outskirts had washed away. I set off and passed that dirty place Wagan, and on to Ber.

Ber had survived well: it was a very old village, though so small, and had a higher middle than some. Nor had it grown recently, so there were no outlying houses to fall down. I went into the bazaar, and was greeted with enthusiasm. Yes, the road we had built had been fine, but now it had been partly washed away. Never mind, when the water went they would rebuild it.

'Fikr nahin!', 'Never mind!' So many times I heard that from people happy even to have survived, who believed that they would be all right, *Inshallah,* especially if the *Sirkar* would provide food to replace their lost harvest.

The country I rode through, sometimes on part of the road, sometimes wading carefully where the road had washed away, was an astonishing sight. All this wide, featureless country was a waste of water, with only an occasional tree, or spoil bank, or collapsed house showing. There was no breeze at all, the air was oppressively humid, the sun shone without pity from a white sky. It was not so very hot, or the day would have been mortal.

I rode into Kambar, where my naik greeted me, reproaching me that I had not taken him with me. People came back from the Protection Bund saying that I had ridden away alone. I apologized to him, pointing out that he had no horse, that anyway he had had his adventure, riding out of Shahdadkot. He had reason: he could have borrowed a horse, and it was his duty to be with me. But I was glad that I was alone. I gave him Horse to ride back to Larkana, and myself persuaded the Railway to let me have a trolley.

In Larkana I took a tonga to the bungalow, to change and have a proper bath, if only in a tin tub. I could dress leisurely and have a cup of tea. Tea! Tea without cardamoms! Such a slight luxury was paradisal. So too was the sight of our beautiful drawing-room. But I must go to the Collector, before he heard I was in without reporting.

I was determined to take my hot-weather leave. I had no office work, all disputed sites were under water; no cases, for witnesses and even parties were inaccessible. Correspondences with Government were either irrelevant or needed information also inaccessible. Isvaran wanted reports, and I could give them in person. All I needed was some money from the bank, and I could be away. I was anxious to be away soon, I was not really fit for anything else, and I was afraid that the bridge at Dadu might go if I was long delayed.

In principle, I might go. I could report on the state of the flooding, and that all the Mukhtiarkars had their relief plans well in hand. In fact, no! At the last moment there were food-rationing problems at Kambar, and I was sent to sort it out.

I was just then in a permanent state of irritation: it didn't pay to cross me. (I wonder now how I, who was normally so patient and equable, could have been so bad-tempered as I was then. But I just was.) The problem was such a stupid one: a Hindu relief officer was feeding Hindu refugees but querying every Muslim claim, and a Muslim was doing the converse with Hindus, and refusing them food. I was so angry that I could have knocked their heads together, literally. I scared them into common sense. And was that bridge still holding? Only when I wrote to Joan, or had a letter from her, was I relaxed and peaceful.

As I write about my wandering after leaving the protection bund, I am moved vividly back to that time and that country. What I record as happening, did happen. I may have got the chronology wrong here and there, but not the events. I may have spent three nights in that meander, not just two; but I cannot remember where I could have spent a third, so I leave it. I left the *bund* in the middle of a bad bout of diarrhoea, but with drinking only doctored water, and eating little food, I was cured by the time I reached Kambar. Allahdino should have been with me, it was his job, but I was glad he wasn't. Those few days have left me with a feeling of a very rational and vivid dream.

Back in Larkana, I found that Isvaran was called to a conference in Hyderabad, and insisted that I postpone my leave till he came back. I saw no need, but in fact that was not reasonable: there was just then no Deputy Collector in Naundero, and he could not really leave the District without any superior officer at all.

I knew the water was getting nearer and nearer to Dadu, but he came back by train; the train shuttled back, and then, only then, when I was ready to go, did that sluice blow out. It was useless to be angry. But now I would probably need two whole days instead of a few night hours to reach Joan and the twins. The Railway still had trolleys— they must have brought in extra ones—and I knew there was a motorized one, but that was kept for their own officers, so they let me have an ordinary one. I would have to pay, at least for the crew. Never mind!

I loved riding on those trolleys, seeing the country, feeling the breeze they created, so near the ground that there was always a feeling of great speed. The normal crew was two, but four for a long journey like mine. A railwayman came with me, inspecting the line, which would reduce the cost. Two men ran behind on the rails, pushing, and every half hour they changed with the other two. They wore shoes, which surprised me, for usually they would be barefoot; but they explained that in the cold weather, or early in the morning, they would be barefoot, but in the middle of the day in the hot weather the rails were so hot that their bare feet would be blistered.

On the way we had an odd encounter. We met a trolley going the other way, and, of course, stopped and exchanged courtesies. He was a policeman, son of one of the Bhuttos, coming home from Bombay. I had heard of him. He had been charged with murder, but acquitted on a plea of self-defence: he had been caught in bed with another man's wife, the husband had attacked him, and Bhutto had shot him. Clearly it was self-defence; it was just lucky he had his pistol with him. But the case made him unacceptably notorious in Bombay, so he was back in Sindh.

He had not come alone: with him was his new wife, said to be a famous Bombay actress, but all we could see was a long white *burqa* with a toe sticking out. She might be revealed to thousands on the screen, but not to a white man and a bunch of 'coolies' on a trolley. We left them, with some pithy comments *sotto voce* from my crew. They might be illiterate, but they knew all about a story such as this, touching the most powerful local family. I laughed. They knew I had heard.

On we went, with flood water on our right, dry land towards the river on our left. We came to the Dadu bridge, looked at it, decided that the double bend posed no problem to a trolley, so ran into Dadu station in time for me to catch the Karachi train. I paid off my crew and told them I would be back in about two weeks; they might even be there to meet me.

I should have called on Gallagher, but didn't want to be angry again; I wanted to forget about the flood altogether. Nor did I want to miss the train. I got on board and went to sleep.

We reached Karachi in the small hours. It was raining, had been for a long time. (There were twelve inches in twenty-four hours, a whole year's normal total.) Everywhere seemed to be flooded, and at that time there were neither taxis nor gharris. The waiting-rooms were full of women and children, so I sat on a trolley and waited for the dawn. I smoked and watched the rain, seeing the rails being slowly covered, and feeling that perhaps I couldn't get away from floods. It was ironic, but at least it was no concern of mine.

At last I got home. I learned to speak English again. I paraded my sons about in their pram. Lady Dow had given Joan the freedom of the Government House gardens, and we took them there. I met His Excellency, told him about the floods, gave him my ideas about what I thought would need doing once the water had gone.

I met the Clees, and then had a long interview with Taunton, the Chief Secretary, and pressed for a Reconstruction Programme, with a Special Officer to look beyond flood relief to the opportunity provided by all the land washed clean of salt. Described the foul, salt-polluted water rushing through the breach in the Flood Protection Bund. Special staff, special programme, dedicated funds, special measures to take advantage of this unique situation.

I could hardly expect him to commit his Government, but I was sowing seed in his mind, and not planting it too deep. On the other hand, I wanted to scotch the tales I knew would be spread about me, that I could not deny, would not want to deny, that on occasion I had acted with a high hand. I hoped I made it clear that I was in the tradition of the ICS officer who was perfectly capable of tackling any problem he had to face, acting within the law or not, for the public good, 'under colour of his office'. I made it clear that I felt that I was best fitted to be this Special Officer, as I had implied to the Governor and to Clee. I probably did myself no good at all: this junior Assistant Collector talking so big to the top brass.

All this took several days, and just as we were deciding that we would be our private selves, Isvaran called me back again, urgently. The call had come through Taunton, so there was no way to avoid it. I sent Joan a note from Dadu, and thereafter it would be several days before we heard from each other.

I inquired what the emergency was. Isvaran told me he wanted to go on tour. I had lost half my leave, and taken two days to get back, just for that. Must I always be in headquarters when he was out, even within the District? What would happen when my real touring season began? How well justified was my feeling about him! Perhaps he suspected what I thought of him as Collector, and felt he must exercise authority. I sat around brooding. I went to the Club. I spent time working out what I would do if I really was given a special job, with money to spend. I wrote it all down, and sent it, very officially and confidentially, to Taunton, through Isvaran.

There was no response. I was so worried at the way time was passing with nothing done, or planned, except for a little money for famine relief, that I wrote to Joan with my worries. The letter is dated 20 September 1942, (so the twins were two months old: my time had passed quickly).

So far nothing has been heard from Government as to what it intends to do about the floods. And the interim period is beginning. Are we to give free grants of land for this rabi crop, or not, and funds for reconstruction? Is wheat to be encouraged rather than other crops? Are village sites to be moved, or not? Is there to be any resurvey at all? Already some areas are coming out of the water; in a fortnight there will be a lot, and we don't know at all what Government intends to do.

Quite literally in Karachi no one has done any more yet than allot some money for food. I am writing again, but feel that already it is too late for any planned reconstruction to be undertaken.

...If you see Taunton you can mention it—all the questions, I mean, don't press me for the job anymore, or he'll get fed up.

It astonishes me today, reading that, to think how the wife of a junior officer could even think of tackling a Chief Secretary, or that her husband could be so rash as to ask her to do it. It was, I suppose, part of the mystique of the

Indian Civil Service. We were both members, there was no
problem of seniority or subordination. But there were areas
in which one need be careful.

Perhaps my confident approach depended on my belief
that I had done pretty well at Kambar. I had prevented a
bad riot; I had entertained the Viceroy without a hitch,
with a lot of game, and with a notable picnic. I had seen
my sub-division flooded with no loss of life at all, and myself
in the middle of all the danger spots. The Quetta Mail did
not bog down, and it was Gallagher's fault that there were
floods in Dadu. If only the Brohis and Mengals had attacked
and been beaten off heroically! As it was, who could say
that there really was a threat? Or that earlier there really
might have been a riot in Kambar? As for the floods, I had
ridden about cutting bunds and flooding land, often the
land of important people, and had cleverly escaped from
Shahdadkot and flown to Karachi, a means not available to
many people. Moreover, I had been rude to a Minister,
and threatened his friend.

Before I could brood for too long, Isvaran came in, full
of orders for me. He had only been as far as Kambar and
Naundero—indeed, to go further he would have needed a
horse or a boat—but he knew everything. Most of his orders
needed only information that I could give him. Some, like
bringing in wheat from Warah to Larkana, were quite
impracticable; but one would get me away: I was to go and
evacuate Ghaibi Dero.

Isvaran had not actually seen the place, but it had been
reported that the Nawab needed help. I explained that
there was an easy way from the Dero to the hills, so he
agreed that I should clear my office before going. My
Chitnis showed me a sheaf of demands for information
about the floods, information that could not be had till at
least the water had receded, so I told him to sit on them all
until I came back again.

A letter from Joan: Framji had written that the peak of
the flood had passed, and the main current had at last

moved away from the breach, so that he could make progress with the closure. There was also a nasty rumour that I was to be transferred as Personal Assistant to Holt, Collector of Sukkur. He had asked for an Additional Collector, which would have been a post on senior grade, but was being given this Assistant instead. Why he needed this extra help I couldn't tell: when I was there with Dermont Barty, Ansari had managed perfectly well. And why me? Why not for me the reconstruction job for which I was well suited? A Personal Assistant was usually a junior Deputy Collector, not an ICS officer.

It seemed that my negative analysis of my work at Kambar was to be the operative one, or that Gokaldas harboured bitter resentment. But this was only rumour, and rumours usually proved false. So I left, worried but hopeful. The railway line was still open for trolleys, constantly repaired with extra ballast as the lapping water washed it away. This time a Railway official was travelling, so we had the motorized machine. Still it had a crew of two, to throw stones at pye-dogs which attacked it all along the way.

In Kambar, Ali Ahmed had now organized rationing well, giving food only to proven refugees. There was, in fact, no shortage: the object was to preserve the surplus. I had brought a load of ration cards, and he issued them to refugees, but we were both dubious of their value: one needs more than cards and a list to set up an effective rationing system. But he had locked away enough stocks to set a controlled price and forestall a black market. There was no way just then for any but the smallest quantities to be moved away.

As for Ghaibi Dero, I supposed that people would go to the hills. But a lot of boats had been brought up from Manchar, and a ferry service was running the other way. Government had hired some boats, and I had one. I went to Dostali, found that everyone who wanted to get away could, and collected all the ripe grapefruit from the bungalow garden and sent them to Joan. They reached her after four days. I left Ghaibi Dero to its Chandio guards.

The boats from Manchar came with their Mirbahar crews. Some were on government contract for officers such as me; others were freelancing. They came by rail, and launched themselves as soon as they found water deep enough. They needed only to buy food sometimes when they were near a shop. They did all the carrying where bullock carts couldn't go. Mine was a contract boat, its crew were twins, Khan Mahomed and Mahmoud Khan; they both answered to Mamoo.

The boats were high-bowed punts, like those at Drigh— which were doubtless among them. We set off for Shahdadkot, overtaking boats heavily loaded with goods, passing others with passengers. There was an organized ferry. It took us five hours, but they took much more.

Shahdadkot was a wreck. It stank with rotting rice, and doubtless other things. All the paddy mills and grain stores in the lower town had collapsed, and even the brick houses higher up were cracking as the earth beneath them melted. There was still a river running between the town and railway station and police headquarters. Bernard Budd had asked me to get out all the wheat I could for him, and certainly there was plenty of it stored above flood level. But the railway was cut to pieces, and it took a little boat, carrying no more than half a ton, five hours to cross the flood; loading and unloading made one trip a day's work. Bernard had his own boats, fetched from the river, but it was all too expensive. Moreover, the grain would still be there when the railway reopened. It was a strange situation. Boats brought fresh fruit down from Quetta, fresher and cheaper than it was in Larkana and Sukkur, much cheaper than in Karachi.

I stayed in the Tolani house, surrounded by water, but firmly founded. I was entertained by the Tolani bad hat, Satramdas, who was a cheerful ne'er-do-well, full of bawdy gossip, even from Delhi. He had, in fact, just come by

various means from Karachi, and told me, on good
authority, that there was going to be a Special Reconstruction Programme with a fund of two *crores* of rupees.
(About £1,500,000. It was an enormous sum, so much that
its size made its truth improbable.) Rumour said that I
would administer it. So I left Shahdadkot full of hope. But
I wished the figure had been more credible.

However, the Mukhtiarkar and the police inspector were
happy with their charge—in fact, they were having an easy
time.

On the way back we met a boat from Mirokhan—there
was a veritable network of services!—which told us that one
of the small food stores in an abdar's hut on the bank of
the Warah Canal was being undermined, and might fall
down. I sent someone along the bank to Mirokhan, where
there were still people, and by the time I had got the hut
open there was a reasonable number for a distribution: no
time for any careful screening, I divided people up into
groups and gave them a bag of rice each, to divide, a turban
full of gram or lentils, and a handful of chillies to brighten
their lives. There was one bag of chillies, which I distributed
myself.

I had never handled chillies. The memory of that
occasion is so vivid that I never did again. I was hot and
sweaty, all pores open. I plunged my arm into the little
sack and doled them out, a handful each. First there was
an itch, then a pricking, and then such agony as to make
prickly heat seem by contrast a gentle tickle. I had to finish
the job, appearing unmoved—well, not too deeply moved—
before I could go and douse the fire, and scrub and scrub
till there was no more than smouldering heat, and clearly
my arm was not going to drop off.

The Mukhtiarkar arrived on his horse. He noted down
the groups that had had food, to avoid giving them a
double ration. He told me that one should not plunge
one's arm into a bag of chillies: surely everyone must know
about chillies? He was a little resentful that I had

encroached on his sphere, but could hardly say so to his superior officer. However, I apologized, there had been no time to spare; we gave him news of the flood, and parted friends. Then, to justify me, the side of the hut fell out.

It took eight hours to reach Kambar; in full sun, no shade at all. I was wearing sandals, and even my feet were burned. We saw so many boats, some with awnings over family groups, some laden with goods. I took more photographs. I had missed the top of the flood, by now it was slowly going down, but even so it was awe-inspiring. What it had been when only the tops of the tallest trees were showing, I must imagine: I was on the Dhamrao then. As the country looked now was impressive enough, and I had the whole of that peaceful day to appreciate it. We were in no hurry; we even tied up to a tree for a picnic. I had been given a flask of tea, but the Mirbahars would not touch it, they preferred water from over the side, said it was sweet and good. Indeed, it was probably as pure as any water anywhere else in the District. But a cigarette each they would accept. As we moved along I just sat, standing if Mamoo saw anything he thought worth a picture. I photographed them as one of them punted, and then they demanded one of both together, properly clad with clean white turbans, tall and slim. I have it still: later I sent a copy for each, addressed to the post office at Dadu, for their homes were always moveable with the seasons.

I discharged the two Mamoos at Kambar, but they would not go home: they would stay, and expected to make so much ferrying that it wouldn't matter if at the end their boat had to stay.

Back in Larkana was a letter from Joan, full of hope for me for the special job. Framji had been called in to Karachi to report to the Prime Minister, and had spoken about the need for a special reconstruction programme, and had mentioned me as best fitted for its care. Allah Baksh Soomro, the PM, said to him, as he had said to me, that he was all in favour, but there was no money. Taunton sent

me a DO saying my name was being considered. Joan had
met Jack Phelps, the latest, and last, British recruit to the
ICS in Sindh, who had told her he was being posted to
Kambar, but didn't know about me. Joan's letter and
Taunton's were several days old.

There came the direct, the real news: the first, derisive
rumour was the truth: I was to go as Personal Assistant to
Holt at Sukkur, on the junior scale of pay. There was to be
no Special Officer, no special project at all, just a little
money to relieve famine.

I was bitterly angry, and disillusioned. But it had all been
Gazetted. Only inwardly could I rail, and it would do no
good at all. Clee said I might get something better soon,
but he had also said not long ago that he was short of ICS
officers, and then sent me to Sukkur to be a glorified clerk,
so his note was doubtful comfort.

But at least we would all be together. If I had been
posted in a special job we would have been in an awkward
situation, for Framji would need his flat, and there was no
way that Joan could get to Larkana with two babies, at least
till trains were running again. Perhaps the unhappy posting
saved those babies' lives.

Since then I have often wondered why the prize posting
was dangled before me and then taken away; why
reconstruction was ever proposed. A minimum help was
provided, no more, and people were left to pick themselves
up and rebuild their houses and their livelihoods, as had
happened in India a hundred times before. I was silly to
think that, at this late time in the British Raj, things might
be different. Money must be found to rebuild roads and
railways and canals, but there was no more. Perhaps my
transfer was not just a condemnation of my actions.

So my intimate association with the great flood ended,
with no fuss, no celebration, no congratulations at all.

As soon as Jack Phelps came to take over, I said good-bye
to Isvaran, politely, no more. I expect he was as happy to
see me go as I was to be away from him. He certainly had

not helped with my project, and may well have helped with my transfer.

My only mementos of the great flood are a number of photographs and one very large green bottle.

15

DOWN, THEN UP

So I packed up all I could carry with me and left all the rest—furniture, books, linen, crockery—to come to Sukkur when the railway was open again. My car Jack Phelps could use till it could reach me. I returned Horse to Naundero, with some appropriate fee. I went one last time to the Club, and said good-bye to all our friends. All I left was touring crockery for Jack, and the wheelbarrow for the mali.

Jack Phelps arrived, he met my office staff, and we had a formal photograph taken, with proper garlands. I gave him my charge notes: an excellent staff, no arrears of work, no current cases, none likely to arise till the water was gone. He was, in fact, in charge of a vast lake, with odd trouble spots like Kambar and Shahdadkot, but with a good set of Mukhtiarkars. And good friends at the Club. O'Flynn had gone to the Railways, but his Deputy would do very well.

I went for the last time on the trolley to Dadu, and on the train to Karachi for my joining time on transfer: no need now to fear a recall, and no need either to hurry to begin this shadow of a job. I reached there before my letter did, so I could read it myself, and re-ignite my indignation:

Damn Taunton! The special job may have been a castle, but I have a letter from him saying that my name was being considered for it, so it's unjust to turn round on us and accuse us of daydreaming...

Let's not bother about the job. We go to a better station, this is the last month to pay for the car, and next month I get an increment too, +Rs 92. And above all we shall be together, and shall not have so much touring to keep us apart. Great dishonour, but I could not love my honour much, loved I not you far more. And in a week I shall be with you.

We were short of money, though in fact doing better than most of our contemporaries: Joan was a notable economizer, and we were abstemious. My Service was supposedly very well paid, but inflation had beaten all of us. High pay was one of the factors that kept us honest, but it didn't operate any more. Had we not had the incentive of a tradition, we would all have been 'bent', but I never heard of any of us who were. As I wrote to Joan: 'I can't complain officially about our finances. I wouldn't, anyway. Clee and such would merely say they told us so.' Which, indeed, was true...

The move we proposed, with two delicate, three-month-old babies, would not, I think, be countenanced today. In the conditions we faced in India at that time, it did not appear such a very risky venture. Moreover, Framji needed his flat, with Jeanie coming home; and the Reinitzs promised to come and stay with us as soon as we had a place of our own, with our own furniture. But in fact they never did: Hugo was the doctor most sought after, most hard worked, in all Sindh.

Joan had been in Karachi for most of the year; she had many ties to break. My meetings with the Governor, Taunton, and Clee were inevitably formal and bleak. I must not be angry and insubordinate, they could hardly be apologetic. Farewell meetings with their wives were not so stiff. The most Taunton would say was that the next time there was a senior-scale acting job I would have it. I thought: maybe. I still had his letter that hinted at the special post that never was.

We said good-bye to the Shahbans, and I saw Afroze and her baby. Afroze had grown up from that giggling, dumpy girl who had married Nazir: perhaps he had seen how she would grow, for now she was a specially beautiful young woman, a paragon of her race, as was Margaret Cargill of hers. In my opinion, anyway.

Margaret Cargill came in to compare her Simon with Adam and David. April Swayne Thomas gave me her portrait of Joan, and promised to stay with us in Sukkur.

And so on, and on, and on. We scattered farewell cards all around, as one did. The Soomro Ministry had just fallen, so there was no need to call on Ministers.

My leaving Larkana had been simplicity itself compared with the problem of moving the whole family from Karachi. Nawab was not going with us, but Mistri, who had gone to help Joan when she had to do her own catering, would stay. We would have no bearer in Sukkur, for my Khandu was in fact a Larkana patewala. But we would have Candy.

Candy deserves very special appreciation, for she was to be with us for a very long time. She had come straight from being a servant at the Convent, and was going to the *jungly* parts of Upper Sindh, leaving the sureness of the Convent behind her; leaving her two sisters, her auntie, and a young man who on and off was courting her. She had faced the criticism of ayahs she met, for being on at night, being underpaid, not working fixed hours. All true. But Joan pointed out that she was living like the family, all found, that when she had appendicitis she was treated privately, that she had time off when she wanted it—usually! She was dressed 'european' and the clothes were provided. And so on. The grumbles died away: she was a nanny, not one of those 'sari-ayahs'. On the whole she was happy, and as time passed she was more and more attached to 'her two sons'. There were no other twin sons about: that helped.

Candy, with her Convent upbringing, was immensely modest: Joan said she kept her knickers on even in the bath. 'Madam, I have no new knickers for hospital!' 'Candy, you won't wear them, anyway'. 'Gee, Madam, shame! I'm not going!' But she overcame her shame, and went. While she was away her sister Regina stood in for her. If Regina failed, there was always Matilda.

Later, she married and had a daughter, at about the same time we had one too. So, as she said, she then had two daughters to add to her two sons. Adam and David loved her dearly, and so did we. And Judith when she came, to join Candy's own Rebecca. We wanted to take her to England when we finally left Sindh, but had to decide that England would be too cold and unfriendly a place for her; also, she had her own family. We always kept in touch with her, and years later, when Judith was grown up and Candy an old lady, companion to an old lady in the Gulf, Judith met her there, all unannounced. Her cable had not arrived, so she asked her mistress if she might see her; it was proposed to summon her, but Judith said, 'No, don't do that. She is Candy, I will go to her.' She did, and Candy's startled greeting was, 'O, Madam!' Were mother and daughter so much alike?

Candalina Miranda: very dark, with it beautiful; something Portuguese a long way back. One of the very special people we knew in Sindh.

Somehow we were all packed up. The Railway had claimed that the breaches would be bridged by November, but even their own engineers didn't believe it. So we took the Lahore Mail, with a compartment for all five of us, our many-packaged *saman* in the van in Mistri's charge. We were in the coach that was cut off at Rohri and shunted across the bridge to Sukkur, where Harland Holt met us.

Our situation was the converse, as it were, of that in Larkana: we had the Old Circuit House as our official home, and it was ready for us. But we had no furniture, so we must stay with the Holts in the vast Collector's Bungalow. This was only till the Railway was running, but that was delayed again and again, and we were with the Holts over Christmas and into January, which was trying for everyone.

The Holts had little Bobbie with them, but we added babies and nappies, smells and crying. There was room in that great place, but none suitable for a créche. The Holts were very patient with us, but I expect they were as happy as were we when at last we could move to our own place.

We were together now for eight months; for six months in our own home, longer than ever before. But it was an uneasy time. My job was nothing: doing what work Holt decided he didn't want to do himself. I was a district magistrate, but not many cases would come my way.

If my transfer had been intended to humiliate me, it had been entirely successful. I couldn't understand why Holt needed a personal assistant, ICS at that. Sukkur was on the periphery of the Hur trouble, there was only small flood damage, and it had no border with Balochistan. Holt agreed that I should go to see how Framji was getting on at the breaches, so I was ferried across the gap in the Shikarpur road and found him at Chak. He was full of confidence now. The River was falling, and the current had moved away. His timber dams were holding, and being backed by earth; and the winter gangs of Pathans with their donkeys had arrived. He was promised earth-moving machinery from the Americans at Karachi. He felt very differently from the time when he had written to Joan in September. Then it was: 'The current is still maddeningly strong, and everything is conspiring to make the work increasingly more difficult... the work has to kill me before I give up, or others give up against my advice.' Victory was in sight: he had no complaints against anybody. Indeed, he had won against all the odds, when all the experts had foretold that he would lose.

The Americans arrived in January, with their scrapers and loaders, the Pathans moved off to do the usual winter maintenance work, and left that part of the river protected by most magnificent bunds, the best in Sindh. But this mechanized repair set the Quantity Surveyor a puzzle. He knew how much soil a donkey could carry, how many loads it took to build a yard run of bund. These machines used much more, they compacted the soil far more solidly than did the little hooves of the Pathan donkeys, and he had to construct a revised formula. But the final result was very pleasing to the engineers.

Not till January did our furniture arrive. Meantime, we met Sukkur society, and celebrated Christmas. We had left places where we knew so many people, but here we knew hardly anyone. Joan left Karachi, where she had friends of all races; but whereas here I did have a job, of sorts, she only had babies, endlessly those babies to care for. So the change was much worse for her. In Larkana our friends were all Indian, with their Clubs there and in Kambar. In Karachi Joan hardly ever went to the Gymkhana.

The Sukkur Gymkhana was of the old-fashioned up-country kind, hardly changed by abandonment of the colour bar. The men were almost all officials, the women were almost all of the kind that made Joan hesitate about marrying me at all. I have no clear memory of any of them, except of Jane Holt: we became very fond of her.

In the month up to Christmas I discovered the reason why Harland Holt wanted extra help, not, I suspected, among those urged on Taunton. He was reorganizing the whole of his office record according to a theory of his own. Instead of revenue cases being filed each under its own head, they were all put in one file, correspondence in strictly chronological order, so that several inches depth of paper must be searched to follow any particular case, and the same for every subject heading. Great heavy files, carefully tagged by some wretched clerk whose career depended on his not missing a single reference. By the time I left the reorganization was not complete, and I doubt if it ever was. I can safely suppose that Holt's successor had the tedious task of untangling those vast files..

The atmosphere in the Collector's Bungalow was distinctly strained. We had no bearer; Mistri had come with us, but was living with his wife at the Old Circuit House, and his were not the skills of a bearer, however willing he might be. I had one patewala. We depended on the Holts and ourselves for every service; in fact, on Joan and Candy. We liked the Holts, but they had their own problems.

Christmas at Sukkur was much as it had been when I was there four years before, except then there had been a colour bar, but no ban on club 'treating', which was ordered by Harland, as District Magistrate. Surprisingly, it was quite effective. Of course, one could treat a friend, but the old custom that everyone must stand a round died, which suited a poverty-stricken Personal Assistant very well.

Sukkur had become a station for a section of the newly-formed Airborne Division, and as far as we ever discovered, they were all colonels. We never met any other ranks, officers or privates. Nor do I know what they were doing: military security, no doubt. They all had hostilities-only commissions, and were unlike the regulars I had met. We met them at the Gymkhana, and they greatly enlivened it. There were four: one, Lachlan, was admired as a hero of Dunkirk, but I never met him, or another now nameless. But there was their medical officer, Peter Thorne, young, bright, and charming. And there was Denis Arber, a wit and a diplomat.

Peter Thorne quite bowled Joan over. She was having a very trying time, with endlessly feeding and washing the nappies of two tiny babies too weak to be allowed to yell, with no house of her own, and, apart from Candy, only unfriendly servants of my superior officer, resenting instruction from an inferior memsahib. Peter Thorne appeared at a time when she was very vulnerable.

Often we had argued that there should be no legal bond of marriage: mutual affection should be enough. Our society required the bond, but within it there should be freedom. But when that freedom threatened me, I did not like it. Our ethic notwithstanding, I was worried. Perhaps it was just as well that Peter was posted away to Kohat. There were letters—years later, when the war was over, when we had left Sindh, we still wrote to him—but we never met again.

Denis Arber was truly a wit. Our standards were not perhaps of the highest, so it was not difficult to stand out, but Denis was kind-hearted with it. There was no malice in his wit, and that winter there was need for kindness in the Sukkur Club. He introduced the Club to childish games, and one such pointed the difficulty of mixing English and Indian culture, for the roots of a culture are in childhood. We had very few non-official Indians, but there was Naraindas, a barrister trained at the Temple. We played the game of finishing an epigram: A stitch in time? Saves nine. Too many cooks? Spoil the broth. A few Narain knew, many, naturally, he didn't. A woman's crowning glory? Her hair, of course. But Narain gave it thought: her thighs. Denis turned it off, said he was being funny, but Narain was serious. Hindus take sex seriously, do not hide it away and let their children grow up in ignorance or prurience, like the English did in those days. Narain didn't know the roots of English culture, would have been shocked to know its attitude. And the misunderstanding was reciprocated. To think of the facts of life being hidden from the young! It resulted in repression and guilt. There would be no idea of 'soiled goods' among Muslims or Hindus. Virginity was at least as highly valued, pre-marital sex far more severely punished, but at least their children learned early what it was all about.

At first we were not very happy in Sukkur, I mourning the special post that never was, and in one that meant nothing, Joan with two babies providing more anxiety than anything else, and a society of which very few evoked any empathy with us. But in January we could move into our home. The Railway opened, and our wagon arrived. I hired bullock carts, and bit by bit they brought our furniture toilsomely up the hill to the Old Circuit House, and we furnished another home. Never since her marriage had Joan had one ready to move into! Nor was it an easy affair.

In fact it was very awkward. I had no office *naik*, only one patewala, no sweeper, no bheesti, no bearer; only Mistri and Candy. If I appear greedy for help, be it remembered that we had a thunderbox, a tin bath, and water only after long sustained work on a small pump. The kitchen was as usual, a brick bench with chullas. The floors were of well-worn rough tiles, never free of dust, but shortly to display an unexpected merit. In England, with contemporary modern equipment, one could have managed well enough—a few years later in England we did, without any servants at all.

Life began to look better. On our hill we caught every breeze that blew, we were above the dust of the town, and out of the morgue-like guest-rooms of the Collector's bungalow. My Kutchery was over there, so we had a room for Candy, even her own bathroom, though its chief use was as laundry for the twins.

I had little to do with running the District. One of the Deputies was Nur Mahomed from Larkana, the other Fateh Mahomed, whom I never met. Holt never called a district conference. My concern still was with Karachi, and my indignation at what I felt was my shabby treatment. After all my work in the floods, which was surely worth commendation, I deserved better than this. (But undoubtedly I had flooded lands of powerful zamindars, and offended a Minister.) I had written to Taunton and to Clee, and been promised something better soon. But they had let me down before.

Clearly in Sindh ours was an 'unbuttoned' Service cadre. I doubt if, in any other province in India, an officer only three years in post would have dared to write as I did to his superiors, both with over twenty years' service, or have had a friendly reply instead of a severe set-down. But Sindh was so small that relationships were inevitably closer than elsewhere.

A man arrived from Karachi to be our bearer. He had no 'chits', but Candy knew him: he was a Christian, and his was a sad tale. He was born a Hindu, but wanted to marry a Christian girl. He knew nothing of the complications of the religion, but was happy to convert. He went to the nearest church, and became a Methodist, only then discovering that it was useless: the girl was a Catholic. He knew Candy, so came to Sukkur to try for her; but she was a Catholic, too. She said that he was a good boy, might do for bearer, so we took him on. Bernard Budd's bearer was a Christian, as we knew. Daniel was his baptismal name.

Daniel's bad luck went further. Frustrated, he bought his sex. After a little he complained of pains, so we sent him to the Civil Hospital, which diagnosed syphilis. Confidentiality has its limits, and we were told. How far syphilis might be infectious or contagious we did not know, but weren't going to take any risks, with either the twins or Candy: we gave him two months' pay and his fare to Karachi, and sent him back. He sent us a pathetic, and memorable, postcard: 'I had pain in organ ball, that is all.'

Daniel must have slipped in through a gap in the grapevine. As soon as he went, a successor appeared as if summoned: a tall, gangling Punjabi, with a mouth full of snaggle teeth, who spoke little Sindhi, so Joan with her Urdu could talk with him better than I: Illahibaksh. His teeth made him splutter wetly now and again, but that was a very small drawback, and from the time he found us in Sukkur he was with us until finally we left India altogether.

April Swayne Thomas came to stay; her Karachi studio gave her something to do while her husband was away on his mysterious duty. She was charmed by our hill, with its view all round and right across the river. She must visit Sadh Bela, which we had been promising to do ourselves for a long time. It was a notable island shrine of the Hindus, a place of pilgrimage for Khairpur and Sindh.

We were ferried across, though with no one so sophisticated as a guide. Perhaps the shrine would not have seemed so very unusual to a Catholic from Italy or Spain, where churches were highly decorated, as it did to us from the cold Protestant churches of the north: it was astonishing. Any sort of decoration was acceptable, were it of precious stones or metal, or of the most tawdry tinsel. There were little chapels for every god and goddess in the Hindu pantheon, there were special places to make offerings to the lingam and yoni in their corners, for those who sought fertility, and everywhere the smell of oil lamps and guttering candles and sweaty bodies. There seemed to be no care for cleanliness, holiness was all. There were great smoke stains on the walls, torn decorations, and on the floor, by the walls, the signs of continuous betel chewing. We were interested, but not pleased. In our eyes this shrine compared ill with the austerity of those of the Muslims.

Our twin sons brought Joan and me much honour: to Joan for her fertility, to me for my virility. As if we had arranged it. Otherwise, they were more a matter for anxiety than for pride; their care was a burden. During the day Candy was a very competent nurse, but at night we took over. Joan was still feeding them, but they were at best slow feeders, and had sometimes to be, as it were, force-fed. For a long time they were weighed before and after feeding, and altogether, there being two to deal with, loose bowels, careful bathing, and endless nappie-changing, Joan had no time to be bored. Perhaps the worst time of all was when they couldn't suck, and milk had to be expressed with a horrid little pump and then offered to them to drink—a painful process.

We developed a simple technique for the night watches, which depended on the otherwise troublesome, uneven surface of the floor tiles. The boys were put in their pram, under their mosquito net, it was put at the side of our bed, where one of us could reach the handle. I don't remember if we worked shifts, but one of us, through our own net, would push the pram, with carefully regulated force, across the rough floor, up a gentle slope, rocking as it went; it would stop, and gently rock back. Its motion was a wonderful soporific. It returned and hit a hand. If all was quiet, one could sleep; if one child cried, another gentle push would rock him to sleep again, and with luck he would not wake his brother.

It seems that most babies choose a comforter. Ours chose towelling, cold-weather nappies. (Not the hot-weather muslin ones.) Each knew his own, and was deeply offended to be offered his brother's. There was always an uneasy time after the nappies were washed, till they had been sniffed and rubbed and sucked and had their proper smell back. There was fun, with all the exasperation, for they could sleep all day, ready to keep us awake all night.

There was a day when a cobra was seen sliding out of the drain from the bathroom. Remembering Kipling's story, I suggested we find a mongoose, but such an animal was not known in Sindh: a better idea was to find a snake charmer. I came home from the office one day and was told that a charmer had come, had found a snake, indeed two, had caught them and taken them away. First he had searched the compound to look for hiding places. Then he set himself down and began to pipe. Wonderful to relate, a snake had appeared and reared up in front of him, alarming everyone, and he had put it in his basket. Just in case, he went on piping, and another appeared, he caught it, and then he said there were no more. Unfortunately, he had been paid before I had arrived: we should have insisted that we keep the snakes, they were ours, on our property, and we had paid him for finding them. In fact, I believe he had 'salted' the compound with his own snakes, tame ones. But what really worried me was that, if we had been tricked, there was still a real wild snake around. But we never saw a snake again, so perhaps my scepticism was unjustified.

A travelling 'mattress-beater' arrived. He travelled around with his single implement: a kind of very long, single-stringed guitar, and would tease out our cotton mattresses, felted over time. He had to have a room to himself, and there he settled down, taking in the mattresses one at a time. He tipped out the flock in a heap, stuck his instrument into it, and twanged the string, feeding it with flock all the while. The room filled with cotton lint as his twanging broke up the flock, and it was astonishing how much came from one thin mattress. How the cover was filled and quilted again I don't remember; but afterwards the mattress was soft and comfortable again for a time, and all the dust and dirt it had collected was left on the floor. He spent more than a day with us. And he was well worth his pay.

We drove to Shikarpur—the road was mended by now—for Joan to see the Eye Hospital, and to meet the Hollands for a special purpose. Sir Henry had retired and his son was running it. We went round the Hospital, seeing everything as I had seen it before. I was on official duty, and I wanted to help. I talked with Dr Holland: direct Government help might compromise its charitable status, so in the end we decided that the best thing would be for the Collector to make a public appeal to all charitable persons to be generous. Dr Holland wrote down all his most urgent needs.

We had our own, private, purpose. Adam and David had a small problem: their foreskins were tight. We could, of course, go to the Civil Hospital in Sukkur, but feared a breach of confidentiality, and news spreading that the Memsahib believed in circumcision. Once that was whispered round there would be no use in denying it. It was no great matter, but there was no principle, and we would not appear to take any side. Anyway, at six months, and not very strong, they should wait for a year.

In Sukkur we went round Mangharam's Biscuit Factory, where Seth Mangharam had installed the latest machinery just before the war. His biscuit was Energy Food, which we knew well, for it kept fresh, better than any imported ones: the Seth claimed that it was 'as good as Huntley & Palmer's'. His factory was certainly as good, if not more modern. I could tell him that my father sold most of his flour to Huntley & Palmer, which connection pleased us both.

He also made sweets. He gave us some of his extra strong peppermints, and ever afterwards we kept some. I used to buy them in seven pound tins, and they were a marvellous comfort in the hot weather. He made 'Sukkur Rock', like English seaside rock, and its making was odd. Also, I had often wondered how the sugar was put round almonds, and here I saw: a small concrete mixer was charged with nuts, a very stiff syrup was added and the machine was turned. After a prescribed time it was emptied, and there they were, evenly covered, any colour you liked, smooth and shapely, just as in the shops.

Sukkur had its cinema, but nearly all were Hindu films. We saw one American fiction, famous in its day: *Flash Gordon's Trip to Mars*. It was shown in English cinemas in ten-minute instalments, programme-fillers, but here the twenty instalments were shown in one, and took two hours. There were odd breaks in the story, lapses in timing and logical sequence, but, from the audience reaction in Sukkur, that didn't matter at all. Most were believers in magic, and science fiction was just one of a kind.

We acquired two spaniels from the Bhutto kennels, supposedly pedigree springers, not very convincing to look at. But Bella early took distemper and forthwith died. Minna must surely be strong to have survived, but in Sukkur she developed rabies. How, we could not tell. She was put down, and I, the only one who had handled her, had to have an injection. At the hospital I had to wait while an abdar who had been bitten by a rabid horse had one of his massive doses. The horse had bitten a thumb right off. It seemed I was lucky, and only needed one, but that meant 10cc just under the skin of my stomach, horribly painful till it was dissipated.

In Sindh rabies was endemic, and there was a routine procedure to deal with it. If anyone saw a rabid dog he would shout a warning, it would be taken up all around, cars would hoot, and it was astonishing how quickly the streets emptied. Word would reach the police, and special marksmen would come out, find the dog, and shoot it. Unless another was suspected, life was back to normal as quickly as it had stopped.

Little Minna was too small to do more than threaten to bite; she was put down before the virus had spread far. But I once did see a rabid dog in extremis. He was twisting about as if trying to bite himself, slavering, giving an occasional high-pitched yelp. He would run a little, then start the squirming and yelping again. In the end the police cornered him and shot him.

By May it was growing hot, and Joan took the twins away to Karachi. She was to stay with Colonel Eminson, the Civil Surgeon, who had a big house and no family. Zoe Gallagher was there too. Gallagher had been moved from Dadu to Upper Sindh Frontier, in place of Bernard Budd. (So what view had been taken of the flooding of Dadu? I just don't know!) Our six months together were finished, and Joan was not regretting going away. Karachi was much cooler, and she had many friends there, particularly Hugo Reinitz, to help her with his advice for the babies. She had not really enjoyed Sukkur, and didn't like its society, once those colonels had gone. My job would keep me with that same society, which exasperated me, too. Of course we regretted being separated, but now we were getting used to it; perhaps the first golden glow of marriage was fading a little, but with that we were becoming more mature. Now the stream of letters began again, and we could take out our ideas and dust them off till they were clear and shining, a little altered, but fully genuine.

Joan went down on a day train, no air-conditioning, but I made sure that at Rohri she had a block of ice, to be renewed at Nawabshah; I knew that by herself she would have saved the cost, so I spoke severely to Candy, to have the ice for the sake of her sons.

In Karachi, Joan met barely-disguised surprise that the twins had come back alive, that they had even grown. She had gone away six months before, well-wished by friends who to themselves spoke of tragedy, and who now welcomed her back with the greater enthusiasm.

All over India there are the sad graves of children a few days, or months, or years old, who had surrendered to the hard climate, to the ills from which they had none of the inborn resistance of Indians with generations of selection behind them. The risks were not so much from rabid dogs and snakes and mosquitos—care would protect them from such obvious dangers—but from the hidden infections in food and water, and from deficient diets. Adam and David were also very premature; seen in Karachi before they went to Sukkur, anyone might fear for them.

Perhaps it was as well that we had been away from the gloomy prophets. We never doubted but that they would survive and grow up. It had been hard work, chiefly for Joan and Candy, but if love and care and nursing meant anything, they would be all right. They were rickety, they had persistent diarrhoea, but they grew, they were stronger, and in Karachi was Hugo: if anyone could consolidate the victory, he could.

By the time Joan left Sukkur, I knew very well that she was over-tired, run down, and periodically worried about the twins. Apart from me, there was no relief. A change, a cooler climate, and a rest were badly needed. Her first letters to me were not happy; she weaned the boys, and for a time suffered all sorts of ills: bad periods, aching teeth, boils, and dengue fever. But she had no house to look after, and she soon recovered. This was a very old bungalow, shared with Zoe Gallagher, run for Eminson, a bachelor who came and went at all hours. I was told that when I came I must bring a zinc bath, so that she could have a separate bathroom; and a bicycle.

It was I who was having an easy time, yet I was rash enough to reproach her for drinking too much! Causing

prickly heat. How had I the nerve? But I was properly put
down. (She found smoking a comfort, then, but that was
before tobacco had acquired its lethal reputation.) The
boys improved, and with them Joan's spirits. Hugo took
them in hand, with a tonic for Joan and a special diet for
the boys: cod liver oil, of course, and what Joan called
'white sauce'. There was milk, and a little butter, and corn
flour. Their trouble was not dysentery but weak bowel
muscles. To give them a chance to grow strong, kaolin was
prescribed. We looked it up: it was china clay, highly
absorbent. If treated properly it would make cups and
saucers, and given in small doses to a baby it clogged his
bowels and gave his muscles a chance to grow. I suppose
that in these days it sounds like witch-doctoring, but it
worked. Laundry work was significantly reduced.

I sent her a bicycle and she rode about Karachi, to save
the cost and inconvenience of gharris, but it was not
approved of. But she was always lively and cheerful, and
those two little boys were now looking so well. It was just
like Joan Pearce, she would do anything. She got away with
it, too.

But there was no job for her. Then she met the Boltons.
Jerry Bolton was Finance Secretary, and had persuaded
Government to exercise its emergency powers under the
Defence of India Act to buy up the rice crop before it was
all exported away. He wanted an economist, and who could
be better than a Cambridge graduate? But it was not so:
her academic skills did not fit, and anyway the salary was
much too small to keep two households beyond the hot
weather. Bolton set up his purchasing organization, but
found his economist elsewhere.

The ICS and, indeed, other Services, kept an eye on
those twins, and Joan had to be careful not to justify any
charge of neglect. They were seen around in their pram,
and occasionally the whole family would be out in a gharri;
or they could be seen playing on their dhurrie in the
garden. There, they needed watching, for they were swift

crawlers, and could quickly move off the edge and into a flower bed, ready to eat anything handy. There was bound to be a mistake some time. Joan was out, Candy had gone in for something, when Jo Menesse, wife of an engineer, came to call on them. One was asleep, the other was trying to eat a nim berry. Total neglect, most irresponsible, nurse should be sacked. Candy was back at once, but it was no good. The story was round in no time, though in fact it didn't stick. For one thing, everyone knew Candy, and Joan's opinion of her. For another thing, a nim berry never did anyone any harm. Furthermore, Jo had no children, and was known to be jealous of Joan's.

We liked Jo Menesse, but we never forgave her for that.

I had had to take my leave early, to take over from Holt when he went to Kashmir on leave. I had hardly got to know my sons again when Gallagher arrived. He had left his District without notice, without permission, and gone into hospital in Karachi with an ulcerated leg. I was called by Charles Clee, told that Upper Sindh Frontier could not be left void, and I must at once go there and hold charge— not act as Deputy Commissioner, just be present there. I was angry, respectfully angry, if that be possible. Clee and Taunton had promised so much after Larkana, and now this, not even a proper posting. Clee promised that I should not suffer, but Joan was sure I had not been firm enough. I could only plead that I was not made that way. I could only hope that my virtue, in not making any public fuss, would win me justice. (Justice, in a matter of official postings? There was an odd thing to expect!)

Nazir and Afroze came in, and Framji from his breaches, and Joan roped them all in to tell tales of my virtues; she would herself spread this talk among the wives. I would be either set on a pillar or ruined. But I had to go to Jacobabad just the same.

Last year I had lost my leave because of the floods; this year because Gallagher had abandoned his District for an ulcer. Lots of people got these Sindh sores without making

this fuss! But I went. Soon afterwards, Joan wrote that
Gallagher had come to the bungalow to stay with his wife,
which was natural. But he had this ulcer; ulcers were highly
contagious, and he was in a house with three small children.
If he wanted to infect his own child, that was Zoe's concern;
but she would be very nasty if he came near her two.

Gallagher stayed on in Karachi for a time, supposedly
sick. He had a high opinion of himself, unrecognized by
anyone in authority. In the end Sindh could do nothing
for him and he went back to Bombay.

The loss of half my leave was specially hard for Joan.
The special things we had planned were no more, leaving
her with an ordinary, repetitive round till she could join
me, and even for that she didn't know where we would be.
The Reinitzs and their friends became ever more important
to her, and she was always sure of a welcome with Bashir
and Bilqis Malik, and Jeanie and Fram. The Shahbans
always welcomed her, and Afroze was there with little Tariq.
She found them better friends than all the service families,
except for Margaret. She could seldom entertain in return.

After Joan left Sukkur I had begun to acquire more work.
At last Holt accepted that he need not be continually
looking over my shoulder. When he did, I several times
told him he could have the file—the enormous file—and
deal with it himself. If I was to work, I would work in my
own way. But jointly we pushed a Collector's powers under
the Defence of India Act to the limit, or beyond. We
acquired a supply of wheat 'using barter, smuggling, and
threats', even buying stocks from Khairpur, and incurred
the wrath of merchants hoping for a high price when
controls went and trade followed 'ordinary channels'. Holt
had threatening letters: 'You dirty rascal, you bloody
bugger, you bully, you Britisher—quit India!' We stored
enough to last till harvest, and for a time locked away much
more. Government buyers came, and were told, 'Sorry, the
Collector has it all,' but when we had had our fun we

released the surplus to the Government buyer. It was all an antidote to the heat.

The Hur rebellion was finally crushed. The Pir Pagaro's desert stronghold was captured, the Pir was put on trial for multiple murder, waging war, and other things, was found guilty, and executed. And that, it was hoped, was the end of the Hur sect. His fort was destroyed. It was not looted: all his belongings were collected, listed, brought to Sukkur, and put in a godown which was put in my charge, and I was fascinated by the prospect of seeing them. But most of the stuff was junk, so I supposed the real valuables were stored elsewhere. There were old clothes, bales of damaged cloth, pieces of furniture, clockwork curios of all kinds, enough to keep a psychologist happy for a long time. There were five old cars, any new and useful ones had disappeared. There was a great deal of the famous lacquer work that I found it so easy to dislike: several enormous swinging cots constructed of turned and lacquered wood, inevitably looking as heavy as they were.

The whole inventory was to be sold, and I and some now forgotten expert did the pricing. I thought of buying one of those swinging cots, but what would we do with such a thing in England? And how could we get it there? (But probably museums would have fought for it.) Instead I bought a big cotton dhurrie. There was an enormous standard electric fan, with a circulating action, and a device that sprayed scent through it. Such a fan would be a boon for the Club, it was only Rs 100, about a tenth of its shop value, and Harland proposed that we buy it. Sven Kruse, manager of the cement works at Rohri, and endlessly feuding with Harland, voted against that: said he would resign if we did. (Some of us thought that an added reason for its purchase.) We bought it, and he didn't resign. It couldn't be used for some time: it used DC current, and the Club had AC, but in the end we found a converter. The vote went against operating the scent spray.

The feuding in the Club was tiresome. Once the Great Fan Battle was over, another arose. Alcohol was very short, but Sven found a black-market source. Harland must, as District Magistrate, oppose its use. I refused to join in, and was accused of disloyalty. But of course I was on the side of the law. I pointed out that I hardly used alcohol at the Club, and high prices would stop me altogether. Harland proposed that we all put our monthly ration into the bar, but again I found that unfair. (I see from a letter that our bar bill for April was thirty-five lemon squashes. Our ration we drank at home. But it doesn't appear very sociable.)

There was relief coming from all this friction. I would take my leave, and then both Sven and Harland would go to Kashmir, and I would be Acting Collector.

As Harland Holt became neglectful I acquired more interesting work, and I took on one unusual and only semi-official affair myself. I was approached, very tentatively, by a young Hindu, a known 'trouble-maker', who had heard that I had been round the Mangharam factory, had seen what it was like; did I know how badly its workers were paid? I did not. Banaram was a bright young man who was interested in hard facts, not to be put off by cliché or rhetoric. He could give me facts, he certainly engaged my sympathy, and he asked me to urge Seth Mangharam to pay his men better. I disclaimed any power to do that, nor, indeed, did I think that the Seth would pay more just because I asked him. What Banaram needed was a trade union for the workers, and then, with their support, he could make their claim. I explained about membership, dues to create a fund, a Secretary—all the trappings of a British trade union. I explained it as a sort of academic exercise—in no way could I claim that it was a function of my office. But Banaram set to work: he recruited members—the whole work force—a Secretary, the structure, the Rules, and his minute book, and came to see me again. Everything was in order, and I told him so. 'Now I can call a strike,' says he. I protested that that was not the way to do things; a strike was the very last step to take. (Moreover, if it were publicly reported that the Collector's Personal Assistant had advised him, it would be very awkward for me.) So, instead of a strike—but how he loved the idea!—he worked out what he would demand for his members in pay, in hours of work, and so forth, and presented their claim to Seth Mangharam. Had it not been known that Banaram had been talking with me, he might have had a very rough reception. As it was, the Seth came to see me, we worked out what he was prepared to concede to avoid a strike, and the offer was sent to Banaram. His Committee accepted the offer, and everyone was happy. So reasonable an outcome was impressive.

Banaram had been lucky; I also, in not having to act beyond what was reasonable to ensure peace and good order. Later, he went on to unionize the workers at the Cement Factory, but Sven Kruse was quite different from Seth Mangharam. He was apt to be a violent man, and I found that he had arranged with Judge, the Police Superintendent, to use the police to break up meetings and have Banaram beaten up. I was a District Magistrate, and I could give orders to Judge: I told him that he must not interfere unless there was a threat to public order, in which case he should act as a neutral force, there only to keep the peace. The new union flourished, there was a settlement, and the workers benefited: the Cement Company could well afford to pay better wages.

It would not be usual for a union to have authority on its side, on the side of the exploited worker, as I was. When I was moved from Sukkur the bosses probably recovered, but I hoped that what the unions had won would never be entirely lost. Had there been a strike of which I had fore-knowledge, I might have been in trouble, but I was lucky. The possibility did not bother me much; I was ICS: we were used to doing what we thought was right, regardless of possible trouble. Truly, we were an arrogant lot!

My actions did not make me popular at the Club, so I spent most of my evenings at home, reading, listening to music, and writing long letters to Joan. I found a local headmaster who was happy to help me with my Sindhi, for I became ambitious to become an Interpreter. This was simply personal ambition: there was no money in it, only a note on my record if I passed. The fact that Harland Holt jeered only made me the more determined.

Fram finished his triumphant work on the breaches, and Jeanie came to take him back to Karachi. Peter and Margaret came and stayed with me, and what were they doing in Sukkur? Later, perhaps, it was explained. They bullied me: I refused to be forceful about everything, as they seemed to be. Joan would agree that I did not push, as they said I should. But it just was not my way, and I was not to be persuaded. I would push my powers to the limit in my work, but not just for a job. I was quite priggish about it.

I cleared my desk and went down for my two weeks of Upper Sindh leave. I took a zinc bath with me, let the Railway think what it liked. When I returned it would be as Collector, if only for a month, but I was promised that when Holt returned there would be this much better job that I had been promised so firmly. So I arranged that all our belongings should be packed up, and moved into the Collector's Bungalow till I left.

A few beautiful days, with the boys more a pleasure than an anxiety, with cool nights with Joan, and friends to meet again. Then came the urgent summons from Clee. Protests, and anger behind his back, did no good. Gallagher must be replaced. I must go to Jacobabad and 'hold' the District till he returned. I was to hold charge, I must not change any of his dispositions, nor make any of my own. I was not to 'act', Gallagher would doubtless be back before Holt went on leave. There was no point in arguing with a direct order, but at least this better job would be found for me afterwards, and my leave would be made up some other time.

I returned to Sukkur, from where I commuted to Jacobabad. The ancient Residency there was ruinous, and one end had been damaged by an earthquake and demolished. The compound was a jungle. None of the buildings was safe, and the town was a disgrace. I asked the office about these policies that I must not change, asked to see the files. There were no files: Gallagher's method was the reverse of Holt's, and his orders were all verbal, and his Chitnis were not sure he understood them anyway. I talked with Andrew Davies, now Police Superintendent, and his orders were verbal too.

But Gallagher did not come back, and I was left 'holding' when Holt went on leave. Peter Cargill was posted to Sukkur, the 'act' promised to me, and I protested. Peter was my junior anyway, why couldn't he hold USF, while I moved back to act in Sukkur? If Gallagher did come back, would I revert to be Personal Assistant to my junior? But Clee said he couldn't change officers about just to suit them. Perhaps Peter had been working for this act when he and Margaret came to stay.

Gallagher finally left Sindh altogether, and I was posted, not just to act, but simply as Deputy Commissioner, Upper Sindh Frontier District. While I was in limbo I was not at all happy. It was very hot, everything was in a tangle, the town filthy, the bungalow a ruin. Residency? It didn't deserve the name! Great chunks of plaster fell on my bed when it rained, and I had to poke the rest down. I stuck stamp paper across the cracks in the walls, and checked them every day. I wrote to Joan all about it. In the town the streets were rivers of mud. John Jacob was an engineer as well as a soldier; he had built gullies and sumps; he had built the Residency; he would never have suffered a mess like this.

16

JACOBABAD

When I was confirmed as Deputy Commissioner, my sour criticisms faded: the Residency was a grand old building, just neglected. The town should have a proper administration. The *jungly* compound would be fun to explore. There was romance in being on the Frontier, 'sitting in Jacob's chair'. John Jacob had himself built the Residency; in fact, he had built this whole town, once the little village of Khanghur; it was an 'antiquarian's paradise', I was told, but I must make it properly habitable.

The Residency was built wholly of mud brick, walls two feet thick, double verandahs all round, projecting in the front to house his Clock. The Clock was seven feet high, in a glass case, and everything had been made by himself. It told hours, minutes, and seconds, the days of the week, the date of the month, and the phases of the moon. It was driven by weights which sank into a water-tight well. It ran for thirty days, and had its special caretaker, hereditary, I believed. It kept excellent time. I stood by the clock and looked along the verandah, and was reminded of the arcade of an ancient church.

The two main rooms, dining-room and drawing-room, were very large and very high, ceiled with unsquared teak beams and rafters, with a thick thatch of jungle grass plastered inside and out. At one end of the drawing-room was a large fireplace, at the far end of the dining-room was a portrait of John Jacob, with his sword at one side, and on each a trophy of *jezails*, hand-made muskets won from the hill tribes. Beyond the drawing-room there was nothing: a whole suite of rooms had been demolished after an earthquake, so for all its grand appearance, it had no more rooms than our bungalow in Larkana. Nor would the PWD spend any money on repairs: it was condemned. But I managed to squeeze enough from them to stop the roof leaking, or, indeed, from falling in on me.

Gallagher had done the most ridiculous things. He had prohibited the export of cattle, a hopeless order to enforce. The roads could be patrolled, but the whole frontier was open, and cattle didn't like the roads; moreover, it was only legitimate dealers who wanted to take them out. He had appointed a Mukhtiarkar with a large staff to organize the purchase and export of wheat, while the Agent of Jerry Bolton's Purchasing Board sat idle. Orders were all verbal, so I cancelled them and saved funds at the same time.

Then there was our own money problem. We were very short, every officer was short. I wrote to Joan about all the people I heard of selling their cars as inflation bit. Our dear Chev must go, and I asked her to advertise it in Karachi. But, before I was formally in charge at Jacobabad, the chief Khosa Sirdar saw it, had heard that I wanted to sell, and offered for it: Rs 5,000. A marvellous price; but by now it was a unique car, and, battered and shabby, was still elegant. I had not yet taken charge, so Clee approved the sale. Fifty beautiful Rs 100 notes. I wrote lovingly of them to Joan, sent her a cheque for a thousand, and told her to buy a new dress, and some pretties to please me. We could, if we wanted, lay out some money on this grand new residence.

It was already furnished, but the furniture was very heavy, very dark, stained and painted teak, high Victorian. Our furniture would fit there very ill, and something must be done about that. The dining table would seat twenty, with chairs to match its massive size. Ours would be lost in that great room, but it would fit very well in the drawing-room, so we could live there almost entirely, keeping the grandeur of the dining-room for some possible grand occasion.

In the bathroom was a shower, fed from a tank on the roof that was laboriously fed by the bheesti. This was a great luxury; but its temperature was determined by the season, so was always wrong. There was all that superficial grandeur, yet we still used a tin bath and a thunderbox. The kitchen was, of course, standard; there was no refrigerator, but a large ice box holding a whole block of ice, on which bottles were laid, and gradually melted themselves in. Very seldom was fresh food kept from one day to the next, even in the cold weather.

The Residency itself was near the middle of the compound. There was a gateway towards the town, and another towards what had been the Cantonment, now long gone; but neither had a gate. The surrounding mud-brick wall was tumbledown. Much was jungle, but there were servants' quarters, my Kutchery, and the Record Room, judged unsafe to enter. In the jungle I found Jacob's dovecote, for he used pigeons for his communications. The fives court needed plastering, and the swimming-pool had been fatally cracked by an earthquake. I never saw the tomb of his horse, Messenger, though I have seen a picture of it: a plastered brick pyramid, outside the walls.

In front was a garden whose grass and trees were famous. If one were homesick, one might imagine a patch of English parkland, though the trees were small and the grass was the local, very coarse kind called *drubb*. It could be watered, so it was green in the hot weather, when everything else dried up. The grass was mowed by sheep, and after a time we acquired two fat-tails to do the job.

Fat-tailed sheep, *dumbas*, were greatly favoured as pets in Jacobabad; their quality was judged by the size and thickness of the tail, which was pure fat, with a few membranes to give it cohesion. As the tail grew, it obstructed the rear orifices, and several times I saw a specially prized and well-loved pet with a little two-wheeled carriage attached to lift the tail from the ground. How mating was managed I never asked.

Upper Sindh Frontier was the only District in Sindh with a Deputy Commissioner who had the same powers and responsibilities as a Collector. It was, also, the only District with a Residency. I was very junior to be a confirmed District Officer, but that was all right: I sat in Jacob's chair, had his whole tradition behind me, and it was very strong. But still I had a Personal Assistant.

There were many physical reminders of John Jacob, apart from portrait and sword and the Residency itself. There was a cantonment for the Special Force, a small cavalry unit, the final local reminder of Jacob's Horse, which became the Scinde Irregular Cavalry. The Scinde Horse was one of the crack regiments of the Indian Army, was converted to tanks, and was in my time fighting in the war in Africa.

The strength of the Special Force was two *subedars* and fifty *sowars* in two troops, commanded by a Risaldar. When I arrived one troop was away on duty in the Hur area: turn by turn the troops had served throughout the Rebellion, and the Risaldar told me it was a popular duty, a relief from endless parades and exercises. When the Deputy Commissioner toured, he would take with him a mounted escort of two *sowars*, and this was a popular duty too. The DC was welcome to ride one of the horses, or to take horses riding when he was in Jacobabad, or go to the parade ground and watch the work; or he could play polo or *nezabazi*, which was tent-pegging. All such things provided his men with an interest, which was very desirable.

All day when the DC was in residence the Union Jack flew in front of the Residency. A squad of police came at sundown to lower it, and I tried to be near, with my topi, to take the salute and to inspect them. At night sentries patrolled before and behind, and at dawn they paraded again to hoist the flag for the new day. I might well be in bed on the *thalla*, and my presence was carefully ignored.

It was all very pleasant—and unnecessary in the eyes of anyone with no feeling that a tradition should be preserved. This was the safest border in Sindh. On the other hand, perhaps it would not have been so secure had it not been known that there was a well-trained and equipped cavalry force at once available.

Less than a century before, this had been a wholly lawless border, until John Jacob, with his swift-moving cavalry on one hand, and the prospect of a safer and more comfortable life on the other, persuaded the tribes that there were better ways to live than by raiding and being raided by other tribes. The skill, the courage, and the success of his policies are all detailed in the Record of the Scinde Horse. He was an engineer as well as a soldier. He cleared canals, cut roads through the jungle, and settled people on the land, safe from raiders. He surveyed all his area, by the use of the chimneys, the very last of which to survive I had seen with Dermont Barty near Sukkur. His tomb was at the far end of the main street, and often I went to look at it. Let the streets be never so filthy, the tomb was always neat and clean. Often there was a bunch of flowers laid on it. I discussed their significance with Ali Ahmed, Deputy Collector of Khandkot, whom I had known as Mukhtiarkar of Kambar, and whom I had recommended for promotion. He supposed the offerings were from women wanting children, but I pointed out that Jacob had never married, had no known offspring. So we decided that they were just as likely to be from women who had had enough of child-bearing, and came to the tomb for help.

Even my Superintendent of Police was in his first District post, so Jacob's spirit bore a heavy load from our common inexperience. All I knew of Andrew Davies was that he had been Joan's assiduous courtier of a year before in Karachi, and that he knew no Sindhi. He depended on his Inspectors and subedars for information, which was dangerous, for they might be biased towards one tribe or another, towards one grouping or another. But there was something in the police of the Jacob tradition, too, which saved Andrew from being grossly misled.

On my first arrival, Andrew told me of a long-running feud between two branches of the Burdi tribe that threatened to break out into violence. I thought till then that each tribe had one Sirdar, but now I learned that there could be more, but only one would be chief. Khan Bahadur Jaafar Khan, Member of the Assembly, chief Sirdar of the Burdis, was being challenged for leadership of the tribe by Sirdar Mahomed Khan. There was a danger that the feud, which had been running for forty years, might come to a head, that Mahomed Khan might make a bid by force. Jaafar Khan had been spending much of his time away at the Assembly, which on the frontier was considered a pointless activity, keeping him away from his tribal duties. The Burdis lived on both sides of the border with Balochistan, and a battle could cause complications with the Political Department.

There had been murders, seductions, raids from one side or the other; the latest offence was that Mahomed Khan had killed Jaafar Khan's prize ram. This was not in itself a very serious crime, but it was a studied insult, implying a loss of power and potency. The Chief Sirdar's *izzat* had been befouled, and must be avenged.

The Criminal Law of British India would find it impossible to deal effectively with such a case. The Sindh Frontier Regulations found no difficulty. I called the parties and, sitting as a jirga, a tribal court, I secured from each a list of supposed crimes and insults. Each was then given the list of the other and asked for comments. As District Magistrate I could do this, and expect to have an accurate response. It was an element of Baloch custom, probably still is, that all offences, criminal and civil, can, provided they are covered by the rather vague mantle of Custom, be compounded by a money payment. So, with a list of offences and final agreement as to their truth, and taking account of any special factors involved, one could set a figure for each party to pay the other; even murders could be dealt with thus, without troubling the niceties of British law.

So my Shristedar and I totted up the sum each sirdar owed to the other, struck a balance, and Mahomed Khan paid up. Only one detail of the accounting do I remember: the death of Jaafar Khan's ram cost more than did the abduction of a girl from Mahomed Khan's village; but this was because she was happy to marry the man who had abducted her. Had she been unwilling, the charge would have been very high indeed. In fact, it might have led to the very battle the *faisla* was intended to prevent.

There was an odd contradiction between the supposed •ruthlessness of primitive tribal custom, than which Western law was so much better, and its ability since time out of mind to produce a peaceful and truly civilized settlement. This *faisla* was formalized with due ceremony: a moulvi came with a Quran, and in the presence of myself, my Shristedar, my Personal Assistant, Madadalishah, and the Havildar, the two men embraced as brothers, and each in turn placed the Quran on his head and swore eternal friendship. Friends of both parties were there as witnesses, they praised God, and themselves swore friendship. The Shristedar made a record of the agreement, the two Sirdars signed it, and I witnessed their signatures. That settlement lasted for all the time I was in Sindh. Perhaps it really was permanent. In this one single thing I can claim to have done something worth while.

Letters began again. The boys flourished, and so did Joan. She knew of my confirmation before I did, for she knew all the ICS gossip. I wrote of my last drive from Sukkur to Jacobabad and back at a triumphant 30mph, which was very good on that road, and after the car's hard life. In fact, I had an excellent wife, I loved her, and I wanted to see her again. Quite often she wrote that she loved me; so perhaps I was 'a good husband, as husbands go'.

Joan provided me with direct liaison in Karachi. When Bolton complained that his Purchasing Agent could buy no wheat, she went and had a drink with the Boltons and explained, far better than I could in a formal letter, the problems I had with all Gallagher's verbal orders and with his scheme to take the grain to the river and send it to Sukkur, (where Holt didn't want it). So he was patient until I could get the Agent working. She told me of the new second-hand-car control that was coming.

Bolton's control system was on the whole highly effective; but not this car control, which was forced on him by Government, which decided to control prices and prohibit export. Each make, each model, was priced by its age, and what a schedule that was! Promptly, no car was anywhere. openly for sale. (But the Chev was already sold.) A car has four wheels, it can go on any road, and it only had to get out of Sindh to be free. Later I heard that Bolton's Civil Supplies Department never even tried to enforce the control.

Sirdar Abdur Rahim Khan was very happy with his Elegant Chev. It became truly elegant again. He sent it to Karachi for overhaul, and when it came back he drove in it to call on me; really, to show it off. I found no difficulty in envying him. It had been restored to all its elegance, and I walked round admiring the brand new tyres and covers, and the little flower vases fixed to the instrument panel. I stroked the new paint, and abjured the driver to be very, very careful. I threatened to prosecute him if it were scratched. There was a moment's alarm, until the joke was seen. Then it pleased everyone. But how very envious I was!

When I was at last confirmed in office, I was surprised at how quickly I, a new arrival and an unknown quantity, seemed to become well-liked. Then it became clear that Gallagher had become extremely unpopular, of uncertain temper and unpredictable action. No one had wanted to speak a word about it until it was certain that he would not return. I benefited: I was said to be like Jacob Sahib, than whom there could be no better man. Gross flattery, to be indignantly denied, but pleasant to hear, nonetheless.

I met another Khosa, Mahomed Amin, the only Communist Member of the Assembly, who had just been released from gaol; what his offence had been I don't now know, but certainly nothing disgraceful, or the other Khosas would have kept him away from me. He had been released when he agreed to join the Muslim League, so his trouble must have been political. I could talk with him, jeer gently at this Communist member of the League. He could laugh. We could even argue about ends and means. Somehow he persuaded the merchants of Jacobabad that my presence was good for them; perhaps it was, after Gallagher. He presented me a cheque from them for Rs 25,000, an enormous sum, which argued the relief of Mahomed Amin and the merchants at the change of officer. He wanted me to remain, or Bernard Budd to return. He said the money was for me myself. Had I been able to think of anything specific that he or the merchants wanted from me, I would have returned the cheque with indignation, but instead I gave it to the War Fund, in his name. He didn't like that, but surely Russia was on our side now?

Once I was confirmed in charge, I set about preparing for the family. I was helped by my discovery that all the furniture was hired, so I sent it all away except that for the dining-room and bedrooms. The vast drawing-room would comfortably take all our own furniture, and part of it could be separated off by the long cupboard to make a dining-room.

It was disconcerting to find that this grand Residency could hardly accommodate a family as small as ours. The best I could do was to keep one bedroom for us, and the other and the dressing-room for Candy and the twins. At least there were two bathrooms; and if Candy preferred it she could have the Annexe. The PWD agreed to install electricity there, but I doubted if even that would persuade her to accept it: the thought of all those wild tribesmen of the Frontier scared her, and sleeping by herself in that isolated place would terrify her.

Our furniture arrived, in two lorries, very modern. But the family, coming up from sophisticated Karachi would revert to thunderbox and tin bath, with the doubtful luxury of a shower which ran warm when we wanted it cold, cold when we wanted it hot, according to the weather.

Now that I was confirmed I took my transfer leave; it seemed a little odd, for I had already held the post for six weeks, but I went to Karachi and found how *jungly* I felt. To see Joan well and the twins bigger and fatter was happiness enough. Any hopes of a job for Joan had faded, so I must hope that she would find Jacobabad good, though she would be the only Englishwoman there, and the only woman I had met was Dr Jessaram at the Zenana Hospital, who was very much a serious Hindu professional. There was Andrew Davies, whom she knew well, but who might easily become a pest. In Karachi we did all the things we had done before; and then we must say good-bye.

There was a complicated packing to be done, but we finished, we got it down to the Station, and there was Bashir Malik to help us. It was a monumental departure. We had a coupe to ourselves on the Quetta Mail. Illahibaksh saw all the baggage aboard, in all its miscellany. There were bags and bundles, a big cotton dhurrie, two little chairs, one bought in the bazaar, one I had made—a child-size thunderbox, a playpen, the pram, and a beautiful teak cot with a frame for the mosquito net. And Candy's and Illahibaksh's *saman*, too. There were Americans, travelling air-conditioned, of course, who wanted to help, but we feared their exuberance, their keenness to see this bit of British Imperialism: an officer taking his family up to the wilds of the Frontier. We let them think ours was wild! We could all get into the coupe, with necessities such as bundles of nappies, always to have one quickly on hand. The Stationmaster came to see what might delay his

precious Mail, saw Bashir, and was reassured that he would
prevent any delay to the crack train of his division.

In the end everything was stowed, all farewells were done,
and we were away. There were so many foreign travellers
now who would see as unusual and dramatic what had been
commonplace all over India for a long time. Joan, who had
by herself made other journeys like this, was well-organized.
This time there was no crisis. Even the boys were quiet,
amazed at what went on.

Through the night we took cat-naps, a boy waking for a
drink, Candy coming in and going to another compartment
at one or another station; a child might cry, but was soon
comforted, his nappy changed, and soon sent to sleep again
by the rumbling and gentle rocking of the train. All so
ordinary, except for our grand engine rushing through the
night.

I had always found railway stations seen in the middle of
the night relaxing, even though they were seldom quiet.
Dim lights, in a pitch-dark countryside, people talking,
sometimes a hubbub when a child or a bundle was missing.
Then quiet again, till at the blast of a whistle, with hissing
and thumping, that beautiful great steam locomotive pulled
away, slowly gaining speed.

We crossed the Lansdowne Bridge very slowly and, after
a noisy stop in Sukkur, the train ran very carefully on the
new embankment at Ruk. I had crossed there when the
track ran on huge piles driven deeply through the
floodwater into firm ground—an extraordinary feat of
railway engineering.

We reached Jacobabad at dawn, and it seemed that the
whole of the Revenue Department was there to welcome
us. It was Saturday, but they had to come for this. Deputy
Collector, Mukhtiarkar, Chitnis, and Shristedar who would
come later to tell me about the District; PA, Havildar, and
all the patewalas. Andrew had come with some police, to
keep order, and he had his car.

Everyone wanted to see the two boys, but they were asleep: all that showed was two small bald heads; Joan and Candy took them away in the car, and I set about dealing with the vast *saman.* The Stationmaster came to see what was holding his train, and I apologized. No matter, said he, the driver could easily make up his time on the straight line across the *pat.* He wasn't going to make a fuss when all local officialdom was there.

Tongas drove away with the baggage and Illahibaksh and Mistri. I thanked everyone for the welcome, and took another with Mahbubalishah. At the Residency he went off for a nap before opening the office. I was left alone.

There was the sentry; I returned his salute, and told him to carry on. I saw the sentry at the rear turn at the end of his beat, come to attention, and turn back. So we were quite secure; even a Governor could not be safer. I hoped Candy was reconciled. I wished we had come from the other end of the Residency, and not past the ruined end, though it was not entirely new to Joan. There were lights on, but no sound. I went in, and there they were, sitting quietly at the table, drinking tea. The twins were on the couch asleep, a little blanket over them and a rubber sheet under.

We put them to bed under their net, we saw that Candy had all she needed, and then at last got to bed ourselves.

I must have slept a little, but I woke, dressed quietly, and left them. I went back to the drawing-room, and there I found Illahibaksh with all the baggage spread round him, as if for a sale, looking hopeless. Where could all this go? But never mind, and would the Sahib like *chota hasri*? He surely would, so I ate toast and drank coffee very pleasantly.

I sat quietly again, hugging myself. How could anyone ask for more? A loving and beloved wife, two beautiful sons, Deputy Commissioner of the Upper Sindh Frontier District, not only on senior scale, but with a special allowance, and living in the only Residency in Sindh.

There was the sound of marching men, and the jemadar came to the front, with his guard, collected the fourth, and paraded them in front of the flagpole. I collected my topi and went out. As he hoisted the Union Jack I saluted it, and then inspected his guard. I took their salute, they marched away, and another day had begun. The flag told the world that the Deputy Commissioner was in residence.

When I went on tour there would be no guard, no flag flying. But I talked the matter over with Andrew Davies. This guard was, like the Special Force, a relic from the time when there really was danger, so near the frontier, with Baloch tribes all around. They were still there, but no longer the fierce raiders of a century before. My family would not have been there had it been so. But Andrew agreed that there might be anxiety, that since the family would often be at home when I went on tour, he could provide the guard then, too. However, we both agreed that it would be most improper for the flag to fly unless the *Sirkar* itself was there.

It was a Saturday; I had only to talk with Chitnis and the Shristedar about a tour programme, and then there was the rest of the weekend to settle in.

We all squeezed in; Candy and the twins had one bedroom and a bathroom, and were not comfortable. Then a baby cobra was killed in the bathroom, and general opinion was that the mother would come to look for her child. Candy by now had found that the tales of fierce tribesmen were quite false; she decided that the cobra was a greater danger, so she and the twins moved to the Annexe, which became the *Baben-jo-Ghar,* The Babies' House. Andrew agreed that the beat of the sentry should be extended to its front, and all was well. The Residency at once became a pleasant and gracious place to live.

Two days in the office, and then a solemn beginning for my first tour as head of my own District. Otherwise, also, it was different from other tours: I had different functions, and I moved by rail, with a mounted escort. I camped along our own narrow-gauge railway, whose stations were conveniently spaced: I could camp at each alternate one on the way out to the terminus at Kashmore, at the others on the way back.

I didn't want to leave Joan too long in this new place, so I cut my tour short. From Dostali I took bistra, patewala and Chitnis with me and, of course, one of the troopers, and rode the train to Kashmore. The Risaldar had been insistent that I must never be without my escort, he anyway insisted on coming, and it was his turn on the train.

I inspected the Treasury, its books, and its balances of both cash and opium stock. I made 'gaol delivery', for the *habeas corpus* element in British law was a valuable element of the Criminal Procedure Code: it was a reform of the previous uncontrolled methods, and no longer could a prisoner be left languishing in gaol, forgotten because some policeman or magistrate or powerful man had a grudge to satisfy. The gaol Register must be produced, the cells inspected, the prisoners seen, and any complaints heard. Only then could the Register be signed. If things were unsatisfactory, a prisoner could be transferred to another gaol, or released on bail. The Mukhtiarkar's record would thereafter bear a very black mark.

But the Kashmore gaol was clean and empty. The town was small, and felt very isolated: a promontory of Sindh, as it were, with tribal Balochistan to the north, the Punjab to the east, the River to the south, and only the little railway for escape.

One night there, and I took the train back to my camp. For breakfast the Mukhtiarkar brought me tea and a cold omelette with a buttered chapati, specially cooked for me by his wife. The driver allowed me to ride on the footplate.

The cab was surprisingly large for so tiny an engine, but even so it was crowded, with the stoker having to get at the fire-door to feed in his large logs. I asked the driver how fast the train could go, and he offered (I forget the Sindhi idiom of his reply) to whack her up and see. This he did, and we swept along with a great thudding rush, under a heavy pall of white smoke. The countryside seemed to flash past, and the whole train rocked from side to side; passengers looked out in alarm, hardly reassured to hear that the Deputy Commissioner was himself driving; but that he certainly was not. I looked at the speedometer, then at the driver: was it in good order? Of course it was, and it read twenty-three miles per hour. He whacked her up a little more, we passed twenty-four, and then he shut off steam and the speed dropped to eighteen.

I congratulated him on his fine engine, and for an exciting ride. He did not go faster, he explained, because he had two problems. One was that he might not be able to stop in time; the other was that the last time he had passed twenty-five mph a coupling rod had fallen off, and he and his mate had had to walk back over the track to find the linchpin that had fallen out, and then carry the rod from where it fell a quarter of a mile to the engine, with the passengers jeering at them as they passed with their heavy load, sweltering in the heat. Had that happened today, he would have been shamed before the Sahib; but he showed me that he carried a spare pin now.

So we rolled sedately into Khandkot, and there I left the engine. My thanks and my congratulations were both wholly sincere. The Mukhtiarkar met me with a cup of tea and a special Sindhi bun, baked for me specially by his wife. Perhaps Kashmore had wired ahead, and perhaps the wives were rivals.

At Khandkot, as at Kashmore, I had the taluka Treasury to inspect. At this time of year, when last year's revenue receipts had been sent in and the new year's had not yet been received, the totals were conveniently low. But rules were there to be followed, and all the books must be checked. Individual cash totals must be totted up, for each denomination of notes and coins, and after a few treasury inspections I grew good at totting. I was shown the totals of notes, took a bundle at random, abstracted some, also at random, and set the clerks to count. When they had finished we counted my samples, added them in, and hoped and prayed that the total tallied with the book, that we had the right answer. We did, we always did, and I could find no trick to it. After all, the Hindu mercantile castes were particularly good at accountancy; and if a man wanted to practise fraud, there were more profitable and safer ways than by cheating the Revenue Department.

The Treasury also held the taluka's ration of opium, which was a government monopoly. This may seem strange today, but so it was. I had to check the record of receipts, disposal, and the balance in hand, which was weighed in my presence. There was a very small tolerance for evaporation. I must note, investigate, and report any unusually large disposals.

It was odd stuff, it had a strange, fungal smell, and looked like a lump of very stiff black treacle toffee, but was slimy rather than sticky. I felt no temptation at all to try it; I never saw it anywhere else but in a Treasury.

This source of opium linked the Revenue Department with the liquor shops, and it was the District Magistrate's job to issue their licences: these were auctioned, but an applicant must have suitable premises and be of good character; then the licence would be issued to the highest bidder. It was always possible that a 'ring' would be formed, and all the bids would be very similar and very low; if this were suspected one could call for fresh bids, and arrange for an outsider to offer a true price, and either win, or secure a proper price from the broken ring. These liquor shops sold beer and locally-distilled *arrack*, made variously from molasses, from rice, and from various pulses, supposedly from legitimate stills. They also sold the opium, and cannabis in several forms: it was drunk as *bhang*, smoked as *ganja*, and seeds were sealed in the little beedis with the loathsome smell.

There was no direct control of these drugs, so there was no black market, nor any violence connected with supply;

the hemp was locally grown, control of the shops was light. The police might report excessive petty crime, or an officer might inspect a shop and find too many hemp-drunk men lying there, and then the shopkeeper might find his licence cancelled. He had every reason for care. For anyone with a moral objection to drug-taking, this was all very shocking, but if one just wanted untroubled communities where there were few sources of pleasure available, the system worked well.

It was novel and satisfying to be dealing with all the matters that came up from the sub-divisions and talukas, and sending them on myself to Commissioner or Chief Secretary, with no other officer intervening. I could require reports, without necessarily having to procure the information myself. I could quickly have developed a swollen head, had Joan not been on hand to deflate me.

We planned nothing for ourselves for Christmas, the boys were too small. We might make a party with Andrew Davies and the Assistant Political Agent, but then he was going off to Sibi. So Candy was our concern. Jacobabad was a poor place for a young girl to celebrate, but we found a Catholic family on the Railway who were going to Sukkur, and would look after her. Perhaps we would drive to Sukkur with Andrew when she came back. No longer was she scared of the fierce tribesmen—she had quickly found that there were none. She soon had all the patewalas her friends, except the Havildar, whose dignity would not bend. Lal Buksh was a sort of aspirant patewala, and he attached himself to Candy as help and protector: Lalu.

Looking ahead, there was the Horse Show looming in January, and after that the Viceroy. Two Viceroys in less than two years! We wondered, were we being honoured or victimized? But this visit would be easy: this new Viceroy would come by air and leave by air, all in one day. The Horse Show was a different matter.

The first step in preparing for our domestic side of the Show was to explore the shop of Hassanand Popatlal, the one 'European style' shop in Jacobabad—it even had a glass window. But its days of prosperity were long past. Popatlal should have been renamed Ichabod. There was a time when Jacobabad was a military cantonment, with troops stationed there with British officers, and sometimes their wives. But this closed down in 1923, and was all demolished except for the Mess, which continued for a while for officers passing through. Now even the old Mess had gone.

Popatlal had bought up all the stock of tins, and we went right through it. Tinned salmon—what luxury!—sardines, corned beef, peaches, baked beans. Things we hadn't seen since the war began. Popatlal pointed out how well-filled they were, so full that the tops bulged. We saw little that we dared buy; instead, we advised him to get those tins out of the shop, lest he suffer a nasty explosion.

Later, Popatlal thanked us for our advice. He told me he had punctured a tin of salmon and taken an eyeful of liquefied fish. It smelt nasty too, he said.

One item he had: bottles, found in a cupboard in the Mess. They were very cheap, being old stock. We agreed to buy it all if it were any good. There were two bottles of wine, but they had gone back, very far back, after twenty years in a cupboard in Jacobabad.

There were, too, two glazed earthenware flasks, with handles and narrow necks, a blue glaze, and a vaguely baroque, eighteenth-century look about them. One had lost its stopper and was dry, but the other was sound. It contained a syrupy orange liqueur, and had lost nothing over those years. This flask became The Liqueur, and was dispensed by the thimbleful to special friends on special occasions. It lasted till just before we finally left Sindh—it was Pakistan by then. We wanted to share the last drops with the Reinitzs, but by then the flavour was somewhat sophisticated, and the Reinitzs rejected it. Some of the big black ants had eaten their way through the stopper, and before drinking those final drops we had to strain the ants out. The added flavour must have been formic acid, but we drank it nonetheless in memory of special occasions.

Popatlal could get us stores from Karachi, and he had a cold room, a modernism we found nowhere else in Upper Sindh, but considered essential by Joan if she was to cater for a big Horse Show Party, the biggest, the oldest, the best in all Sindh. Popatlal could get a special ration of gin and whisky and beer from Phipson in Karachi, and some he would keep on his own account, in case any of our guests felt so generous as to give us some. Gin was distilled at Nasik, beer was brewed at Murree, but Scotch whisky was imported, and was very scarce. We would not inflict on our guests the White Hart brand distilled in Quetta. I had from years back Dermont Barty's opinion, and later myself met its flavouring, dropped from a train.

While I was on tour Joan had been improving her riding, so that when I was in we could go riding together. The Risaldar was very happy to help her, and chose a suitable mount: a bay mare, Mumtaz. The sub-cavalry mounts of the Special Force were tall for an average-sized woman, but Mumtaz was the smallest, and Joan came to love her dearly. The Risaldar rode with her, but when he heard from my escorts that I was reasonably proficient, he was very happy that we should borrow horses and do their exercising for him. He would guide Joan round the town to the Parade Ground; of course he would not take a lady the short way, through the brothel.

When I came in the Risaldar asked for an interview on a very delicate matter: the Memsahib did not grip the horse tightly enough to ride well, what did she wear under her jodhpurs? He could not question her, but her husband could. I said, just knickers. He suggested very long woollen drawers, but I could do better than that: next time Joan went riding she could grip well, with a pair of my long-johns, till we could get smaller ones from Gangaram in Karachi. There was no more chafing, nor embarrassment for the Risaldar. But Joan thanked him very cheerfully and openly for his suggestion; he probably blushed, but appreciated it, too. He was new to this frankness of white women in talking about such delicate matters.

Now we began to prepare for the equestrian side of the Show. There were numbers of trick-riding competitions, and for some there were classes for visitors. For women there was 'bending', slalom-on-horseback, and the potato race, for which a potato was put on the top of a bending pole, and must be collected from horseback—or from the ground if it were knocked off—and taken one by one to a bucket. It might bounce out of the bucket, too. Joan became creditably proficient at these races. For men there was *neza-bazi*, tent-pegging, a standard exercise for a unit of lancers. The peg was made from the aerial roots of palm trees, which could be lanced without splitting. It was stuck in the ground, and the lancer must lift it and carry it away, as in battle he would spear his enemy: let his lance trail to clear the point, and then sweep it round to hold aloft. I became pretty good at that; beginning with a four inch peg, I progressed to two, and then I could even lift a one-inch peg most times.

I have seen tent-pegging done at a trot, and at a canter, which needed much skill, though in war the enemy would hardly have waited for the lance. At a hand gallop it was different, and never have I seen anything like the heart-raising speed and skill of the troopers of the Special Force riding down on the tiny peg. The rider raised his lance high in the air at the salute, called his war-cry, '*Allah-ho-Akbar*', and set his horse at the full charge at the tiny, distant, hardly visible mark. The horse loved it, too. The lance would come slowly down, level, then lower, and then right down to spear the peg. The rider let his arm go limp as he passed the peg, trailing the lance, then raised it behind him and swept it round to his front, hoping the peg was impaled on it. Very seldom it was not. The best troopers could lift a half-inch peg, even one buried and shown only by a tiny hill of chalk. I must try to emulate the experts, but though I never got beyond the one-inch peg, and sometimes missed that, I could have the excitement of the charge even if I missed altogether. I could lift my lance high with the peg on its tip, trot to the saluting base, and warm to the cheering crowd. Only, there was no crowd, and this was only practice. There were just two or three troopers watching, calling 'Shabash' even if there was no peg there.

When the Cavalry Sports were held, there would doubtless be grumbles that Joan and I had an unfair advantage. But the Special Force didn't see it that way: it was only right that the Deputy Commissioner and his wife should win, to sustain their *izzat.* Joan would have Mumtaz, I would have Prince, a gelding who had toured with me, who was my favourite. For a short tour to Garhi Khair Mahomed I rode him from Jacobabad—the camp moved by rail—so I knew him well.

Sirdar Bahadur Sirdar Abdur Rahim was the chief Khosa sirdar, unknown to me when he bought the Chev. He had promised a special tamasha, to celebrate Christmas, as our but not his holy day. He was a proper chief of his clan, not interested in politics. He could accommodate even the Communist Mahomed Amin, because he was a clansman. Just for the evening we would leave the boys with Candy, and Andrew would drive Joan over. (I must have a car soon!) We were not told the nature of the tamasha, it was to be a surprise.

It began quietly in the Sirdar's otak: here were chairs and tables set neatly along the walls, carefully squared round the beautiful carpet in the middle. Joan went behind the purdah to meet the Begum Rahim Baksh, while we drank sweet drinks and ate nuts. Afterwards Joan told me that there were children there, and other women, but, compared with the grand otak, the Sirdar's domestic arrangements were drab and a little mean. On the other hand, perhaps in his private life he had no wish to live grandly. We inevitably compared this Khosa home with that of the Chandios at Ghaibi Dero. Joan's meeting was not very informative, halting Urdu talking with Balochi Sindhi, but, she said, friendly.

When it was dark the real tamasha began: the Sirdar had hired a famous firework maker, and he would put on a very special show.

There were rockets and bangs and catherine wheels, but the special item was a race between rocket-driven cars. These were the size of a child's pedal car, built all of bent cane, very light and strong, with squibs tied round the wheels, and linked by a fuse. There were four, each driven by one big rocket in the stern, no brakes were possible, there was no steering, no way of stopping them once the fuse was lit. The course was about a hundred yards long, with a blank wall at the end. The Sirdar's party was on one side, a crowd of townsfolk and children on the other. The cars were differently coloured, and clearly a good deal of wagering was going on.

Four drivers were stripped down to short drawers, with none of the usual loose clothing to catch sparks. Each had a portfire, and each carefully lined up his car to face the end wall exactly: at the Sirdar's word they all lit the fuses. There was a hissing, a pause, and they were away.

After only twenty yards one of the cars on our side hit its neighbour, which landed upside down in the track of the offender; a most remarkable somersault. They charged each other, and their rockets kept them locked together.

The other two raced on, neck and neck, till one veered off and ran at the crowd; with shouts and screams they tried to give it room, but some were overrun. Meanwhile the last car ran on, crashed into the wall, and burst into flame, a clear winner. The two that fought each other were also flaming wrecks, but the one that had burst through the crowd sped on till its rocket died, the only one to survive.

This was a magnificent and exhilarating spectacle, appreciated by all, for, apart from three boys and a man slightly scorched, no harm was done. And, as the Sirdar pointed out, had they been real cars with real drivers there was no doubt that people would have been killed, so this way was much better. There was a flaw in his logic, but my Sindhi was not adequate for me to dispute it. Moreover he had certainly shown us something special, and he was my host.

The evening ended with a feast of *sujji*, *dumba* mutton grilled on spits round a heap of glowing charcoal. On this cold, clear evening, on cushions in the open air, we sat round a fire that was welcome now but would have been unbearable in the day. We gorged ourselves with this hot, tender meat, eaten with fresh, puffed chapatis, washed down with sweet fizzy drinks. Each of us had a little towel— very necessary with no tools but our fingers, and meat running with fat. Perhaps it sounds rather gross and greedy; well, none of us were heavy eaters normally, and we had very few luxuries. There was, of course, no alcohol, and Andrew regretted his flask, left at home, but I was glad of it: even the smell would have been an offence to the Sirdar.

There was also my comfortable knowledge that the Sirdar was so great a man, chief sirdar of the Khosas, the biggest Baloch tribe on our Frontier, that he could never be suspected of seeking favours.

The twins called, and Joan went back to Jacobabad with Andrew. We were both thankful that Andrew's flask was at home. I stayed on to finish my work next day, and before leaving I called on the Sirdar to thank him for the best tamasha we had ever had, and to compliment him on the condition of Garhi Khair Mahomed, his own village, which was a model of good governance. Even the mess left by the race had been cleared away.

In Jacobabad there was all the planning for the Horse Show to be done, and this occupied the spare time of all of us till the Show began. I was *ex-officio* President of the Horse Show Committee, but my staff and the Mukhtiarkar knew just what to do, with nearly a hundred years' records to guide them. From year to year there was little change, and a new Deputy Commissioner would be a brave, and probably foolish, man to make any but the smallest changes.

The Horse Show—still continuing as the *Mela*—had a very serious central function, though it was also a useful outlet for government propaganda, and there was a social side which made it, for Upper Sindh officialdom, the most important event of the year.

The most important side was the horse market. This began in John Jacob's time, for he needed remounts for his cavalry, the Scinde Horse. It was an Irregular Cavalry Regiment, the best in India, and let no one imagine that 'irregular' means in any way indisciplined, or detached from the regular army, or badly equipped. It means that instead of the troopers being mounted, equipped, and clothed by the Army, each must provide his own horses and equipment—often from pride better than the official supply. This was the reason for a market for horses developing in Jacobabad, and so breeders from the hills found a good market for their stock. By the time I was there the demand was for 'sub-cavalry' horses, of a size suitable for the Special Force and the many zamindars who took pride in their mounts. The various Frontier Militias had a standing invitation for their officers to stay at the Residency when they came to buy. This year there was Colonel Keating, tall and distinguished, from the South Waziristan Scouts, and Captain Sutton, short and horsey, from the Zhob Militia. Keating was a dandy; he told us who in Savile Row made his suit, which sporting tailor in Jermyn Street made the loud checks of Sutton's, and that mine came off a peg somewhere.

We didn't see much of them. Each had his risaldar to help him, they spent all day trying and buying, and left. The risaldars stayed on to see the horses put on rail, and all this, the chief single transaction of the Show, was finished before it had properly begun.

Our time was not entirely taken up with work, or, indeed, with tamashas. Once food and drink for the twins was organized, we had time to explore places and possibilities. I showed Joan the dovecote, now the home of wild pigeons, the ruined fives court and swimming pool, the dangerous Record Room. She met Dr Jessaram at the Zenana Hospital, and we went to the Club. I remember going to meet local society there—almost all officers, of course—but apart from its tennis court, it had no meeting place. Joan met the headmaster of the High School, but there was no hope of a post there. He had no use for an expert in English literature, nor for an economist, nor for anyone to teach more than the simplest arithmetic. Our exploration had discovered little but ruins, so this Show, and another Viceregal visit, must provide a lot of occupation.

There was an odd incident which showed how uneven was local knowledge of mathematics, with an example from, as it were, the deep end. I had to recruit a clerk for my finance branch, and Madadalishah and I constituted a selection panel. We set the young man all sorts of simple mathematical problems, and he got them all right. His mental arithmetic was extraordinary. Then Madadalishah produced a quadratic equation; the boy took time over this, but then came out with two answers. Madadali had himself worked it out on paper, and the boy was right. I didn't think one could do quadratic equations in one's head, and suspected that perhaps Madadali had primed him. We adjourned for lunch, and I told Joan of this remarkable boy we were recruiting, who could do quadratic equations in his head. She said it was not possible, that Madadali was helping the boy to trick me. She set a similar problem herself, worked out the answers, and I recalled the boy to solve it. Which he did. Marvellous! Less than a minute and he had both answers, and there was no possibility of collusion. So he got the job, and my doubts of Madadali were unjustified. I don't know if the boy was otherwise brilliant; he may have had this one mental quirk and been otherwise dim. On the other hand, he may have had a brilliant career. But calculators will have devalued such a talent.

We rode round Jacobabad. At Joan's request I took her the quick way to the Parade Ground, the way through the brothel where the Risaldar would not take her. We were impressed by the state of the area, by far the neatest and cleanest part of the town. We took the twins out in their pram. Joan and I, with Candy pushing, a patewala and Lalu for escort, we paraded right up the main street, past the Exhibition Ground, past the Cinema and the Park—how grand it sounds!—to show to the people that they really were babies, that we all trusted everyone. And nobody took any but the most casual interest. Well, at least it showed that the burden of Imperial power did not weigh very heavily on anyone. We saw the Tomb, and as before there was a bunch of flowers. We turned back home, seeing now the Durbar Hall and the Zenana Hospital; but there were no crowds to control, even though they had had time to collect, even though this novel little vehicle must have been strange to most of Jacobabad. In fact, we had had a pleasant walk, with no excitement at all.

17

THE RAILWAYS

The Kashmore Railway was very much our own. It began in Jacobabad, travelled the whole eastern part of the district, to terminate at Kashmore, on the extreme eastern boundary with the Punjab. Its gauge was 30 inches, so narrow that its wagons looked as if they would topple over if too much weight were put on one side.

There were, I suppose, arrangements between the agents and the North-Western Railway to deal with risks, track safety, and rolling-stock inspections, but I never saw any sign of interest in this little railway being shown by the main line. It had been built by MacKinnon MacKenzie, managing agents throughout the East, and was still owned by them.

Always the passenger train had one wagon empty, the freighting of it the perquisite of the running crew. Whenever I travelled on it, I noticed men lining the track just outside the station, where there was an uphill grade. One by one as the train reached them they jumped on board and took a free ride. Just outside the town the line bridged a branch of the Begari canal, and on the return journey, just before the bridge, bundles would go flying from the train to land on the bank, followed by the unticketed passengers, who jumped into the water. There was a time, though, just before the new *abkalani*, when the canal was dry, and this particular free ride was not possible.

Often the train ran late, due to one hold-up or another. The most awkward was when, in a sandy desert tract, a storm had buried the rails with sand, the wheels lost them, and they had to be very carefully persuaded back. Every engine carried heavy jacks and baulks of timber, in case of need. I once saw how such a mishap was cured.

We all at one time or another cursed that railway. We all were proud of it, and loved it dearly.

There was, I believe, no other railway like it anywhere. Now it is gone. Instead of the little top-heavy engine with its tender piled high with a load of wood for its furnace, there is a common diesel motor, on a broad-gauge track, crossing the lonely border at Kashmore, carrying on like any ordinary railway to join the main line at Multan. Trains now will be travelling too fast even on the up-grade out of the station for anyone to jump on, or off into the canal. And there will doubtless be ticket inspectors, who never troubled our little line.

The passenger service was perhaps something of a joke, but valuable nonetheless. The real work, the work for which the line was built, was to fetch out all the rice and pulses grown along the Shahi Wah, the big old canal that ran from the river at Kashmore, along the Balochistan border, and along both sides of the Begari, so covering much of Sukkur district. By no means could it be called a strategic railway, but its existence, its promise of movement by police or even cavalry, had a calming effect on the Bugti, who were always restless, and other tribes that straddled the border.

The main line to Quetta was the cause of constant worry to the police. All trains stopped at Jacobabad, and a few miles beyond the station was the boundary with Balochistan. If the police sought a man they were entitled to cross the border 'in hot pursuit', but for that they would need to be on the train, or in a car, conditions that seldom occurred. Jhatpat station was just over the border, and once there the quarry could disappear; the territory was nominally under the Khan of Kalat, but actually ruled by the Political Agent at Sibi, whose Assistant of Jhatpat lived in Jacobabad. His was an uncomfortable position, outside his territory, with no local influence, belittled and disliked in his office by the local Baloch, who claimed to be badly treated whenever they crossed the border. This was probably untrue, but on the other hand these politicals seemed to show little respect for either law or custom. I had crossed swords mildly with Tony Drake when he held Jhatpat, but we had remained friends. Now there was a new man, Alan Dredge, and I had to get to know him.

My introduction to his official self was unfortunate. A merchant of the town came to see me with a plea that I should in some way stop his going to Jhatpat: he had been summonsed to appear as a witness in court before the Agent. The summons was in order, and I pointed out that anyway he was a witness for the prosecution, so what harm could come to him? He said he would be imprisoned, if Government lost the case he would certainly be imprisoned. Nonsense, said I, and with my reassurance, but very unwillingly, he went. That evening a man came, in tears, to tell me that his friend really was in prison. This was hard to believe, but when Alan came home I asked him, and it was true.

How pleasing it was to be righteously indignant! One of my people imprisoned for no reason, and in denial of my assurance to him! The reason I was given was that the case had gone on longer than expected, the merchant's evidence had not been taken, and the best way of making sure he was in court next day was to put him in a cell. It did him no harm, it even saved him expense, why should he, or I, object? But object I did: what about the man's reputation, what about his family? What about my own reputation, who had given him assurances? I demanded his immediate release, that very night. (But that in fact was just not possible.) I made some caustic remarks on different ideas of British law, and hinted at protests. Indeed, I could have reported to the Chief Secretary, who would possibly have protested to the Agent, and there would have been trouble for Alan. But in fact the man had taken no real harm, he had a dramatic story to tell rather than a blot on his reputation. I had had a very satisfactory interview, and had increased my *izzat* in the town; moreover, there would be times when Alan and I would need to work together, particularly in interpreting the doctrine of 'hot pursuit' liberally.

There was a specialist crime centred on Jacobabad. A freight train going to Quetta would stop, thieves would 'case' the wagons to find one loaded with miscellaneous goods, and board the train near that wagon when it left the station. Once it was clear, in the open *pat*, they would break in, toss out whatever they could, jump off and walk back, collecting anything worth while. Once the train reached Jhatpat the rifled wagon would be discovered, and the police at Jacobabad would be wired. Police would set off from both stations, recovering anything the thieves had left; there was little hope of catching the thieves themselves. There was no difficulty of hot pursuit, and I daresay the police parties would, when they met, share any worthwhile finds. Certainly nothing much of value reached Jacobabad, but I remember one recovery that was notable: a case of bottles of 'whisky flavouring' with a packet of White Hart labels, exact copies, except for that name, of the White Horse label. They were clearly meant for the distillery in Quetta, which made that deadly stuff, and doctored the alcohol with this essence. The product was easily saleable now that import of the true brand was a tiny trickle. I met a man who had tried it, and his opinion was that two bottles would send the strongest man blind.

Even in those days Jacobabad had its airstrip, a simple cleared strip with a little coarse grass, but mostly the gravel of the *pat*. The Racecourse circled it, and at the side was a little hut. It was maintained by the RAF as an emergency landing strip between Karachi and Quetta, and they kept a fuel dump there. One day, before Joan had come up from Karachi, Andrew was notified that a flight of Hurricanes would land to refuel, so we went down to see, with three police sepoys in the back of the car. We watched them come up from the south, first tiny dots, growing bigger extraordinarily quickly. They flew in a vee, circled us, changed to line ahead, and landed in a great cloud of dust. They came up one by one to the refuelling point, took on petrol, waved to us, and were away: a great roar of engines, an even greater cloud of dust, and by the time we could see anything they had formed up again and were flying fast towards the hills, the noise fading as they grew small until we finally lost them. We went home. Those beautiful machines brought us for the first time into any real touch with the war.

Not till a year later did we hear any more of those planes. Only one of the five reached Quetta. The others lost their way in the hills, ran out of fuel, and crashed.

18

THE JIRGA

Unlike the rest of Sindh, the Upper Sindh Frontier District had its Deputy Commissioner instead of a Collector, though all their powers were the same; and its Residency. It also had the Sindh Frontier Regulations.

The Jirga System was the judicial bequest of General John Jacob, who in the forties and fifties of the nineteenth century had settled the frontier between Balochistan and Sindh.

The Baloch tribes of the hill areas were accustomed to raiding into the plains of Sindh; Jacob first defeated them in battle, then suppressed their raiding hobby by constant mounted patrols by the regiment he raised, the Scinde Horse. The speed of action by his patrols was astonishing, helped by his pigeon postal systems between outposts and Jacobabad. We had seen his dovecote.

He was artilleryman, cavalryman, engineer, and surveyor. He built roads, cleared jungle, repaired the old canals and kept them running; he surveyed all his area. He made it more comfortable to farm instead of to raid. He also built the Clock.

Hugh Lambrick, whom I knew well in Sindh, was a descendant of John Jacob and wrote his biography, which is as absorbing and exciting as any fictional book about the heroes of British India. Jacob's memory lived on in my time, so that the Upper Sindh Frontier District was considered a suitable post for a young and inexperienced officer: he would be sitting in Jacob's Chair and, so long as he dealt with people reasonably and honestly, they would overlook many mistakes.

When I was in Jacobabad there were many Baloch tribes with concerns on both sides of the border, which to most was an entirely imaginary line. They had had their own system of justice, their own courts, the jirgas, since time out of mind, and when the legal system of India was formalized in the 1860s it was felt inappropriate, indeed impracticable, to include the Baloch customary system. On the other hand, the tribes would find it impossible suddenly to accept the strict rules of British law.

So the Sindh Frontier Regulations were enacted, and under these the Deputy Commissioner, in his role as District Magistrate, secured law and order in his District. But the Regulations covered only the Baloch and their own tribal customs. For all his other 'subjects', the DC had to operate the Indian Penal Code and the Criminal Procedure Code. There were, fortunately, more Baloch on this frontier than there were Sindhi Muslims and Hindus put together, which happily made ordinary legal work light.

The various tribes, or clans, themselves provided the members of the jirga from among their Sirdars. There were several jirgas for minor cases, the Shahi Jirga for important ones; and over all was the District Magistrate.

Rules of evidence before a jirga were practically non-existent: hearsay and evidence of general repute were admissible, and even evidence from a member of the jirga itself. There was no fuss about whether or not a question was leading. As in any court, evidence was given on oath, but a jirga could, as an ordinary court could not, require a party to the case, or a witness, to swear on the Quran. Refusal so to swear would tell heavily against a witness, but even so he could argue that he refused not because his evidence was false, but because he feared to endanger his immortal soul by accidentally saying some little, irrelevant thing that was untrue without his knowing it. Such a heavy oath was not always a simple way of finding the truth.

Minor cases only came to the District Magistrate if one party were dissatisfied with the result. He could not reverse the decision, but could return the case for further consideration, perhaps with comments on the interpretation of evidence or custom. The comments would doubtless have been formalized by the Shristedar, who was himself the real authority on custom. If the jirga maintained its first decision, the DM must accept it. (He might, however, have information of feuding, making a change of membership of the jirga desirable before its reconsideration!)

Under the Regulations, the District Magistrate had extraordinary powers. He could arrest either party, or a witness, without any warrant, to ensure attendance. (But I had been highly indignant when the Assistant Political Agent Jhatpat had exercised just such power to arrest a Hindu!) He could sequestrate the property of an absconder until he surrendered. If a fine were unpaid he could, without any special process, forfeit goods. He could exclude a man from his village. All this sounds draconian, and so it was; but swift justice was extremely important: delay might result in a plaintiff taking action himself. Among the Baloch it was all so well known that exercise of these powers was seldom needed.

The chief problems the District Magistrate had to face were the definition of Baloch custom, and whether it could be invoked in a dispute between a Balochi and a Sindhi, Muslim or Hindu. This was my Shristedar's field, and he took an academic as well as a practical interest in it.

I found jirga work far more interesting and satisfying than ordinary cases under criminal law, which most District Magistrates did not have: I had no sub-divisional officer for the Garhi Khair Mahomed half of the District, so I had to take the cases that would have been his. For the jirga there were no complicated judgements to write, which would so often result in an unsatisfactory conclusion based on the existence or absence of 'reasonable doubt'. Nor did I have to listen to the obfuscations of pleaders trained in the minute legalism of the Indian Bar.

There was another important difference from criminal law: the basis of Baloch custom was the right of a man to preserve his and his family's honour, his *izzat*. This could be held to justify what otherwise would be criminal, and a demand for compensation for an insult that was not criminal at all. So justification could be claimed for anything from murder to personal insult. Disputes over ownership of land or other property, over marriage settlements and inheritance—a jirga could deal with them all. It could, within its sphere, take the place of a civil as well as a criminal court, but Custom must be involved, and there were frequent disagreements as to whether such and such a case was covered.

There was no death penalty, and the aim of sentencing was to avoid imprisonment if at all possible: if a man were in gaol his family starved, and whoever had a claim against him gained nothing. Punishment by a fine and compensation for the person who had suffered was far preferable. There had been a time when an offender could be held in servitude for a period, but that had been stopped.

So many minor offences there could be, and from any of them, if not swiftly dealt with, a feud could develop, growing over time into a series of blows and counter-blows, the origin long forgotten, the end violent and bloody.

It was a feud of this kind, within the Burdi clan, that I had to deal with by a *faisla*, an agreed settlement, when I sat myself as a jirga, still only holding charge in Jacobabad.

It was a saying in Sindh that all murders arose over water or women. Baloch custom had nothing to say about water, but about women there was plenty. News of a murder meant almost certainly '*karo-kari*' (a man blacked, a woman blacked). If a woman be taken in adultery and herself and her lover killed by her husband, that is according to Baloch custom, and the husband has committed no offence. Indeed, if he failed to kill them his honour was besmirched. If he killed the man and kept the woman, because he valued her beauty or for some other reason, he was dishonoured, and the killing of her lover would be viewed differently: he would be ordered to pay compensation to the dead man's family. Whether or not he killed one or both, the killing must be done in the heat of passion upon finding them. If he hear of it from someone else, or ran off home to fetch his big axe, his *khuni khudr*, then his action would clearly be premeditated murder, which was not customary; he would be prosecuted in the ordinary criminal court. Further, the criminal law could not be entirely pre-empted, and under the Regulations a 'customary' murder could be punished by seven years in gaol for each death. (Fourteen years was a far higher punishment than the five years a First Class Magistrate could impose!) There was no provision for an appeal against sentence, only for an application to the Revenue Commissioner for revision.

There were many possibilities for disagreement on interpretation of details of customs. The jirga members, all sirdars of their tribes, all experts in interpretations which might vary from tribe to tribe, spent a great deal of time in reaching their decisions. They were sent to me, and I had the essential advice of my Shristedar, acknowledged to be the greatest expert of them all: it was his job.

Once I had confirmed a jirga finding, or decided a case myself, there was no appeal, except to the Revenue Commissioner, who could not overturn a decision, but only order reference back for reconsideration. If I refused to change my decision, and he felt strongly that I was wrong, he could, at the last, transfer me and appoint someone more amenable in my place. This would be a very extreme step to take; I am glad it didn't happen to me.

The system generally worked smoothly; the Frontier was peaceful and there was no excessive crime, though there were a few difficult cases. In one, the guilty man and woman had escaped, the one from the district, and was untraced, the woman to her parents' home. The jirga set a sum of compensation to be paid by the adulterer to the wronged husband, recoverable from his family; the wife was divorced, and her husband retained her *daulat* since she had dishonoured him, and also herself. I agreed with the jirga. The woman's family appealed to the Commissioner, who told me to look at it again: he considered that the *daulat* should be returned to the family as the woman claimed to have been forced. I consulted the jirga, and we decided that the order was right, complied with custom. We would not change. I reported this, agreeing with it, and the Commissioner accepted the decision. He did not disagree strongly enough to transfer me.

I was senior enough now to write to my Commissioner using his Christian name, a significant step forward for me. I wrote a demi-official letter to Charles. I pointed out that the jirga and I were unanimous in our decision, that his disagreement was on a doubtful item of fact, where local knowledge was more likely to be accurate than his judgement or mine, and that rejection of the jirga's finding might weaken the authority of all these influential sirdars. This might reflect disastrously on the maintenance of law and order among these fiercely proud tribes. I laid it on strongly. There might even have been some truth in it, too.

There was another case which became a local *cause célébre*. A man raped a nine-year-old girl, her father came on them, chased the ravisher, and killed him. The girl's mother found her and took her to the Zenana Hospital—she was shocked and badly injured when she fought the man. Her father came to the hospital, ostensibly to comfort her. Instead, he killed her as she lay in bed.

The jirga took a long time over this case: there was no dispute about the evidence, the father admitted both killings. The ravisher was killed without any premeditation, the girl as soon as he could get to her. The little girl had been dishonoured by being raped, she had coupled with the man, her family was dishonoured too. The jirga reported that this was all according to custom: the ravisher was dead, the father could go to gaol for three years for that. There was no one to be compensated, and the father had the right: he had committed no offence.

When I read the report I was so very angry! I called the Jirga and rated them bitterly, those grand bearded chieftains, and I, a foreigner, only a year in their territory. (I had need of the Shade of John Jacob!) I told them that if this case accorded with their custom, then their custom was bad. How could a little child resist a grown man? How could her being forced dishonour her or her family? It was her father who, by killing her, had dishonoured himself, and if the Jirga continued its support for him, then it would itself be dishonoured. While still my fury lasted I wrote to Clee express, with the record, reporting the action I was taking, and that I was arresting the father on a charge of murder. I had him arrested and charged with premeditated murder under the Indian Penal Code, the case to be tried in some other court.

The Jirga left. My Shristedar said he was shaking with anxiety: had any of those Jirga members had a gun or a sword, he feared I would have been attacked. I was still shaking with shock and anger myself, for my faith in the basic justice of Custom had been damaged.

But on both sides emotions calmed. I met some of the members, and apologized for the violence of my speech. Some of them, on the other hand, thanked me for preventing them from doing great harm to their tribal reputation.

The father was tried, found guilty, and hanged.

The Pakistan Government has withdrawn the Frontier Regulations. Probably it was time, for they were, in fact, a makeshift method of maintaining order among a traditionally disorderly people. But it worked pretty well in its time; and if the Regulations have been replaced, as I understand, by Criminal Tribes Regulations, and that punishments are those sanctioned by Quranic law, then the Baloch may well regret the loss of their customary procedures and penalties. Moreover, the Baloch were not in my time any more criminal than other societies in Sindh, and in some ways their customs were less brutal and more socially conscious than the laws of British India. Nor has the status of women improved much beyond their position as chattels of husband or father; in some ways I think it has regressed.

19

THE HORSE SHOW, 1944

Being *ex-officio* President of the Horse Show Committee was by no means a sinecure. The Programme was much the same year after year, but there was another programme, with times for inviting judges for the various competitions, for notices to be published inviting entries for the competitions, times for the District Officers' Party and the Shahi Jirga's Party, Rules for the Baloch Races. Nearer the time we had to decide which Sirdar should host the party, a decision requiring tact, and knowledge of who had hosted it before. Also, we must decide what film to show, and which of the 'entertainments' on offer we should accept. The Police and the Special Force must agree on their programmes for their sports. I found the clarity of thought and efficiency of planning most impressive. It was a pleasure to chair such businesslike meetings. I might find the lack of any plans for meetings about 'rural uplift' and agricultural improvement disappointing, but would not, new as I was to such an organization, try to change anything—this year. The war was going well, the Germans had surrendered in North Africa and were being driven out of Italy, while the Americans were rolling up the Japanese in the Pacific, and they were being defeated in Burma. So the film we chose was *Desert Victory*, for the Indian Army, and especially the Scinde Horse, had been involved in that. For entertainment we chose a Variety Show.

It would be tedious to detail our programme for the week: the programme notice itself can do that. President of the Show may sound just an honorific title, but he—I— would have a busy time, for I must see at least a little of the stock classifications, of the judging of all the classes, of ploughing competitions, and at the end must make a suitable speech when I presented the prizes. At the same time I would have my own private party.

We had to invite our guests and arrange to accommodate them. Having only half a Residency we needed tents, our own and some we borrowed. Many of our friends were too busy, but some came at least for some of the time: Nazir and Afroze for two days, over from Sukkur, bringing Jane Holt, though Harland was too busy; John Petty, our Forestry Officer; David Halford, now in the Finance Department, and his girlfriend Joanne Collins; Denis Arber of the Airborne Division; April Swayne Thomas, avid to learn about Sindh; Robin Keith, whom we did not know, just up from Bombay and, which we could not know, destined later to take over from me. Eric O'Flynn came, and Reggie Simpson, but they were police, and Andrew Davies' guests. All of these had taken, or would take, some part in our lives.

The logistics of our own party at the Residency were in their way as complicated as those for the Show itself, and we had no advantage from previous experience. Most of the work inevitably fell to Joan. Providing some sort of cover from the weather for our guests was a small part of it. But at least a problem that would have appalled a housewife in England did not arise: each guest would have a bistra, towels, and the like, so we need keep only a small reserve of bed linen. For staff we had the patewalas, always helpful if inexperienced, and Mistri and Illahibaksh recruited mates from them. The cooker was provided with extra chullas, from somewhere commodes and tin baths arrived, and bheesti and bhangi had full-time work; and did it very thoroughly. I remember no serious hitch.

For catering, Mistri was full of confidence. He and Joan worked out a daily menu—there is still a copy of it—more varied than at first seemed possible. There were recipes from Grete Reinitz, a recipe from Jeanie, who could not come because Fram was away in Bengal showing them how to close breaches in their bunds, which they had not considered possible till he closed more difficult ones in Sindh. From somewhere we acquired an extra ice box, to take all the extra ration of drink we had been able to squeeze out of Phipsons for the Show. This menu surprises me now, with the record of luxuries I thought we could never buy in the war. Some, perhaps, had been acquired from American PX stores through friends: the Americans seemed to suffer no shortages. Joan and Mistri were happy with what could be had locally, or brought up from Karachi. But there were cornflakes and baked beans, even ham and bacon, unavailable since the war began, except to the Americans, who even had ice-cream shipped in a tanker across the Pacific, or so we were told. The menu notes 'sausages (one tin)', which is rather sad. But there were prawns and fish brought up in ice from Karachi, butter and cream on ice from Dokri—my contacts were helpful! We had our own ice-cream machine. It is very noticeable that there are no Indian or Sindhi dishes at all. This would be a very British party.

In the morning there was coffee or drinks under a shamiana on the lawn, making all the care taken of it worth while, for this one week. It has always been my feeling that after a party there is nothing better than to be meeting again next day. When people went to sit under the shamiana they would find two little boys already there, on their dhurrie, just beginning to stagger about, even growing a little hair, pleased as puppies with the attention they received, and accepted as their due. Candy also received due praise, and how proud she was, for some of the guests had seen the twins when many thought they would not survive, and now they flourished; and much of the credit was hers.

I had my varied duties around the Show, Joan had the catering and housekeeping, with her special care for the twins and to be sure that Candy was happy: it was a wonder that we found time to enjoy our guests, but enjoy them we did. I even had time for a few photographs.

Such fun we had! There was no one over forty, no top brass or '*burra sahib*' to constrain us. I was just over thirty, Joan twenty-eight, and we were younger than most of our guests, except, of course, Afroze, mother of two, still only nineteen, and growing still more beautiful. News of the war was so optimistic that it was acceptable for us to celebrate and be cheerful in a way that would have rung false a year before. There were a few military officers, but as a whole we were determinedly civilian.

Throughout the Show I was concerned chiefly with its agricultural side. I asked the judges general questions: what was the quality of the stock? What improved machinery, fertilizers, seeds, were on offer to the cultivator? There seemed to be none, and it was all very disappointing. Looking back, I expected far too much, I was insufferably priggish, and yet I had to be suffered. So I collected points that I would put to the Committee for its final report, proposals for more adventurous items next year. This Show was, after all, chiefly for agriculture, in an area with little other industry. Surely here was the ideal place for innovation. The Show was itself created by John Jacob, and he was a great innovator.

I was no judge of horses, but I could tell if a cow looked like being a good milker, if a bullock looked strong, if a bull had points worth selecting. But whereas many of the horses had pedigrees, the cattle had none. Even at Dokri, recording for selection of breeding stock was inadequate.

Sheep came under cattle. The ones in the Show were all *dumbas*, and quality was judged entirely by the size of the tail, a standard that I could not take seriously. Goats were kept for milk, and many went for meat at an early age, as *sujji*. Some attempt was made to breed for milk, but there were no records, selection was by reputation.

There were buffaloes, kept just for their milk, which in my opinion was poor stuff: buffalo butter was white, and tasted white, not like the yellow English butter I knew. (What I did not know was how that colour was enhanced artificially!) Also, the Indian buffalo was an ugly beast, black, patchily hairy, usually covered in mud from its wallow. It was a very mild-tempered animal, quite unlike its fierce African cousin. I just did not like it, was not interested in it, which was very unprofessional of me.

Noticeably absent was the pig, which was, quite simply, anathema. Here was a big difference between the condition of the Muslim farmworker in Sindh and his Christian brother in the west: one of the greatest assets of the English farmworker was his ability to keep a pig on his scraps and have its meat. A farmer who would not let his men keep a pig would be avoided by the best of them. I had seen pigs, but poor-looking beasts, kept only by the very lowliest of Hindu outcastes.

I spent a lot of time at the Show Ground watching the judging, which went on and on, day after day. The judges went solemnly round, disrupted often when a horse-breeder decided to ride a horse right through, to show off its paces to a buyer. The judges learned patience. The police spent a lot of time there, too, for it was always a place where pickpockets and con-artists and general *badmashes* gathered. By the end of the week the police cells were full.

There was a great deal of noise, sudden shouting that turned out to be a friendly argument, one or two individual fights that were much appreciated, but never a threat to the peace. It was as though a truce had been called on all the temptations to Baloch wickedness. Only the pickpockets flourished.

One serious alarm there was: a Hindu boy disappeared, his parents raised the alarm, and the police were told that he had been seen at the station with a known 'undesirable' from the hills. Foolish man! In Jacobabad were the District Magistrate and the Political Agent with his Assistant, and there was the telegraph. Police were ordered to Nuttal and Belpat, on the far side of the *pat*, the train was searched, the boy and his abductor were sent back to Jacobabad under guard. I would have the trying of the man, in an ordinary court, for abducting little boys was not a recognized Baloch custom.

In the dawn the child was reunited with his parents; aunts and uncles, brothers, sisters, and cousins were there with their cries of relief and welcome, all adding their tears of joy, and smothering him in swathes of saris. Then they let him go to his parents, and he had his reward: harsh words about obedience, while they 'slapped him around', as the sub-inspector told me, till he wept more than they had done. In his opinion the boy would never wander again. The man was put in a cell, to be tried when the Show was over.

There was to be a Variety Show, staged in the Durbar Hall. It had been well publicized, with emphasis on the chief act: two *Danseuses Francaises*. Just what a French Dancer was, who knew? But the French were known to have easy morals, and dancing was always exciting. So the Hall was full. At the back were respectable bearded Muslims and stout Hindu merchants. In the middle sat our house parties, ostentatiously displaying our tickets. In the front, on benches, sat the younger gentlemen and all the local bright sparks.

There was juggling and conjuring, a small troop of Kuttak dancers, not very good, I was told, though I enjoyed it; then some *qavali* singing, which the Muslims appreciated enthusiastically, for they were well-known, well-loved songs.

At last came the *Danseuses Francaises*. Their entrance was greeted with gasps, and then with moans of desire. Truly they were French, or mostly French. They were fair of form and face, and their hair was shining gold. They were indubitably young, and very pretty, if you liked a girl to be plump, as the audience clearly and vocally did. Muslims do not, or anyway at that time did not, cat-call a woman, but there was a low continuous mumble of '*Wah...wah...wah...*' Moreover, there was plenty of those pretty bodies to be seen, and more was suggested. Their feet were bare, their toe-nails were painted, and they wore anklets of little bells. Their hareem trousers were of sheerest muslin, underneath they wore tight little pants, visibly blue; their midriffs were bare, and they wore tight blue satin bodices. This confection was crowned by two pretty faces and long golden hair, with round jewelled caps over all. They were carefully and modestly made up. They were a sensation.

Of course I remember them. I was a happily married District Officer, but those girls would have been a sensation anywhere, let alone on a rather lonely frontier. Andrew, sitting beside me, was fidgeting alarmingly; he told me that he was going to invite them to the party afterwards. I pointed out to him that Mrs Das would be deeply offended, and he must not. Nor, most certainly, must he ask one of them to go home with him. For one thing, it would destroy his reputation; for a second, there would probably be a riot among the young men in front; and for a third, he might catch something.

The girls danced a little, they sang a little in French. It was very bad, though that mattered not a jot. Men in front began to throw things, which alarmed the girls till they discovered that the missiles were bank notes wrapped round rupees. Those young men never saw a woman, except their mothers, their sisters, and their wives, or very little girls. These two were, also, entirely unlike the ordinary Indian prostitute. They had no need to sing or dance, let them just gyrate slowly.

The dance show threatened never to end. The manager had to come on and promise that, after an interval so that the girls could rest, they would come on again. Only thus did he avoid a riot.

There was an interval, and people went out into the night. But I was worried, and needed to consider things; I should have consulted Andrew, but he was in no fit state, very angry with me. Men might fight and kill over such girls. I was not a moralizing prig, I just didn't want any trouble. It seemed far more likely that these two girls would be abducted than any Hindu boy.

I went to talk to the manager, who was very pleased with a profitable evening. I told him that he and his troupe must be clear away very early in the morning, and that for the night he must take precautions. Would he like a police picket? He told me not to fear kidnap: he was well aware of the danger, and kept his own muscle; he pointed the three of them out to me, and they certainly looked adequate. As for the girls, they were already fixed up, and there would be no more trouble. They had accepted the best offers, and would be ready to go first thing. Each would have a 'piece of muscle' to keep an eye on her. No, there was no compulsion, they liked the money, they liked the varied experience. When they had saved enough they would, unfortunately for him, leave and get married. His job was to keep them happy. So I left it at that.

In their second act there was no throwing of money: they had made their choice, and disputing it would mean facing that tough muscle. Their admirers must be satisfied with just looking.

I heard afterwards that their fee was Rs 1,000 each, which in 1944 was real money. At that rate they might soon marry. I wished them well.

I could go to supper with Mr and Mrs Das—he was the Executive Engineer—with an easy mind. Andrew was glum, but there was nothing to be done about that. (He could not have matched that fee, anyway.)

Joan had been helping Mrs Das, who had never entertained a lot of Britishers before, had no idea what they would want to eat. Was she a vegetarian? She was. So, she should provide only her own vegetarian dishes, samosas,

pakoras, curry puffs, the sorts she had eaten at the Karachi
Club. It would do these meat-eaters good. Small plates and
paper napkins. Perhaps a little gin and whisky—we would
all be tactful in this abstemious house. After supper Denis
Arber told a memorable, half understood story, all
innuendo, on the lines of Burton's *Thousand and One Nights*,
disparaging the great of the land, particularly of the Army.
Joan was quick at understanding, I a little behind her; some
never understood at all. Andrew was not paying attention.

That was the first of our parties. The Police and the
Political parties followed, much the same, for the guests
were inevitably much the same. Elsewhere the real Show
carried on, taking no notice of these irrelevancies.

I was anxious to watch the ploughing competitions. As
ever, I was the improver, still thinking about that little
Ferguson tractor that I hoped one day, after the war, to
introduce into Sindh. But again I was badly disappointed.
There had to be two classes, one for the traditional plough,
which was no more than the beam with a narrow steel
chisel that did no more than a light cultivator; the other
was the improved one Agha had displayed at Ghulamullah.
It was just the same: its breast and share were in one piece,
it turned a sort of a slice, but still there was no coulter.
That was no drawback on the clean land of the Show
Ground, but in the field, facing stubble and other rubbish,
there would be a problem. I made a note. I remembered
that I had made the same note at Dokri. The ploughmen
were skilful enough, indeed, they needed to be, with those
tools. Perhaps I could help them to better ones. But they
had used the old ploughs for so many generations; who
could trust these new ones? When I gave the prizes I made
a little speech. After the war I would show them a machine
that would enable them to sow four times, ten times, as
much *rabi* seed as they did now. Perhaps they believed me;
perhaps the ground was not wholly stony.

I presented all the prizes for horses and cattle. I spoke
with conviction about the cattle, urging the keeping of

records necessary for any improvement, the selection of particular points and their preservation, for recording pedigrees as for horses. For the horses, I admitted ignorance and made a little flattering speech: I rode horses, they were beautiful beasts, even the losers at this Show were beautiful. I congratulated the winners, told them that they were true breeders, that good breeding would lead to ready sales, and so on... and on... It was such a relief to be enthusiastic, even though I knew that any of those fine breeders would have been happy to cheat me had I not pleaded ignorance.

Friday was the climax of the Show for visitors. There were the Police Sports, and the Special Force 'event', followed by the District Officers' At Home, which was very much a class affair, for Sirdars, other big landowners, the panchayat, and other big merchants; Joan and I were inevitably chief host and hostess, but fortunately had had to do nothing but pay our share of the cost. (The rasai fund helped to keep that low.) It was organized by Ali Ahmed on the parade ground.

The District War Committee met at the Residency, and there I must make another speech, all patriotism and optimism. I quoted the number of recruits for the armed forces—very few—and money raised, which was an unusually large sum, due to the generosity of Mahomed Amin Khoso and the merchants! The war was going well, we must continue our support, and so on... and again, on...

The Police Sports were the concern of Andrew Davies and the Risaldar. I had seen police sports before, but for me the part that was Cavalry Sports was special.

The Police were vital to the District; the Special Force, now that the Hur trouble was over, might be considered merely decorative, but I was proud of it. Also, its being there might play a part in our security. It had little to do, and the Risaldar was lavish in his provision of mounts for our guests. At the Sports there were special classes for guests, and they were given time and mounts for practice. We amateurs were not to be shown up too obviously against the expertise of the troopers.

There was little competition for Joan in the ladies' races. Joanne Collins, who had asked for a 'big, weak horse' when she went hacking, entered, but drew back at the last minute, which was probably just as well. We had wondered if she was a suitable mate for David Halford, which was presumptuous of us, and wholly wrong: they married, they have stayed married, and I expect she has made him a 'good wife, as wives go'. And he as good a husband. Did the Service feel it had a right to decide on a man's wife? And a member so junior as I, at that. No one dared question my decision.

There were several who would ride in the men's race, and in the *neza-bazi*. Visitors must, of course, be given the choice of mounts. I hoped to have my favourite, Prince, but David chose him. Had he perhaps seen me practising on him? Among the guests were several army officers, and enough for a good competition. Who won the flat race I don't remember; I expect I would have done so had it been me. But the *neza-bazi* went on and on, competitors dropping out as each missed a peg. In the end, only David and I were left. David had done it before, and had *my* horse; I had had plenty of practice and rode another horse chosen for me. We were down to the last, the one-inch, peg. David rode down first, lanced it, and carried it triumphantly past the grandstand. Then I settled, the horse settled, and I held him back for a moment before I let him go. At full charge we went, my lance high in the air at first, gradually falling, level... keep your eye on the peg... lower still... right down and lance it. Arm loose, lance trailing, then swung round and lifted high with the little peg securely on the tip. Pull up gently, ride round to the stand and accept the cheers. Just as it should have been. But there was no peg: I had hit it, carried it, but it had fallen off; and the cheering died. So David won. I must slink back on the far side.

Joan won her bending and her potato race—I have a photograph of her. She took one of me, charging down on the peg. But I did not win. It was just as well, or I might have been accused of fixing the result.

The Special Force troopers then showed us how it should be done: four charged down in line abreast, then four in line ahead; all hoisted their one inch-pegs high. Then finally the pegs were buried, with only a little heap of chalk on each. They lifted them all, they trotted past the stand and saluted, and we all cheered and cheered. It was exhilarating, so exhilarating that Adam and David wet themselves, which was not usual in these days; but Candy had come prepared for it.

Then there was fancy riding, with the lines interwoven at speed, and trick riding, the rider took up his carbine, leant down and fired under his mount's belly. A man was caught up from the ground at full speed, another leapt from his own horse to another. It was unfortunate that his own horse, excited by its freedom, bolted through the crowd, and we feared injuries. But there were none: it was a rule that Indian people in crowds were never hurt. It was because they all, Hindus and Muslims alike, had such undoubting faith, a faith that we Christians lacked. (A little scorching at a rocket-car race didn't count.)

The next day, the final day, came the most stirring and riotous event of all. The Baloch Races were held on the track circling the airstrip; there were only two qualifications: the rider must be Baloch, and the horses must use the Sindhi *pund*. So really it was a trotting race. This was the pace all our tapedars used on their ponies, but in this Race there were real horses, and they were ridden at a full and ferocious charge.

There had to be two heats, so many wanted to show their rivals what they could do. Once the starting line was full the ones left out were stopped, with much beating and shouting, to await a second heat.

Perhaps these were Balochis as John Jacob had known them, save that there were no guns or swords, only quirts and their strong shouting. There seemed to be no rules; if you could reach a rival you could quirt his horse, or even himself, and equally he would ride you off if he could, right off and into the crowd. Twice round the course they went, and on the second circuit there were loose and fallen horses to negotiate, but the pace never slackened. Only six from the heat would get into the final; only eight finished.

The second heat was very much like. The final, with only twelve riders, was much more orderly, the riders were the most skilful, and more concerned with winning than with beating up a rival. They moved at astonishing speed. I had never thought the *pund* could move so fast without breaking into a gallop, which would disqualify the horse. The favourite won—of course he did—a large dark man from the hills. Joan gave him his prize, and Alan Dredge told me loudly that, had he been over the border, he would at once have been arrested, he was a much sought-after *badmash*. But here he was safe, we did not want him, and once back on his home ground he would disappear.

Horse-racing in England, so carefully regimented, is to me flat in both senses.

Last came the Residency Ball. The furniture in the drawing-room was all moved out or back to the walls, drinks were set out on our own table, and chairs and couch put in the inner verandah, where the light was dim and the heavy, solemn ticking of the great clock would soothe stretched nerves or inappropriate excitement. Food was laid out in the dining-room, under the eyes of John Jacob in his portrait, and we hoped he would approve, for we had carried on the tradition that he had begun. Probably even the food would have been familiar to him, for there was little that was exotic; it was simple and entirely British, as the menu shows, though meringues and sundaes from Vienna would have surprised him.

John Jacob would have found his drawing-room almost unchanged. We had a big fire of logs, perhaps one or two vases of flowers. But we grew few flowers: I have a picture of Denis Arber posing behind some promising hollyhocks, but you can't put hollyhocks into vases. There were no windows, so no curtains, only three doors to the verandah. We had no pictures for the vast expanse of the walls, but we were all used to that: the room must justify itself by its proportions, its grand, teak-beamed ceiling, and its teak floor, specially polished for the dancing. At the edge of the Empire one did not expect prettiness. We all felt at home.

Then we danced. Between us all there were plenty of records, some right up-to-date in 1944; waltzes and foxtrots, veleta and tango, Astaire 'hits' and something for a Palais Glide; there was an excuse-me dance and then we did a conga; we wove about in the garden till the music was inaudible, dancing back till we could hear it again, hoping that we were still in time. (How simple and innocent were your grand-parents' amusements!)

The music was from our portable gramophone, playing softly with its fibre needles, but only the sophisticates from Karachi would wonder at it. Couples slipped onto the verandah to cool off, and Joan went to look after the twins so that Candy could come and watch and listen. She loved dancing, but I was not so bold and unorthodox as to dance with her. Perhaps I should have done, but to think of it now is much, much too late.

I had warned people that if they went right outside they were likely to be challenged by the sentry. For those who did not know, this gave an exciting feeling of the danger of being so near the Frontier and tribal territory. It was entirely bogus, but nevertheless romantic.

Ours was not the sort of party to go on all night. The food was always there, and the drink: now, at the last, there was no need to keep anything in reserve. At midnight came coffee and a hot rum punch. Joan came back, we had one last dance together, and she went to bed. I, too, had had enough of dancing: I found a vacant couch on the verandah and cuddled up there with Bunty Thompson. By then cuddling was about all we were capable of; we liked each other, we had had fun, and were both a little tipsy. So we just sat there quietly.

We went back inside, and I found that the party was like to die on us. Everyone was tired, sleepily tired, so we all had the last dance and then sang Auld Lang Syne, as was proper.

There was nothing wild about our Ball. With Mr and Mrs Das there, and Ali Ahmed, my Deputy Collector, that would have been offensive. We were not of the right age, anyway. But none of them danced, and all three were a little shocked by the way men and women held each other close. Ali Ahmed later told me of his surprise at the way husbands seemed not to mind seeing their wives in other men's arms. I had to assure him that it signified nothing, was just a matter of different customs.

Everyone went away, and I was left with Illahibaksh to see what we could do to straighten things up. At about two o'clock we gave up.

I went to bed without waking Joan. I didn't sleep, I kept mulling things over till I heard marching feet and an order. I got up to look: it was dawn, and the guard was parading before going off duty. I went outside, but could hardly take the salute in such a slovenly state. The flag was raised for a new day and the guard marched away. I really had kept the party going till the sun rose, if only in my head.

Everybody left, early by car, later by train. By midday there was no one left to lessen the gloom of anti-climax, so we asked Alan and Andrew to lunch to clear up the leftovers. Then there was the dismantling to do. But before that I must think of our staff: our visitors had left something more tangible than thanks. Illahibaksh and Mistri had been individually rewarded, and were very happy with that. I had been left with a sum to distribute among the others.

Here was a problem. There was Mahbubalishah and the patewalas, the dhobi, the bhangi, and the mali. The Havildar naturally expected to receive most, by reason of his rank; in fact, he had done very little to help, and had had an easy time, with no formal callers, no cases, very few petitioners; his chief function he saw as giving orders to his patewalas. He should have least, but must have a little more than his subordinates, for discipline's sake. The fact that he annoyed me with his conceit, and that I liked the patewalas, particularly Aadam, was beside the point. He would have a particular shock when I gave the bhangi, an outcaste Hindu, the biggest share, but he had certainly worked hardest, with thunderboxes to clean, and baths to fill and empty, and hot water to have on hand at all times. I thought that if Mahbubalishah were to protest openly, I would ask if he would have liked to do the job himself, but that would have been unfair, and anyway he did not express his shock openly. Dhobi got something less than bhangi, and mali a little. I explained how I had judged the shares of each.

Tents came down, furniture, crockery, and cooking pots were returned to their owners, and routines were reinstated. Only the shamiana was kept on the lawn, so that the twins could be outside even in the middle of the day. The two *dumbas* returned to duty, but they were tethered well away from the shamiana: the boys must be kept away from the fascinating little black marbles the sheep dropped behind them.

This was a blessed Sunday. By next day all would be normal, only memories and a few photographs to come when I could get them developed. We could turn to the next thing and forget about it all. But over fifty years on, fifty years after the end of the British Raj changed the whole nature of the Horse Show, I wouldn't want to forget it. I feel a deep nostalgia for that Show. We had helped to make it work, it was continuing a century-old tradition which had a purpose that was still very much alive. We had assisted in history, and wouldn't want to, never could, forget it.

After everything was over, the Horse Show Committee met for the last time before it went into aestivation for six months. We noted any mistakes that might need changes, we decided that we must be very careful in choosing an entertainment, and, at my insistence, decided that Government must be asked for something more positive than horse and cattle shows to persuade farmers to look to their farming methods and perhaps improve them. Then we congratulated ourselves and voted thanks to everyone, but everyone, who had been involved.

That was really the end.

After the Show I went on tour; Joan stayed in with the twins. Several times I came in by rail for the weekend, for we were both suffering reactions from the Show. While it lasted, all ills were suppressed, but afterwards, as Joan's letters to me on tour show, we were not well. Her letters were sometimes only scraps of paper, finished in a hurry and irritation as the *kothar* demanded it at once, lest he miss the train. None of mine survived, which is a pity; Joan's are, as often before, headed only 'Teatime, Monday', or just, 'In haste'.

At about this time the twins were ill, too. Adam developed malaria, but he later recovered completely; David had jaundice. For all the care taken, there were gaps, and illness could sneak in. But even greater care could deal with it. Joan developed gingivitis, and we had to borrow Andrew's car to take her to Vishindas at Sukkur to put her teeth right. (We must get a car!) I had malaria seriously: that is, it might strike at almost any time, though between attacks I was perfectly well. I had, the Civil Surgeon told me, the 'benign tertian' kind; this meant that there was a severe attack, a day's recession, and a return on the third day. It could be very bad. Once, when I was driving, there was a sudden violent ague, and I could have crashed had my foot not slipped from the accelerator. To me there was little benign about it; perhaps it just meant that I wouldn't die of it.

But we had quinine to control it. After the Japanese war began, quinine tablets were rationed, but we were lucky. Each District was given a stock to distribute, and Gallagher had tried, without success, to sell his instead of issuing them free. In the office safe I found very little secret record, no reports on staff, but the whole stock of quinine: the safe was stuffed with as many packs of 500 big pink pills as it would hold. I kept them for the Revenue Department, sharing them among the Mukhtiarkars and Ali Ahmed and my own office. And keeping back enough for ourselves.

Quinine certainly helped. The raging fever, the shivering cold, could be ended by a heavy dose, followed by a 'laudable sweat', so heavy sometimes that it soaked through those thick flannel pyjamas I always carried round, on my uncle's advice, seemingly so superfluous in the heat of Sindh, but used so often that their pretty blue colour became a leprous yellow. But the quinine left the sufferer deaf, dizzy, and lethargic for the day before the next, milder attack, which the quinine also dealt with, and then freedom. Till next time.

For company Joan had Mrs Das, so cheerful, so happy in her domesticity; so boring. And there was Dr Jessaram at the Zenana Hospital. She was a character new to us in Upper Sindh: a fully-qualified lady doctor. In England at that time there were not so very many women doctors; in India far less, and probably no Muslims at all. Dr Jessaram was plain, she was tough and competent, and she had plenty to talk about. She and her family must have been very determined for her to qualify at all, and then she was posted in this little hospital in a small isolated town where western medicine was still fighting the *hakims*.

One weekend Joan called me in: Dr Holland was on his way to Shikarpur and would come and circumcise the boys, suffering from their tight foreskins.

We had hoped to have the little job done without publicity, but we could hardly expect Candy to keep quiet about it, and however we might insist that it was being done for purely hygienic reasons, everyone would surely believe that the motive was religious. All Muslim boys were circumcised at about this age, with great solemnity. Hindu boys were not. We certainly avoided any suspicion of ceremony, but the assumption would remain. Not that it really mattered.

But there was no lack of care for the little boys. I stayed at home for the operation, and saw the results. Had there not been so much pain and screaming—they were too young for an anaesthetic—we would have thought it funny. (Not till later could we laugh). The tiny penises were fully erect, quite rigid, each with a knob of bandage on the top; like a pillar with a turban on top. For a day or two, life for everyone around them was miserable. They did not wet themselves, or their nappies, or their little pants; they just sat on their pots and yelled, with no result. I was back on tour when Joan wrote to me that their bellies swelled till she feared a return of their previous bowel problem. Then, after the soreness passed, after there had been a copious outpouring, all was well, they healed, and the bandages came off. But there I was, away from it all. How easy it was to plead important work and avoid trouble!

On one of my weekends at home, when Andrew was in too, we went to Sukkur, to the Gymkhana, to meet different people. Not to involve ourselves, just to meet. We didn't know the Collector now, though he was of my Service: Parpia, a Parsi up from Bombay. I wondered how he would cope with the Sindhis and Balochis of Upper Sindh? He probably saw his posting as a reprimand for something. How would I cope with a transfer to the Presidency, even if it were considered a reward? By now I would want none of it.

The Club closed at about eleven, and by midnight we were on the road home. Andrew was routinely fairly drunk, so I would drive his car, with himself asleep in the back. But this night he did not sleep. He began to climb over to be with Joan in the front. So we had him in the front, and he promptly began to climb into the back with her. We thought of Joan driving, while I got in the back and fought Andrew, but he was bigger than I; that way disaster threatened. So we stopped again and surrendered: Joan got into the back with Andrew. He had won; he pointed out that it was his car, anyway, it was only fair that he should decide who sat where. (We MUST get a car!) That left me to drive in peace, ignoring the odd smacks and protests from behind. Joan could deal with Andrew, and if she needed help I could again stop, and we would deal with him together.

Driving in this land at night was an eerie experience. There were no lights at all, anywhere, till we passed by Shikarpur town. Even the villages were quite dark. The railway paralleled the road, and once a freight train roared by, its searchlight giving us warning, its tail-light glowing red till it faded away, leaving us with nothing but the little pool of our own lights, with no sign that there was any existence beyond their feeble beam.

Past Shikarpur the road was of earth in those days, with the usual cart ruts, but plenty of room to avoid them. We need not expect to meet any traffic. A mist slowly enveloped us, but it was not damp, it was dust. It grew thicker and thicker till I could see for only a few yards, and then at last I could see the tail of the convoy. I pulled out to the side to overtake and blew the horn, which must have startled those sleeping cartmen severely. I bumped along till I saw the jemadar's lamp, gave a final blast, and we sped away.

'We sped away.' Speed is a relative term. Averaging anything more than fifteen miles an hour in the dark between Shikarpur and Jacobabad was good going. We bounced gently along, past the Thul road, where Dermont

Barty and I had been caught by rain camping in tents. Then there were no more carts with all their dust.

All fell quiet in the back, so I switched on the roof light and looked in the mirror. Andrew slept with his head on Joan's shoulder, she sat upright, her eyes wide open. She just smiled at me, and signed to be silent, so I drove on. We crossed the Begari bridge, and were home again.

We drove Andrew to his bungalow and delivered him to his own sentry and his bearer, and walked across to the Residency. Joan turned off to look at the *Baben-jo-otak*, and I walked on and answered the sentry's challenge. While I waited for Joan I looked at the long, long arcade of our verandah, silent under the moon, with just the faint light that always burned at Jacob's Clock.

Joan came over: their night-light showed them both asleep, and Candy too. On a cot on the little verandah was Candy's faithful guard, Lalu, who always stayed if we were out. So Joan told him quietly to go to bed.

Illahibaksh came in from the back as we went in at the front. Should he make some tea? We decided not: better we go to bed. So it was just a shower, and then to bed and to sleep. Joan slept and I lay by her, and she had my arm round her now. No more thinking of that poor, frustrated man. My own dear wife; my own dear sons.

After the Show, and until the Viceroy came, Joan had a lonely, exasperating time. I was on tour as much as possible, but she had two babies to look after with numerous willing but incompetent servants, in a tumble-down bungalow, be it never so prestigious. She had no company but Dr Jessaram: for a man to visit a lady while her husband was away would have been most improper. When I grew priggish about Andrew's incompetence, she laughed at me and even defended him. When I accused her of frivolity, she laughed again.

I was very happy, with my own District that I was getting to know, and for which I was developing the sort of unreasoning loyalty which I gathered was the standard reaction of any ICS officer towards his District. To someone coming from Bombay, all Sindh was a hard place, and the thought of Upper Sindh Frontier was wholly horrible. In Sindh we sneered at the soft climate of Bombay. To me, my District was coming to appear the best of all possible charges.

Every wife of every District Officer doubtless suffered as Joan did at this time. But if she could not enjoy the camping, at least she could be sure that, with two small babies, she would not have to stay for the hot weather.

20

ANOTHER VICEROY

This Viceroy was travelling by air, which introduced new routines. First, an RAF officer arrived to inspect the airfield. Then a signal station must be set up, for His Excellency must be kept in constant touch with Delhi.

Lord Linlithgow was the last of the aristocratic Viceroys, for whom life and work could proceed at the speed of a train and the post, perhaps sometimes of the telephone. He had a train to live on, and a large entourage of staff. The new Viceroy was a soldier, familiar with aeroplanes and the radio. He would come with a Secretary, one ADC, and a personal servant. He would live on the country, as it were. His would be literally a flying visit. We had heard of Lord Wavell: officers passing through had considered him the best of the British generals, his plans in Africa ruined by Churchill's orders. Churchill was a wonderful propagandist, but as a strategist he was a disaster. We would be happy to entertain Lord Wavell.

The inspecting officer came and went in a day, but the two signallers were to stay for a week; their orders were to stay at the Barracks, but there had been no barracks for twenty years, so they were to stay at the airfield, and would bring their rations with them. Joan wouldn't have them stay all the time in that little hut, so they could stay with us. As usual. Their rations included a seven-pound tin of corned beef each, which would have been edible for not more than a day, and some American K-rations. Joan appropriated the rations, and would feed them. Those tins would have been a god-send a month before! We had not seen K-rations, scientifically measured, easily portable food for one meal; there were sweets, chewing gum, even khaki toilet paper. A fascinating acquisition. The signallers were a pleasure to have, and in effect only one at a time: one must always be on radio watch.

According to the little grey book of the Programme, Wavell would be in Jacobabad for only four hours. He would arrive on our airfield from Karachi, go straight to Sukkur, back to Jacobabad, where we would welcome him at Jacob's Tomb, he would have lunch with us, grant a few interviews, and then fly off to Delhi.

I was very indignant. I had not been consulted about the programme. The timing was much too severe: twenty minutes to inspect the Tomb and drive to the Residency. (Having welcomed him, I must show him the Tomb, and somehow get ahead and welcome him again at the Residency!) Everything was timed exactly, and if there were delay somewhere else, his time would be cut down. If he saw the Clock, there was no time for him to examine it; if he heard of the twins, he would have no time to see them. The Risaldar wanted to salute him, but there was no time. However, we had one advantage that other visits lacked: from us he would fly straight back to Delhi, and delay in Jacobabad would only make him later there.

I wrote asking for amendments. The ADC was most unwilling to upset his timing, but he agreed that there must be a little flexibility. His Excellency could hardly avoid seeing the Clock, and should be briefed about the Special Force. I said nothing of the twins: the Governor and Lady Dow were coming too, and Joan would speak of the twins with them at lunch.

I could have ten minutes for him to inspect the Special Force, and he accepted an unusual order of seating for lunch, to accord with the tradition that the Deputy Commissioner must always face the portrait of Jacob at the end of the big dining-room. I have preserved the plan for that unusual seating, with the Viceroy in the middle of one side of the table, the Governor on the other; I, according to custom, was at the head, the most junior officer at the foot. (Oddly, that officer, ADC to the Governor, was Roger Collett, known to me at school, whom I hadn't met since then.)

Joan, of course, had all the work. The house must necessarily be ideally clean; His Excellency might not mind a little dust, but Lady Dow would, and was not the sort of person to overlook it. The table must be set just right. Our cutlery might be plated, but for the important guests we brought out the beautiful smoked glass. Joan and Mistri were experienced in catering for big parties, and for the great. Lady Dow had written to tell Joan what to serve, but she took no notice of it: that menu had Lady Dow's own digestion in mind, and she would doubtless have her pills.

Andrew and I had to welcome the party twice, the first time when they arrived from Karachi, when we were just introduced before they set off for Sukkur. We were to expect one Dakota, but two came: the ordinary workhorse of the Army, but Wavell abhorred fuss. We were in good time at the airfield, to be given a message that departure from Karachi had been delayed. We ignored it, which was just as well, for there came another message: they had made up time and would be early. So much for the pretty timetable. We were very glad of the signallers.

The Governor presented me, the Inspector-General presented Andrew, and off they went. Six cars: first a pilot, an escort, a 'spare car', and three for the party. Andrew was worried lest his men might have allowed a bullock cart convoy to get on the road, but I pointed out that only the pilot would have a clear run, the Viceroy's car would be befogged by the dust of three cars ahead... Either they would be choked or boiled, or be spread over a long, long stretch of road, hoping that the dust would settle.

We waited for the dust to settle and followed, Andrew fearing some unforeseen disaster. There was none, and at the Begari bridge we handed over to the Sukkur police. We picked up Andrew's men on the way back.

At the airfield the signallers were pleased: the Viceroy had inspected their listening post, further upsetting the programme. Did the ADC really think that His Excellency would not inspect a station away in the desert like this? He was a soldier, known for his care for his men.

The cavalcade was on time next day at the Tomb. Wavell was in uniform to salute a famous brother officer of a century before, and asked about the usual bunch of flowers; the chowkidar was there and said they were put there by girls wanting sons. I explained the alternative theory, Jacob having been without issue. His Excellency did not commit himself. I left them there—I must get ahead of them, to welcome the party and introduce Joan at the Residency. When they arrived His Excellency stepped up on the *thalla*, and, timing it beautifully, the Risaldar with a troop of the Force behind him, pennons flying, came round from behind the Residency, faced the *thalla*, and gave their cavalry salute. The Viceroy returned the salute and stepped down, he chatted a little with the Risaldar and then inspected his men, the remnant of a great regiment which still existed, the only cavalry in Sindh, recently on active service itself. We all felt honoured.

The ADC looked murder at me, but could do nothing. He was beaten.

We had given the Viceroy our bedroom and bathroom— indeed we could hardly offer less—and he asked why he was not having the Annexe. I explained, and he insisted that he must see the twins. So Joan had to be called in a hurry, we came on Candy all unannounced, and she was flustered, at first did not realize that this was the Viceroy. The twins were asleep, and she offered to wake them, but he said no, they would surely yell, and probably wet themselves. So they never saw the Viceroy.

There were interviews before lunch, and I had noticed with regret that the first was Nawab Ghaibi Khan Chandio, he being the senior sirdar but, at the same time, the fattest, the most stupid, and least helpful of the Baloch. The interviews took place in my office, and I sat with him to interpret; I noticed on the desk a copy of Wavell's book, *Other Men's Flowers*, and hoped that this would be his present for me and Joan. But he left it there, and after his plane had gone I went to look for it. It had gone: Havildar said a sahib in uniform had come and taken it away. I thought it might come by post, but it never did. So perhaps the ADC had his revenge; rather petty, we thought. But I had truly made a mess of his programme.

There was time for a drink before lunch, and HE was willing to save a little time by taking his drink out to the verandah and examining the Clock. He asked its keeper how he had changed for the new century, but he did not know: his father was keeper then. He was a teacher at the school, and spoke good English, which helped a lot. He worked out that all that was needed was the change of one number. But what about Leap Year? February was just past, and the date was correct. I had to admit that the keeper had explained how it was done, and I had changed it myself, so that it had appeared to be magic. The keeper kept quiet: he had been very much annoyed with me, but could do nothing. At least I had apologized for the trick.

It was strange how, of that Viceregal party of ten, we knew six. Tim Crosthwaite was on the Viceroy's staff, Dermont Barty was the Governor's Secretary, and his ADC, Roger Collett, had been at school with me, though much senior. I asked him how he had become an ADC, for in those days such sinecures were reserved for wounded soldiers. He explained that he was wounded: playing rugger somewhere, he had cut his leg on a piece of rusty barbed wire, it had turned septic, and now he limped, he hoped not for ever. Joan talked with Dermont Barty; Anne and Jennifer were well, they would stay in Karachi for the hot weather. No, the twins would not stay in Jacobabad, but we hadn't decided yet where they would go.

Thanks for the lunch, probably better than any in Government House Karachi, with Lady Dow choosing the menu. Good-bye to Lady Dow and Joan, and we others all drove to the airfield...

There were formal farewells, and the Viceroy followed his officers to the plane, a very ordinary Dakota, no badges or flags, no guard to salute, just a police guard standing back. We all stood well back, and I warned my Governor that Jacobabad had a very dusty airstrip; even with the warning we were not far enough away, and when the plane started there was an undignified retreat.

The Governor went back to the Residency, assembled his party, and they left for Karachi. And that was that.

Wavell had wanted little fuss; he could hardly have had less. Life returned to normal with hardly a bump. One day, and routine was reinstated.

I had work to do on tour before the canals filled, and with the *abkalani* the hot weather began. Joan in Jacobabad had electricity and ice, but still in that triple-walled house it was hot. And apart from domestic and nursing work she had nothing to do. It was my usual problem: how could she be happy with nothing else? I had no electricity, seldom any ice, but I had work that I enjoyed, and the continuing satisfaction of exercising authority. In spite of the coming hot weather, I was secretly happy at the thought of another year at least in this District that I was beginning to know. I dared not speak of such a possibility with Joan, and disliked not being candid.

But there was a solution to our problem. We would go to Dalhousie. Jane Holt wanted Joan to go to Kashmir, but it was expensive; Jane's offer of teaching, Joan felt, would be more like being a nanny for the brats of officers' wives than real teaching; and it was a long way off. Mrs Stiffles in Dalhousie ran a hotel, she would have room at the end of June. That was too late, but the family could stay with Jane till then. If only the Holts had not been going to Kashmir! Karachi would have been acceptable for all the hot weather, and our friends were there.

I came in early from my tour: Joan wanted a few days together before we were separated for four or five months. They were good days, though already hot, and I would go with them to Karachi for a little. I was justifying my seniors who claimed that an officer who married early was for years useless. But I would deny that I was entirely useless. Anyway, it was all too late, and I could not regret my dear wife and sons; whatever they might say, I would certainly sacrifice my duty for my family, though I saw no reason for the choice to arise.

Meanwhile, Jacobabad grew hotter. We went to Karachi. We had a coupe on the Down Mail from Quetta. Candy's bag was in with us, and she could be sometimes, at other times in a ladies' special. If necessary, she could stay, and I would squeeze in with men. We were going down by day, so Joan made no fuss about having a block of ice. At the station was the usual crowd to see us off, and as usual passengers leant out to ask what the fuss was. It was the Deputy Commissioner with his family, getting out of this hellhole. (But in Quetta they didn't know what hell was.)

The paddies were flooding, the rice was just showing green. We crossed the Begari, flowing full, we passed Shikarpur—there was no one there we knew. We crossed the canals at Ruk, all rebuilt and the railway running on a proper embankment again. In Sukkur I greeted Mr Birkett, the Stationmaster, and then very slowly we crossed the Lansdowne Bridge. After Rohri we were in a foreign country till we crossed the River again at Kotri and rolled down through my first Sub-division, where Joan had first camped with me, scrub desert till we reached Malir, and then journey's end at the Cantonment Station.

We were late at Karachi, but Bashir met us, procured us porters and gharris. The boys were asleep, so they had to be carried to the Holts' house opposite the Gymkhana.

The first part of the journey to a cool place was over, and already we felt a breeze that caressed, unlike the burning draughts of Jacobabad.

So many people came to see the little boys who had almost been despaired of a year before, and now were strong and lively. They even had a little hair, lint white, and looking as if it would blow away. We could watch Candy preening herself in the showers of lavish praise. Particularly, the Reinitzs came, and Hugo examined the boys all over, as he might some precious china vase, to see if they had suffered any harm. But even he was satisfied.

I had only a few days, and then I was back in Jacobabad, and the stream of letters began again. I had only one short time on leave to look forward to for the next five months, which had not seemed so bad in prospect, but now looked unbearably long.

Joan's letters were reassuring. There were people she knew in a place she knew. It was cool, there was green grass and green trees, and the boys were well. Candy was happy, too, with her auntie and her sisters to meet. Joan had left Jacobabad tired, frustrated, worried for the children, bothered by the heat, but after a week her morale had recovered. Lady Dow was welcoming and friendly, far more assured now that she was herself First Lady. She invited Joan to Sandspit, and her gardens were always open to the twins. Lalu had gone down to help Candy, and for the first time he saw the sea. Joan wrote that his astonishment was unforgettable: how was it that the land, the firm, dry land, even the hills, could end just like that? Why did not the water, always rolling in, in big waves—and the monsoon rollers were really big—flood all the land? What he was told I don't know, but I'm sure that talk of tides and moons would make little headway with Lalu.

From Karachi Lalu went with Joan to Dalhousie, and there he saw real mountains, and they scared him so badly that she sent him home, to the safety of the flat, hot plains of Sindh.

I supposed I could manage the heat alone again. If I wanted to stay on in Jacobabad I must, and without grumbling, though the heat was, as always, the hottest ever. A man could put up with living alone in a rather squalid state, for he always had his work, but a woman would have nothing to do but watch her children, as so many in the past had done, watch them sicken and perhaps die. All over India there are those pathetic little graves, but none in Jacobabad, perhaps because there had seldom been married Deputy Commissioners, perhaps because our heat was so fierce that by no means would a family have stayed there. Had there been even one of those infant graves, I think the place would have been condemned by Joan for any part of the year.

Aadam would take paid leave in Dalhousie, and replace Lalu. (I give him two 'a's to distinguish him from our own Adam.) We met the train at Rohri and I went into the coupe to greet my family. For this journey Candy could stay in it all the time, which kept them all happy. The water from their ice block was drained away, and a fresh block put in the little toilet, but not for long could I stay there, nor must Joan come out. The temperature was a pleasant 90°, quite cool, for on the platform it was over 120°. (120°F is about 45°C.) Rohri station is in an airless canyon cutting through the limestone rock, known sometimes to equal even Jacobabad for heat. As was usual in those days, the air-conditioned compartments were full of Americans. British officers also travelled first class, but the Army did not pay for air-conditioning. Economy was not the only reason: experience had taught how dangerous air-conditioning could be, and after a time the Americans might learn. Meanwhile, Rohri was prepared.

It was known that Rohri was a place where it was well worth while to watch the platform, and not just to see an officer saying good-bye to his wife. No: the sight worth seeing was the Americans. They were always enthusiastic to see India, and would get down to look. They screwed the

temperature inside down to a comfortable 75°, and, hit by
the sudden impact of a 45° rise, promptly collapsed as if
shot. Their mates stayed inside. But always a powerful
orderly was there for the Mail, to pick up any bodies and
carry them into the recovery room.

The 'recovery room' was a shelter made of *khus-khus
tatties*, thick walls and roof made with the aerial roots of
palm trees, highly absorbent of water, constantly wetted,
and having an inside temperature of about 100°. Patients
were taken in, warmed up to this median temperature,
carried quickly back to their compartment, and told to stay
there.

Their door was shut, the show was over, all the heads
along the train were drawn in. We kissed good-bye for one
last time, and the Mail moved slowly on, its beautiful
locomotive belching steam and smoke and, as it were,
shouting as it picked up speed.

The Residency was very empty. In the District, Andrew
Davies had managed to miss the heat he dreaded, and the
new Superintendent, Sirdar Abdur Rahman, was unknown
to me. The new Assistant Political Agent, Henry Hall, had
gone to Quetta. His wife Margery had annoyed Joan as we
were arranging for her hot-weather retreat by lauding her
own loyalty: she would go where her husband was sent.
Who would not, said Joan, if he was sent to Quetta?

So I was left the sole representative of the British Raj.
Not that that bothered me: if Joan wasn't here I could do
very well without those others. There were six weeks of the
true hot weather ahead, and then I would see them again.
I would discover if what I might call the spirit of John
Jacob could survive the devastating heat, as he had done
for ten years.

All alone, I had a full domestic staff, which was
ridiculous. So I used one small corner of the big dining
table, as more convenient for the kitchen than ours in the
drawing-room. I used one easy chair in the drawing-room,
under one of the fans, with a little table fan to help it. I

would have a shower, nominally cold, would dry myself and run, literally run, along the verandah to get under the fan before I was soaked with sweat again, wet as though I had not towelled at all. Had I not drunk so much I would have sweated less, my prickly heat would have been less, but a dry skin was even worse. I had a voracious demand for limes; sometimes I would add a little gin, but I didn't really like it, and there was no one around to encourage social drinking. Andrew Davies was probably right, the hot weather and the drinking necessary to him would probably have destroyed him.

I slept on the *thalla*, under a net, with a fan inside on a stand. I became used to the pacing sentry, whose beat had been shortened now, with no one in the *Baben-jo-otak*. He probably hated my being there, for never could he take a rest lest I be awake. If the light at the Clock went out it would mean that the power-station had broken down, my fan would stop, and I would surely waken. These were the nights when my knitted woollen 'body-belt' was vital: lying naked, even a sheet was almost too much to bear, and if one sweated and then the fan came on again, a chill was very possible, but not with that woollen kidney protector.

Work took on the hot weather routine. The Office and the Courts opened very early, hoping to close by two o'clock for a siesta, and if necessary reopen in the evening. This was no good to me: I tried it, and fell into a heavy sleep, waking to a bleary lethargy that made real work impossible. So I would have a midday meal and then carry on, and everyone must conform. If they didn't like it, that was just too bad.

Karachi never recognized any change: the Secretariat still wanted immediate replies, not allowing for the difficulty of collecting information with the heat so discouraging. The pattern of crime changed, too. The ordinary villains were lazy, but the warm nights seemed to encourage the wives and daughters who would be unchaste, so that *karo-kari* murders were more common. It was always a wonder to me how bold those girls and young men were, risking death, meeting usually in the warm darkness, but surely aware that it was almost impossible to move anywhere unseen.

There was also frequent trouble over water once the paddies were flooded, channels being opened or closed to one man's advantage and an indignant neighbour's hurt. Tempers were short, often there were fights, sometimes near riots, occasionally killings. My new Superintendent was a revelation after Andrew Davies, with quick and accurate intelligence, followed by swift action.

Through the routine shone the bright shafts, when letters came from Joan and from Home. The Second Front had opened, and all our families were safe and well and hopeful, more realistically than their earlier stubborn disbelief in defeat.

In Burma, in the Pacific, the Japanese were being pushed back, and in Sindh the Hur trouble was effectively over.

In the rest of India, the chief anxiety arose from the unpredictable actions of Mahatma Gandhi. Imprisoned at last, probably as he had intended, he fasted. His fasts had their effects. A threat of fasting to death could stop a riot, but now his threats were taken seriously by Delhi. Were he to fulfil that threat—and he came near to it—there was no telling what might happen. In my safe were careful instructions as to what action a District Officer should take, and, since there might be little warning, there was a code word to make instructions operative. My code word would come by telephone, through police headquarters, and any intelligent sepoy who had been following the news could guess what this single word meant. But in Sindh there was no apprehension of serious trouble: we had a Muslim League ministry, which might even welcome Gandhi's death, though no one would dare to say so. Anyway, there was nothing to be done but wait. And the message never came.

Our Club met on most evenings. We had no building, we collected chairs and tables and sat outside near the tennis court. We didn't play tennis either, for the court was concrete, and till after seven o'clock it was so hot that it burnt one's feet. We talked shop and world news, we drank soft drinks, and sometimes someone would bring samosas or pakoras. Sometimes Mistri would make little fancy cakes, from Vienna via Karachi; but orthodox Hindus were doubtful of their propriety, and those not so orthodox did not like to parade the fact, so only a few of us ate them. Being assured that they were *halal,* our Muslim members would take a chance.

We didn't have a bridge four, but played a sort of whist, and *vingt-et-un* was understood by everyone; but never for more than one anna stakes.

When Joan was in Jacobabad Dr Jessaram would come, but not after she left. The Doctor went on leave herself, and a *buddli* arrived at the Zenana Hospital: Dr Butani, pretty, young, tall, and willowy—and reserved. With no other women at the Club, no one expected her to come. A pity, but she came to me—a necessary formal call. She was very nervous; perhaps the Deputy Commissioner, from his high position, would take advantage of her? He would not. I was not really tempted to risk my reputation by laying siege to her virtue, but I could not help being aware of how long Joan had been away. If only she could be induced to smile at me... Of course, there could be nothing but fantasy, the imaginings of a young man left lonely in a hot climate. Several times we met, always on business, and always she was nervous; nor did she ever smile. Not once.

Soon after Joan had gone to Dalhousie, another lady came to see me, with a petition, and she was quite different. She was a young whore from the brothel; she was less heavily painted than the girls there usually were, for, as she said, they knew that the sahibs didn't like it, and she wanted to please. She was representing them all; their trouble was that all their wealthy clients had gone to Quetta, so they wanted to go too. They had business there, as much as any merchants, more than the zamindars who got licences to go. They were loyal, they were not spies.

A year before, the Army had required permits: they wanted no unnecessary people in Quetta, and the Deputy Commissioner had been told to use his discretion in issuing them. Norman Gallagher had issued permits to Sirdars, and to half a dozen whores, selected by themselves—my office told me this—but by one means or another all had in the end got there. By professional free gifts, no doubt. I explained that now there was no need for a permit, they could go when they liked. She lingered on, she struck a pretty pose, until a shocked and indignant Havildar came in and hustled her away.

Perhaps her visit was her own idea, perhaps a joke. A whore is by no means stupid or without humour. What a triumph it would have been to seduce the Deputy Commissioner! And indeed, as my usual source of gossip, Mahomed Din the mechanic, told me, in the past it was not unknown to have happened.

At last I bought a car. I had sold ours before prices were controlled, now I used the control system to acquire another. Mahomed Din had heard of one for sale, had seen it, and said it was good. A Chevrolet again, but older than the Elegant Chev. The price quoted was, of course, well above control, but when I offered the control price the owner could not very well refuse. I made him sell—that was the law. It was nevertheless a great *zulum*. Never mind: at last I was mobile again.

It was hot before Joan left for Karachi, and later it grew hotter still. I registered 128°F. (Sometimes it went higher, but not while I was there.) The fields were not yet fully flooded, and the air was so dry that what one drank evaporated through the skin at once. A car must not be left in the sun, or the carburettor would dry out. Don't touch the paintwork, for it will blister your hand. It was said that an egg would fry on the bonnet, though I never tried it.

The big tank built by John Jacob was getting low, and wells in the villages were themselves getting low; everyone was growing anxious, but comforted by the ancient men who were confident that they never did run dry.

Before they dried the canals were flowing full, the rice was all transplanted, and over all the land were great swathes of pale green, broken by clumps of grass or shrubs on the banks of watercourses, and by the lines of trees on the canal banks. Everywhere was completely flat, everything was so still that it seemed nothing would ever move again. Then a little breeze would stir the grass, a cool breeze now, comparatively cool, not much above 100°; but with the flooding the humidity increased till it seemed the air was near being water vapour. That was what reduced the temperature, but it brought mosquitoes and prickly heat and cholera.

Only early in the morning was the air fresh, and it became my custom either to drive to the Special Force and ride there, or share in exercises, or ask for a horse and ride round near the town, with my escort, of course. If I drove to the Force I would go the short way through the brothel, when the girls were all at their housekeeping; in the evening they would be preparing for business. There was nothing furtive about it: theirs was a respectable community, and they were close and loyal to each other. I understood that they had no need for pimps, but there were always one or two tough-looking men about, to discipline uncooperative customers. Each girl had her own place, and they were all oddly like bazaar shops: open fronts with wooden shutters, with a big bed visible in the background; the owner would sit in front for all to see and make judgement. In some there were children looking from a window upstairs. It was, in fact, a very clean and respectable place, and the best-kept part of the town. There was no threat to the peace from there.

One was endlessly drinking; maybe a little whisky or gin, but they were not essential. I would have endless bottles of soda or jugs of lime juice. It was the water that was needed, for it came straight out again. We lost a lot of salt that way, which I always thought caused the prickly heat, the salt irritating the pores. In the war in Burma, the army held Salt Parades, to make sure the lost salt was replaced. In England it seems very odd to me that people are advised to eat less salt! We liked our food well salted. And in cool places people from the heat could be recognized in a sure way: 'He drowns his drink.'

This humid heat was the bad time. If the fan stopped at night I was at once bathed in sweat, and often even if the fan recovered I could not sleep again. Once—or it may well have been so many times as to become a habit—I put on a dressing-gown and went to the station to see the world go by, to assure myself that there was that other world. I knew the timetable, I knew when a train would stop, and I would be there. At the end of the night was the Down Mail from Quetta. There was always a crowd waiting for it, but a railway station at night, when there is no train standing, is a quiet place. The lights are dim, people are talking quietly, the night seems to have quieted even the children. The coolies sit back waiting, and the Stationmaster—it would be himself for the Mail—just glances from his office occasionally. The food-sellers are preparing, and I can get a cup of tea on credit, for I am known; the cardamom tea of the railways, with well-boiled milk. No one takes notice of me.

The searchlight would appear in the far distance, before any noise could be heard, for the line was very straight. The station would wake up, and what had been a quiet place would become a riot of noise. I wondered what people who looked out thought of this lonely figure in a dressing-gown just standing and watching. I always hoped to see someone I knew, but never did. After the train left the quiet returned, and I walked home, thinking that perhaps I had looked quite heroic, alone in this isolated outpost. But more likely people just wondered who that silly fool might be. Never mind, I had seen that there was another world, I had been close to that great steam loco with its four-coupled drivers, one of the finest ever built. Back to my bed, I could sleep again.

Local society was brightened by the arrival of Sitaldas Khemani, whom I had met when he came to set Larkana Municipality to rights. He had done that so successfully that he was now a Rao Sahib, and he had come to do the same for Jacobabad, which needed him more even than Larkana had done. On my first arrival I had reported that the town was in a mess, and this was the result.

In fact, the canals were running well, and water supplies were assured; there was a good Police Superintendent; crime was no more than usual; and now we had the best man to deal with the Municipality. I could claim that my district was clearly being well run. For the moment. One must never suppose that the moment would last.

As soon as Joan was settled in Dalhousie she began to urge me to come: take leave early, rain is expected before the middle of July. So I would go; I would split my leave and go again to bring the family home. I needed permission to leave my District, but that was formal: it was assumed that I would not leave it in crisis, and I could put Madadalishah in charge. The paddies were all flooded, water levels at Attock were normal, and even if there were a sudden rise, I could be back home before the high water reached Sindh. Madadalishah would be very happy to hold charge. Poor Madadalishah: I am afraid I was of little value to him in his career. I lacked a Deputy Collector for Garhi Khair Mahomed, and could have put him in *de facto* charge, but I could not imagine his being an effective executive officer. I had known several Deputy Collectors, the best was Ali Ahmed Yusifani at Khandkot, and Madadalishah could not match him in any way. Moreover, he was vain, stupid, and conceited. His manner and his dress sense also irritated me. He wore his suits, waistcoats and all, even in the hottest weather, when I wore only a shirt and shorts.

He had to, for his gold watch-chain and the handkerchief peeping from the breast pocket. He had an ample belly to display that chain: on one end there was a watch, and on the other was a large selection of ear and nose spoons. I had never seen such implements before, so he explained what they were for. They were on a ring, some were plain silver, some were decorated and probably valuable, and they were of every size and shape of scoop. He would sit in the office in his special chair, and, as I spoke or read aloud from a document, he would rub an ear, then thoughtfully, carefully attending to me, select a spoon and poke it in; he would turn it about, withdraw it, and examine his catch before wiping it off on his matching silk handkerchief. If work needed doing on his nose—and it often did in our dusty climate—he would again select with care, and operate politely behind his hand.

The weather was very hot, I was separated from my family and easily irritated, but I felt that I could hardly protest at his toilette. So I held myself in, and disliked the poor man the more.

He was a great dandy. The aesthetic principle for his dress was that everything must match. His very best suit was purple, not quite roman purple, something a little muddy and approaching blue, so striking that I can still conjure up a picture of him wearing it, sitting in his chair, handsome belly spread so that he could toy with the gold chain. His shirt was deep lavender, his tie had purple stripes. His socks were mauve, and even his shoes were of deep purple patent leather. A symphony in purple, completed by that little pyramid of a purple handkerchief poking from the breast pocket. In the middle of the hot weather. I was expected to admire it, and of course I did.

There came a time when Madadali reinforced my view that he was not suited to an executive post, and this not because he lacked any of the knowledge required by a Deputy Collector, but because he lacked judgement, and the 'civilized' attitude towards women that was in my opinion essential. I regretted the purdah, but accepted it as a deeply entrenched custom, one which even most women accepted. But his ideas went further, unacceptably further.

He asked for compassionate leave to go home to deal with a domestic problem, and of course it was granted. One should never probe into such a reason: Muslims were almost pathologically secretive about their family life. In Larkana my naik, Allahdino, had asked for leave because his wife was ill, and on his return I asked, was she now well? He smiled brilliantly and answered that she certainly was, it was a healthy boy, and both were well.

Madadali was away for a week, and when he returned I asked him if all was well. Yes, it was: his female cousin had reached marriageable age, and he had had to marry her himself, lest her share of the property go out of the family.

Quite simply, I did not like him. I disliked his dandyism, his little habits, and now his attitude to this young girl. Probably his colleagues saw nothing untoward in his behaviour, and probably in asserting himself he made things worse. He was certainly more competent than I allowed, and he was doubtless aware of my feelings, However, my feelings about his shortcomings did not stop me from leaving the District in his charge. I listened to Joan's arguments, and set off for Dalhousie.

21

DALHOUSIE

I had to change trains twice for my journey, at Rohri and Lahore, but it was an easy journey, for I had no one to care for but myself. I could eat at Spencer restaurants at stations, or even from the platform vendors, food that would never do for Adam and David. I had only a suitcase and my Father's bistra and a box of oddments for Joan, including two balls of hand-spun *dumba* wool. Nor for me was there any crying in the night.

I had a long wait in Lahore, but sadly not long enough for me to go and look in the Museum, Kim's 'Wonder House', with the great gun Zam-zammah in front of it.

The railway crossed the wide plain of the Punjab, with perennial irrigation almost everywhere. All the land was divided into rectangular fields, and they were growing rice and wheat and cotton, recognizable by their differing green. This was land that would grow two crops every year, and the rabi was not limited by drying of the water. There were several canals to cross, each as big as any of ours, and even the bullock carts were much bigger, with large spoked wheels. I could reassure myself: everything was so wide that it was just a bit boring!

Past Amritsar came the terminus at Pathankot, and there I had to change to a bus. The road up to Dalhousie was very narrow, wide enough for only one vehicle, so traffic moved in convoy. The convoys left each end at the same time and met and crossed in the middle, at Dunera, where the ground had been cleared and levelled. It was no good being in a hurry; however quickly you reached Dunera, you must await the convoy coming down. To set off before it arrived was probably fatal, for there were few passing places, and if you met, either you must reverse to Dunera, or your car would be put out of the way: tipped down the *khud*.

Dunera was a cheerful place, full of 'hotels', which were just teahouses, and a resthouse left from the days when the road was travelled by mules, and reaching Dalhousie from Pathankot took two days.

For me, fresh from the plains, it was all wonderful. For a time I could look back and see the dusty plains through a haze, but soon that view was hidden as the road twisted, and we were deep in forest. In Ziarat there was forest, but there the junipers must stand apart from their neighbours, with plenty of ground to catch the scanty rain. Here, the trees were set close, giant cedars, the deodars that supplied sleepers for the railway. The forest had no end, but sometimes there was a gap, and I could see another ridge across the valley, and another beyond that, all covered with these wonderful trees, making a continuous cover of bright, dark green, the land losing visible shape as it rose, finally hidden by mist, or it might even have been in cloud.

We passed through a Gurkha camp, with huts and messes, and the herd of cows that Joan had told me of.

And then we arrived. Even I, travelling alone, needed help with my *saman*, for I had woollen sweaters and stockings and underclothes. I had packed them, dripping with sweat, in Jacobabad, and here I was, already wearing a tweed jacket. How thankful we were for those airtight trunks which for years now had preserved woollens from moths and those little beasts we called woolly bears! (I believe they were the larvae of what we called, equally unscientifically, silver boys.)

The coolie knew the hotel, he took my stuff there on his little barrow, and there they all were. They all looked happy, too. Again I was something of a stranger to the boys, of less

importance than Aadam, but getting to know them again
would itself be a pleasure. Joan was better, too, and relaxed
now, in spite of hill diarrhoea, which everyone seemed to
suffer from, and not to worry too much about. Caused by
height, and doubtful water. Anyway, the boys had grown,
though for them there was the anxiety that their bowel
problem could return. Candy took them daily to a nursery
school, and each day they took a spare sun-suit; each day
they needed it, and I have a picture of Adam, coming down
a chute, wearing a Mickey Mouse suit that certainly wasn't
his.

We would walk down to the Club, which was on a shelf
looking over a deep valley towards the north, where, beyond
the mist, were the real mountains. We would collect the
boys from school and take them home for lunch. That
dining-room had an iron roof, and on most days the local
troop of monkeys would visit. Suddenly there would be a
crash, then another, and one by one the monkeys would
land on it. There was a baby monkey, and Adam and David
wanted it, while I was made uneasy by the cunning leer of
the troop leader when he looked at our boys: perhaps he
was planning an exchange.

But first I must unpack, and give everyone the little
bazaar present I had brought. Then there was the wool,
grown on our own sheep, hanked, washed, and wound into
two big balls, one creamy white, the other grey flecked with
black: payment for the dismantled loom. When I left Joan
began to knit, and when next I came there were two
sweaters, David's grey, flecked with black, Adam's creamy
white. They were very proud of those sweaters, and wore
them till their chests grew so big that they couldn't get
them on. Very warm they were, though a bit rough, they
said, to their skin.

Joan had a lot to tell me, about the new place, the new
people, the hotel. I had little for her. She had not much
liked the 'hot weather widows' she met from the Punjab,
and her friend was the widow of a soldier killed in Burma;

she had a son, Michael, who was the great friend of our boys, and Alma Payne became Joan's. Alma was Anglo-Indian, therefore despised by those temporary widows, which outraged Joan.

But the cheerful spirit of Karachi had faded. This was beautiful country, but she could not see much of it. Her room was uncomfortable, the hotel food she was sure was mostly re-cooked, and in the hotel was a large and noisy Muslim lady with two even more noisy and troublesome sons. There was Alma, there was Candy, and there were picnics, but that was about all. And Candy was an anxiety, for Aadam could hardly chaperone her, and she must be allowed to go out by herself. She had met some Catholics in the Army, but that did not necessarily guarantee that they could be trusted with a lively girl like Candy, who was so very innocent.

So my arrival was especially welcome, even though everyone had to squeeze up to make room for me. Joan had written that she had ordered a load of logs for her little fire, which promised a cosy time. Instead it rained, as she had warned me it might, and we had to stay in, reading, listening to music, playing silly games with the boys. Those games sent them into fits of laughter, goading each other on, as it were, till they collapsed in hysterics, recovered, and began all over again.

We did nothing much, but it was a good week, ending tensions, relieving worries, pleasuring ourselves by walking about with our two beautiful sons, hiding, perhaps, our pride in them. By the time I left we were both in better health, perhaps just by reason of being together.

I went down the hill with memories of walks round the peak on which Dalhousie was built, of wandering in the little bazaar which clung to the hillside below us, of sitting hoping to see the high mountains if sometime the clouds blew away.

Next time I would stay longer, and then we would all go home together.

I arrived at Pathankot as it grew dark, and sat in a darkened carriage waiting for the lights to come on. It was very quiet, all the rush and noise of boarding was over, and as I looked out I could see wavering sparks of light as fireflies wandered along beside the track. I had never seen fireflies before, and was happy to watch in the dark: the light would have put them out.

The train started, but still there was no light. I became all Sahib, and a bad-tempered one at that, leaving his family and the cool breezes of the hills for the furnace of the plains. I pulled the cord—I had always wanted to do that—and the train stopped with a jerk. The Stationmaster came and asked what was the trouble; I told him, I told him forcefully, and he sincerely regretted it; he would telegraph along the line, and surely there would be a spare one at Amritsar, but he had none. He restarted the train, and again I stopped it: it should not go, said I, till I had a light. Poor man; now all along the train were interested faces at the windows, people calling to each other that it was only a bad-tempered Sahib, and laughing. At me! In the end a bulb was produced, and I let the train go. Someone else must have travelled in the dark.

All night I travelled alone, supposedly glorying in my assertion of the authority of the British Raj. In fact, I became more and more ashamed of myself. I, supposedly so sympathetic, so understanding, so genuine an advocate of racial equality, had done more harm to Anglo-Indian relations by one silly display of bad temper than any ignorant Army officer could do. Such autocratic behaviour was expected of the Army: never of the ICS.

I left the train as inconspicuously as I could in Lahore, I hid myself in Spencer's restaurant, and caught the Quetta Mail back to Sindh.

That incident, all in a setting of fireflies, has stuck in my memory when much else about Dalhousie has not. I did not tell of it in my letters to Joan. Only now, fifty years on, do I tell; I was so very deeply ashamed, and even now I blush.

I left Joan with an insignificant cold, which led to ear-ache, an abscess, and deafness, though she didn't tell me till it was all over. My own insignificant cold turned to fever, and I didn't tell her of this either. My 'benign tertian' involved such violent shivering that I could hardly write at all. For some reason, now beyond my understanding, Joan wrote in a letter, 'I'm amazed at our getting ill at all.' Perhaps she just meant to reassure me, for in fact it was a wonder that we were so often well: the cool damp of the hills in July was hardly more healthy then the hot damp of Sindh when the paddies flooded. Perhaps we were both determined that we would beat these ills of the British in India. So long as the two boys were well, we were satisfied

Adam and David had their second birthday; except that there were nice presents, it meant nothing to them, for all Candy's careful explanations. She was herself becoming disillusioned: she told Joan that she would buy herself a gramophone, more reliable than any man. Adam and David now took Michael Payne to their school, which was, indeed, a marvellous school. It was run by a woman, 'Froebel-trained', with four of her own children, and always spare sun suits.

Joan was not very happy in Dalhousie: she found no friends among 'these awful memsahibs', she seemed not to perceive herself as one of them, and felt they cut her off from making Indian friends. For my part, I felt that perhaps this would shed a pleasant light on Jacobabad, where all our friends were Indian. But she did not want to come back there: she urged me to ask Clee for a transfer.

That I surely could not do, not just like that. For one thing, I had been there for hardly a year; for another, and notwithstanding the heat, I didn't want to move. I just hoped that after the cool of the hills, coming back to Upper Sindh Frontier when it was cool would change her mind. There was no sense in winning a transfer to anywhere else in Upper Sindh, almost as hot, wholly strange, and without the prestige and romance of Jacobabad. The change, when I brought them all home from that cramped cottage and the recooked food to all the space of the Residency and her own cook, would, I was sure, reconcile her.

Often I had hoped to be summoned to a Conference in Karachi when Joan was there, and there never had been one. Now one was called for all Collectors when she was far away, but at least it was pleasant to be cool for a day or two, and to stay with the Reinitzs. We all conferred with the Chief Secretary about law and order, and with the Finance Secretary about the procurement of foodgrains on Government account to help with the Bengal Famine.

I made a special point of seeing Charles Clee, because he, as Revenue Commissioner, was the dispenser of transfer favours. I had promised Joan. I doubt if he found me very enthusiastic, or that he thought me deserving of special favours for being so foolhardy as to start a family. Anyway, he could only suggest the possibility of some other Upper Sindh District, nearly as hot as Jacobabad and we strangers. I didn't mention Joan's drastic alternative: that we say be-damned to the war and the bit of my career remaining, and go home. I very much hoped that cold weather in the Residency, and all that that implied, would soften her heart.

22

AIRBORNE INVASION

Not long before I went to Dalhousie again came the high point of the season: an extraordinary event, more extraordinary in its way even than the Viceroy's visit. A Strictly Confidential letter arrived from the Chief Secretary, copied to the Revenue Commissioner, the Inspector-General of Police, and to my Superintendent, Abdur Rahman.

It was proposed to carry out an airborne landing in Jacobabad; two officers, one Army, the other Air Force, would come to select a site. They would stay in the local hotel. (When would Karachi learn that there was no hotel?) Meanwhile, Abdur Rahman and I were to consider suitable sites, and send our recommendations.

Secrecy was all very well, but it would have helped to know how many landings there would be, what would happen to the men, what sort of country was wanted? And what, apart from entertaining us, was the demonstration for? Did the Services want secrecy or publicity? No help came.

We were left to do our best, work it out for ourselves. We had no country like the green fields and woodlands of Europe, nor like the dense jungles of Burma. In fact, the only reason we could see for the choice of Jacobabad was that we had the only airstrip between Karachi and Quetta.

We did our best: we identified an area south-west of the town, waste, scrubby land with the nearest we had to jungle.

There was better jungle along the river, but we argued that
the danger of drowning was high, and there was no quick
way from there to the airstrip for the retrieval of the
parachutists; we didn't report this idea. For the 'jungle'
strip we added a note that wild boars were known there. As
an alternative there was the airstrip and the racetrack round
it, completely bald gravel and soil.

The two officers arrived, embarrassed to find that they
were inevitably my guests at the Residency. In fairness,
Abdur Rahman should have had one, but his whole
household was *purdanashin*. However, he came to dinner,
and we tried to pump some information from our guests,
with little success—not, we thought, for security reasons,
but because they knew very little anyway. They did say,
however, that publicity would be welcome. So was the
intention to impress the 'tribesmen' in case of trouble, and
as a preventative for after the war? Perhaps. All they needed
to do was to select a site.

Abdur Rahman took them to see our chosen sites, and
they chose the airfield. They were concerned lest men get
lost in the jungle. Our jungle was only a few feet high,
grass, desert shrubs like aloes and oleander, with the
occasional acacia tree, and watercourses to fall into. And
perhaps wild boars. Having made their choice they
returned to Karachi.

We sent word round about this special tamasha, worth
anyone's while coming down from Quetta for. Then we
pondered on its purpose. There seemed no relevance to
either European or Burmese conditions, so it must be a
warning to the tribes in the hills. But why not fly in from
Quetta? Perhaps someone remembered the disaster of that
flight of Hurricanes. There was no trouble expected near
us, so why a warning? The trouble was in other parts of
India: a parachute drop there might be useful. We gave it
up.

The day arrived. Several officers arrived from Karachi,
by air, to watch the show—thank heaven they would return

the same day. In plenty of time we went to the airfield, and found a large crowd. Everyone became quiet, there was a far-off humming, growing to a growl, to a great roaring noise, and three Dakotas appeared, circled the airfield, and the drop began.

One by one they turned in from the circle, flying at about 3,000 feet, a dozen parachutes blossomed, the plane flew away, and the next one dropped its load before any of the first had reached the ground, and then the third. All were in the air at the same time, but the murmur, even laughter, of the crowd fell silent as one parachute failed to open, and plummeted to the ground. There was a murmur of shock and sympathy for the poor smashed body, but then men rushed up and began to open it: it was a container whose automatic chute had failed. Pity changed to uproarious laughter as the tension relaxed.

Thirty men there were, and they began to gather up their parachutes. We listened to the comments of the audience. There was a good deal of mock pointing of guns, of clicks of imaginary triggers and then bangs. 'Much easier than duck!' 'Time for left and right and a second gun!' 'Easier with a rifle!' 'A dozen rifles and not one would escape!'

The plan had been that the men would quickly come together and take cover. They came quite quickly together, but there was no cover, no cover at all except the airfield hut, and there we, the supposed enemy, were crowded. So they lined up, marched to their officers, saluted, and waited for the planes to return. One by one they landed, picked up their loads, and flew off home. The officers thanked us and themselves flew off. We had expected comment, but there was none.

But the spectators thanked us: well worth coming down from Quetta to see, they said, and went their ways talking about it. There was nothing left but some odd litter of broken K-ration cartons dropped by men eating while waiting for the planes.

Abdur Rahman and I had to report to our superiors our opinions of the affair—confidentially, of course, but our reports might well reach the Air Force: we should be cautious. So we regretted ignorance of its objective, but considered that as an attempt to awe the 'tribes' it was a total failure: the general opinion was that half a dozen riflemen could wipe out the lot, mostly before they landed. We suggested that if there were to be any official report to the Press, it should follow the line that we were going to take locally: that these were recruits, practising how to land without crippling themselves. We heard no more about it.

23

DALHOUSIE AGAIN

Perhaps I was growing inured to the heat, for I stopped complaining. Perhaps the District really was happy and peaceful, for I have no crises to dredge up from memory. There was the airborne exercise, hardly relevant to my story, but otherwise the few weeks before my second leave in Dalhousie have nothing to tell.

In this time two other planes landed on our field: two fighters on their way to Quetta, landing to refuel. When I got the message, I asked Mahomed Din if he wanted to see them—he was knowledgeable about aircraft types, what were these? Thunderbolts, American fighters, each with a heavy radial engine. Mahomed Din was dismissive about them—their engines were only a dozen two-stroke motor-bike motors set in a ring, air-cooled, very simple. However, he came to see them. Big, heavy planes, nothing like those beautiful doomed Hurricanes. We met the pilots; one engine had a bit of trouble. Dino looked at it, diagnosed it, and said he could put it right. He took the car and went to fetch his *subcheez*, all his tools. The planes stood at the end of the runway, for the pilots dared not taxi to their take-off point with the engines still hot: they were air-cooled, and the air was anything but cool. We sat in the shade of the hut and smoked. They asked about Mahomed Din, did he really know what he was doing? I said he probably did, he was a very good mechanic, he knew their motors were just motor-bike cylinders bundled together, and he had diagnosed the trouble hadn't he? So when he returned, and when the engine was cool, he repaired it; nothing big, a broken spring, and of course he had one in his box of oddments. He didn't want payment, but the pilots gave him a dollar coin, to hang round his neck.

They were ready to set off, and I asked, did they have compasses? They had not, but they had something new to Jacobabad: directional radio. So that accounted for the discs on a pole that had appeared on the airfield hut; it was very secret, but could not be hid.

The two planes took off in the inevitable storm of dust and roared away to the north-west, towards Quetta and a cooler place.

I had another attack of malaria, but a mild one: with the surrender of Italy its wonder drug had become available, and Hugo Reinitz had sent me some: mepacrin. It was not a cure, but it drove the virus into the spleen and kept it there, dormant. It had the bizarre effect of turning one's skin bright yellow. My fair skin—and I was not tanned, one did not bathe in the sun of Upper Sindh—developed a delicate shade of yellow, bright on my finger- and toe-nails. But Indians developed a very bilious colour indeed. Never mind: it was a very welcome relief, gave a wonderful boost to one's morale. My yellow skin returned to normal, but I had yellow nails till the colour just grew out.

Again I entrusted the District to Madadalishah, left instructions that for our return everything must be specially clean and bright, and set off for the hills.

I had no good news for Joan about a transfer, but with optimism bolstered by the effects of mepacrin, with her recent letters speaking of good health and growing boys, I hoped that she would be reconciled to staying on.

The corn was ripening in the Punjab, and for the first time I saw fields of cotton, lavish white heads, like a thin snow-shower. At Pathankot it was cool, and as the road rose it grew cold. The rains were almost over, and in the cottage a fire was welcome, and at night a blanket, even two.

We walked the boys to school, we went to the Club, perched on its little ledge hanging over the valley, and we walked them home again. Once, on a day to be remembered for ever, a special 'white stone' day, there was a break in the clouds, then the mist burnt away, and there, full in front of us, with the sun shining bright, was the whole range of the high mountains, glittering under snow all along the peaks. News spread, and others came, to watch silently. We just sat and looked until the clouds rolled back, and all was grey again.

We walked, we picnicked with the boys and their friend Michael and his mother Alma. We had one special one on the flat top of our little peak, where there was a clearing among the trees. The boys collected pine-cones and twigs, and Joan lit a fire; we all sat round it, pretending we needed it because of the cold, and to scare the wild animals away. But Joan had prepared something more adventurous: for a night or two we could leave the children with Candy while we went for a trek—a very short trek.

About twenty miles away was the capital of Chamba State, and halfway there was Khajjiar, a well-known beauty spot, a little hamlet in a wide, open meadow with a lake, unusual in this land of endless cedar forests. There was a *dak* bungalow–here the postman still travelled on foot, for there were no roads at all. Joan had booked it for us for two nights, with one night between, when we would stay at Chamba. She was told there was a resthouse there, but knew no way of booking it, so we would take our chance.

So we left the boys in the care of Candy and Alma, with Aadam for their security, and set off. We needed only a small pack and raincoats; umbrellas would have been more sensible, but we had seen people with them, and laughed, for the umbrella seemed so much the mark of the English bourgeoisie, and the thought of them in those stately cedar forests was ridiculous.

Khajjiar was as beautiful as we had been told, a place the like of which we had not seen since leaving England. We came out from the trees, and there was this green meadow, rising and falling till the trees began again half a mile away, clothing the hills to their tops. The grass was very green, the little lake was like a mirror, and there was no sign of any life. But the bungalow was open, the chowkidar expected us, and even after only ten miles we were tired, for my habit of life had little need for walking.

There was curry and fruit for supper; we took our tea to sit on the verandah, wrapped in blankets, and contemplated the moon, shining on the soft grass like silver. And then to bed. No cries in the night, no other noise, no need to get up till we wanted to. Boiled eggs, chapatti and butter for breakfast, and tea again. No need in the world to hurry.

On we went next day, back into the forest and then out into open country. The road was a mule track, and indeed after a few miles we met a party, two mules with several hillmen, and, of all things, a white man. He was very suspicious of us: 'Who are you? What are you doing here? Where do you come from?' We saw no reason at all for him to be so suspicious, but we were polite. We were going to Chamba, we were on holiday, we came from Sindh. 'Why come to Dalhousie?' He seemed oddly ignorant; however, I explained that Sindh was very hot, I was Deputy Commissioner of the Upper Sindh Frontier, from Jacobabad, the hottest place of all, and that Sindh had no hill station of its own.

This seemed to reconcile him to us; perhaps the word 'frontier' impressed him, though probably he had no idea how little our frontier resembled the turbulent places he was imagining. He was Political Agent for Chamba, a man worth knowing in those parts. Since we did not appear to be spies, or meaning to exploit his domain, he was willing to be friendly. We all sat down and had tea, and when he heard that we had nowhere booked to stay, he gave us a card with a message for the major-domo. We were to stay in the State guest house, to be entertained there by the palace staff.

All was friendly now. After two miles we should be able to see Chamba, so we said good-bye and walked on. What a thrice-blessed young man he was! How pleasant it was to travel, not in hope but in certainty.

After two miles we came to a grand view of the capital, as he had said we would. What he had not said was that it would be on the far side of a ravine, and that on our side the track fell steeply down a precipice over a thousand feet high. At the bottom ran the Ravi, one of the great rivers of the north; but the flood time was past, and from so high above it was only a little rock-littered stream.

Our legs felt more practised in walking now, and the way ahead was downhill, no great problem. There lay the palace, and the town centre, perhaps four hundred feet above the river, no great climb.

But this was not walking, still less running, for running would have pitched us right down the cliff. One step at a time we went, weight landing on one foot, hard, the other down, and one's whole body jolting down onto it. That descent used muscles we hadn't known were there, and overworked them grievously. By the time we reached the river bridge at the bottom we ached everywhere. On the other side was a climb; climbing was easier, but nonetheless it would need more effort. We sat at the bottom wondering if we could find enough.

Clearly we must, and at the top would be rest, and tea, and the State's welcome. So we did; but at the top was a long flight of stone steps. We set off slowly, but after a few steps Joan sat down. It was no good, she said, her legs had seized up entirely. They had, too, literally: they just would not bend. So we sat on the steps for a time, while I rubbed her legs, and then set off, with me supporting my lady, painfully slowly, in grave danger of falling together and rolling down to the river...

Sheer obstinacy, and the hope of a chair and tea, kept us going; we reached the top, and there stood the major-domo, a forbidding figure in a long silk *achkan*, with a tight turban, woven with gold thread, wound round a little embroidered cap. He was obviously prepared to condemn us to go away, to go down those steps, down to the river, and away. But I gave him the card from that estimable young man, and all was changed. We were welcome, we could certainly have a room for the night. He would send us food and tea, and we could have a bath—a hot bath! He said he had noticed that we were a little stiff—how, indeed, could he have missed noticing?—there was a masseur in the Palace, would we like him? Indeed we would! But, he warned us, we would have to pay.

He could have charged what he liked.

We drank our tea, we had our bath, and the masseur arrived. He worked us over, helped by the bath; our muscles stopped aching, and our legs worked again. We had a meal, and had to decide: do we go to sleep, or do we look at this place? That was a difficult choice, for we felt generally lazy. But there was a guide book, and after studying it we decided that there was too much to be left for the morning.

Chamba was a surprise. I suppose Balochistan made me assume that wherever there were hills the people would be Muslims, but in Chamba it was not so: the Raja was a Rajput, his people were Hindu. This accounted for the haughty visage of the major-domo: he must be a Rajput, and the Rajputs were a proud race. But the Rajputs lived in Rajputana, in Central India. How came there to be a Rajput here? We asked, but were given little real explanation: there had always been Rajputs here, the Raja's family was Sikh, and he still had kin in Rajputana. His family had arranged for him to marry a princess from Jaipur, and his sister had married back there.

So the temples here were Hindu, though it seemed that the hill people had added some of their own special gods to the pantheon. These temples were not so flamboyant as we would expect, but they gave unusual prominence to the lingam and the yoni: they were represented on a giant scale outside one temple, but outside another were a delicately shaped lingam and a yoni in the form of a tiny pool of running water.

Surprisingly, there was a Presbyterian church, and a Church of Scotland mission. How, and why, had the Scots come so far? Were they making converts? Had some people come here to settle? We found no one to tell us. The Scots were greatly enterprising all over India, but there seemed little to attract a foreigner to stay in Chamba.

We went in to supper, and in that fine guest house we felt sadly under-dressed, but in spite of that we were housed in luxury. There was a drawing-room, with a fire lit specially for us; we would have gone straight to bed, but felt that it would have been ungrateful to leave it unused. So we sat by it for a time, and then wandered round looking at the pictures, of Chamba, of the river and the hills, portraits of the Raja and his family. This room was furnished with high victorian taste: it seemed that any rich or noble family wishing to appreciate western style must choose that particular period, often, unfortunately, sacrificing the Victorian virtue of comfort for mere ostentation. Perhaps the fact that this was the period of the greatest glory of the British Empire of India had something to do with it. Carrying it to Chamba must have been a monstrous task.

We went to bed, and listened to the silence. We felt more alone than we had ever felt, and revelled in it, but with a little underlying twinge of conscience for neglecting the clear duty of parents. We were able to suppress the twinge firmly enough to spend a beautiful night, and to wake feeling that the climb before us was not after all so daunting.

The temples at Chamba were unlike any in Sindh, though our experience was small: Sadh Bela was the only large one we knew; but we had seen pictures of large ones elsewhere in India. These were tall polygonal towers, built of wood on stone bases—they were, after all, in the middle of one of the great cedar forests of the world. Over twenty feet high, they were crowned by caps with wide eaves to

shed the rain. The craftsmanship was beautiful, the
decoration was restrained in contrast to the usual rather
tinsel-like decoration inside, though here it glittered less
than in the only temple we knew.

The Palace was on one side of a rough paved square, the
temples on the other, creating a most elegant centre for
this State capital. We were allowed to take photographs
but, for security reasons, not of the Palace. What danger
was envisaged we did not understand. Chamba was hardly a
worthwhile target for an air raid, had no imaginable
strategic importance; but we obeyed.

The village was terraced down the steep hillside, with
the bazaar between it and the terrace. Here, the shops
kept goods only for local demand. Thinking of the trouble
and pain of getting here from the outside, he would be a
foolishly optimistic shopkeeper who would acquire stock,
with much labour, on mule-back, for visitors. We couldn't
even find any little thing to take back for the family. So
although the bazaar held nothing to interest us, its simple
cleanliness, its steep paved street, washed frequently by rain,
charmed us, comparing it as we must with Sindhi bazaars
with their little septic puddles.

Even the Raja must walk if he wanted to go anywhere:
this was no kingdom for effete royalty. The Raja and all his
staff must have had very sturdy calf muscles. Perhaps there
was a palanquin for the ladies, but we never saw one. His
little army would be manned by the hillmen themselves.

We said good-bye to the major-domo and to the solemn
vakil, signed the visitors' book, one of very few, far
separated entries, and set off. We scrambled down to the
river and, after our massage, faced the opposing cliff
undiscouraged by the height, triumphant when we reached
the top. Eight thousand feet up, we were slow, but the rest
of the way to Khajjiar was level, so we paused to look at
Chamba's own mountain, Dain Kund, as we had promised
we would, and admired it, admired even more the cedar
forests which reached nearly to the top. We ate the

sandwiches we had been given, and drank water from a spring. Surely it could not be polluted from so high up.

We walked gently back to Khajjiar for the night, and then back to our cottage and our dear boys, and all the responsibilities their care involved. There were walks and picnics, there was the last day at school, with sentimental good-byes. We packed up to go home, said tearful good-byes to Alma and Michael, with an urgent invitation to come and stay with us when it was cool, and we set off.

Joan was glad to be away from the re-cooked food and the blue milk—just too late it was discovered that the churn was being topped up with water on the way up from the Gurkhas—and more especially she was worried about Candy, who was ill, and unhappy, and nervous: quite unlike her usual self. She was not even sad at leaving her soldier friend. Let us get home, she said, among friends, then she would be better.

Somehow there was much more to take down the hill than had ever come up. With the four of us and Candy and Aadam we nearly filled the bus. At Pathankot I apologized to the Stationmaster for the fuss I had made last time, and he forgave me; he said that this time there was a very good light. As before we had to wait for the train to start, but this time there was no need to mind the dark: the boys sat and marvelled at the little flashes of light that wandered along the train.

Somehow we managed to move ourselves from one train to another at Lahore, and finally, in a cool September morning, we reached Jacobabad.

Again there was a crowd to meet us: the Mukhtiarkar, the Havildar with his patewalas, Illahibaksh and Lalu, and Mahomed Din with the car. The boys were awake this time, excited without being noisy. At first all these people worried them, but then they joyfully recognized Lalu; truly they knew Lalu, who had, after Candy, been their best friend till a few months before.

As before, the noises brought faces to the windows as the sahibs on their way to Quetta were told that it was the Deputy Commissioner bringing his family home from the hills. As if we were royalty. (There is no denying that my head was swelled!)

As before, Joan and Candy with the boys would drive ahead. But Adam and David knew Lalu, they were big boys now, they were not sleepy, they would walk home with him. It was not far, Aadam could go with them, so we let them go. We did not want two noisily enraged little boys to spoil our homecoming.

I would step very carefully; I must praise nothing, but let Joan just notice, let the comforts of our own place, of properly cooked food, of the cooler weather—but warmer than the hills—of our own friends instead of those awful memsahibs, do their work, and reconcile her to our still being here. Dr Jessaram was back, having managed to leave the whole of the hot weather for that unsmiling, stony-hearted *buddli*, who had now gone. The Halls would be back soon, but there was no Engineer, and Abdur Rahman's wife was in purdah. Joan must call on her, and that would need tact, but Joan could never be a *grande dame*, and her Urdu was good now. Then there was the Club.

There were a few days of peace, preparing for us all to go on tour together, and then came a shock. Candy went to see Dr Jessaram about her sickness, and the news was that she was perfectly well, just pregnant.

Joan had given Candy warnings, but clearly not enough to pierce the darkness of her Catholic ignorance. Oh, yes, Candy knew who the father was, he was a nice boy, but she certainly wouldn't marry him, and anyway, who could know where he was now? Nor was she going to have a baby, that would be too, too shaming. Long separation from religious disciplines had clearly weakened her morals.

Certainly neither Dr Jessaram nor Hugo Reinitz could help now, so Candy went off to visit her auntie in Karachi;

she hadn't seen her for a long time, and she would know what to do.

So she went away. The boys moved into the spare bedroom next to us, and during the day Lalu would look after them, with Joan near at hand. We explained that Candy had gone to see her family, which puzzled Adam and David. Candy was a part of their family, they understood that; Alma and Michael were a family, though small. How could Candy have another? We tried to explain, but after a little we gave it up. For a long, long time we heard nothing, till we feared she was never coming back. For the boys, hope must be kept alive. 'Soon, soon she will come.' Soon was a new word, defined only when she actually came.

I rearranged my tour, and went to the west, where I had to do the remission work. I rode between camps and came home by rail for the weekends. I left Joan with the car so that she could take the boys around. She took them to the Special Force, where they watched her ride, and the men ride, and where the Risaldar told them all the grand things about horses. They talked readily now, a mixture of Sindhi, Urdu, and a little English for their parents. They saw the Tomb, and insisted on leaving their own offerings. Joan drove them to the Begari Bridge, where they saw all the bullock carts go slowly by, and they waved at the drivers, and the drivers waved cheerfully back. Joan explained that on the other side of the bridge the land did not belong to me, which surprised and puzzled them.

At last Candy came back as, of course, they had always known she would. But their enormous pleasure showed that perhaps there had been a time when they were doubtful, that they harboured a suspicion that they would never see her again. She had had a rough time, but their pleasure recovered her spirits

Now we could take the promised tour along the railway, our own railway. We had to go quickly, because Christmas was coming, and soon after was the Horse Show, with the Governor coming soon after that.

This tour needed careful planning, for everyone would move by train, my family and staff, the Office, and the whole touring *bundobust*. We took up almost the whole of the one coach with a first-class compartment on our little train. Bungalows were close to the line, and where they were not, tongas had to be arranged at the station. As usual, Joan was left with the detail, while I, happy to be in duty bound, had to ride between camps to do my work. Whether or not mine was the easier part was immaterial; it must not be said that an officer neglected his duty for his family. It should all work very neatly, and Ali Ahmed at Khandkot could be trusted to see that it did. If the train didn't break down.

So we all set off, I early on Prince with my escort, everyone else from the station, with all the world to help and to watch. I wish I could have witnessed that departure. But, as on every following day, I was peacefully away inspecting crops and liquor shops, schools and maternity homes. There were exactly fixed times for visitors, and petitions, and courts.

The first camp was at Odhano, and I set off early to be at the nearby station to meet the train. I was punctual, but the train was late. Nor were they on it. So, had they all missed it? No, said the driver, but my Havildar had told him to stop where the line ran very close to the bungalow, and they had detrained there. I rode back; I was very angry with Mahbubalishah, I rebuked him for his effrontery, for he had done it in my name: I would have a lot of apologizing to do, he must not go on in this way. But I had missed all the commotion of settling in, so I soothed him by saying what a good idea it was, and that I would arrange for a stop here when we moved.

The Havildar behaved as if he owned that railway; indeed, he had used it for touring so often that he probably felt that he had periodic controlling rights over its running.

There was another occasion when the camp was moving,
and I waved at the train as it went by. A little further on I
saw it stopped in the station when it should have left long
before, so I rode up to ask what was the trouble. The driver
told me that the Havildar had told him to stop, the sahib
had looked tired and might like a ride. The sahib would
not, and this time was happy to berate Mahbubali loudly
and publicly. I told him he must stop trying to run the
railway; if a freight train had been following and had run
into the back, what then? But he was a proud man, he
could not be set down like that. No freight train had come,
had it? And he only did it from his care for me.

We went as far as Khandkot, headquarters of the Deputy
Collector, and there we all had tea with Ali Ahmed. His
wife was in purdah, so only Joan met her. She also inspected
the Maternity Home, and met the midwife, the forceful
lady who wanted her daughter to be a nurse with Dr
Jessaram. But although Joan was happy to congratulate her
on the state of the Home, she made it clear that Dr
Jessaram must herself see the girl, that Joan could not be
used to influence her. I went with Ali Ahmed to Ghouspur,
where the Governor would have a shoot, and on to the
River, for me to see the cultivation in the *kutchas*, to make
notes for my case for the creation of short-term
smallholdings, and to demonstrate the inefficiency of share-
cropping in such land. A most satisfactory little survey.
There lay land that had borne good crops, side by side with
land just as good which was held by a zamindar, but was
waste because the share-croppers did not find it worthwhile
to cultivate it.

Joan had wanted to go all the way to Kashmore, to the
end of the line, but with the Horse Show coming there was
not the time to camp on the way, and I could hardly ask
the Mukhtiarkar to put up the whole family for a night. So
we turned for home.

The great thing about touring by rail, by a railway like
ours, running right through the middle of the District, was

that one did not need to make a circular programme, with camps appropriate for moving the *bundobust* by camel. At Khandkot we all boarded the train and went home together. Only the horses would take two days, and the *sowars* assured me that that would be a great treat. Joan rode out with me once or twice on pertal, and herself thought of riding home, but it would have been too far, and, as with Kashmore, she was disappointed of the treat. We all trundled back together.

The boys had seen the free-loaders board the train as it left Jacobabad, now they would see how they dismounted. The canal was not running now, but there was still a large, deep pool under the railway bridge, and we told them to watch. First the bundles flew to the bank, and then the men jumped. Adam and David began to cry—the men would drown. But then they scrambled out and collected their bundles, we laughed and told them it was all a joke, so they laughed too. In fact, they overdid it: they rolled about laughing. Maybe they didn't quite understand it, but if we laughed it must be all right. Their momentary worry past, they became hysterical with relief.

There was little we could do to celebrate Christmas. Candy would go to Sukkur with her friends. When she came back, we thought, we would go to Sukkur to see the New Year in, but then we considered who there was with whom to celebrate: there was no one. So we stayed at home, we thought of our families, still asleep when our New Year began, and I tried to teach Joan the hymns of my Methodist forebears—what I could remember of them. 'How many pass the guilty night/ In revelry and frantic mirth...' So did not we. 'Come let us renew/ Our journey pursue...' That was more like it! We ended in a welter of homesickness, Joan six years from home, I seven, and no real prospect of quick return. We had doubtless changed; they, living through the war, would have changed more, and Adam and David knew them not at all, were known only from letters and little snapshots.

Between ourselves, too, there were changes. The golden aura that had surrounded us when first we met was a little dimmed, the surface scratched. Joan had changed more than I—she had to. The girl endlessly seeing new things, fearing only boredom, had become a woman with the heavy responsibility of children, children whose early life had been difficult indeed. She had become a highly competent organizer, no one, nothing could dominate her. As for me, I had probably changed much less, because my world had changed much less. But we were happy. There had certainly been annoyance, even anger between us sometimes, but on principle we never let the sun go down on wrath. Perhaps I really was a good husband, as husbands go; and she herself such a wife. We had had difficult times, but by now the worst seemed to be over. And we had had some wonderful experiences together.

24

1945

At first my request for an administrator for Jacobabad had been refused: there was, of course, no money. But as soon as the Governor decided to camp there, some was found, and Sitaldas was appointed: for the Viceroy there was no need to bother, he was not interested in small towns, but for our own Governor at least enough must be done to clean the place up and avoid sarcastic remarks about slums. And Sitaldas was the right man to send; he was also welcome in our Club, and for help with the Horse Show.

It was, I think, inevitable that the enthusiasm we felt during our first Show could not be equalled when it came round again. On the social side it was from the beginning doomed to disappoint, so few of our friends could come. But on the professional side my proposed alterations bore fruit, almost too heavy a crop.

No horse buyers came from the Militias this year. There was no Engineer in post, and Abdur Rahman's family was in purdah, so there were only two parties. A surgeon from Quetta stayed with the Halls; John Petty stayed with us while he looked at his forests; at Charles Clee's request we took in Roger Thomas, and very happy we were to do so. He was that unusual person, a British zamindar, with a very large estate in the Punjab. There were two others, whose names I forget, whom I must call the Soldier and his Wife. They were wished on us, with the idea that a time away from Karachi with its excitements and temptations might prevent their marriage from foundering. Some sort of compliment, we supposed, but they gave no help at all to our party.

John Petty came with a special purpose. There was said to be growing in Sindh a climbing plant rich in latex, which might be used to provide India with its own source of rubber. All District Officers had been told to look out for it, but none had found it. John searched the forests along the river and found none. Strangely, a year later, when Joan and I were dining with him in his Karachi flat, he showed us the plant, twining round his verandah: the only one ever found in Sindh. That was very appropriate; it was, moreover, quite useless: it had a pretty flower, but little latex. And was the only one.

Our Show Committee was pleased with itself. This year's programme was far larger than the previous one, with all sorts of officers coming to give addresses on relevant matters. We were pleased, but a little cynical at the number of people who found time to partake a little in our Show. There were twenty-two public addresses! Had they nothing to do in the Secretariat but write speeches? I must, in justice to these experts, listen to all I could, but by the end of the week there was a sad falling off in attendance at their meetings. Nevertheless, we sent them all home full of praise for the way the local zamindars appreciated what they had heard. It seemed that no praise was too fulsome to be suspect. And we, the local establishment, sincerely wanted to make our Show more and more relevant.

We had expert judges for all the animal and industrial classes, who could not be suspected of any bias, so saving a deal of disputation. But next year we must have live demonstrations of all the techniques discussed.

We had a very small house party, but several guests for a day. However, for them there were simple rules for Joan's catering: no pig meat for a Muslim, no beef for a Hindu, keep at least one vegetarian dish handy, and give a Christian—or ourselves—anything no others wanted.

There was time this year for Joan to go round the Show
with Adam and David, enjoy the praise they evoked, and
leave them sometimes for Candy to show off. Praise meant
nothing to them, their wonder was at so many new things.
The Variety Show this year was a live animal circus, which
for a time turned their chatter into astonished silence. The
tiger in his cage worried them, but no, he would not be
getting out. His owner swore he was as gentle as a lamb,
but those of us who looked at him detected a spiteful look
in his eye; he looked anything but gentle. Or perhaps it
was an ancestral distrust of tigers. He must certainly not be
let out.

The Officers' Sports were a washout. Margery Hall
decided not to risk her neck, the Wife was in no fit state to
ride, even had she wanted to, so Joan could only ride over,
to rather subdued applause. It was a sad finish. For the
neza-bazi, competition was a little greater. The Soldier was
no more fit than his wife, but John Petty would ride, and
Henry Hall and his guest from Quetta. But none of them
was practised; I rode Prince, and Abdur Rahman, who could
have provided real competition, was so much concerned
with his Police Sports that he had no time.

I lifted and carried all the pegs; so I should, but
nonetheless the applause was enthusiastic. For the Deputy
Commissioner, doubtless, for the triumph was not so very
great. Joan said the boys didn't seem to understand about
winning. They had to be persuaded to join in the applause.
The Police marched and counter-marched; they gave a lathi
display; they arrested a 'criminal'. It was all highly
competent, but I had seen it all before. I had seen the
Cavalry Display before, too, and even watched the practice,
but because of the jingling harness and flying pennons, the
horses so beautiful, it never ceased to thrill. They charged
and counter-charged, they charged through each other,
and then trotted to the far side of the ground where they
picked up their lances. The two troops met, wheeled left
and right to join, and the Risaldar rode to the head. Then,

with pennons flying, they trotted, ten abreast, to the grandstand and gave their Grand Salute. My most vivid memory of all: John Jacob would have been pleased. Everyone was pleased. My sons were awestruck, with only an occasional word. In fact, the whole show, ending with fifty horsemen advancing on them, was too much. They wet themselves. It was excusable, and we overlooked it.

There was a *malakhra* competition, which I missed: this formalized wrestling bored me. But a *kabbadi* competition at the school was another matter.

Kabbadi is a grand game. For one thing, it can be played on any piece of flattish ground; for another, no equipment is necessary. I daresay there are rules for the size of the pitch, the length of a game, the number of players in a team, but I didn't know them, and it seemed that so long as numbers were equal on each side, it didn't matter how many there were. A game could go on till one side had only two men left, or there could be an agreed limit. On the pitch, just three lines were marked, with lime, or even with a stick dragged in the dust.

A challenger would leave his base, cross the mid-line, and challenge the enemy to catch him, while he tried to catch one of them. Either might happen, or the challenger might—often did—run out of breath and retreat home. The point was that he must only use one lungful of air, so he must forever mutter '*kabbadi...kabbadi...kabbadi...*' to prove it. Each time a challenger retired, with or without a capture, the other side challenged. Each team member had one turn. In words it may not sound exciting; on the ground it was. Clearly the merits of a player lay in his agility and the size of his lungs. Some of the subtleties of the game were explained to me; there were, doubtless, others of which I was unaware. Jacobabad High School was the Upper Sindh Champion, so I was seeing the best. But perhaps even better was that there were no costs, no costs at all, and this was important, for in Sindh, with a Muslim League Ministry, education was not highly regarded: old-fashioned Muslims would argue that since the Prophet, may he be blessed, was reported to have been illiterate, there was virtue in illiteracy itself. (The Jakrani Sirdar, Darya Khan, adhered to this school. He also believed that the Prophet (PBUH) never cut his hair, nor washed more than the ritual ablutions. As a result, the Sirdar looked and smelt terrible. He should have sat on the Shahi Jirga, but the other members would not have him.)

The Baloch Races were run with the usual mayhem and shouting. There was one private race, between two top breeders, each backing his own horse. This was as orderly as a race should be. I don't know who won, and nor did Abdur Rahman, though he loved racing. The chief race was not so fiercely contested as before; perhaps, with no buyers from the Militias, some breeders had kept away.

I must explain the awkward matter of Joan's judging of the handicrafts. Not that her decisions were questioned, they were all accepted as proper, but she had openly admired some of the winning exhibits, and was told that, of course, they were all for sale. So she bought a piece of dyed cotton, embroidered by hand with a device like an embryonic *fleur-de-lys*. Also, a knitted woollen jacket, with pockets and long sleeves, knitted all in one, with no stitching at all. This was astonishing craftsmanship, but it fitted me very oddly. Joan was very pleased with her purchases, but the awkward thing was that the owners did not really mean to sell: the offer was purely nominal. Joan would not return them: they had been winning the prizes for years, she said, and their departure would encourage new entries. There was certainly merit in that for the future.

The Show was perhaps better than last year's, though not the social side. With no great difficulty I have ignored the Soldier and his Wife; indeed, we saw little of them except when there were drinks under the shamiana, and at any other time when there were drinks. I suppose they came for meals, but mostly they stayed in their tent.

There were two Officers' Parties, very quiet. The last, at the Residency, could not this year be called a Ball: it hardly deserved to be called a Dance, with two women and five men. No veleta, no excuse-me, certainly no conga. It looked as if it would finish very early. The surgeon went home to bed. The Halls danced together, and Joan with John Petty. Roger Thomas and I walked outside, talking my 'shop': share-cropping on his farm, kalar in the Punjab; I let all the bees fly from my bonnet.

It was quiet and still and cold, very peaceful. Suddenly there were screams, and a great roar. 'It's the tiger! He's got loose! Duck down!' This was from Roger Thomas, who said he had heard one before. We crept to the compound wall and looked over; the roaring was coming from the same place, so the tiger was not out. His cage was just outside, and there was the manager shouting at the chowkidar, who shouted back: he pointed at the Soldier, who was groaning loudly, and whose wife was having hysterics. The tiger was growling and licking his bloody paws; the man's right arm was a bloody mess from elbow to hand, the skin in tatters.

With all the noise it was difficult to think. First the arm must be seen to, then there could be explanations. The manager fetched a clean towel to wrap up that ghastly arm, the police jemadar arrived and was sent to tell Dr Jawa to open up the hospital for surgery. Everyone had come out from the Residency, so Joan took the hysterical woman away, and Henry Hall went to rouse the providential Quetta surgeon.

We abandoned our party; the surgeon said he must set to work at once, so I drove him and the Soldier to the hospital, which, glory be, was all lit up, Jawa waiting. He could be proud of his swift action, at such an hour, and fortunate in that the Surgeon had inspected it, by invitation, on the previous day, so it was unusually clean and neat.

Roger Thomas was left to find out just what had happened. The couple, pretty drunk, had come to the cage and that foolish man, seeing the tiger peacefully asleep, had, said the chowkidar, poked him awake with a stick, 'this stick,' and then, to show off, had reached in to stroke him. The tiger was very annoyed, grabbed the arm and dragged, the man dragged back, and with the help of the chowkidar and the Wife, got his arm away. But those fearsome claws had torn the skin to ribbons. It was just lucky that no large vein or artery had been cut.

Thomas could see no reason to blame either the chowkidar or the manager with anything, but later we would take statements for a proper inquiry. The Soldier and his Wife were both drunk: he deserved what he got. Moreover, he had spoiled our party. Of course, our party was dying anyway; but at least this escapade would make it notable.

At the hospital the surgeon put on his gown, a bit ragged where rats had got at it. He saw to all his instruments being thoroughly sterilized, and pulled on his rubber gloves, which crackled ominously. And as the patient was being prepared for Jawa to give him an anaesthetic, all the lights went out. The hospital was lit up all over, and the fuses could not stand the extra load of the theatre lights as well.

Not for nothing were we used to the power station failing, and very quickly pressure lamps were brought— one of these needed constant pumping—and a man was sent to fetch the Sikh electrician. Word went out to switch off all lights outside the theatre.

Antiseptics and sterilants have changed a lot since then. Jacobabad depended on picric acid. I have read about the stuff now: it is a sensitive explosive, but we in our ignorance noticed only that it turned everything yellow. Perhaps the Surgeon knew; if so, he didn't say.

He tucked bits of muscle back into place, he dragged ragged edges of skin together, and stitched and stitched, and finally it was done. His opinion was that the arm was safe, but he doubted if all the fingers would work. And there must be a danger of infection, so the patient must be taken to a better-equipped hospital as soon as possible. He was full of praise for Dr Jawa.

The Surgeon disrobed, and looked, amused and unsurprised, at his hands all yellow where the gloves had leaked. He saw his patient into bed, and then we drove to the Residency, where he had a fine big drink. Joan brought in the Wife, sober now, and no longer hysterical, to be reassured by the Surgeon. Joan had heard all her story, and doubted if even this would help to redeem that endangered marriage.

I wish I knew that Surgeon's name. The job he did was not, perhaps, particularly intricate, but he showed mastery of what one might call jungle surgery, and was untroubled by our shortcomings.

The obvious way to get the man quickly to hospital was by air to Karachi. By six o'clock I felt that I could properly ring Charles Clee at home, and ask for a plane.

When Clee came on the phone, irritated at being woken so early, and on a Sunday, I just stated baldly that a man had been mauled by a tiger, and I wanted a plane to get him to Karachi quickly. 'A tiger! In Sindh! You must be drunk, Pearce!' But I had his friend Roger Thomas with me, who assured him that it was true. Clee's response to me rings clearly in my ear today. Our party was anything but drunken, but we had made another bit of Jacobabad history.

An hour later news came that an ambulance plane would arrive at about ten. Joan helped the Wife to pack up their tent, and told me later that she had found five empty gin bottles there, and one half full. They had brought four, and still needed more, so they had bought two from Popatlal—the two he kept for us. They needed a bottle a day; no wonder we saw little of them, and never sober.

The Surgeon examined his patient, pleased that he was to go so soon. He drove with me, the Wife, the patient, and all their belongings to the airfield, and as the plane took

off, we both breathed thanks to heaven, and went home
for a beer.

Joan had had all the Wife's story: the Soldier away too
much, the Wife bored and having too free a time in
Karachi. But it didn't seem that the therapy we were meant
to provide had been successful: too much gin, probably.
Perhaps this injury would help, though it didn't seem likely.
In fact, just over a year later I met the Soldier in Karachi,
and he still had his arm. It was swollen and discoloured,
but all joints were in working order, he said. He had the
address of the Surgeon, and I hope he thanked him.

They never thanked us, nor did they leave anything for
the servants, but perhaps the manner of their going could
excuse that.

While we drank our beer, Adam and David came with
Candy to play under the shamiana, and that Sunday
morning, lazy after the toilsome night, was very pleasant.
Abdur Rahman had to hear about it, and would see about
an inquiry. Ali Ahmed came, on his way home to Khandkot.
Perhaps Dr Jawa, to listen to his praise. After lunch, John
Petty went, and then a plane arrived to take Roger Thomas
back to the Punjab. A zamindar so modern that he had his
own aeroplane! I thought of the Sukkur zamindar,who had
complained to the Viceroy that there was nothing to spend
his money on. We were given a flight round our District,
the first time Joan had ever flown, the first time I had been
awake in the air. Most clearly I remember the sight of the
River, with its unpredictable wandering course, and all the
kutchas laid out, nothing hidden. How much might have
escaped assessment? A photograph might be interpreted to
tell us. That was a thought worth storing.

That was the end. A meeting of the Show Committee
summed things up: no more circuses, more demonstrations,
less talk. Circular to the Militias telling them what fine
horses would be on offer next time. Thanks to everybody
from everyone. We would collect a bigger party next time.

If there was a next time for us. This Horse Show deserved no white stone.

The Governor would arrive on Thursday, and he would be with us for two weeks. It was a little unfair to have arranged his programme so soon after the Horse Show, but we had had long notice of it. It was a very long camp for one District, with an extraordinarily large list of interviews; but in Jacobabad he would meet most of the Baloch sirdars, and important merchants too.

It was anything but a busy camp, with two whole days in the middle with nothing fixed at all. He did not visit Jacob's Tomb, nor did he inspect the Special Force. He had his own household in the District Bungalow, he had no need to share mine. He inspected Begari Head, as all the top brass were accustomed to do, and where Abdur Rahman and I welcomed him to our District, and then for two days His Excellency did nothing but grant interviews, and I nothing but take Her Excellency to inspect the Local Board Dispensary and the Khandkot Maternity Home; there the midwife failed to impress her. There was a shoot at Ghouspur, where I suppose I stood by—I have no memory of it—and there were two whole days when the little grey book says nothing but 'SUNRISE/SUNSET'. His programme was filled with very little. But when the party moved to Jacobabad it was the Deputy Collector, Ali Ahmed, not I, who said farewell at Khandkot, after a personal interview, which was a notable, and for him very promising, innovation.

'The Deputy Commissioner will accompany His Excellency throughout, except where otherwise stated.' I was glad he had a light programme. The War Committee, the District Local Board—I was always there, and remember nothing. I went round the town when Sitaldas showed what he had done in a short time. Joan looked after Lady Dow, who had even less to do than Himself. She met Dr Jessaram and inspected the Zenana Hospital, and otherwise seemed to spend her time on the Residency lawn. Adam and David

were all that we could have hoped for. The last time Lady
Dow had seen them they were sickly babies, likely to die;
now they were two and a half, running about, talking
endlessly, very ready to be friends with this stranger. Candy
came in for appropriate congratulations, and they all sat
under the shamiana and drank squash.

I remember just the unimportant things, such as Roger
Collett's complaint on being taken through the brothel.
When he had tripped on the steps of the Durbar Hall and
upset the solemn procession, he had laughed as if at a
joke; as we drove through the brothel he had commented
on its neatness, and wondered why these women sat in
empty shops. When the answer came to him he was silent.
Afterwards he complained to me, I should have warned
him: an ADC should not have allowed his charges to be so
embarrassed. I pointed out that the Governor was not
innocent, he should see all sides of life in his province, and
would probably have been annoyed if he had been
deliberately diverted away. As for Lady Dow, I didn't
know...

The trip through the brothel was to watch a polo match.
I do not think His Excellency was so very keen on polo, but
at my suggestion he had in his programme an appointment
to watch a *kabbadi* match at the High School, and that was,
I think, as great a success with him as it had been with me.
Lady Dow was there, and noticed that it was a game for
everyone, not just soldiers and wealthy civilians, and the
better for it. Lady Dow did not like the grand ladies of
Karachi, who resented her being herself the Chief Lady.
She told Joan all about it, for in that, as in several other
things, their feelings were shared.

There was lunch at the Residency, but this was in effect a
family party, only the Dows, Dermont Barty, Secretary;
Roger Collett, ADC; and Abdur Rahman; then we must ask
the Halls, as they were representing the power over the
border. It was a party small enough for general
conversation. I recall none of it, but I imagine Lady Dow

must have told her tale of the 'jungle picnic', and I the story of the tiger in Sindh. Even the food pleased Lady Dow, and indeed, her digestion had been considered, she being the chief guest.

Dermont shepherded people away so that I was left alone with Sir Hugh. This must be for a special reason, for I was not marked in the programme for an interview. He unbent, and talked about the all-India situation, off the record. The 'Cripps Proposals' were quite dead, whatever the Hindus accepted the Muslims rejected, and vice versa; Wavell was making no progress, and was, he thought, being undermined at home. But as soon as the war ended there might be real advances towards independence, even if the Japanese war dragged on. The ICS must look to its future. Probably he was talking like this to all of us.

I think Sir Hugh already knew he was going to Bihar; he was too able a man to be wasted in peaceful Muslim Sindh. Had he not known, he would hardly have talked as he did, to one of his junior British officers.

He asked what were my ideas for myself. Well, I thought that nearly five years straight in Upper Sindh was enough. I deliberately said nothing of children, I could leave that to Joan. So, if I were transferred, what job would I like?

This was extraordinary. I knew that Peter Cargill was capable of asking, and I was not, but I never supposed I might be asked myself to choose my job! After all, the whole of the Bombay Presidency was available if Sindh did not want me. I suggested the Food and Civil Supplies Department, the new tool of administration for which I was quite well fitted, with experience in the purchase of foodgrains, and even of things like toiletry. (My experience with Kishenchand Punjabi might even be useful!) Or there was Agriculture.

We left it at that; he would see what could be done. I suspected that really he wanted to see how I would react to a decision already tentatively made. Perhaps my enthusiasm for Jacobabad had led him to think that I wanted to stay. If that were so, I would have courted marital disaster.

There was a second partridge shoot, with Sirdar Bahadur Sirdar Rahim Khan Khoso as host: at Kadirpur, the *jungly* area that we had offered to the RAF for their parachute drop. Unlike Ghouspur, where the birds were walked up over open ground, here the beaters must beat towards the guns. There was a strict rule that in such country there must be no firing at ground game. I explained this—some of the party might not know—and warned that there was ground game, hares and wild boars. It was well to avoid the pig anyway, for a 12-bore would not stop an adult, and if a piglet were hit its mother would be horribly dangerous.

I stood behind the line of guns, and was given one of those little wire chairs. To sit on? If I liked. To ward off a boar, perhaps, or to stand on and hope he wouldn't see me as he charged by. For any of these purposes it was doubtfully useful.

Of course, it must be the ebullient Roger Collett who saw the hare, found the shot irresistible, and loosed off. There was a yell, and everything stopped. A beater had been hit, had been thoroughly peppered. The jemadar and his beaters weren't going to work any more, it was too dangerous.

We looked at the victim. Luckily there were no wounds to his face, his eyes were all right, and his mates admitted he was not likely to die. I promised he would be all right, I would take him straight to the hospital, the doctor would patch him up, and I would bring him back in sound condition. If the Governor Sahib's shoot was ended now the *izzat* of all of us, particularly of their own Sirdar, would be blackened. The Sirdar Sahib backed me up, the man would go in the Sirdar's own car, the Dipiti Sahib would go with him. But they would not beat till they saw their man again, able to stand up. So it was left: the shooting party would have their meal, and I set off, driving, once more, the Elegant Chev. Jawa had another opportunity to show

his skill. He dug out the pellets, nine of them, and stopped
the bleeding. We got the man a new shirt and gave him
some laudanum. This made him sleepy, and I drove him
back. Dr Jawa came with us to see that all was well.

All was indeed well. Between us we stood the man up,
and the jemadar lifted his shirt and saw the little dabs of
cotton wool; he counted the holes one by one, aloud: nine.
I pointed out how clever the doctor had been, how lucky
the man was with his fine new shirt, and hinted that the
sahib who had shot him would undoubtedly be generous.
(I would make very sure of that.)

In the end the beaters were reassured and the shoot
went on. But what a disaster it would have been if it had
ended like that! What a disaster for the Sirdar's honour
and mine. It might well have prejudiced the Governor
against both of us, and it was all the fault of his own man.
But the Sirdar said that in his experience that kind of
excuse would not help with important people like
Governors.

It was decided that the wounded man should not rejoin
the line; in fact, he was asleep, and Jawa whispered to me
that perhaps he had overdone the laudanum for a man so
meagre as this.

So the shoot ended with success: a good bag—I don't
even know what a good bag would have been—one boar
seen but avoided, one hare given a scare but escaped.

The camp ended. Next evening Their Excellencies left
for Sibi, for a sort of State Visit to Balochistan, just for a
day. Abdur Rahman and I said good-bye at the station; all
the excitement of a Governor's departure provided a more
colourful entertainment for passengers looking out than
even our arrival from Dalhousie. Joan and Candy and the
boys came to look on, just for the fun of it.

It was a proper tamasha: police everywhere, Abdur
Rahman in full uniform, I in my white topi, Government
House *chaprassis* in scarlet turbans and belts, their

Excellencies and their staff in evening dress. The best tamasha Jacobabad had seen for a long time.

Today, it must seem almost unbelievable: there was war raging to east and to west, in most of India there was civil disobedience often relapsing into violence, with Governors ruling by decree under emergency regulations, while here in Sindh, near the supposedly disorderly tribal frontier, a Governor and his party could meet the people—if only selected ones—and watch games with crowds around them, with small measures of security, only our local police and a few in plain clothes. We had no apprehension of danger, and there was none.

It is not unbelievable: I was there. Wherever His Excellency went, I went. People may not have turned out to cheer him, but they turned out to cheer whatever show there was when he was present. He could finish his tour drinking coffee under the trees on the lawn. It happened, we thought it could never happen again, and it never did. Not while the British Raj lasted. Once the country was independent, it would be a different matter.

The Governor and all his people left, and the administration was put in gear again. There was still inspection work to do, and I made a short tour to Garhi Khairo. I met the Sirdar Sahib, and we talked of his shoot that had so nearly ended in disaster. I was, in effect, saying good-bye, depending on the Governor's hints. For my last tour of all we would camp to the east, along our own railway, but this time the whole family should go to the very end: we would camp for a night at Kashmore.

So we did, and on the way back the driver whacked her up again, but the boys very positively refused to ride in the cab. All went well until we were quite near home, then there was a crack, and our coach keeled over at a most alarming angle. We, the Havildar in the next compartment, and several clerks leant out and yelled at the driver, and further along people leant out and yelled: they thought we were enjoying the speed. But finally the strange angle of our coach was noticed, the driver's attention was attracted, and he stopped. He and his fireman came to look, and the fireman, unwillingly, urged on by the driver's pulling rank, crept underneath to have a better look. The bracket at one end of a bogie had snapped, and the bogie had jumped up through the floor. It had hit Mahbubali's bottom: it was lucky he was well covered, or he might have been castrated.

Then we could admire the ingenuity of the running crew. They fetched jacks and planks and baulks of timber; they strengthened the floor, they jammed wood blocks between the spring and the frame, and bound it all in with rope and wire. They declared that now all was well: at low speed we could reach home. But Mahbubali would not sit there any more.

For the last time we watched the free riders jump off; the pool would soon be too small for jumping, until the *abkalani* came round again. And we would not be there.

One investigation I must make before leaving Jacobabad: I would enter the old Record Room, see some of the ancient files, and particularly find the Record of the Scinde Horse, which I was told was there. I was warned officially not to go in: earthquake shock had made it very unsafe, and it was kept securely locked. None of the record was current, but that precious Record of the Scinde Horse would be lost if no one rescued it before the final collapse.

The Engineer would not go in. Indeed, I entered very gingerly myself, prepared to retreat at the slightest creak. But there were none. So I stood and looked at all the old records of the District, shelf upon shelf, many dog-eared, all carefully tied and tagged. Some of the tags were legible, some not. I found the Record near the door, and since all seemed safe I proposed to explore further. But then I noticed that, although the legs of the stacks all stood in little water pots, as government regulations required, the water had dried up long ago, the termites had crossed the barrier and had got at the wood. It was probable that the stacks, and not an earthquake, would finally be the reason for collapse. And if I were to pull out a file and so upset the balance, I might myself precipitate it. So I left it. With great care I took out the Record, nothing else. Most of the old files would be very old, files that ordinarily would have been 'weeded' long before, had anyone been willing to risk getting it out.

The Record of the Scinde Horse was a disappointment, not for its content, which told of the extraordinary feats of Jacob's cavalry in his own time, when he was settling the border, but because this was only a typed copy; the original was in the museum in Karachi. I read it through, and left it in the safe for my successor.

Soon after the Governor left, I had a letter from Dermont Barty advising me not to make any firm plans for the hot weather. This was followed by a confidential DO, very personal, from Charles Clee, with facetious remarks on how dangerous was my District. One man nearly killed by a tiger, another nearly murdered by gunfire, all in the same month. This needed no reply, nor did other unimportant chat. Then he said that the difficulty of my coming to Karachi was that there was nowhere for a family to live... He just left the remark hanging, but the hint was strong enough for me to write to Nazir Ahmed, and ask him to try to find somewhere. Lack of a home wouldn't stop us.

My transfer order came: Additional Director, Department of Food and Civil Supplies.

My successor would be Robin Keith, who had come to our first Horse Show, and who was unmarried, so the PWD could at last pull down the old Residency, and he could live in the Annexe; no more need for a *baben-jo-otak*.

We had a farewell party with the Municipality, now under Sitaldas, and, just as for the Governor, with the zamindars. The Shahi Jirga took tea with us, followed by a studio photograph. I still have that picture; I can still name most of those sirdars. There is, too, a photograph of all the senior Revenue officers, Ali Ahmed, Madadalishah, and the Mukhtiarkars, and all my office staff, Havildar and patewalas.

Doctors Jawa and Jessaram are in it too. Joan and Adam and David are, of course, included. Every time there were garlands, even small ones for the boys; garland after garland, we supposed the gardens of Quetta must have been stripped of sweet jasmine and marigolds. What were more lasting were addresses printed on silk, heaping on me praise that I hoped at least in some small part I deserved.

There was still no place for us in Karachi, but an empty house would soon be ready, and Nazir and Afroze would squeeze up for a few weeks and take us in. So again we packed up everything, put it into a van, the car onto a flat truck, and were ready to leave.

Robin Keith did not come, so I must leave my charge notes in the safe. There were my notes on staff—all good—and the secret codes, all locked away. The key must go to Clee.

Everyone came to the station to see us all off. We were leaving so many friends. Lalu was there, of course, and we hoped the boys would not realize that they were losing him, or there would have been floods of tears. And it was well that Robin Keith had not arrived, creating a problem of divided loyalties.

We boarded the train, loaded again with garlands. There were *salaams* and *namastes* and hands shaken all round. As usual, other passengers looked out, for the Stationmaster held the train a little for us. Then we were away. The dawn came up, but there would be no flag hoisted at the Residency till Robin arrived.

I feel a jolt to my heart even now as my thoughts move back to that time. I could have wept. I probably did; and though Joan was very happy to be going at last, she probably wept a little, too.

I was very low. I had spent most of my short service in Upper Sindh. I knew the people and appreciated them and their country. Of course the climate was tough, our living conditions in many ways primitive, but there was even a sort of pride in all that. For two years I had been Authority in my own District, and that was a heady diet for someone unusually junior to be tasting. Now I was surrendering it for a soft life, one among many with authority superior to mine. Perhaps, too, I was a little apprehensive about fitting into the sophisticated life of Karachi. For five years I had spent no more than a few days at a time, once or twice a year, in what one might call 'society'. I was regretting the kindness, the helpfulness and loyalty of friends and staff in Jacobabad, whom I might never see again.

25

KUTCHERY ROAD

The sadness of departure gave way to anticipation of arrival at a place that would remain cool when Jacobabad grew hot and then hotter, where Adam and David would find friends, and where Joan would at last be able to get a proper job, and meet friends she had known on and off for years. If Adam or David were ill, there was Hugo Reinitz, who knew all about them.

Already Joan had approached the Convent School. There was a new Mother Superior, and the objection made to her employment five years before was no longer valid: she already had children. Moreover, teachers as well educated and experienced as she was were as precious as jewels. Candy was happy, too: she could see her family and her boyfriend, if he were still interested.

We would live in a semi-detached house down a narrow walled lane off Kutchery Road. The whole place was enclosed by a wall: house, servants' quarters, garage, a fine paved yard, and a very small garden. Open a door in the wall, and there was a wide maidan, flat and bare, beyond it the hump sidings of the railway, and beyond again the salt marshes with the forts of Manora on the horizon.

Never had our home been ready for us to move in; this time we squeezed in with Nazir and Afroze—and however could we repay such kindness?—while the house was cleaned by Illahibaksh and Mistri and our furniture retrieved and supplemented by hiring. Then we moved in.

We would live in a house very much like an English suburban semi-detached villa, as far as could be from the grandeur of the Residency, but what luxury! For the first time we went upstairs, inside, to bed. The floors were tiled, upstairs and down, and there were ordinary casement windows. From our bedroom we could see right across to the sea beyond Manora. We had a bathroom with a real enamel bath, and hot water laid on; only from an electric heater, which heated very slowly, but hot! No need for a bheesti. There was a shower and, the greatest luxury of all, a flush toilet.

Cockroaches! We had never lived with cockroaches before, Upper Sindh was too hot for them. It was also too hot for fleas and bedbugs, and the little insects we called silver boys, whose larva was the 'woolly bear' that lived on animal fibre—wool, for choice.

A refrigerator we had, and a proper sink for washing up, and cupboards very convenient for china. But the kitchen was away across the yard, and still was equipped with chullas. There were no verandahs—the constant west wind would have blown straight in—but now there was somewhere for Joan to hang her curtains again, especially that prize-winning embroidery from the Horse Show.

There was a room for Candy, one for the boys, and their own bathroom with a little bath for them and their laundry. As for Candy, she would use the big bath, but she complained bitterly about this: she needed a shower, and the shower was only cold. It was very difficult washing in that big bath. Of course she must keep her knickers on, no matter that the one little window was high up, the glass obscure. No decent, modest Catholic girl should be altogether naked!

It was a very ordinary little house, wholly unromantic, but, after the glory of the Residency, how very convenient!

Joan was to take the top form at the Convent for London Matriculation (External) in Mathematics and English Literature. Mathematics was easy, but for English we must have Shakespeare. The *Times of India* offered the *Complete Works*, in two volumes, specially cheap, and we accepted. I was then told that I was expected to buy other books, but objected that there was no condition. After a bit, the *Times* gave up trying... Then the school added history to the syllabus: British history, with a little European, less Indian. I would have to refurbish my memories, not from university, but from school.

We settled in, and this new life could begin. I was no longer a magistrate, there were no petitioners coming to the door, no business visitors. No Havildar or naik to protect our privacy. People concerned with my work met me at the Office. Never again would a Sirdar come to the door, all smiles and welcome, just to give good wishes, tell me how the crops were coming along, or ask me to camp near him next time. At home, domesticity pure and simple. I had become a commuting Secretariat Officer, so despised before, and Joan had become a schoolteacher. Candy became an orthodox, over-worked, nursemaid.

Karachi was full of soldiers, all in transit for the Pacific war. (The German war was over just before we arrived, so we missed all the celebrations.) The Americans looked after themselves, they were well-paid, well-housed, and their PX stores provided them with everything imaginable they might want. Their beautiful uniforms, their money, and their novelty gave British Other Ranks no chance with the local girls. Indian units did not stay long, they went off quickly to their regimental bases. British officers were well-provided for, automatically accepted into local British society, but other ranks of the Army and the RAF had a miserable time. They were housed under canvas in any open space, and their messes were under canvas, too. They had no privacy, little to do with their free time, and very little money. Their uniforms were inevitably shabby, and since they were in small specialist units, there was no call for military pride. However people might sneer at the British memsahibs—and we were guilty of it ourselves—they could be relied on to deal with a situation like this. They opened a day-long canteen staffed by volunteers. They met the soldiers and talked with them, helped with letters, admired photographs of their families, and danced with them. Those young men were frustrated and homesick, and what may look like patronage was enormously valuable for morale, and simply, kindly meant.

Joan had her work and her family, but she helped, too. Particularly, she danced: she was a good dancer, and she loved it. (I was not a good dancer.) At the fixed dances she danced with any partner who asked, but she found David, who became her special partner, and she his. He was a simple lad, a signaller; he had no idea why he liked dancing, or why he was good at it. At home he played the trumpet in the Salvation Army. They danced a marvellous rumba.

There was another young man. He was no better a dancer than I, but he was bright, and vaguely leftish. He held the lowest rank in the RAF: Second Class Aircraftman, 2AC. Probably he could have risen, but all he wanted was to get out. Rafe Meredith, bitter at the way the war was wasting his time. There was a girl back in England whom he was training to be the perfect wife for himself; he claimed that she was highly intelligent, which we thought made her unlikely to play his Pygmalion game. (In the end they both married someone else.) So Rafe and I would just sit, arguing or watching Joan and David dancing, which was a great pleasure in itself, in silence.

In July, Adam and David had their third birthday. They were old enough to know that it was for some reason specially their day. I was determined that it should be celebrated with a special present. All through my extreme youth I had yearned, hopelessly, for a pedal motor car. Now I found not just one, but two, one blue, the other green. They were second-hand, and never had been elegant, but my two should not suffer the disappointment that I had felt. They had expressed no yearning, but never mind that.

In public one must always agree that one's offspring are highly intelligent, but we were always a little doubtful about Adam and David. With us and 'our people' they were bright enough, but with outsiders they were not talkative: they preferred to talk to each other in their secret and unintelligible language. They knew how a bicycle worked, they had seen Joan ride hers, but these cars had no bicycle pedals...would they ever understand these levers? I was too big to get in to demonstrate. So each was given his car; they got in and just sat. We went away while they puzzled.

The cars steered with a wheel, there was no brake, to stop one back-pedalled—only there were no pedals. After a while there was a crash, and shrieks of laughter: one had run into the other. They were careering about the yard, a menace to all us adults. It had taken them about three minutes, so they were by no means stupid.

It was a very simple test, but comforting. Their different characters showed, too: David would steer very carefully just where he wanted to go, whereas Adam, Candy's 'crackpot', just set off and went hell for leather wherever his fancy led. That was the most successful present I have ever given to anyone.

In the Pacific, the Americans were slowly occupying island after island, the Japanese defending fiercely, sometimes literally to the last man. Then news reached Karachi merchants of violent explosions on mainland Japan: of first one city and then another totally destroyed. They must be greatly exaggerated, but at least were very heavy blows.

Then, suddenly, it was all over. Rumours of whole cities being destroyed were true. Not till later did we all realize the enormity of those first nuclear explosions.

In Karachi, full of troops no longer needed for the war, transport planes flew home half empty, and a rumour spread that the RAF would be used to lift Dutch troops to the East Indies, to reoccupy the previously Dutch islands. There was near mutiny in the RAF at Drigh Road, and in the American Air Force at Mauripur. But Americans began to go home, and the rumours about transporting Dutch troops were denied and proved untrue.

Then the Indian Navy took a part. We had confidential news of trouble at Bombay, which might spread: above all, we must emphasize that ships had 'refused orders', it was not a mutiny. Moreover, the trouble was not political, it was due to bad management.

There was a frigate tied up in Karachi, for repair, and its crew mutinied 'in sympathy'. It was a ridiculous mutiny, but could be dangerous if any determined man took control. Word arrived in the Office that the ship was threatening to fire on the town. Since our building was in the middle of the commercial centre, and we supposed the mutineers would aim there rather than on houses, we sent all the staff home till events made matters clearer. I went to a house in the Cantonment which had three storeys, and where there was a man I wanted to see anyway. That ship really did fire on the town. We heard a bang, and were in time to see a cloud of smoke rise over Bunder Road. Three more bangs, and three puffs of smoke. Then it was all over. There came news that the whole of the dock area was surrounded by a battalion of the Black Watch, in Karachi on the way home.

Next morning the ship surrendered. It had remained tied up alongside the quay, and in the night troops had crept up and set up machine-gun posts. At first light they could see that even the gangways were still rigged. They had no choice but to surrender, 4-inch guns were useless against machine-guns, and the ship was boarded and 'captured'. Only the second time, I think, that a warship has been captured by boarding by the Army; the other time was in the French Revolutionary War, when French cavalry captured a Dutch ship by charging over the ice.

I went to Bombay to represent Sindh at a conference about supplies. We discussed many things, but chiefly I was concerned with selling rice and buying cloth, so with me went Gangaram, the Elgin Mills agent, and an agent from our Purchasing Board. We had a leisurely sea voyage and two days' work. We were not trying to barter, but just to see that there would be smooth arrangements for trade. We and Bombay knew just what we severally wanted; it was a very successful conference.

When I arrived home I found that Rafe had moved in with us, was sleeping in the spare room. His tent, he said, was a ruin, so he just went there in the day for his drills and duties. I went to the office all day and came home in the evening, like any commuter. We spent the evenings playing with the children, reading, or listening to music with our muffled fibre needles. I didn't really like having a lodger.

I must tour round Sindh to check our purchasing agents and inspect our storage depots. I suggested that Rafe might like to come with me, to have a free tour of the province. He would like to very much; he got leave without trouble— the problem for such units was to find occupation of any sort for the men.

Perhaps Rafe would have preferred to stay with Joan, possibly she would have preferred that too; on the other hand, more probably she feared lest he find some reason for not going. Only I was clear in my mind. Liberal ideas were all very well, and they worked, but there was no sense in over-straining them. If Rafe couldn't come I would change my tour till he could. We three got on well together, on the whole, but it was an odd period, full of tensions. We could talk and laugh about most things, but not about this girl that he claimed to be training to be his wife. He took Joan as his exemplar of an ideal wife. But even though he set her on a pedestal, still he was coming away with me.

We set off by train for Upper Sindh. At Larkana there was a 'Lahore Shed' to be examined. This was a huge arch,

could be built to any length, could be entered at either
end, or both, and must be rat-proof. No need to bother
with insect pests in Upper Sindh. The arches were
constructed on geodetic principles, which made possible
the use of very short wood units, so very cheap. It was
roofed with wire netting overlaid with *bardana* and then a
thin coat of cement. It was just what we needed for rice
storage, and in fact several were built.

I could have taken Rafe to Jacobabad, but I had too
recently left, it might have been hard for me, and
embarrassing for Robin Keith, so we didn't go, but went
straight on to Sukkur, to talk about wagons for rice, and
how much storage was necessary. Mr Birkett was still
Stationmaster, and invited us to the Institute. Rafe, of
course, made fruitless passes at Norma Birkett. But the
beautiful dark Snowdrop had gone with her family on
transfer. Kate, the pretty telephone girl of years before, was
there, but married now, and careworn, with a jealous
husband careful to keep her away from these dangerous
young men.

One more day, and we took the ferry to Sadh Bela. Rafe
was enraptured by all the many gods and little shrines, the
brilliant decorations, however tawdry, and the strange way
that Hindu pilgrims, clearly come for spiritual help and
comfort, were noisy, spat betel juice, and dropped paper
wrappings everywhere. There were also noisome corners
obviously used as urinals. But Rafe saw the glamour, loved
the intricate carving, and the little bells and cymbals tinkling
for no clear reason, liked the people, whole families
searching for their particular god or goddess, with hordes of
little children running round between peoples' legs.

We took the train for the east bank of the river. We
crossed the great bridge at walking pace, lest it fall down,
and changed at Rohri. The little *khus-khus* hut was not
there, not in the cold weather.

I had one more place to stop: Nawabshah, where we had
a wheat store. I didn't know the place; indeed, I am

extraordinarily ignorant of that side of Sindh, which is its most modern part, at that time newly won from the desert by the Barrage, and very recently torn by the Hur Rebellion. Mile on mile of wheat and cotton, rectilinear fields, interlaced with the new tree-lined canals and distributors of the Barrage. Had I ever been posted there, I would doubtless have found it a satisfying area, as I did Upper Sindh Frontier, but that was now too late.

Our wheat store at Nawabshah was a very simple structure. On a large scale, its principle was the same as that of the big clay jars used throughout Sindh for families to store their grain. The grain was tipped in at the top, and came out through a little hatch at the bottom. The Government store was a long range of 'silos', each holding about ten tons. It was on a solid mud-brick base; the wheat came in bags, was tipped in by a hatch in the top, and came out through a little hatch at the bottom, high enough on its base for a sack to be filled there.

There was in Sindh a wandering tribe, the Ods, whether Hindu or Muslim I know not; they may even have been animists—they certainly lived close to nature. They were builders, and their speciality was the equivalent in mud of shuttered concrete. To build, all they needed was a good, clean space where they could make their mud, and some straw to chop into it. They must know the height of the wall to be built, so that they could calculate by their secret formula how thick the base must be. They moulded their mud into a continuous strip, about nine inches deep, all round the base, and when that strip was hard enough they moulded another on top. And so on. When the wall was finished, they would wet the outer surfaces and smear over all the joints and cracks. This was said to last as long as sun-dried bricks. At Nawabshah we would test the theory, for one of our stores was built by Ods, the other with sun-dried bricks, *kutcha* bricks.

The grain was very secure, so long as the bottom hatch was strongly locked, but the loading was tedious. Each bank of silos was about eighty yards long, with twenty silos. There was a stair at each end, so a man must heave a two-maund—84lb—sack onto his back, climb the stair, and carry it along to the hatch: upto 40 yards from each end to cover the twenty silos, 35 trips for each silo. Maybe the coolies valued the work, but it would kill them early. I would propose that we buy, or get made by any decent mistri, an elevator, mobile but hand-operated, that could move along the bank, take bags straight from the cart, and deliver them straight to the hatchway. Indeed, I would be happy to design one myself, from memories of English stackyards.

We returned to Karachi, I to report to the Department all my ideas, collected from our agents, from examining the storage depots, and with my proposal for an elevator, Rafe to report to Joan all the marvels he had seen—marvels to him, to me familiar sights, but seen to a greater depth from having to explain them to someone endlessly inquisitive.

News of posting awaited Rafe: he was to go to Ceylon. Ceylon is a beautiful place, much to be preferred to anywhere in Sindh, but he didn't just then want to go. Go he must, but he would write to us, and we to him when we had an address. From Ceylon he was sent to Shaiba, a staging post for the RAF in the middle of the Arabian Desert. Then he went home and was demobbed, as in the end all the soldiers were! He did various things, and married, but not to that ideal wife. They went to Canada, and he became Surveyor to a small town near Toronto, and once even came over and stayed with us.

We valued Rafe. There were not many in the armed services who impressed us (but we did not meet so very many). There were Peter Thorne and Denis Arber, both colonels, and Rafe Meredith, Aircraftman 2nd Class. No others. Of the three, Rafe was the most notable.

When I came in from tour, the important news for us was that the Key Leave Scheme was approved, and that we would be going home in the spring.

The Key Leave Scheme deserves comment. At the beginning of the war all leave had been stopped, and as a result there were ICS officers who now had credits of upto two years—some should have retired, but were kept on— and even juniors such as I were entitled to a year. There were seniors who would have been happy to take their whole due, leaving juniors to fume with indignation. But the maintenance of efficient administration must first be considered: at this critical stage in the negotiations for independence, the Service must be kept up to strength. So the Key Leave Scheme was worked out. Leave was rationed; extra was allowed to anyone willing to take it in the winter, but generally, no officer would have more than six months at once; a certain advantage was allowed to families. So we felt pleased with our allocation.

I was in bed with a chill—perhaps one of those benign bouts of malaria—as I listened to the news of the first post- war British election, the astonishing news that Labour was winning—had won—had won with a landslide! Churchill, the great war leader, had been rejected.

To India, this meant that Independence was not far off. A little later, Churchill proposed that India be held by force, but this was dismissed as pure rhetoric: India had a promise. If it wanted to stay in the Empire, it was welcome, but there could be no use of force. Moreover, the Army that had just won a war would probably mutiny if turned on India. And what of the great Indian Army? Staying by force was nonsense. All the new Prime Minister, Attlee, wanted, was to settle India's problems quickly. Lord Wavell was still Viceroy, still trying to get Muslims and Hindus to agree on a formula set by Churchill, possibly deliberately unworkable. He was making very little progress.

Peace was breaking out everywhere. In my Department, it was likely that emergency powers would soon lapse, and then it would be a matter of persuading ministers of our value. More generally, the Indian Civil Service must consider its position. It was an Imperial Service, covenanted

to the Crown. (So also was the Indian Police.) An
independent India might not want us. Perhaps a few agreed
with Churchill, but most recognized that independence
must come, and many juniors like me would welcome it.

Soon after the war ended, the Governor invited all the
Sindh ICS for a weekend. (The spacious days when there
would be a whole week were long past.) We held a meeting
of our Provincial Association to consider our future, as a
Service and individually. We were told that our Service
might be ended abruptly, or some of us might be allowed,
or even welcomed, to stay on. We must take particular care
for our Indian members, who might be considered traitors,
having served the Imperial power: measures must be taken
to prevent victimization. Pension and provident funds must
be made absolutely safe, if necessary being funded by the
British Government.

The capital funding of the Family Pension Fund was
massive! It was a beautifully crafted scheme. There was of
course a lifelong pension for a widow; payments for
fatherless sons to the age of twenty-one, to cover a university
education; a fatherless daughter would receive a sum on
her marriage, and a pension for life if she did not marry. It
was a contributory scheme, the contributions fixed to suit
an officer's salary. The thought of a handsome capital sum
if the fund were wound up was seductive, but the actuaries
pointed out problems, which made everyone change their
minds. They quoted cases still current under the East India
Company scheme that had been wound up in 1858: two
officers married in old age, each had a daughter, neither
of whom had married, and they were both still receiving
pensions ninety years later. So ours must remain a pension
fund. I explained it all to Joan, who took little persuasion
to prefer the pension. Should we have a daughter, and she
live unmarried, she would be drawing her pension well
into the next century. (Come to that, Joan might herself be
drawing a widow's pension then; but we let that possibility
lie.)

There is a group photograph of the Sindh ICS taken at this time. We are there with Adam and David; Nazir and Afroze with their Aftab, the Bartys with Jennifer; Peter Cargill is alone, without Margaret or their Simon. They were separating.

This time, the end of the war, was hard on marriage. The Cargills were perhaps too clever, too determined and selfish, each too attractive to others, to survive. But they were among our best friends, and I determined that this separation must be stopped. I would try to sort them out, to stop this nonsense; but in fact that kind of tactic towards such characters was not really possible. It was Margaret who most concerned me: we were always good friends, we tolerated each other's foibles, I was very fond of her, and her beauty disarmed me entirely. In Peter, I had to tolerate his arrogance, and, indeed, was also jealous of his self-confidence. Margaret was living in a flat next door to us, and I went to see her, to reason with her, perhaps to rant at her, to plead with her not to leave Peter. But he was already there, and as I waited to go in I heard Margaret say to him: 'For heaven's sake don't quarrel, or we shall upset Roger!' She would protect me—I might be upset! It was clear that I could do nothing, I was silly ever to have thought I could.

I *was* upset, and for a long time. Margaret went away, and Peter would tell me nothing. Perhaps Margaret still lives, still beautiful in old age. Perhaps she will even read this and remember.

We often met Nazir and Afroze, for we were all in Karachi at once. Several times they invited us to the Karachi Club, with Bashir and Bilqis, and once Afroze danced with me. Nazir was dancing with Joan, so it was only fair. We danced a foxtrot, but Afroze made it very clear that there must be no hugging. Arms length was best, arms bent was permissible, but nothing closer than that. I loved Afroze too much to risk her indignation, particularly with onlookers who would love to gossip. Standing up with me was brazen enough. Once or twice they went with us to the Gymkhana, but they didn't really like it. They might be adaptable and liberal, but tipsy officers displeased them. They displeased us, too.

We met the Reinitzs and their friends. We sailed in the harbour with anyone who wanted a crew. Joan taught and I went to the Office. Otherwise, we were happy just to watch Adam and David grow.

26

THE DEPARTMENT

In the Districts, Collectors—and the Deputy Commissioner—learnt a lot about the Food and Civil Supplies Department, for we met it at its sharp end. We provided estimates and forecasts of crops, we reported on quality and arranged transport, and we helped the local agents of the Purchasing Board. Now I was working at the other end.

First I had to learn a plethora of acronyms. There was my own, which introduced me to all the others: SPB, the Sindh Purchasing Board, which bought the whole available rice crop for export on Government account. Then the KIMA, the Karachi Indian Merchants' Association, a powerful body which disciplined its own members and represented them with Government; my direct concern was with its laboratory, where samples of grain were analysed for quality assessment, and whose integrity was never questioned. There was KSIAM, the four big flourmills, Karachi, Sindh, India, Asia Mills. (I did once ask what would be its name if a fifth were built. The logical answer I received was that there wasn't a fifth, so why bother?) Later came the KRCRA, the Karachi Ration Cloth Retailers' Association, and a somewhat vague RSA, Ration Shop Association.

For transport there was the KPT, Karachi Port Trust, and NWR, the railway, with which my contact was the DCO, the Divisional Commercial Officer, who happened to be Bashir Malik, a great friend of both Nazir Ahmed and me.

I was constantly concerned with these bodies. In retrospect, it has struck me how little we of the Sindh Government had to do with European commerce in Karachi. Undoubtedly there was an association of European, even British businesses, but I know—I knew—nothing of them. There were the big firms of managing agents: MacKinnon MacKenzie (owners of our beloved Kashmore Railway), Matheson Lang, Volkearts, which was Swiss, and exported the raw cotton, and a Greek company, Ralli, which specialized in shipping. I had occasional dealings with one or another, chiefly concerning transport, but their main concern was with raw cotton and, although that was Sindh's greatest export, we took no interest in it at all: we were responsible for supplies to the civilian population.

There were two other acronyms that were important in setting buying and selling prices: they always had been since rail and modern transport arrived, and still are: 'cif'—cost, insurance, freight—and 'fob'—free on board.

The only thing we bought in bulk, apart from foodgrains, was *bardana*, sacks for the grain. They were bought from Calcutta, fob, made from jute grown in Bengal; or the jute cloth would be imported in huge rolls to be made up in Karachi. The sacks were not of very good quality, they would not do for flour. Sometimes we bought second-hand, but only for very low-grade grain. Anyway, when the sacks reached the village shops there was far better use made of them.

In all this trading and control there was one man who encompassed all areas of commerce: Jamshed Nusserwanji Mehta. He was quite old, unusually tall, an extraordinarily energetic and knowledgeable Parsi. He was a member of almost every commercial body in Karachi, even the European ones. He was dressed always in white, with a Gandhi hat, and his complexion was so white that it appeared to be dusted with flour, which, he said, was appropriate because his chief interest was with the flour mills. He was forever rushing into the office of one or other of us with exciting news, urgent proposals, or warnings of disaster. But he was always welcome: he was so cheerful, so knowledgeable, and never once did he seek any advantage for himself personally. He really was sincere, truly honest. Often he might have mocked our ignorance of his trade, but so long as he considered that we were working in the public interest he overlooked that, and was unfailingly helpful.

The Food and Civil Supplies Department was quite unlike the traditional departments of Government, Home, Revenue, Public Works, and Agriculture. We were seldom even concerned with them, only with the Finance Department: we were commercial, we made money, far more than we cost the Treasury. As a result, we were not so strictly controlled. We were heavily staffed, too, with three Indian Civil Service officers, one from each community, Hindu, Muslim, and English: B.R. Patel, Director, and Nazir Ahmed and I, Additional Directors. (There were many Patels in the ICS, at all levels, throughout the Government of India and the Provinces.) Our office was not in the Secretariat, but in a rented building in the heart of commercial Karachi, near the Merewether Clock Tower. The ground floor held private offices and shops, and the stairs were stained with betel juice in a way that would never have been tolerated in a 'proper' government building. Our patewalas wore no badges, were only distinguished from ordinary visitors because we insisted that they keep their clothes clean and neat.

There was little old or established regulation to control us: only wartime rules. We could control prices and distribution, we could buy and sell anything that could be defined as civil supplies. We were responsible for the enforcement of price control on second-hand cars, and when I gave my own opinion of its merit I was quickly told that it had been forced on the Department, which did nothing about it unless there were specific complaints; a great relief.

I arrived soon after the death of Jerry Bolton, who had set up the whole method of operation of the Department, and who was a great loss. The new Finance Secretary was David Halford, whom I knew, but he was too much of a traditionalist for our sort of operation.

A noticeable and notable feature of this government involvement in trade was the complete honesty among themselves of the traders with whom we dealt. If Government—personified in us three Directors—were stupid or ignorant we were fair game, though very quickly we would hear of the game and could put a stop to it.

My new post was entirely different from any I had held before, and involved a complete change in my perception of the characteristics of the two chief religious and ethnic communities. In Upper Sindh the Muslims were vastly in the majority, and we accepted that they were on the whole straightforward and honest, the more trustworthy the further down they were in the social scale. They were generally illiterate, they valued education very lowly, and they were not smart enough even to be successful criminals. From this generalization there were, of course, numerous exceptions, from leaders of criminal gangs to university professors, Quranic teachers, Members of the Assembly, and Ministers of State.

Hindus likewise could be categorized, again with numerous exceptions, as mean, tricky, and most generally as moneylenders who squeezed their poor creditors to the limit.

Contemplating now the injustice inherent in those views, I conclude that at any time my assessment of an individual was apt to be coloured by the temperature outside.

In my job in Karachi, I was concerned almost entirely with the commercial population. There was a large European population with which my Department had few dealings, several Parsis, and a few Muslims, some from outside Sindh, from parts of India where Muslims were in a minority and traditionally in trade. But the great majority were Hindus, and my opinions changed abruptly and drastically. These Karachi businessmen were knowledgeable, skilful, and honest (according to accepted commercial lights). Among themselves they had to be reliable, and had discovered long ago that it paid to be so with government officials who had entered by force, as it were, into the heart of their trading. We three at the head of the F&CS Department began ignorant and had to learn very quickly, and we did, by watching, by inquiring, and by setting up systems that would expose sharp practice. That sort of ability was, after all, an element in the mystique of our Service; another was that we must be, and must be seen to be, always, without fail, honest.

Much of my time for some months was spent learning 'the trade'. Sindh produced a very large amount of rice, consumed very little: it was a wheat-eating population. The Purchasing Board bought the whole of the vast surplus for export, so I must know how quantities and qualities were assessed. As consignments arrived in Karachi, I would check a percentage for their weight, to compare it with the weight on the purchase note, and for this I had to learn the method used. The rice was always in bags—therefore our large demand for *bardana*—and from each consignment bags were chosen at random, on one side a slack one, though not so slack as to be obviously leaking, and on the other a plump one, though not one so fat as to be obviously overfilled. Both were weighed, and the average of the two was accepted as the bag weight of the whole consignment. I was glad that we had no means to store or transport grain in bulk! The assessment of quality was more difficult, and most of the work of the KIMA laboratory concerned this: not just for rice, but for wheat, millets, pulses, and more complicated things like cotton and sugar. But at first for me it was only rice. A sample was taken from sacks chosen at random, its size depending on the size of the consignment. The sample was weighed, halved, perhaps quartered, and one part would be divided among several assessors.

Some of the merchants who had enlightened ambitions for their daughters would pay for their training as doctors or nurses or teachers; most were happy that they should prepare themselves for marriage. But some girls wanted something between, and KIMA provided the means in its laboratory. These girls were the assessors; there were a few boys, but I was told that the girls were much better.

I was taken to see. There was a long bench under windows facing north, each girl sitting with her own space and light. They were all busy with their analysis: one might sense our presence, look round and smile, or frown, and turn back; another would straighten her back, close her eyes and flex her fingers; sometimes there would be a short chat, even a laugh. There was a supervisor, but she was not there to drive them on—the girls were, after all, daughters of her employer—rather was she looking for the girl who was perhaps unwell, and needed to be taken from her bench to rest.

The laboratory was a merciful rest from the raucous noises of the street outside. There was only the tiny click of the rice grains as they were pushed about, and the rustle and the quiet words of the girls themselves.

Each sample was analysed, grain by grain, each pushed to its proper heap: whole grains, halves, quarters, three-quarters, even eighths. Beyond that there was 'dust' and any rubbish, very carefully collected. These last were as important to the sample as any other. All the samples would then be collected, each size of grain would be weighed separately, the rubbish and the dust too, the proportions in the whole sample calculated, and on this was decided the quality of the whole consignment.

I never heard of any analysis being questioned; there was a system for arbitration, but this was for price disputes. No one ever questioned the integrity or expertise of these girls.

There were two varieties of rice grown in Sindh: sugdasi, white rice that the better-off ate, and kangni, red rice, which cropped more heavily, the rice of the poor. It grew mostly in Lower Sindh, it was the kind I had seen when I had the Thatta subdivision. Sindh did not grow the best of all varieties, basmati, which came from United Provinces and was the rice of the rich (and, I believe, the one Mistri bought for us). I had asked at Dokri why Sindh did not grow basmati; they did not know. In fact, it had been tested before, and proved a failure, and our researchers had lost the record. However, they might try again.

Assessing the quality of wheat was much simpler. Sindh grew a bearded variety, for me difficult to differentiate from barley in the field. It went through no process like the paddy husking; samples were judged by eye, even the rubbish was not eliminated. But Government only bought a stock judged adequate to discourage hoarding and so maintain a reasonable controlled price.

The big Karachi mills had experts who could value by eye. For Government that was not enough: we had to check the sight estimate by analysis. The rubbish was weighed, the whole, plump grain, the broken ones, and the shrivelled. Weights and proportions were calculated and a price agreed. But we did not buy wheat for export, only for our buffer stocks. Wheat had to be moved to areas such as the west bank of the River in Upper Sindh, where it was ground in *chakkis: chakki aata* was considered the best flour of all: wholemeal, stone-ground (the *chakkis* were just like the water-powered ones we had seen in Balochistan, but engine-powered). Even in Karachi, with its great mills, there were *chakkis* making flour for the discriminating.

In Karachi there was a large demand for bran and 'middlings', which was the fine dust extracted from wheat with the bran. There was little demand for white flour, the inevitable result of taking away the bran and middlings. It was used by Europeans, and some was needed in Bombay, but there was a large surplus which must be sold somewhere. The Persian Gulf would take it all, at almost any price, but we dared not send it without approval from

Delhi, and the Government of India took a lot of persuading before it agreed that it could go.

'BR' and Nazir Ahmed decided that I must deal with the matter, since my father was a flour miller, which was fair enough. So I went to consult with one of the mills. It was a magnificent place, equipped with the most modern roller mills, and about ten times the size of my father's. I knew a little of the 'extraction rates', and learnt more. For wholemeal flour the extraction rate was nil: the highest extraction rate to produce passable white flour was 60 per cent. The bran and middlings were needed for the vast number of horses and milch cattle in Karachi, but their value was low; profitable sales for the white flour were essential, and at this time Central and provincial Government regulations prevented the mills selling it themselves. So I had to work out extraction rates with the four mills, basing the decision on demand and on prices of the different products of the wheat. It was all so different from my father's problem: his market was for white flour, and there were no horses. But he wrote and told me that he had the same problems with extraction rates.

The Government of India approved our proposal to sell to the Gulf States; the question was, who should have licences? I proposed the making of a simple choice: each exporter with a record of the trade should have a licence in proportion to the size of his trade pre-war. KIMA was, of course, involved in discussions, and pointed out that that would give valuable licences to people who might now not be trading at all, and would on the other hand exclude newcomers.

The easy way would be for the flour to be bought by the Government from the mills, and sent on Government account, which would be very profitable indeed. But we felt that we should not attract attention to another such deal after the trouble with the Bengal famine, so we should issue licences on payment of a fee. In effect, we would auction them. This charge would do no harm to Sindh or

India, nor would it raise the price of flour in the Gulf States: it would be paid from the profit margin. There must be some limit on the profitability of the trade, or the temptation of the mills to use a high extraction rate would become irresistible. The danger was that a licence would be so valuable that corruption might creep in to our own administration.

I worked out details with KIMA, but when it came to the actual grant of licences, there was scope for judgement, and for impropriety, (shall I say.) As I expected might happen, I received an offer of Rs 5,000 (about £375) that I might give to the charity of my choice, for grant of a licence for a greater amount than the merchant would normally expect. I asked him to choose the charity, he left it to me: I told him, the Pinjrapore Association, and that it should be in his own charitable name: I ensured that he did so. He received no licence at all for that period. He had in fact been nominated by his friends to try me, but had not expected the outcome, good for his public image, disastrous for his business. I was never 'tried' again. The merchants were told what quantity of flour was available for export, what was the licence fee, and were left to share out the licences themselves. Jamshed Mehta learned the story, from the millers' side, and was hugely amused. I, who took my work and my professional integrity rather priggishly seriously, was not.

I must explain the Pinjrapore Association. It was an Association for the Protection of Ancient Cows—so it was described to me by one of the devout Hindus who ran it. They could not bear the way that old cows, past milking, past breeding, but which for religious reasons must not be killed, were just left to die miserably. (Young bulls were sold outside Karachi to people who had no qualms about castrating them and using them for draught). The Association owned a large area of scrub land outside Karachi, and there the old cows were taken; there were a few men to look after them, they grazed where they could, and when there was no grazing, some grain offals would be taken in to them. They finally died peacefully and were cremated, as was proper. The odd thing was that the Association was renowned for the quality of its milk. In other words, a little peace and food and kind treatment was rewarded by their return to their previous life of milk production.

By the time I joined the F&CS Department, its most exciting and productive period was over, and its creator, Jerry Bolton, was dead. From BR Patel and Nazir Ahmed I had the full story of the Bengal Famine of 1943-4. This part of its history does not seem to appear in the books. There was not, in fact, any great shortage of rice, but the Bengal administrative system, based on its Permanent Settlement, did not have the same requirement that its officers tour and learn about their Districts as did the Governments of Bombay and Sindh. There was no power to prevent hoarding or control prices, and we understood that it was price, not actual shortage, that was causing starvation.

The Sindh Government turned to the rice trade initially to secure the quick movement of stocks of grain. The Sindh Purchasing Board set a generous price, took delivery, and shipped it to Calcutta, selling at a price fob; that is, the Government made no profit, though it did set the price at such a level that it would not lose.

In Calcutta, the merchants who bought it at once set their price as high as they thought their market would stand, making enormous profits and doing the starving poor very little good.

Sindh protested, but the Bengal Government regretted that it had no machinery to control prices or set up food shops or ration supply. To Bolton the answer was obvious and simple: Sindh should charge a price which, considering insurance and freight costs and the final retail price, would leave the Bengal merchants a reasonable profit. Sindh made an enormous profit, so great it was even—perhaps specially—kept secret from ministers.

Calcutta complained to Delhi, and Delhi told Sindh to stop profiteering. Sindh pointed out that it was sending rice as fast as it could, that its price was not raising prices in Bengal, and that if it sold at cost price this would not benefit the final consumer. Calcutta was told that it must open control shops, and as soon as it did so we cut our price to the bone. The control shops, provisioned initially from Sindh, broke the hoarding market and the famine was soon over.

I would not claim that Sindh broke the famine by itself, but it certainly played an important part. Moreover, the knowledge that there were always state-owned stocks in Sindh discouraged any future attempts at price rigging.

Sindh had its reward: the Barrage debt was paid off ten years early, and there was still a substantial capital sum set aside for post-war development.

Though the famine was over, the government-financed grain trade went on. The rice came to Karachi, was assessed for quality, and stacked in the railway goodsyard. It stood in great rectangular, pyramidal stacks, raised a little from the ground on dunnage. The stacks were secure from theft, for the railway kept a close watch: not so much against theft as against fire. The chief commodity stored was cotton, thousands of bales from Sindh and the Punjab awaiting shipment to Bombay.

In Bombay there was an active 'futures' market; gambling there could make a man a 'paper millionaire' in a day, for the trading was all done on margin. If there was a big fall in prices on the Bombay cotton exchange, the railway police in Karachi doubled their security: it was much better to claim insurance on stocks destroyed by fire than to deliver at a price below that of its purchase. Our rice was very safe.

Cotton, for security, was held in godowns, so our rice must stand out of doors. There was little danger of rain, and the quantities were so large that we did not insure. But pests were another matter. I don't think Warfarin had yet appeared, or rats would have been no problem: as with fleas and bedbugs, weevils could not stand the heat of Upper Sindh, and rice from there was free of pests. But if the rice was from Lower Sindh, or had to be stored for some time, they were sure to move in.

Gobindram, the expert I had met in Shahdadkot, set to work to find a control. He discarded several as being too dangerous, killing the pests, but also the rats that ate the doctored rice. I kept reminding him that a total kill was of less importance than the safety of the human consumer. We had plenty of cats to deal with the rats.

In the end he came up with one which he assured me he had tried on rats and mice, with no ill effect. (The delicate little mouse is tougher than the big fierce rat!) It was benzene hexachloride at a very high dilution; it killed the larvae and very young weevils, and the adults did not live long anyway. We tried it, sprayed onto the surface of a stack, and the larvae and hatchlings visibly died. We never heard that any people did.

Many years later I used the stuff, by then called Gammexane, to control weevils on apples. It was labelled with a skull and crossbones, I had to use protective clothing, and must not apply it within six weeks of selling, nor during blossoming when bees were about. I didn't die either. I used it at much higher concentrations than we used for rice, but even so, perhaps we were just lucky.

On one occasion there was rain. It was not heavy—it only wetted the exposed sacks, and all the bottom tier of each stack—but taken overall, the dampness resulted in a net gain in weight, which was retained until the stock was sold. And we had saved the insurance premium. Nevertheless, we decided that we could not risk a heavy downfall, so we bought a stock of big tarpaulins, and arranged to borrow Port Trust staff to cover the stacks when rain threatened. We dared not leave the stacks covered all the time or they would have heated.

There was an acute petrol shortage, which for a time put the little trams off the streets, but then a gas alternative was provided by generators towed behind on little carts. It was tried for taxis, but that was too dangerous, so there were not many taxis running.

Fuel was very short, but charcoal was needed in Karachi for cooking, and coal for the power station, the railways, the big Dalmia cement works on the edge of the hills, and some small industries. They all produced vast quantities of dust, which could surely be made into briquettes. The only machine to appear made them one at a time, but the women of Lyari, used to making dung cakes, were happy to make them of coal dust. It may sound male chauvinistic to give a woman this dirty job, but the women of Lyari saw no problem, and were certainly thankful for the extra money they made. I could even get the dust delivered free to them—power station and cement works were glad to get rid of it.

My Minister, Mir Mahomed Khan Talpur, was a pleasant, gentlemanly person. He was well educated in the Islamic fashion, but was sadly ignorant of commercial affairs. He had very large lands, but could not understand my objections to share-cropping with his haris. It had always been like that, how could it be bad? He was really quite unsuitable for his particular Ministry, though he was extremely proud of all the powers he had, and of the state trading enterprise that he did not understand, except that it was highly profitable. He was wealthy enough not to be tempted to share in that profit, but was always happy to exercise his powers under the slowly-dying emergency regulations. He did not quite understand that now that there was no war, no enemy, trade with foreign countries was bound to be much freer, and that imports and exports were now governed by exchange rates and the balance of payments, not just of Sindh, but of all India.

He had friends in India, and already some were moving to areas that would be Pakistan, if Pakistan ever came about.

He sent one of these to me one day with an order: I should issue an instruction that all imports of tobacco, in bulk or manufactured, must pass through this friend's company. I knew nothing about the tobacco trade, so I asked the friend about it: he told me it would be enough if a notice were served on the British and American Tobacco Company, with orders to Customs and Excise, and that the Order be gazetted.

This was a case where great diplomatic care was needed. I did not want to call my Minister a fool, nor to issue improper orders that would make him and the Sindh Government and above all me, look foolish. I needed more to change my Minister's mind than just my opinion that his powers did not in these days extend so far. I stalled, told the friend that he must wait while I prepared the order and had it verified with the Mir Sahib. I drafted an order and sent a copy, strictly confidentially, to the Manager of British and American Tobacco, asking him for comments, said I would be pleased to see him at any convenient time.

His office was in a sumptuous modern block, and I am sure his own rooms were equally sumptuous. But my letter brought him roaring round, up our squalid stairs, and into my mean room, full of files and grain samples, with but two chairs besides mine, one for a visitor and one for a clerk. He blew off at once, and for a time, while his indignation raged, there was no possibility of discussing anything. He cooled down, and I called for my secretary Kimi to come in and take notes. That was a big mistake. I was showing him that even if I was but a poodle of a native (yes, native) Minister, I had a more efficient and certainly prettier secretary than he had. (Kimi was Japanese, a pre-war refugee. She could type faster than any of our young men, she knew shorthand, she could type straight from dictation. I had the job of selecting staff, and naturally I took her as my secretary. She had a sister, nearly as good, not so pretty: she would do for Nazir.)

He became reasonable. He pointed out that even if my Order were to be effective for a time, the only result would be that all tobacco imports through Karachi would stop. They would be diverted to Bombay and would come in by rail, and that we couldn't stop. And anyway, the proposed order was invalid, and if I acted on it, it might ruin him, but it would make my Government extremely unpopular.

I could not but agree with all he said. I asked him to write it down and let me have it at once. Kimi had a shorthand note of our discussion, and he should have a copy of that.

The manager's letter came on the same day. And everything remained secret. I didn't want anyone to know of the matter, except Nazir and BR, but to get it settled before leaks occurred. So I saw the Mir Sahib next day. I told him of my discussion, gave him the note of it and the Manager's letter. His powers might be questioned, and anyway tobacco would soon arrive from Bombay. There would be dealers ruined in Karachi, we would be very unpopular with a lot of people who smoked, because prices would probably be raised, and it wouldn't do his friend any good in the end. It was a pity, it would have been satisfactory to have controlled tobacco that way—the Mir Sahib, I knew, did not smoke—but it did seem better for his friend to look elsewhere, and if he had any ideas I would try to help him. The Mir Sahib decided to tell his friend that, because the foreign company would not co-operate, he considered it better to drop the idea. I assured him that he was being very wise.

I was learning. When dealing with a Minister, diplomacy was necessary and could be very rewarding. He must be persuaded that what I wanted to do was in fact his idea; and if I disagreed with something that he wanted to do— and with the Mir Sahib that was almost anything—I must persuade him that it was his own cleverness that spotted the flaws in it.

But this was a time for thinking about leave rather than fencing with a minister. The Department was getting on very well so long as I spent a reasonable time there. No longer was work so urgent that I would stay there for lunch. Round the corner was a 'hotel' that produced wonderful curries with beautiful nan bread that could be collected for me to eat at my desk. Curry smells were nothing unusual in that building! I sometimes regretted that light work gave me time to drive home and miss my peaceful curry picnic in the Office.

Then, as work grew less, my leave was gazetted: I would not be replaced and, when I returned, BR Patel would go to Bombay and Nazir Ahmed and I would be Joint in the Department.

This was fine for me: for the family, they would not come back. Joan would lose many friends, above all the Reinitzs, but they promised to go and stay with her. The boys didn't truly realize what it meant. They were excited by the promise of going on a big ship, but could not encompass the thought of never seeing Candy again. Joan was happy to be leaving India, and anyway there was the boys' education...I would not stay on for long, independence was surely not far off, and we could now look forward to a year or two apart with equanimity, whereas six years before even one year was unimaginable.

Sindh was so much a part of our lives, indeed, was the whole of our married life, that we hardly believed that it was really ending. I would return, and Illahibaksh and Mistri would still be there, but Candy would be someone else's nurse. Life even for me would be quite different. Of course we would all write to each other, friends would go and stay with Joan; but we didn't really believe it. At the Office a group photograph was taken of my going, as if even I was not coming back.

We selected all that we must take, and the rest went into the Commissioner's godown. All the farewell calls were made, to the Governor, the Commissioner, my Minister, and all our friends; the *Burma* docked, and we went aboard. The *Burma* was a little ship, too small to have been used as a trooper. For others it was austere, but to us, recently from the wilds of Sindh, it was luxurious: there were eggs and bacon, kippers, and real butter! We travelled 'posh', we lounged and talked and helped the boys to play with plasticine. We dined sometimes at the Captain's table. It was a very long voyage, dodging about in the Mediterranean to avoid the minefields, but if one looked on it as a cruise, what could have been better? This deserved one of those white stones.

Southampton was badly battered, disembarkation a riot. The boys were endlessly astonished: by white 'coolies' at the docks, by grass growing up hillsides, so very green, by the enormous red buses in London, and all the strangers who were Joan's and my dear families. They were all so loving; but where was Candy?

From Joan's family in London we went to mine at Shelford, more relatives, even a cousin. But there were only four months for us to find somewhere to live and settle ourselves in. Joan would have to learn about rationing, how to run a house all by herself, and we had to find a school for the boys.

We bought an old car, we even bought a little house near Cambridge, and furnished it after a fashion. Joan became pregnant. The Holts were in England, and Jane would stay with Joan, be there for her baby. But then Jane changed her mind: to be shut away in the country with her boy and the much younger twins, with Joan as her responsibility, and an English winter in prospect, was too much to face: she went back to Harland, and everything fell apart. We had lacked foresight, complications promised to be too great, so we would all return to Sindh together.

We left all those loving relatives, we even left our house to be sold by my father. We sailed in an overcrowded ship that had been sunk in the war, raised and repaired, painted white all over its upper works, painted over the massive rust. Not even a cabin for us together. There was plenty to forget about that voyage that ended our leave. But at least we reached Bombay safely

There was still a long, long railway journey ahead of us, over a thousand miles through the middle of western India, with two changes and two nights and days in the train or waiting on platforms or, we hoped, in waiting-rooms. Nor did we have a bistra with us, with night clothes and bedding: there was no need for such things in England. This was the line north from Bombay, through country that was full of history, country that was first green and fertile, becoming drier and more desert-like as we crossed Rajputana. Joan and the boys were exhausted, and slept. I watched the country till it became dark, and then I too slept. At one large station I got down to look at the engine, larger even than ours in Sindh, and, suddenly anxious, went to see if our baggage was on board. It was, for we were in the care of Grindlays again, and even at the two changes I had no need to worry.

We revelled in luxury and ate in Spencers' dining-car on the train. We had a coupe to ourselves, with a washroom, and it was pleasantly warm: wash hands and face and teeth, there wasn't much more possible. When Adam and David woke for their supper they were charmed by it all, especially having to run along the train to the dining-car, and then run back at another station. Once we were aboard, the train still had twenty minutes to wait, but we were not allowed to get out: what would they do if we were left behind?

Sleeping again all night; but I woke for the stations. Railway stations at night have always held for me a special charm—all the riot of passengers boarding and leaving, all the cries of food- and tea-sellers, and then quiet as the flag is waved, and the engine whistling as it pulls away.

We changed at Marwar to the Jodhpur Railway: a metre-gauge railway, smaller than the main line, but even so, larger than our Kashmore Railway. How it did rattle! The

line ran through desert, and the coaches were made as
dust-proof as possible which was far below perfect. But we
were lucky, near the front of the train, before the cloud
was established, so at last I saw real desert, like the desert
of Thar, which made up much of Sindh. We saw the palace
of Jodhpur in the evening, and in the night passed near
the ancient fort of Umrkot, where the great Akbar was
born.

Two men got in, for we didn't have a coupe now, and
promptly lit beedis. Joan and I hated the smell, but usually
put up with it. Now she was pregnant, and would be sick.
Would they please stop? They would, to please the lady. So
I, too, must be smokeless all the way to Hyderabad. There,
we were in Sindh, very nearly home.

It was very odd: who, after the green fields and soft light
of an English summer, could really welcome the harsh sun
glare and dusty plains of Sindh? But I did, the more since
my family was with me, when I had expected to come alone.
Nothing now could be wrong.

Nazir and Afroze knew that we would all be coming, and
that our old house would not be ready for a few weeks.
That would not have mattered for me alone, but now there
was the whole family. They did not this time have to squeeze
up: the flat below them was being kept for the latest ICS
recruit, Agha Shahi Hilali, and he was happy to wait for a
bit till the house was ready and our furniture back again.

Illahibaksh arrived, expecting me, welcoming us all, and
then Candy heard that we had all come.

She arrived a day later. We saw her coming along the
street and sent the boys out, no reason given, and watched.
They saw her, and stood still as though thunderstruck. They
held hands and burst into tears; Candy saw them, ran up,
and enfolded them, and she burst into tears too. There
they stood, three silly ninnies, crying and howling, and
passers-by stared in amazement. They recovered their wits,
and then for them everything was as it had always been.

Candy was married now, and she was pregnant, too. But, said she, not to worry, *fikr nahin*, her husband, Augustine D'Souza, was a cook, not so good as Mistri, who had gone home, but he would manage.

Joan had the embarrassment of meeting friends to whom she had bid farewell six months before, but the pleasure outweighed that. We moved back home as if we had never left. Even the pedal cars were still there, but the boys felt they must have shrunk, the fit was so tight.

Joan was welcomed back to the Convent, and the boys went to a little school with Mrs Labouchardiere. She had her own two children, a Swiss girl, a Greek girl, an Indian boy, and our two. She was a trained teacher, and they learned to read astonishingly quickly.

Basil Labouchardiere was an officer of the Imperial Police. He and his wife were Anglo-Indian, adopting their English side, and speaking of England as home. Like us, they could retire to England with a pension, and Basil hoped to be a policeman there; we warned him that Indian experience would not help, might even hinder, and he should not be optimistic. They went, and Dorothy soon found a job teaching, but Basil could not compete with all the young men from the forces. They divorced, and Basil came to see us once, when we too had retired; he had no job, he was hoping to marry again, and then we heard no more. His homeland had let him down badly.

We met the Reinitzs early, and now Hugo was Joan's doctor, in the professional sense. He pronounced her in excellent condition; there was no question of twins this time, and the sex of the child would not be revealed till its birth. He accepted Candy as a patient, too, and was suitably impressed by the way the boys had grown. Life looked very rosy.

Karachi was greatly changed. Most of the British and American troops had at last gone home. Many of the more easily mobile Hindus were going to Hindu India, and it was clear that Hindu ICS officers were being transferred to

Bombay, Muslims from Bombay to Sindh. We all knew that
Wavell's battle to keep India united had been lost, and that
the terms of independence for two separate states could
not be long delayed. So Muslim officers from provinces
which would certainly be in India began to arrive. There
would be a very awkward time between the making of
agreements and their being carried out.

In all sorts of ways, India was growing more and more
restless. In the ICS we heard that in many places the
interference of political parties was making administration
almost impossible. So perhaps I was lucky to be in one of
those despised Secretariat posts. We received notice that
any member of the Service who retired after 1 January 1947
would qualify for compensation and pension, British and
Indian alike. So my own Service was preparing to wind
down.

In the Department we settled our work. We were equally
Joint Secretaries, but Nazir was a little more equal from
being above me in the list ten years before.

There was one change in the office that I noticed at
once. My excellent and beautiful secretary, Kimi Kondo,
had gone. That Tobacco Manager had looted her away as
soon as I went on leave. She came to apologize when I
came back, but I could hardly blame her for going. She
was offered twice the salary, and had a beautiful room and
a brand new typewriter. Even if she preferred me as
employer—and that may not have been so anyway—I could
hardly blame her for leaving the squalor of our office.

In our Food and Civil Supplies Department, we were
conscious before it became publicly noticeable that the
commercial life of Karachi was weakening. Hindu capital,
which was most of it, was being realized and moved out. It
was becoming difficult to arrange credit, and even the
Imperial Bank, we were told, was being awkward about
overdrafts. Half our agents in the Sindh Purchasing Board
had gone, so we had to limit our purchases, and could
foresee the time when we would have to end the system

altogether. The Laboratory analyses were late coming, because each time a member of KIMA went to Bombay we were apt to lose a girl from the analysts.

At the same time it was becoming more and more difficult to procure textiles. Gangaram explained the problem to me: he held large stocks, and financed them on credit, but now no one in Bombay would grant credit to a trader in Sindh; nor did he any longer want to hold large stocks. We looked for a way round.

We could not ask Government to trade with its own funds in textiles; for one thing, the trade was so complex that even the ICS mystique was, we felt, hardly capable of dealing with it at short notice. For another, political opinion was turning against state trading altogether, even though it had been so successful and profitable over the past years. Instead, we must try to use our control over rice exports to put pressure on Bombay to make a bargain, to encourage the grant of credit to textile traders. So I went with Gangaram to Bombay and they agreed to a sort of barter arrangement.

In March Lord Mountbatten became Viceroy. Normally a Viceroy would have long notice of the appointment of his successor, but Lord Wavell received practically no notice at all: he was sacked. I had met him, admired him and his stubborn efforts to win agreement between Hindus and Muslims for a free, united, India. I was shocked at the shabby treatment, and by a Labour Government, too. If it had been decided that policy must change, it was reasonable that there should be a new man at the top, but it was Churchill's insistence that Wavell stick with the Cripps principles that had deprived him of success. He should not have been humiliated. However, I was only a civil servant, I had no right to criticize. But for me Lord Mountbatten, with his handsome figure, his medals, his pedigree, and above all his bright charisma, was a little spoiled.

In February 1947 Judith was born, in the Civil Hospital, full term, a fine big baby, nothing like the tiny scraps Adam and David had been. Again we went to the Bible for her name.

Joan, who had once fed two babies, now had too much milk; but there was a Hindu girl whose milk had not come, so one day when I went to see her she was with two babies again, only one was brown. The other mother watched Joan enviously as she fed them, and this itself cleared her emotional block; she took back her baby and fed him herself.

I sat by the bed, admiring and fidgeting at the same time. There were bedbugs in the cane chairs, and after my visits I suffered. Being from bug-less Upper Sindh we were not used to the pests. But soon Joan and Judith were home, and Adam and David were endlessly proud to show off their new sister. As for Candy, her baby was born very soon afterwards, and, as she said, she now had two tiny daughters to replace her two tiny sons—though the boys were still very much her sons. She, too, went to the Bible for a name: Rebecca.

Joan learnt to play bridge, so far had she moved from her earlier contempt for the game. First we played two-handed, then with the Reinitzs, and then she joined a four of her own. This was a truly international four. There was Grete Reinitz, Austrian; Mrs Maratos, Greek; Mrs Elzingre, a white Russian, a refugee from the Revolution; Joan herself was the only one English. They moved round each other's houses, and apart from the cards there was a fierce cookery competition. Each tried to out-cook the others with her refreshments. There was much dried fruit and chocolate, biscuit or nut crumbs; cream without limit. Such cakes! When Joan's turn came, there must be enough for me, the boys, and Candy each to have a slice. Maratos and Elzingre were fat already, Grete was well-favoured, and Joan had to eat for Judith too, who had a hearty appetite. None bothered with their figures.

At last we bought a dinghy. She was old, heavily clinker built, and no favourite to win races. She was nominally an

International '14', but like all the others locally built, was in effect a Karachi One Design. *Sola*, which means sixteen, was in no way notable, but was our very own. For the rest of our stay in Sindh *Sola*, and the Yacht Club, were the focus of our family pleasures. Joan had her bridge and her teaching, I had my Office, and new ICS arrivals from India with whom to probe the future. Otherwise, and always first of everything, were our children.

At the Yacht Club we could spend our time in all sorts of ways. There was a little beach for the children to play, all four—for Rebecca must of course come too—in the care of Candy, while we sailed. Sometimes we were together, and would sail 'Corinthian', sometimes only one of us could go, and if the wind were not too heavy would sail solo; otherwise, with a tindal, or someone looking for a berth, as in the past we so often had done. From the tindal we learnt a lot about the tidal tricks and wind shadows in the harbour. Each month a pewter mug was awarded to the boat with most points, and O! how we longed to win one! But we never did; perhaps we would not have been good enough, but we could never sail all the races.

I once invited Irene Carneghan, whose policeman husband was away on some special job, to crew for me. Irene also had two little boys, not so small as ours; she managed to be light-hearted and amused in spite of motherhood; Joan was under a lot of pressure at that time, including looking after Irene's children. Irene was a relaxing companion, but she was no sailor. For us, sailing was a serious matter, for Irene it was a joke. If there were no crisis, if I could on occasion manage main and jib sheets and tiller all at once, we were all right. But once there came a change of course near the Club jetty. The wind was not very strong, so I made the main sheet fast while I went forward to set the spinnaker. I gave Irene the tiller: 'Just hold it where it is.' But she put it hard over, she fell into the bottom of the boat, and we began to ship water. Our case was not irrecoverable, I released the sheet and told her to bail, but she was laughing too much for that; she leant well outboard, we took in much more water, and then we slowly sank, though not very far because of the buoyancy tanks; we even sailed on for a little. It was a shameful exhibition, with the whole Club looking on. Irene just abandoned me and swam ashore. Our tindal saw it all, too; he swam out and between us we towed *Sola* to the beach and dragged her up so that we could empty her.

I wouldn't sail with Irene again; but I forgave her. I liked her very much: a bit silly, but full of life, undefeated by living up-country with her policeman, a hard life, and poorly paid. She was a foil for my too serious view of life.

There was a group of civilians of our age who sometimes met for dinner, and to set the world to rights, but Joan would never come. Irene would. Sometimes we would drive out afterwards. Sometimes—or perhaps it was only once— we drove out south of Karachi, beyond Clifton. The houses suddenly stopped: there was nothing beyond but sand, level planes, dunes that shifted as the wind blew, little ripples, little hillocks, valleys only visible because they were shadowed by the moonshine. The occasional desert plant cast its shadow and the moon turned the whole landscape to silver. It was like this all the way to the Delta; and once Joan and I had seen it from the other side.

For me, and I think Irene, it was a pleasant episode; but Joan resented it. Then Bill Carneghan came home, and those meetings ended.

We seldom entertained at home. For one thing, three children complicated matters; for another, Augustine was by no means an accomplished cook. Sometimes the Reinitzs came and played bridge, or Nazir and Afroze spent an evening. We didn't dine out much either.

Occasionally we went to the Gymkhana, where everyone went. Occasionally to the Karachi Club with Nazir and Bashir and their wives. When Nazir and Bashir danced with Joan, Afroze would dance with me, at arm's length. She would face the stares and whispers, Bilqis would not. The dancing grew less as the Hindus left: the one-to-one dancing of the West fitted ill with Muslim social culture. Dear Afroze: from the beginning she was a bold girl.

There were still a few unhappy troops, kept to save their officers from reversion. They still lived miserably in tents, and Joan still helped in the canteen. But we decided to give a party for as many as we could handle. We took advice as to what they would eat and drink and left them to it; about a dozen of them. They had the gramophone and their own records, enough to eat, enough to drink, and a sergeant who appointed himself barman.

It was a good party. A rough, boring life in those ruinous tents had not spoiled those young men. All the bottles were emptied, of course, but afterwards a gin bottle was missing. It was not in fact empty, it had just disappeared. The sergeant had made sure that no one had too much, and arranged that one should disappear. Illahibaksh had seen it go. Perhaps that was how one became a sergeant.

Our family life carried on very pleasantly. Official priority secured for us a brand new Chevrolet. This Chev was a saloon, six cylinders, and bright yellow, which was not a colour we would have chosen. For elegance it could not compare with the one I had to welcome Joan when first she arrived, but it would do very well: we could live with primroses.

The boys had their fifth birthday party, and now were old enough to appreciate their own importance in it. Friends from school came, and we had a roundabout in the garden. This was a tatty affair which an old man with his son was used to setting up wherever a party wanted him. It worked by hand, it had no carousel, but made its own music of squeaks and moans. For the children it was very popular: they could ride free, for as long as they liked. It circled more and more slowly as more and more children piled on.

We picnicked on the shore at Clifton, just clear of the black, mica-laden sand. We went to Hawkes Bay, and sailed across the harbour to Sandspit, once with Lyne, Joan's chaperone on her voyage out, eight years before, when she was going boldly to an unknown country to marry a man she hadn't seen for a year. Now she was a mother with three children, and he was retiring home to England, and still she knew only the one name.

27

INDEPENDENCE

Throughout India, the British in the ICS hoped for a united independent state, but in Karachi, once Mountbatten arrived, all the talk was of a separate Pakistan, and clearly this was coming. I, Secretary of a declining Department in a small province that would surely be in Pakistan, and in a city that might well become its capital—I would do well to accept the reality and work for a smooth transfer of power, insofar as so small a wheel as I could help.

It was—it still is—a mystery to me how Mohammed Ali Jinnah could become the unquestioned leader of the Muslims of India. He seemed such a cold, emotionless man in some ways, with his Savile Row dress and his barrister's language more British than the British themselves. He only spoke halting Urdu. His greeting for us, his officers, was wordless, with our hands shaken. But he was a clever politician, and a stubborn advocate. Mountbatten set a date for the Transfer of Power: 15 August 1947. On that day, come what might, the British Raj would end. To concentrate the minds of us civilians, we were given special office calendars, with a leaf for every day printed with 'X Days to the Transfer of Power'. Every day the time grew shorter, and we could never claim to forget.

British officers must transfer their loyalty or go home; Hindu officers in the ICS had already gone to India; Muslim officers began to arrive. I wanted to stay on. There would be no British Governor in support, and the new

Government's policies might not please me, but surely I could adapt, become purely advisory instead of executive. If Pakistan wanted me, my prospects would be good, for there was a shortage of experienced officers

The very last recruit to the ICS came to Sindh: Agha Shahi Hilali, who had a brother in the Foreign Department in India, and would come to Pakistan; we understood he was an adviser to Jinnah, so we cherished Shahi. He was determined to be a loyal and impartial civil servant. Not so another ICS officer who came from India: Masud was openly committed to the Muslim League, and hated the infidel Hindus bitterly. He supported Jinnah's every idea, even his demand that Pakistan should have a corridor right across northern India, to join what became East and West Pakistan. I felt that here at least I could safely express an opinion: it wouldn't work. Nazir Ahmed, Hashim Raza, and Agha Shahi kept quiet: they also thought it silly, but they had to live there; if I was in trouble I could always retire. Later we learned that Jinnah was told that if he insisted, there could be no settlement, so he dropped the idea.

All the manoeuvering and negotiations by the States are well-documented. The real problem was with those whose rulers were of a different religion from that of their populations. I can write of this because our small group of Sindhi ICS discussed it. The biggest of these was Hyderabad (Deccan), whose population was Hindu, its Nizam Muslim. It was big enough to survive as an independent state, if India would let it. Kashmir had a Hindu Rana and a Muslim population, and borders with both India and what would become Pakistan. Then there was little Junagadh, whose borders were entirely Indian, its population Hindu, and only its Nawab was Muslim, with his Vizir a Bhutto.

Of course, all Muslims made a claim to all the three, either for ethnic reasons or because the ruling family was Muslim. Of our group I was the only one, being British, who could give an unbiased opinion. Pakistan, I thought, should claim that it was the people who mattered, so

Hyderabad and Junagadh should not be claimed, but Kashmir should. This could be seen, round the world, as a high moral stand, and would justify the claim to Kashmir. Nor would there be any loss: Hyderabad could not possibly accede to Pakistan, and although Junagadh could be defended by sea, by land India could—and would—overrun it in a day. In the end, we all agreed that that would be the best policy for Pakistan's negotiators; Shahi was deputed to convey the idea to his brother, who might persuade Jinnah to adopt it. Perhaps Hilali tried. But straight after Independence, Pakistan accepted the accession of Junagadh, and the people there rose up and put their Nawab on a ship for Karachi. Indian troops occupied the town to the cheers of the crowds. A little later there was war between India and Pakistan over Kashmir.

Nazir Ahmed and I abandoned high politics and returned to our proper job of procuring and distributing supplies. It seemed that there would be no end to negotiations, that the final set date would be enforced by the Viceroy.

Then, just before that date, the Radcliffe Report on the Partition of the Punjab was published. It was believed in Karachi that last-minute pressure had been brought to bear on Sir Cyril to put in the Indian part villages that should have been on the Pakistan side of the line, and that without that change the terrible migrations of Muslims and Hindus would have been far smaller, and the slaughter much less. As it was, there was a panic, of Muslims to get out of India, of Hindus to get out of Pakistan. The great migrations developed into an enormous tragedy. No one knows how many died in the long columns of whole families struggling across the dead area between the two States that were attached by gangs of supposed patriots. Perhaps 100,000, probably nearer to half a million. There were trains, too, going each way, and somehow they got through, but not untouched. I was in Lahore, looking for a load of sugar, and there met Bashir Malik. He showed me a train lately arrived. He said it had been full of mutilated bodies, not one alive. There was blood everywhere still, dried black and stinking, with clouds of flies buzzing over all. The train crew had been spared, told to report that it was in revenge. All the murderers were Sikhs, they said, some wearing parts of uniforms.

Trains full of Hindus were going the other way, too, and they were attacked; but in Sindh it was believed that the Muslims were killed most brutally, and always the most brutal of all were the Sikhs. No Sikh dared stay in Sindh after that. But it is unlikely that Muslims were much less brutal: in India there were many reports of young men being 'forcibly converted' to Islam.

Pakistan became independent a day early, so that the Viceroy in person could hand over power. He would do the same next day in Delhi, but there, in the moment of handing over, he would become Governor-General. In Pakistan, Mohammed Ali Jinnah would himself become Governor-General, with the powers of a dictator: the Quaid-e-Azam.

We of the Sindh Government were more concerned with the danger of riots as reports came in from the Punjab than with any transfer of power. But I went with other chief officers to the Assembly to witness the transfer. I did not go inside, but stood on the steps outside, where the great ones would shake our hands before the final public ceremony.

There was no great crowd of people as there was to be next day in Delhi. It had been declared a public holiday, so all the office staffs were there, but the news from the Punjab kept most people at home.

There were two flag-poles set up in front of the Assembly, and a platoon of the Baloch Regiment stood guard. The Viceroy and the Quaid-e-Azam came to the top of the steps, the band—not the Pipe Band for this ceremony—played the British National Anthem while the Viceroy saluted; the Risaldar lowered the Union Jack and carefully folded it away. He marched across and hoisted the new Pakistan National Flag on the other pole, Mountbatten and Jinnah saluted, and as it floated free the band played the Pakistan National Anthem. There was cheering from our little crowd.

And that was that. In five minutes, and after a hundred years, the British Empire of India ended. I saw and heard its ending. But I was tired, it was growing hot, so I went home and had a cup of tea. This was a strange ending for such a great edifice.

One of the reasons for my ever going to India was my romantic pride in the achievements of the British there. Already in 1935 a term had been set to their rule, and I knew it. I knew that there had been dark periods, that commerce and military power were, in the main, far more powerful motives than any search for a just administration. But lower down we had created less tangible, less obvious assets. We would leave behind a civil administration famous for its integrity, with a pool of Indian and Pakistani civil servants whose motive was always to maintain that integrity. Until the British took control, the Rule of Law was known only as an ancient ideal, but under them it became real, even in the States, and under the new States the system, encoded and accepted, was continued, administered by the same civil service, from sub-divisional courts to the Judges of the High Court.

At the end, there were many tragedies as the country was torn in two: small ones of families forced to leave their homes, little local riots, and the enormous horrors of the Punjab. At the very top, in Delhi, there were officers of my service, British, Hindu, and Muslim, without whose work and understanding tragedy might have become catastrophe. For we, the British, must not take sides: there were still British troops, and the two parts of the bisected Indian Army, but they must take no part, lest interference lead to war.

The Empire had ended quietly and unobtrusively, but when the Army left the British were very visibly going. The

Black Watch had served in India for nearly a century, and the last battalion to leave marched through the town with colours flying, pipes playing, crowds friendly and cheering. I was at the docks to watch them embark, to hear the Baloch, also a Highland regiment, there with their Colour troop, pipe the Black Watch Colours aboard the transport: 'Will ye no' come back again?' This was the true end: even the crowd was silent. I was moved to sentimental tears.

This was a time when Sindh was very anxious lest the reports from the Punjab lead to serious rioting. Fourteen Hindus were killed in Karachi, and at once a full curfew was imposed. The riot was really after loot, not blood, and the only body I saw was of an Anglo-Indian at the Post Office, killed by a looter.

Among other things I was Rationing Officer. After twenty-four hours of the curfew I pointed out that people must be able to get food, so I was given armed police and a megaphone to take round shops, announce their opening, and guard them. We told the people that the shops would be opened for one hour, and would then close again. If some were still nervous, they could stay at home and starve for a day or two. Then, after another day, and very gingerly, with police everywhere and troops at strategic spots, the curfew was lifted. Karachi was back to near normal.

The Pakistan Government was set up and began to operate. It was short of everything, from typewriters to office space and staff to fill it. India had a fine governing machine in being, with two awkward wings lopped off. Those pieces had to forge themselves into a new State, the limits of its logistics determined by what it could squeeze out of India. The supposedly impartial Viceroy of all India had become head of the new India. No wonder Pakistan was bitter and suspicious.

Sindh remained nervously peaceful. Hindus were leaving, their property either sold or abandoned. Sources of credit dried up as liquid capital was converted into *hoondis* and bills of exchange that could be hidden in the lining of a coat. Now when I wanted to buy rice I had to pay cash for a proportion of the price, the balance after analysis. Sindhis kept their own stocks, so it was immigrants who suffered and became disaffected. There was an urgent need to get the husking mills working for the new harvest, which meant finding Muslims from India with relevant experience.

Moneyed and educated Muslims from India arrived in Karachi: it was only the poor who had to brave the Punjab border. They took over Hindu houses, either by agreement or because they were abandoned. They were welcomed, for their administrative or commercial skills. Somehow the Pakistan Government offices must be housed, and Sindh was horribly squeezed. My Department was lucky: ours was a commercial lease, and in no way grand enough for Pakistan, so we kept it.

Most of the Hindus from Upper Sindh left through Karachi. They avoided the way out on the Jodhpur Railway because Masud in Mirpurkhas was letting them be looted; his District suffered for this later, but at least he would not allow murder. Sitaldas Khemani came with his family from Jacobabad, where he had stayed in his post as Administrator till the last minute, almost beyond. He came with his wife and children; they had left everything behind except one small suitcase each. They spent the night with us, and we gave them two blankets, because it would be cold on the sea, and most people would be out on the deck. I went with them to the docks to see them off. On the quay were scenes that made me ashamed. There were police, but they did nothing, and the subedar told me he dared not interfere: there were such tensions, such bitterness and envy, that any attempt to bring order might lead to a massacre. So I stood by Sitaldas and his family, and at least no one dared attack them. Soon they went on board in tears, and we saw them no more.

For a time I watched the looting. The looters were Khaksars, so-called patriots tolerated by the Pakistan Government and so, unwillingly, by Sindh. Supposedly they were stopping the Hindus from looting Pakistan, but in fact it was for profit, or from petty spite: books and toothbrushes were taken, gramophones and cooking pots, bags of spare clothes. There was little of value, for these were the poor leaving, with a few clerks and officers like Sitaldas, who had stayed too long in their posts. I wished some of the Pakistani idealists had been there.

I don't know when it was that I realized that now I was a foreigner in a country that I had come to look on as my home. Now in Government I was a mercenary, allowed by courtesy to stay on and call myself ICS, when all my colleagues, full nationals of their own country, were Pakistan Administrative Servants. Only now did I fully realize what had happened when that flag was hauled down. I did not like being a foreigner.

One surprising achievement in transferring power was that we, the British, were now, throughout India and Pakistan, more popular than we had ever been. Officers coming through Karachi on their way to retirement told us of their surprise, coming as were many from parts of India where it had been their job to deal toughly with civil disobedience. Our fears that Indian members of our Service would be mistrusted proved entirely groundless.

Sir Ghulam Hussein Hidayatullah changed from being Premier to being Governor of Sindh, and Mahomed Ayub Khuhro became Prime Minister in his place. The Mir Sahib, still my Minister, wanted to go to England, and Khuhro called me to see him, to see if he should let the Mir go; could Nazir and I run the Department without him, but with the Prime Minister himself in charge? I was very uneasy about this meeting: I only knew of Khuhro's reputation as an unscrupulous and ruthless politician, with criminal reports against him, though none proven. I talked with Nazir Ahmed before I went; he didn't want to go, because his mother-in-law was sister-in-law to the Governor. It sounds remote, but was close enough for Nazir to fear lest he appear interested. It was a strange meeting. We talked about the Mir Sahib: I was asked my personal opinion of him, which cannot have been a usual thing for a Prime Minister to do, talking to a mere civil servant. However, I could be both candid and polite: the Mir Sahib was a very pleasant gentleman, he was honest if one excused small favours done for friends, but he was a little puzzled by the intricacies of the commerce with which his Department was chiefly concerned. Yes, we could manage very well without him, and would be happy to consider ourselves under the Prime Minister's direct control—whatever I believed of Khuhro's reputation, I could not well say anything else. I was astonished then to hear Khuhro talk of himself. He said that I must know of his reputation— indeed, I didn't trouble to deny it—but he assured me there would be no more corrupt practice, no more bribes or improper favours. He would be straight and statesman-like. Of course, I accepted his assurances.

The extraordinary thing was that he lived up to the standard he had set himself. I found him always straightforward but, unlike the Mir, full of common sense knowledge of the work of our Department.

The Mir Sahib left for England. He spent two months there, and returned full of all he had seen. I can see him now: a small man, full of enthusiasm, waving his arms about, telling me of all that he had seen, completely forgetting that I knew the place myself. He had seen tractors, and combine harvesters which I had not yet seen myself. He had seen crops growing on hillsides with no possibility of irrigation, *pukka* roads everywhere, little trains going through tunnels. He had been on the Underground, a whole railway in a tunnel. He had been down a coal mine. He was full of it all. He at last saw reason in my idea that the profits we held from selling rice should be used for development. 'Pearce, we must have a coal mine, too; and factories. Karachi needs an underground railway, now that the roads are full of cars!' With some of it I agreed: there were Hindu properties that should be allocated to Muslim

immigrants who knew what sorts of factory would pay, and
Pakistan was setting up an organization to deal with
abandoned property. There was no traffic congestion to
justify an underground railway, nor did I know anything
about the Karachi subsoil. But we could ask the PWD to
investigate.

We discussed coalmining. At Attock, Pakistan had a little
coal; there had been exploration in the hills of Kalat, but
none had been found; and I reminded him that the Railway
was already changing to oil, because it was not easy to get
coal from India, whereas there was a sea of oil under the
friendly Arab states up the Persian Gulf. So, no coal mines.
And although Karachi is now a vast city with a population
of 10,000,000, there is still no underground railway.
Probably the geology, and certainly the cost, would have
defeated the Mir Sahib. Pakistan has its factories now, but
no more coal than it had then, and very little more oil.

Textiles began to arrive under our barter agreement, so
that we could control prices and set up a rationing system.
This had to be very simple, for a largely illiterate population
which wouldn't understand the stamps of the English
system. We issued cards with holes to be punched, and how
they worked I can't recall, but work they did, well enough,
at least in Karachi; the best we could do for the *mofussil* was
to send consignments to Collectors, *ex officio* Rationing
Officers. I spitefully hoped that in Mirpurkhas Masud would
learn how stupid it was to scare every Hindu away.

Only piece-goods were rationed, made garments were
freely sold. At once we had problems of definition. When
was a 'sari-pair', double length with a double stitch halfway,
a garment, when a 'piece' of fifteen yards? Sindhi trousers,
so voluminous, needed fifteen yards, so did a rough hem
along most of one side and across the middle make two
pairs? In the end we let such fiddles go: if there was enough
on the ration, then those who wanted more could pay for
it.

28

1948

Most British members of the Indian Civil Service, left over
from the Raj, retired and went home. Most business people
saw new opportunities and stayed. Some of them joined
new companies set up by Muslims from India, and some
found posts in the High Commissions. It was said that there
were more British staff in the High Commissions in Delhi
and Karachi than there had ever been to run the Raj. Those
of us who were left could lead an unworried life: if things
went wrong we need no longer feel responsible just because
we were British.

The Home Government abrogated our Covenant, but
promised that no one who retired need be without a post,
either in the Home Service, or in the remaining Empire.
But who would want a post as Administrative Principal, in
an office, endorsing notes from below for decision up
above, when he had ruled a District, or headed a
Government Department?

So we stayed on. Nazir Ahmed became Anti-Corruption
Officer, and indeed there was need for such a post. I was at
last sole head of my Department, though its importance
was sadly reduced. But I was compensated by the transfer
from Agriculture to me of all the development plans. This
was Khuhro's doing: he knew of my previous proposals,
and that there was a lot of money involved; it was less likely
to leak away from me than from Agriculture, subject to
strong zamindari pressures. At last I could begin to work

up my ideas into practical proposals. And the money was there: the profits from the Bengal Famine.

Fisheries were now in my care. Already there were proposals for the shrimp fishery, and to redevelop the oyster beds at Korangi Creek, damaged by an invasion of 'wild' oysters. But I wanted to go much further. The Mohana fishermen of Karachi were highly skilled (their sons were the tindals at the Yacht Club) but they only worked a little way out to sea, as far as they could go and return in a day. We knew that further out there were great shoals of fish, of kinds unknown on land. I wanted to find out about them, and perhaps catch them. I wanted a trawler, and Khuhro persuaded the Cabinet to agree to buy a second-hand one from England. Our High Commission took advice, bought one, hired a crew with a promise of a job or a passage home, and she steamed out. She arrived, and the Pakistan Press made much of the crew, and their feat. I wish I could remember the new name we gave her. She was refitted and went to sea, with several Mohanas as crew, to learn this new skill before the English crew went home. Two Pakistan naval officers went with her. She fished with seine nets, for no one knew yet what the bottom was like, and it might have destroyed the trawl. Nor did anyone know what bottom feeding fish there might be.

When the first catch came ashore there was uproar among the Mohanas. There were fish that no one had ever seen before, and familiar ones in such quantity as no one had dreamed of. They saw their living being taken away. So once the catch had been analysed we gave it to them to sell, with the condition that they tell us of the prices they made.

There were several trips before the monsoon winds grew too strong to risk an inexperienced crew, and we had plenty of figures to work on before deciding how to handle this project. Most importantly, the Mohanas themselves must chiefly benefit, so the Co-operative Department must work on it. Marketing must itself be run by the Mohanas, with business expertise to help. We needed someone to tell us what the various kinds of fish were, which edible, which perhaps poisonous. (I suggested that we try some on the cat. I was asked, whose cat? The Mohanas were very serious people.) If there were some that would not sell they could be turned into fertilizer or stockfeed. The Punjab was always short of sea fish, we could think of refrigerated vans on the railway...perhaps a canning industry... In my head I built castles; on paper I was cautious. A start had been made, but progress would be slow. One could not change the whole industry because of one trawler.

There must be better records for our Red Sindhi cattle breeding, and even for the ugly milch buffalo. Plans were produced for poultry rearing, with several experimental flocks of 'twelve hen birds and twelve cock birds'. I suggested one cock bird, perhaps a second for insurance, lest the hens become so weary with mating that they had no energy left to lay eggs. (I was forgetting my Manual: there should be no humour in Government.)

At Christmas we had a present from Ali Ahmed at Kandhkot. He knew how we liked grapefruit, so he sent us some from Dostali: the trees there had recovered from the flood, and were cropping again. I added another to my development plans.

Christmas was now a minor festival. Muslim holidays were centred round their own holy days, but still the New Year was celebrated: the Christian New Year. This gave Pakistan a problem: it was now a Muslim state, with an enthusiastically orthodox Islamic party. 'AD' had no meaning, dates should be 'AH'—After the Hejra, when the Prophet (PBUH), migrated from Mecca. This was 622 years after the supposed birth of Christ, so the year was properly not AD 1948, but AH 1326. But the Government was firm; it had enough trouble with dates as they were, accepted throughout the world, without the complications of religious pedantry.

I caught a chill at the Yacht Club. It was nothing serious, but then it turned to pleurisy, which Hugo Reinitz dosed with the new wonder drug, penicillin. (It was said that doctors were prescribing penicillin, and only if it didn't work were they making a diagnosis.) I wouldn't go to the hospital, with its fleas and bedbugs, so instead I was nursed at home; and I recovered, more or less.

This was a depressing time for me. Hugo talked of anaemia and the need for sick leave. There would be no difficulty about that; if I wanted to retire, there would be no difficulty about that either, there were plenty who would be glad of my place, there was no need now for any left-over British officer. My Department was being looked over by incoming businessmen like vultures, ready to pick up bits of our Government-controlled activities that might be 'liberated' to private trade.

The Sindh Purchasing Board was wound up. No longer could KIMA provide quality analyses. I finally bought enough rice to cover loans made against its purchase and released all stocks to the trade—a largely Muslim trade now. Then I closed it down; without any publicity ended an organization which over six years had made over three crores of rupees (about £2,250,000) for the Sindh Government, had paid off the Barrage debt, and left a sum which I hoped we could hold for some, at least, of the development programmes.

Cloth rationing ended for lack of stocks. Sale of white flour to the Gulf states was free: they were all firm friends of Pakistan.

The once powerful Department became little more than an office to register stocks and prices. I spent my time polishing my most important development plan: I proposed an aerial survey of the whole course of the River in Sindh. Such a survey would be valuable to the PWD and the Forestry Department and would provide a true picture of cultivation in the alluvial lands, the *kutchas*, of which I was sure large areas evaded paying revenue. I thought the extra information would probably make annual surveys worth while, and the Pakistan Air Force would probably be happy to practise its aerial photography skills. I hoped to create some of my self-employed smallholders, with the help of credit from the Co-operative Department; and if the proposal were a success it could be extended to Government waste generally. Politically I would have been wiser to forget this idea: too many powerful zamindari interests would have seen themselves threatened by it.

29

LEAVE

I got over my pleurisy, all our family was well and happy, and outlooks changed. A happy time began. My own work became less useful, but, with the development plans, I was more hopeful. I would go on sick leave, and Joan and the family would stay in England, which made Joan cheerful. I would return alone for a time, to deal with my precious plans. This time we would organize our life much better: we would rent somewhere to stay while we looked for a permanent home. That would be somewhere in the country, and my idea was to grow fruit, the occupation that would have attracted me had we decided to stay on. We might have ourselves created a citrus orchard. But that was only a daydream. If I retired, indeed, when I retired, it would be to England.

We sold the car; we sold it to a man who said it was just what he wanted: new, striking with its bright colour. He paid an enormous price; to him money was no object, but he must have it now. We knew who he was: he was a gun-runner named Cotton. Hyderabad had still not acceded to India, and he would help an independence movement. I had to have permission for the sale, but Pakistan had no objection: anything that would embarrass India was welcome. He paid cash, but his project failed, and he disappeared, doubtless going to some other unstable part of the world. We bought another car, another Chev, and our oldest yet at twenty-four years old, but it would serve.

We meant to enjoy our last months in Sindh. I would return alone, and I promised—well, almost promised—that it would be only for a short time.

Little happened in my official life. Only with the fishery was there continuing interest. The trawler fished on, the Mohanas began to realize how it could benefit them, and the Mohana boys, the tindals at the Yacht Club, told us of its voyages. I never went to sea myself, Hugo wouldn't let me: how could I claim sick leave if I went out fishing in such a little ship?

But I could sail in the harbour. Seldom could we sail together, and Joan went out more often than I, left to look after the children. On the most memorable occasion, we were to sail together for the Commodore's Prize, the most prestigious of the year. There was so little wind that we decided Joan should go solo, for her light weight and the positive handicap for being alone. I sat and watched. By the last reach she was so far ahead of the fleet that her time allowance was unnecessary; but there was a Club rule that if a race failed to finish by a certain time it was called off, and that time was coming very near. We never wore a watch in the boat, for a capsize would destroy it, and there was Joan, cruising comfortably along, no one threatening her, while time was running out. I went out to the jetty and began to wave; she just waved happily back. I carried on waving, and pointing at my watch, till she took the point, and began to sail hard, as if threatened. As, indeed, she was. She crossed the line, the gun fired for her, and a few minutes later it fired twice to call off the rest of the race.

There were drinks all round, and a little ceremony. There were also murmurs: the race should have been called off earlier, it could hardly be called a race when only one finished... We left them to it; there was no protest, Joan's triumph was unsullied. Some said *Sola* was a slow old boat, how could she have won? But she had, so it must have been skill, and Joan's the greater merit. Anyway, we went straight to the jeweller and got the prize inscribed: a beautiful silver salver, which now sits in the hall, waiting for visitors, a little worn with much polishing. But no one leaves cards these days.

We never won a tankard, the monthly prize, for we didn't race regularly enough. I thought the Prize was our—Joan's—only victory. But later, mixed up with little cups won for pigs, we found two others: the Coe Cup and the Murray Cup. We have no idea who Mr Murray and Mr Coe were, nor what were the occasions for our victories. But here we have the metal to prove them.

Dinghy sailing in Karachi harbour demanded special skills and knowledge, which we had acquired from tindals and from sailing as crew before ever we owned our own boat, and, apart from victories, I can relive the generalized pleasure simply of sailing. The sun shone always, sometimes there was wind strong enough to capsize the careless, sometimes dying away to a flat calm; waves tall enough to come aboard and sometimes mirror-still water, with boats drifting idly.

There were mudbanks to be shaved, with a hand ready to lift the plate, and places where an eddy twisted against the tide. The Mohana tindals knew them all, and we picked their brains. There were, too, the big freighters moored in the stream, to be passed to windward, but not too close, or a back-draught from a towering black hull could stop a dinghy dead. I thought all our knowledge was enshrined only in memory, till we found those little tarnished cups.

My sick leave was approved, and the happy time was coming to an end. I began to tidy up the Department. All the development plans were in the charge of the Prime Minister, and he handed them back to Agriculture. I would not be away for long, I hoped, and when I returned, that was the Department I wanted.

We booked on the *Ascania*, a North Atlantic liner, old, well-heated for the cold, poorly ventilated for the heat. We travelled 'posh', but only because we were on the starboard side. Joan was in a cabin with the children, I in an all-male cabin.

This time very certainly only I would come back. Again there were sad good-byes, but worst of all it was for Candy. Illahibaksh, too, was upset, losing Judith, his precious treasure. I had never thought to see tough Illahibaksh, with his snaggle teeth, crying, but he did. The dinghy was sold; the car was stored for me. I bought a crate such as held American cars of the more expensive sort, and we filled it with our furniture, to await a ship and follow us.

For some reason we flew to Bombay, and only hold baggage went in the British India packet. We had to spend a night before sailing, and faced one last crisis. Our trunks were still in the packet: Grindlay's had supposed we had cancelled our passages home. So I had to hire a lighter, a converted landing craft, cross the harbour to the packet at anchor, and persuade it to give up my trunks. Grindlay's were persuasive, they were whipped out and into my lighter, and we reached the liner just before its derricks were housed. The blue peter was already flying. I left Grindlay's to settle everything, and went to look for Joan. There she was, on the dockside, children and bags all around her, and desperately anxious. Should she board without me, or wait? There were people near who knew her problem, who would be happy for her to wait, leaving our berths for them. But I was in time.

We boarded, the gangway was pulled away, and we stood by the rail: cabins could wait. The little groups that had been sitting on the dock moved away: they had been waiting for some chance berth—someone might fall ill, or break a leg, or change his mind. They had no tickets, they would pay on board; they had minimal baggage—they would happily have boarded with none at all. There was a little cheering, but this was nothing like the happy departures of people going on leave. It was at best half-hearted. Watching India disappear, leaving only the Gateway, perhaps even Joan was near breaking her resolve, not for India itself, but for Sindh, where we had been very happy, where were all our friends.

What a squalid voyage that was! It is an odd thing, but of all my four sea voyages to and from India, only one was pleasurable. For Joan there were two, counting her wartime passage through the submarines. *Ascania* had twice her normal load of passengers, no deck chairs, no deck games, no games for children. Four sittings for meals, queuing for everything. The North Atlantic luxuries were mostly inappropriate, but two institutions remained: hot bovril on deck in the morning, tea in the afternoon. On the first day those at the head of the queue got cups—no one was foolish enough to return them! Glasses appeared, then tooth mugs, fancy mugs requisitioned from children, and finally empty tins. Pineapple tins were best, but any would do; Joan bribed a steward to get two for baked beans, and very soon they were polished like silver. They had one merit: they held much more than a cup.

We must always, in turn or together, keep an eye on the children. If a child moved into danger, anyone might forestall it; if one offered to climb the rail, there would be a rush to stop it drowning itself. But only a child's own parent might chastise it.

The Purser sent round a notice: there were pickpockets aboard, but we took no notice. We met in a group with others going home to look for new jobs. I had a book by William Seabrook about fruit-growing, and that was what we would do. It became my bible, and we would settle near Chelmsford, where was his farm. I knew the rudiments from my father, though that was a generation out of date.

On the night before we docked in Southampton, valuables disappeared from everyone in my cabin, including my watch.

Queue for passports, queue for documents, queue for Customs forms. There was nothing else to do, but we preferred to do nothing, and in the end there was no need to queue. We just wrote, 'Nothing to Declare'.

Two big trunks we had, two suitcases, a US Army box, and clear consciences. But the Customs officer suspected that box, especially when I told him it held only broken toys. The lid was screwed on suspiciously securely, so he must have it opened. I unpacked my screwdriver, prised off the lid, and he began to search. Adam and David climbed onto the bench to help him, happy to explain what everything was, whose it was, how it was broken. People behind grew noisily impatient, but the officer still had hope. He found Joan's ball of wool, as big as Judith's head, made from all the scraps left over from darning and patching and knitting; he banged it, he squeezed it, he got a spike and transfixed it all ways, but in the end gave up. Then everyone had to wait while we jammed everything back in the box. Those impatient people behind us should have been grateful: the officer let them all through unexamined. He looked so foolish, and the boat train was on the point of leaving.

Then we were away, rushing through the country in late summer, with Joan's family at the end of the journey. England was so beautiful, different from the tired country we had seen two years before. But we had little time, everything must be settled, properly this time, before I went back to Sindh. A second-hand car would be at least ten years old, so we would have a new one, to travel round and find a place to live. In the agencies in the West End were the first post-war models. Inside were brilliantly shining cars, and brilliantly shining salesmen, too. We saw a green Austin A40, like our yellow Chev but squeezed up fore and aft. We would have it. But there was a long waiting list. We would pay cash, in rupees, it was for export. (Well, perhaps.) Everything changed: of course we could have one, we could have the one in the window. While documents were prepared a man went to Grindlay's in Whitehall to clear our cheque, and we sat and drank tea: always there was tea in crises. It was extracted from the window and I drove it away. Joan couldn't drive till she passed her test. After all these years! She took it in Chelmsford; she explained that she was used to camels and loose cows, but she passed all right.

We were given vast numbers of precious clothing coupons, for it was assumed that we had nothing to wear, and we shared them with our families. We had a special petrol ration, too, and drove round looking for a home.

In the end we found one: Quilters Farm, near Chelmsford, a little old house sold away from its farm. Near Seabrook's orchards, it was furnished, electricity by generator, its own well. It had a small barn for our furniture when it came, and a very old spaniel called Nell, who had become discouraged from lack of love, but recovered when she received it in plenty. There was a Rayburn cooker, and Mrs Tricker who came in to help. Nothing could be better.

The boys began school, I began cycling over Danbury Hill to learn to grow apples, and Joan took to English housekeeping again.

I went to the School of Tropical Medicine: they passed me as fit, and told me to avoid malaria—did they think I went looking for it?—and gave me a course of the latest drug that they hoped would cure it: Atebrin. (No X-ray; an X-ray might well have changed all our lives.) I booked a flight on Imperial Airways and was ready to go, for this last time.

The Empire Flying Boat was the perfect transport. There was no need to hurry, and it took five days. It never flew high, the pilot showed us the Alps, Vesuvius, and all the North African coast; we flew over the ruins of Tobruk. We spent nights in transit camps. We landed in a lake at Cairo, flew over the Pyramids, and crossed the desert to Bahrain. It was then desert all the way, the dry hills of Persia, the dry, barren hills of Makran, and suddenly we were in Sindh. We passed the Cape Monze lighthouse, the shining salt pans, and then Karachi itself. The plane flew over the harbour, but no longer did it land there, embarrassed by

racing yachts: the dinghies had won, and we flew on to
Korangi Creek, where the Reinitzs met me.

Karachi had not changed much in three months, except
for one thing: Khuhro's ministry had fallen. He had been
convicted of fraud. I was shocked, but it was no big thing:
he had let a friend have a motorbike, from the horrid store
of seized Hindu property, for Rs 100 when it was valued at
Rs 1,000. How could he be so stupid? He could have given
his friend the whole price himself. And when I went to see
him he was angry with me, that I had not been there to
help him, to stop him being so silly. So I might, but surely
he could see the danger himself. However, he was sure he
would be back soon.

Pir Illahibaksh was Premier, and he didn't like me;
moreover, he saw me as one of Khuhro's men, and I could
not persuade him that I was no Minister's man, I was a civil
servant. I became Secretary for Agriculture, with special
responsibility for development plans. But with Khuhro gone
they were 'sat on'.

I stayed with the Simpsons; Reggie was married now.
Barbara had been a Land Girl, on the Bedford estate, and
Reggie had a notable film to entertain everyone: there was
Queen Mary, the Queen Mother, in her battleship hat,
sawing wood for the fire. Reggie was with the Intelligence
Service now, always discreet, but felt able to tell me that I
would be posted out of the way as Collector of Dadu. I had
very little to do. I sailed with Barbara, and saw *Sola*, well
down the fleet; her owner had supposed she was a fast boat
when Joan won her prize, but too late he discovered that it
was skill. I borrowed Reggie's tools and made Barbara a
little loom, working on my bedroom floor, just like the one
I had made for Joan years before.

I had an interview with the Prime Minister. He agreed to
put my proposals for the Karachi fishery and for better
cattle-breeding before his Cabinet. But an aerial survey of
the river, and the creation of small freeholding farmers,
were anathema. Nazir Ahmed advised patience, and so even

did Roger Thomas from the Punjab. But with the threat of
Dadu hanging over me there was no time. I sent in my
resignation. I sorted out pay and provident fund and my
leave credit, and arranged to transfer all money to
Grindlay's in England.

There was a final, very final, round of farewells, of calls
where I must, but from malice none on Ministers, and I
flew away.

I flew in a Constellation: large, noisy, flying so high that
one could not see the ground. (I was one of the few lucky
ones who flew in the flying boat during its short time of
service.)

I left Drigh Road on a beautiful December day. At
Heathrow there was only a row of huts, no reason to linger,
and it was very cold. Nothing to declare; a coach to central
London, the tube to Liverpool Street and a cold train to
Chelmsford. Then a taxi to Quilters Farm in a snowstorm,
where I arrived only an hour after the cable to say I was
coming.

The boys were in bed with a cough, Joan was very tired,
and the house was cold. It was Christmas Eve, and the very
end of our life in Sindh. No drama, no present sadness,
just the pleasure of being all together.

30

COUNTDOWN

Christmas Day, 1948. Early morning and snowing hard. We filled the back of the car with blankets and hot water bottles, buried the children in them, and set off for my old home for the day, for the first real Christmas our children had ever had, with aunts and uncles, cousins and grand-parents; with log fires and roast chestnuts and a Christmas tree.

We set off home as we had come, but now in a freezing blizzard and with extra hot bottles. There was no heating in that modern car: the extra bottles were to melt holes in the ice on the windscreen, one hole ready for use when the other froze over. So we struggled home to Quilters Farm. It was bitterly cold there. By the small hours we were warm and in bed. At the same time the sun was rising in a clear sky over Karachi. It was already risen in Jacobabad, cold and still and sunny, but with nothing like the bitter cold of England.

We had no regrets—or none to which we would admit. We were happy to be in England again.

Looking back over fifty years I find it difficult to believe myself. We had been very happy in Sindh, even in the heat and primitive conditions of Upper Sindh. Our future in England was unsure, but certain to need a lot of hard work and to feel restricted. All our friends were in Sindh, and no more would there be affectionate if inefficient servants.

Above all, no more Candy. If there were regrets, we did not reveal them to each other.

Of course we wrote letters, we wrote to everyone we knew in Sindh. Grete Reinitz wrote voluminously about our friends, and Candy sent long letters written for her, always hoping that 'her sons' would come back.

We bought a small, half-derelict farm, and were busy turning it into orchards when I developed tuberculosis, and all this overlaid my concerns for my plans for Sindh. (Had there been a radiologist in Karachi, all our lives would have been different!) I asked Sam Ridley, still Commissioner, and Nazir Ahmed for news of them. There was nothing. Then in 1956 Pakistan abolished provinces, and the money would have gone. So I gave up.

Hugo Reinitz died, the best of friends, the best of doctors. Grete Reinitz came to stay with us, and we tried to persuade her to settle in England, but she would not. She would go to Australia, a country she did not much like, to stay with her two brothers, whom she didn't much like either.

We wrote to Candy, and sent her presents; she sent gifts to us, too. Her children married and Augustine died. She went as companion to an old Pakistani lady in Kuwait, and there, many years later, Judith met her again. Judith was touring with her ensemble and telegraphed that she was coming. She called on the old lady, who offered to send for Candy; but Judith said, no, she was not a servant, she was Candy. She went to Candy's room, and Candy, astonished, cried out 'O, Madam!' No telegram had reached her, and Judith was of an age comparable with Joan's in Karachi. A few years later Candy herself died.

Nazir Ahmed died, but Afroze lives on in Karachi, I believe. Peter Cargill came once to our farm. Later, as he was coming home for a knighthood, he died. Sadly, I know nothing of beautiful Margaret. Perhaps she will read this, still beautiful in her seventies. I hope so.

It was as well that I did not wait in 1948 for Khuhro to come back, for he retired from politics. One day, walking near Marble Arch, we met him. This gave memory a fierce jolt. He had a pretty girl on each arm, his daughter and a friend from Oxford. He asked us to go to his hotel, but we had a train to catch.

Before long the Indian Civil Service, the finest civil service in the world, will be only a memory, a matter for history books. But I am so very proud that, even for only the last years of its existence, I was one of its number.

EPILOGUE

For the Sindh I knew I have memory, and scores of letters and photographs, carefully preserved, but I wanted to go back, to see again the places we had known. I wrote to the Tourist Corporation, but received little encouragement. Then in 1996 I read a book by Christopher Ondaatje, *Sindh Revisited*: he dared not move on the ground without an armed escort. Where in 1943 Joan and I had rowed a boat under the Lansdowne Bridge to the River above Sukkur, he must not go, for there were snipers on both banks. Where Dermont Barty sat in his office in Shikarpur the Assistant Commissioner still sat, but with a sub-machine gun handy on his table. At Jacobabad, where Candy had wheeled the twins to the Parade Ground in their pram, and where Joan and I rode in the fields around, there was 'total chaos'. It is a very sad picture; I could not afford armed guards, nor hope to find anything I wanted.

I asked the Pakistan Government, the Sindh Government, the Deputy Commissioner of Upper Sindh Frontier for information, but there was none. What I wanted was from fifty years ago, and perhaps 'weeded' from the record. But I was not even told that.

I gave up hope of finding anything from Pakistan, or in Pakistan. But then I asked the British Library: it has the whole of the India Office archive, and recent records for Sindh were in a cellar under the London School of Economics: quarterly Agricultural Reports from 1949 to

1958, and I could certainly see them. Upstairs were busy students clicking away at their computers; down below were endless stacks of books, one small table, a chair, and a lamp. I needed no more.

I found the reports, and I searched through them, happily alone all that day. In forty years I was probably the first person to see them, and very probably will be the last.

I had high hopes that I would find reports of development plans being initiated. But there was nothing. In the following years were reports of crop outturns and the like—and were they still based on the quirky estimates of tapedars?—but they did not interest me. There were proposals and suggestions indicating that Sindh's development plans were not forgotten, but in 1956 provinces were abolished, and all our provincial funds were gone.

At the 1945 Horse Show I had discussed with Roger Thomas the possibility of cleansing kalar land, and in 1950 he wrote a paper about it, so perhaps our talk had borne fruit. But more probably not: in 1953 there was a report of 2.3 million acres of kalar land in the Punjab, and almost as much in Sindh, a third its size; and the area was still growing.

Also in 1953, Karl Kraus wrote of the value of 'demonstrations', and the need for courses for the sons and daughters of zamindars, to learn about the developments in agriculture. Perhaps he had read my revolutionary programme for that 1945 Horse Show.

The difficulty of applying science to agriculture because of the 'vicious' share-cropping system was emphasized, but there was no proposal to create a class of self-employed smallholders. Perhaps such an idea was still too dangerous politically, as I had found it to be. However, there was a report on mechanized farming, so maybe the Ferguson tractor had reached Sindh. (At the same time I was working two of them in England.) But there was no mention of the fate of haris dispossessed by machines.

In 1952 M R Kureshe, reporting on fishing on the Makran coast, lamented the lack of power boats. So had my trawler sunk? In 1957 he reported again, with drawings of twenty-five kinds of fish in the Arabian Sea, but with no plans to catch them. The one clear sign that my Fisheries Department had left a small legacy was that the oysters had recovered from the attack of 'wild' oysters, and by 1953 were flourishing at Korangi and Ibrahim Hyderi. In 1948 we had allocated funds for marketing, and perhaps they still thrive.

There was nothing about poultry breeding, or citrus fruit, or melons, or loofahs. That is a pity: there was no political concern with such mundane things.

So there is very little for which I can claim any credit at all, though there is plenty to show how frustrating it was to try to change anything in Sindh.

In 1997, India and Pakistan celebrated fifty years of independence. India celebrated with enthusiasm and worldwide publicity, but just then Pakistan had little to celebrate. India invited surviving members of the Indian Civil Service to take part in the celebrations, and the fact that I spent my whole service in what became Pakistan, and finally served the Pakistan Government, mattered not at all: my name was still on the Bombay cadre.

Over the half century frail tendrils stretch. In Simla I met Mrs Sarojini Thakur, who had been Deputy Commissioner of Chamba, a District now, a State when Joan and I walked there from Dalhousie; she knows well the vale of Kajjiar where we spent a night. It has become a popular beauty spot, and I bought a postcard of it. It looks just the same as it was in our fifty-year-old snapshot.

In the first gallery of a Delhi museum I found the first artefacts discovered at Mohen-jo-daro; they were taken to their home in Sindh in 1942 for the Viceroy to see, when we saw them too, before they were taken back to Delhi from that lonely place. Again I saw the beautiful necklace of polished agate, onyx, and carnelian, the beads and children's toys, the clay embryo of the bullock cart of our day. There are, too, all the tiny engraved seals, with their astonishing minute carving, the larger ones with pictographs still not deciphered. Pakistan should surely have had them at Partition, but doubtless was concerned with more important things; Delhi will hardly let them go now.

In England, too, those tendrils flower. In the same year I met Zubyr Soomro, whose mother is that same Indra Punjabi, the pretty girl whom we knew in Larkana, who made a notable love-match with Illahibaksh Soomro, head of one of the great Muslim families of Sindh. Also I met the son of Irene Carneghan, who wouldn't take yacht-racing seriously, and still remembers sinking us in front of the Yacht Club. Basil Labouchardiere, the Anglo-Indian policeman in Sindh, at last found his home in England. Others, too. At last I know the name of the surgeon who in Jacobabad operated so successfully on the man mauled by a tiger. Mrs Ledgard has told me that he still recounts the story.

When I had given up hope, there came a letter from Jacobabad, from Professor Muhammed Ismael, retired to live there. The Deputy Commissioner had asked him to answer my letter, but had not sent his comments on. His reminiscences of Jacobabad in his youth—when I was there—depicted a place more luridly primitive than I remember it was, but he sent me photographs of the new Residency, and of the romantic memorial at Jacob's tomb, so he has filled a small gap. Doubtless there will be other reminders, and confirmation, and denials, but some time there must be an end to waiting, and to writing.

GLOSSARY

Aata	white flour (*See, chakki aata*)
Abdar	'Lengthsman', on roads or canals
Abkalani	river flood period
AC	Assistant Collector in charge of District sub-division. First Class Magistrate. *See,* DC
ADC	Aide-de-Camp. Officer in attendance on Viceroy, Governor, etc.
Achkan	long, formal, Muslim coat
Almira	wardrobe; cf. Portuguese *almira*
Amir	title of ruler of Sindh before the British
Anna	small coin, sixteen to the rupee; about one old penny
APA	Assistant Political Agent
Ayah	nursemaid
Baba	diminutive for child
Badgir	wind scoop
Badmash	crook, villain
Bagh	garden
Bajri	millet
Bani(y)a	Hindu shopkeeper, moneylender
Bardana	jute cloth, hessian, grain sacks
Basmati	top quality variety of rice
Bazar, bazaar	shopping centre
Beedi	cigarette of local grown tobacco, with particular smell
Begum	polite prenom for Muslim lady

Behn chodh	serious insult; lit. you raped your sister
Berseem	alfalfa, sainfoin
Bewakuf	fool, lit. witless
Bhangi	sweeper; for all the dirty work
Bheesti	water-carrier
Bhindi	vegetable: 'lady's fingers', or okra
Bijli	lightning, electricity, very bright. *Bijli* butty, q.v.
Bistra	bedding roll
Brinjal	aubergine
Buddli	a change, a substitute.
Bund	bank of river or canal
Bunder (boat)	harbour (boat, barge)
Bundobust	arrangement; organization.
Bungalow	house, usually of one storey
Burqa	all-over smock; outdoor gear for women in *purdah*, q.v.
Burra	big; great, of person
Buttee, butty	paraffin lamp. *Bijli Butty*, pressure lamp
Chakki	grindstone mill; *chakki aata*, stone-ground wholemeal, the very best
Chalumchi	enamel bowl with cover; essential for toiletry on tour or when travelling
Charkha	'Persian wheel' for raising water; animal powered, endless chain of pots
Chaprassi	messenger
Charpoy	bedstead, usually made with webbing; lit. 'four legs'
Chhe	six
Chik	screen, sunblind
Chilli	red pepper
Chitnis	Head Clerk
Chota hasri	first breakfast
Chowk	border post, watchman's hut
Chowkidar	watchman, caretaker
Chullah	slot for fire in traditional brick cooker
Chunna	gram, chick pea

Collector	Head of the District, of Revenue, Police, and almost everything else
Commissioner	superior even to Collector. Head of a Division, of all Collectors in Sindh
Compound	yard, whole of premises
Crore	10,000,000. One hundred *lakhs*, q.v.
Cummerbund	sash, usually for male
Dacoit	bandit, gangster, robber
Dak	post, letters
Darya	river; also name for the Indus
Daulat	dowry; wealth
DC	Deputy Collector, exactly the same as AC, but of the Provincial Service Also, Deputy Commissioner head of District in Punjab, and of one District in Sindh
Deh	sub-division of *tapa*, q.v.
Dera, dero	chief's village
Dhand	lake
Dhobi	washerman
Dhow	two-masted, lateen-rigged, ocean-going ship of traditional design
Dhurrie	heavy woven cotton carpet
Dipiti	local corruption of AC or DC
District	charge of a Collector and District Magistrate
Djambo	oilseed rape
DO	demi-official letter
Dupatta	woman's headcloth
Dosuti	cotton cloth, lit. double thread in warp
DSP	District/Deputy Superintendent of Police. District police chief/deputy.
Dumba	fat-tailed sheep
Dunnage	packaging, stacking material
Durbar	as it were Court of Viceroy or Governor, usually for presenting titles, etc.
Durzi	tailor
Erzdar	petitioner

Faisla	agreement, settlement
Ganja	cannabis
Gasleet	paraffin pressure lamp; *bijli butty*
GH	Government House
Gharri/y	horse-drawn 'victoria'
Gherib	poor, humble
Ghoro	horse; my hired Horse, named 'Ghoro'
Ghur	molasses
Ghuslkhana	bathroom
Godown	warehouse, store; corruption of *gudam*
Goro	red
Goth	village; pron. 'gote'
Gusht	tour, expedition
Haj	pilgrimage to Mecca
Haji	returned pilgrim
Halal	ritually clean; of meat, slaughtered in accordance with Quranic law
Haram	unclean, sinful, opposite of *halal*
Hari	cultivator; in Sindh; share-cropping tenant-at-will
Havildar	military rank; civilian, chief of Collector's *patewalas*, q.v.
HEG/V	His Excellency the Governor/Viceroy. Or Her Excellency
Hoondi	oriental letter of credit
Ichabod	'The glory is departed', I Samuel Ch. IV, v. 21, in old Testament of the Bible
Izzat	honour, reputation
Jagir/jagirdar	absolute land grant/grantee
Jawan	young man, private soldier
Jemadar	corporal, leader
Jirga	tribal court
Jowar	millet
Juari	millet
Jungli	uncouth
Kabbadi	a game

Kachcha	temporary, of alluvial land, mud brick, earth roads, etc. *see, kutcha*
Kalar	salt pollution left by evaporation of water from land irrigated year after year
Kalarish	salt-polluted land
Kangni	red rice
Karia	water course
Khabardar	take care!
Khamisa	long tunic (Portuguese, kamisa)
Khan Bahadur	title: 'Brave Lord'
Kharif	summer crop on all land
Khud	ravine
Khuda hafiz	Muslim farewell May God Protect you
Khuni	murderous
Kishmish	sweet seedless green grapes.
Koi hai?	Who's there? Nickname for Old India Hand
Kot	settlement; fort
Kothar	messenger
Kotwal	postman
Kudr	axe, mattock
Kutchery	office/court
Kuttak	tribal dance, of the Frontier Province
Lai	tamarisk
Lakh	One Hundred Thousand
Lar	Lower Sindh
Lari	bus, lorry
Lascar	Indian seaman, generally from coastal Bombay
Lassi	milk curd
Lathi	iron-bound staff used by police
Lohar	blacksmith
Loofah	vegetable marrow, dried out and used for ablutions
Lunghi	old-fashioned embroidered smock, given as reward for services
Madressah	mosque school

Mahal	revenue sub-division, same as *taluka*, q.v. Only one in Sindh
Mahalkiri	same as Mukhtiarkar, q.v. Only one in Sindh. Properly a Bombay rank
Maidan	plain, open space, parade ground
Mali	gardener
Malta	orange.
Mango	very popular fleshy, yellowish-red fruit
Masjid	mosque, q.v.
Mattr	Peas
Mau chodh	serious insult, lit. Mother-fucker. *See, Behn Chodh*
Maund	measure of weight; in Sindh, about 40lb
Mir	title of member of previous ruling family of Sindh
Mirbahar	tribe of fishermen in inland waters cf., *Mohana*
Mistri	any skilled tradesman. Specifically, our cook
Mithai	sweetmeat made with honey, nuts, saffron
Mofussil	country outside big towns
Mohag	adjoining land, claimed by landowner
Mohana	tribe of sea fishermen. cf. *Mirbahar*
Moulvi	Muslim 'priest'/religious leader
Mukhi	Hindu headman
Mukhtiarkar	revenue officer in charge of *taluka*, q.v.
Mullah	religious leader, usually attached to particular mosque
Munshi	clerk, teacher
Mursi	manhood, potency
Musthi	raw sugar
Nahin	No
Naik	corporal, head of *patewalas*, q.v., of AC/DC
Namaste	Hindu greeting
Nara	channel
Nawab	chief, generally superior to Sirdar, q.v.

Neza-bazi	tent-pegging
Nim	tree with little aromatic berries; twigs used for cleaning teeth
Nullah	channel, creek
Otak	guest room/house
PA	Political Agent in State. Also, Personal Assistant
Pakora	meat or vegetable fried in batter
Paddy	rice fields, unhusked rice
Paisa	generalized term for money
Palla	very popular river fish, much like salmon
Palung	bed
PAS	Pakistan Administrative Service, successor to the ICS
Pat	flat, earth desert
Patewala	lit., badge-man. Office boy/man in government and commerce
Pathan	large ethnic group of hill tribes
Patharidar	cattle-rustler
Perdesh/i	foreign land, foreigner
Pertal	inspection, usually of crops
Pie/pice	tiny coin. 4 pies to 1 pice, 4 pice to 1anna, 16 annas to 1 rupee. In 1940, 1 rupee was equivalent to 1/6a. (old money)
Pinkie	permanganate of potash, used to sterilize water
Pir	holy man. Also, family name claiming direct descent from the Prophet (PBUH)
Pleader	advocate. Pejorative word for solicitor or barrister
Pukka	permanent, hard (of roads), burnt (of bricks). Genuine. Cf. *kutcha*
Pund	trotting pace used specially by ponies of *tapedars*, q.v.
Punj	five
Punjab	land of the five rivers

Punkah	fan. Domestic, fan on frame pulled back and forth. By extension, electric fan, even propeller of ships and aeroplanes
Purdah	curtain, screen
Purdahnashin	woman kept in seclusion
Purwar	Protector (of the Poor)
PWD	Public Works Department. In charge of canals, trunk roads, and bridges, and all government buildings
Qawali	concert of religious and folk music
Quaid-e-Azam	Chief Leader. Title M.A. Jinnah Founder and first Governor-General of Pakistan
Quran (spelt Qoran Koran)	Usually spoken with 'Sharif'; the holiest book of Islam
Rabi	spring crop; different on inundation canals from Barrage canals
Rao Bahadur	title; same for Hindus as Khan Bahadur for Muslims, q.v.
Rasai	customary graft, generally collected by *Mukhtiarkar*, q.v., from *zamindars*, q.v.M to oil the wheels of the administration
Regulator	control sluice on canal
Rishwat	bribery. distinct from *rasai*, q.v.
Rissala	troop of cavalry
Rissaldar	troop commander of *rissala*
Rondavel	round holiday hut in the hills
Rownti	small ridge tent
Sahib	respectful title for official or social superior
Salaam	Muslim greeting
Saman	baggage
Samosa	small curried pasty
Sepoy	soldier, policeman (corruption of *sepahi*, Fr. *spahi*)
Seth	polite address to Hindu businessman, lit., merchant

Shah	prince, ruler. Adopted as family name by Syeds, q.v.
Shalwar	voluminous trousers
Shamiana	tent, awning, marquee
Shristedar	Court Clerk
Sindhi	native of Sindh (formerly Sind or Scinde)
Sirdar	tribal chief
Sirkar	the government.
Sowar	cavalry trooper
Subcheez	everything
Sub-division	charge of AC/DC, q.v., in Revenue Service; also used in other services
Subedar	military, non-com. rank; police, Sergeant
Sugdasi	best variety of Sindhi rice
Sujji	mutton or young goat, cooked by radiation
Swadeshi	hand-spun, hand-woven cloth; hand-made; lit., of the country
Syed	person tracing descent from the Prophet (PBUH) *see*, Shah
Taluka	revenue unit, charge of *Mukhtiarkar*, q.v.
Tamasha	fete; generally festive occasion
Tangi	narrow ravine caused by earthquake
Tank	reservoir
Tapa	smallest revenue charge
Tapedar	in charge of *tapa*; lowest rank of revenue officer
TE	Their Excellencies
Tepoy	small table; 'three legs'; cf. *charpoy*, q.v.
Thalla	platform, patio
Thana	police post
Thunder-box	commode
Tindal	boat-boy; usually a Mohana fisherman's son
Tŏmbu	tent
Tonga	pony trap

Topi	pith sun helmet. Standard wear for Europeans, to avoid sun-stroke.
Tufan	typhoon/storm
Upr	Upper Sindh
Vakil	lawyer, legal adviser
Vizir	Minister, in a State
Wadero	village headman, usually a Muslim
Wah	canal, stream. Also, appreciative applause
Zabardust	bullying, intolerant
Zalim	oppressor; *see, zulum*
Zamindar	landholder. In fact, all land in Sindh, except *jagirs*, q.v., was the government's
Zenana	*purdah*, q.v.; areas for women only
Zulum	oppression, tyranny

INDEX